# Learning

## Microsoft®
## Windows® XP

by Suzanne Weixel

DDC Publishing

PEARSON
Education

## ACKNOWLEDGEMENTS

Thanks to everyone at DDC Publishing, especially Jennifer Frew, Chris Katsarapoulos, and James Reidel. Special thanks to Evan for supplying the photos and to Nathaniel for writing the essays. And, of course, to Rick who held down the fort so I could meet an outrageous deadline.

*Suzanne Weixel*

**Managing Editor**
Jennifer Frew

**Technical Editor**
James Reidel

**Acquisitions Manager**
Chris Katsaropoulos

**Design & Layout**
Shu Y. Chen
Elsa Johannesson

**Cover Design**
Amy Capuano

ISBN: 0-536-81984-X

2004200252

Printed in the United States of America

PEARSON EDUCATION
75 Arlington Street, Suite 300, Boston, MA 02116
A Pearson Education Company

# Contents

## GETTING STARTED WITH OFFICE XP— INCLUDED ON CD 💿

✓ *See page ix for information on accessing the files on CD.*

### Exercise 1
- About Microsoft Office XP
- Use the Mouse
- Use the Keyboard
- Start and Exit Microsoft Office Programs
- Common Screen Elements

### Exercise 2
- Execute Commands
- Use Menus
- Use Toolbars
- Use Dialog Box Options
- Use Shortcut Menus
- Use Task Panes

### Exercise 3
- Use Window Controls
- Zoom
- Scroll
- Use Multiple Windows

### Exercise 4
- Use the Ask a Question Box
- Use the Office Assistant
- Use the Office Help Program
- Use the What's This? Pointer
- Microsoft Office on the Web
- Recover a File

## WORD 2002

### Lesson 1:
#### Getting Started with Word 2002

#### Exercise 1 ......................... 3
- Start Word
- The Word Window
- Change the Word Window
- Type in a Document
- Correct Errors
- Use Undo and Redo
- Save a New Document
- Close a Document
- Exit Word

#### Exercise 2 ............................. 10
- Create a New Document
- Work with Show/Hide Marks

- Move the Insertion Point in a Document
- Use Click and Type
- Save Changes
- Preview an Open Document
- Print an Open Document

#### Exercise 3 ......................... 15
- Correct Spelling as You Type
- Correct Grammar as You Type
- Check Spelling
- Check Grammar
- Use the Thesaurus

#### Exercise 4 ......................... 20
- Use AutoCorrect
- Select Text In a Document
- Replace Selected Text
- Align Text Horizontally
- Align a Document Vertically

#### Exercise 5 ......................... 26
- Format a Business Letter
- Insert the Date and Time in a Document
- Use Uppercase Mode
- Change Case in a Document

#### Exercise 6 ......................... 31
- Set Tabs
- Format a Modified-Block Business Letter
- Shrink to Fit
- Full Screen View

#### Exercise 7 ......................... 36
- Format a Personal Business Letter
- Select Fonts
- Change Font Size
- Apply Font Styles
- Apply Underlines
- Create Envelopes
- Create Labels

#### Exercise 8 ......................... 43
- Critical Thinking

### Lesson 2:
#### Basic Editing Skills

#### Exercise 9 ......................... 46
- Use Proofreaders' Marks
- Open a Recently Saved Document
- Open a Document not Recently Saved
- Insert and Edit Text
- Use Overtype Mode
- Save a Document with a New Name

#### Exercise 10 ...................... 50
- Move Text
- Use Cut and Paste
- Use the Clipboard
- Use Drag-and-Drop Editing
- Move a Paragraph

#### Exercise 11 ...................... 54
- Use Copy and Paste
- Use the Drag-and-Drop Feature to Copy

#### Exercise 12 ...................... 58
- Open a Document as Read-Only
- Open a Document from Windows
- Document Properties
- File Types
- Use Basic Search to Find a File

#### Exercise 13 ...................... 64
- Preview a Closed Document
- Print Files without Opening Them

#### Exercise 14 ...................... 68
- Critical Thinking

### Lesson 3:
#### Formatting Basics

#### Exercise 15 ...................... 70
- Apply Font and Text Effects
- Font Color
- Highlight Text
- Format Painter

#### Exercise 16 ...................... 74
- Use Symbols

#### Exercise 17 ...................... 77
- Bulleted Lists
- Numbered Lists
- Sort

#### Exercise 18 ...................... 82
- Line Spacing
- Paragraph Spacing
- Indent Text

#### Exercise 19 ...................... 87
- Apply Styles
- Create a Style
- Edit a Style
- Reapply Direct Formatting
- Check Formatting
- Select Paste Formatting Options
- Clear Formatting

#### Exercise 20 ...................... 93
- Format a One-Page Report
- Set Margins
- Set Page Orientation

**Exercise 21** .................... 97
- Critical Thinking

## Lesson 4:
### Using the Internet and E-mail; Creating Web Pages

**Exercise 22** .................... 99
- Send E-Mail from Word
- Attach a Word Document to an E-Mail Message
- Send a Word Document as E-Mail
- Receive E-Mail Messages in Outlook or Outlook Express

**Exercise 23** .................... 105
- Internet Basics
- Use Internet Features in Word
- Save a Web Page Locally
- The Favorites Folder

**Exercise 24** .................... 110
- Create a Web Page Document in Word
- Use Web Layout View
- Use Web Page Titles
- Apply a Background
- Apply a Theme
- Preview a Web Page
- Open an HTML Document in Word

**Exercise 25** .................... 115
- Create hyperlinks

**Exercise 26** .................... 122
- Critical Thinking

## Lesson 5:
### Creating Tables

**Exercise 27** .................... 124
- Create a Table
- Enter Data in a Table
- Select in a Table
- Change Table Structure
- Format a Table

**Exercise 28** .................... 130
- Set Alignments within Table Cells
- Align Table on the Page
- Column Width and Row Height

**Exercise 29** .................... 135
- Tables and Borders Toolbar
- Draw a Table
- Move and Resize Tables
- Merge and Split Cells
- Rotate Text
- Wrap Text

**Exercise 30** .................... 140
- Calculations in a Table
- Number Formats
- Cell Borders and Shading
- Sort Rows

**Exercise 31** .................... 145
- Critical Thinking

# EXCEL 2002

## Lesson 1:
### Getting Started with Excel 2002

**Exercise 1** .................... 150
- Start Excel
- The Excel Window
- Excel Menu and Toolbars
- Explore the Worksheet Using the Mouse and Keyboard
- Change Between Worksheets
- The View Menu
- Exit Excel

**Exercise 2** .................... 156
- Create a New (Blank) Workbook
- Create a Workbook from a Template
- Enter Labels
- Make Simple Corrections
- Undo and Redo
- Delete (Clear) Cell Contents
- Save a Workbook
- Document Recovery
- Close a Workbook

**Exercise 3** .................... 162
- Open Files
- Change from Workbook to Workbook
- Arrange Workbooks
- AutoComplete
- Pick From List
- AutoCorrect
- Spell Check

**Exercise 4** .................... 167
- Numeric Labels and Values
- Enter Dates
- Create a Series
- Data Alignment
- Change Column Width

**Exercise 5** .................... 173
- Enter a Formula

**Exercise 6** .................... 176
- Critical Thinking

## Lesson 2:
### Working with Formulas and Formatting

**Exercise 7** .................... 178
- Use Ranges
- Range Entry Using Collapse Button

**Exercise 8** .................... 181
- Format Data

- Fonts and Font Size
- Number Formats
- Percent Format
- Comma Format
- Currency
- Add Color to Cells

**Exercise 9** .................... 186
- Copy and Paste Data
- Relative Reference
- Absolute Reference
- Preview and Print a Worksheet

**Exercise 10** .................... 190
- Insert and Delete Columns and Rows
- Move Data (Cut/Paste)
- Drag-and-Drop Editing

**Exercise 11** .................... 194
- Work with Worksheets
- Group Sheets
- Format Sheets

**Exercise 12** .................... 198
- Critical Thinking

## Lesson 3:
### Working with Functions, Formulas, and Charts

**Exercise 13** .................... 200
- Use Functions
- Common Functions
- Insert a Function
- AutoCalculate

**Exercise 14** .................... 206
- Natural Language Formulas
- Comments

**Exercise 15** .................... 210
- Named Ranges

**Exercise 16** .................... 215
- Understand IF Functions
- Nested IF Functions
- =SUMIF() Statements
- =COUNTIF() Statements

**Exercise 17** .................... 220
- Chart Basics
- Select Chart Data
- Chart Elements
- Create Charts
- Change Chart Types
- Select a Chart
- Resize, Copy, Move, or Delete a Chart

**Exercise 18** .................... 226
- Use Chart Toolbar
- Resize, Move, or Delete a Chart Object
- Change Chart Text
- Enhance Chart Background
- Format Category and Value Axes

**Exercise 19** ..................... 231
- Critical Thinking

# ACCESS 2002

## Lesson 1:
**Getting Started with Access 2002**

### Database Basics .......... 235
- What is Access?
- What is a Database?
- What is a Database Management System?
- How is an Access Database Organized?
- How are Access Tables Related?

### Exercise 1 ...................... 239
- Copy Data Files and Deselect the Read-only Attribute
- Start Access and Open a Database
- Navigate in a Database
- Sort Records

### Exercise 2 ...................... 245
- Enter Records
- Edit Records
- Delete Records
- Print Datasheets and Forms
- Print Preview

### Exercise 3 ...................... 251
- Plan a Database
- Create a New Database File
- Create a Table in Datasheet View
- Change Field Names in Datasheet View
- Save a Table Design

### Exercise 4 ...................... 255
- Create a Database with Database Wizards
- Start Database Wizards
- Use Database Wizards
- Use Switchboards

### Exercise 5 ...................... 259
- Open a Database File
- Create a Table with the Table Wizard
- Start a New Table in Table Design View
- Work with Table Design View
- Select a Field for the Primary Key
- Open a Database Exclusively
- Set a Database Password

### Exercise 6 ...................... 265
- Critical Thinking

## Lesson 2:
**Working with Tables and Datasheets**

### Exercise 7 ....................... 267
- Open a Table for Editing in Table Design View
- Rename a Field
- Add a Field
- Delete a Field
- Reorder Fields
- Change Field Properties

### Exercise 8 ....................... 272
- Switch among Open Objects
- Insert a Column
- Delete a Column
- Move a Column
- Hide and Unhide Columns
- Change Datasheet Column Width
- Freeze Columns
- Remove Gridlines

### Exercise 9 ...................... 277
- Relate Tables
- Enforce Referential Integrity
- Print Relationships
- Close Relationship Window
- Show Related Records

### Exercise 10 ..................... 281
- Critical Thinking

## Lesson 3:
**Simplifying Data Entry with Lookups and Forms**

### Exercise 11 ...................... 283
- Create a Lookup for a Field
- Create a Value List with the Lookup Wizard
- Lookup Field Values from another Table

### Exercise 12 ..................... 287
- Compare Datasheet and Form View
- Create an AutoForm
- Create a Form with the Form Wizard
- Create a Form from Scratch
- Enter Form Design View
- Work with Form Design View
- AutoFormat a Form

### Exercise 13 ..................... 292
- Add a New Field to a Form
- Select Controls on a Form
- Delete a Control form a Form
- Move Controls
- Reset Tab Order
- Change Control Formatting
- Resize Fields and Other Controls
- Align Controls
- Form Backgrounds

### Exercise 14 ..................... 297
- Use Form View Toolbox
- Add Labels
- Adding Lookups to Forms
- Add an Option Group
- Add a List Box or Combo Box

### Exercise 15 ..................... 302
- Work with Headers and Footers
- Display Header and Footer Areas
- Add Page Numbers or Date and Time
- Page Setup

### Exercise 16 ..................... 307
- Critical Thinking

# POWERPOINT 2002

## Lesson 1:
**Getting Started with PowerPoint 2002**

### Exercise 1 ...................... 311
- About PowerPoint
- Start PowerPoint
- The Blank Presentation Option
- Apply a Slide Layout
- The PowerPoint Screen
- Use Shortcut Menus
- Use Slide Design Templates
- Use Placeholders
- Add Slides to a Presentation
- Save a Presentation
- Save File as a Web Page
- Close a Presentation/Exit PowerPoint

### Exercise 2 ...................... 318
- Open an Existing Presentation
- Slide Views
- Move from Slide to Slide
- Spell Check
- Print a Presentation
- Change a Slide's Layout or Design Template

### Exercise 3 ...................... 324
- Work with Content Layouts
- Use Undo

### Exercise 4 ...................... 328
- Move, Copy, Duplicate, and Delete Slides
- Slide Sorter View

### Exercise 5 ...................... 332
- Outline Pane
- Summary Slide

### Exercise 6 ...................... 336
- Import/Export an Outline
- Link an Excel Worksheet

### Exercise 7 ...................... 341
- Critical Thinking

## Lesson 2:
### Editing and Formatting a Presentation

**Exercise 8**......................... 343
- Select Text
- Align Text
- Change the Appearance of Text
- Change Case
- Change Slide Color Scheme
- Change Slide Background

**Exercise 9**......................... 349
- Copy Text Formatting
- Move and Copy Text
- Increase/Decrease Paragraph Spacing
- Move, Size, Copy, and Delete Placeholders and Other Objects

**Exercise 10**..................... 354
- Use Slide and Title Masters
- Slide Master View
- Insert Slide Numbers, Date and Time, and Footer Text
- Format Bullets

**Exercise 11**..................... 360
- Use Rulers and Guides
- Floating Toolbars
- Draw Graphic Objects
- AutoShapes
- Group and Ungroup Objects
- Layer Objects

**Exercise 12**..................... 366
- Customize a Template
- Save and Apply a Custom Template

**Exercise 13**..................... 369
- Insert Organization Chart Slide

**Exercise 14**..................... 373
- Create a Chart
- Create a Table

**Exercise 15**..................... 380
- Embed a PowerPoint Slide in a Word Document
- Export PowerPoint Slides and Notes to a Word Document
- Export PowerPoint Text to a Word Document

**Exercise 16**..................... 386
- Critical Thinking

## Lesson 3:
### Setting Up a Slide Show

**Exercise 17**.................... 389
- Check Slides for Style and Consistency
- Show a Presentation
- Add Transitions
- Advance Slide

- Hide Slides

**Exercise 18**......................393
- Animate Text and Objects
- Preset Animation
- Custom Animation

**Exercise 19**......................398
- Annotations
- Pause and Resume Show
- Add Music
- Add a Movie

**Exercise 20**......................401
- Create Notes Pages and Handouts
- Notes Master and Handout Master
- Pack and Go
- Meeting Minder
- Incorporate Meeting Feedback

**Exercise 21**......................406
- Set Up a Presentation
- Set Up Show Dialog Box Options

**Exercise 22**......................408
- Save a Presentation as a Web Site
- Publish a Presentation
- Make Your Web Presentation More Efficient

**Exercise 23**......................412
- Export to Overhead Transparencies
- Export to 35mm Slides

**Exercise 24**......................415
- Critical Thinking

## CHALLENGE LESSON— INCLUDED ON CD 💿

### Lesson 1:

**Exercise 1**
- Locate Data on the Internet
- Make Web Data Available for use Offline
- Edit and Format a Table in a Word Document
- Send a Word Document via E-mail

**Exercise 2**
- Locate Data on the Internet
- Enter Data into an Excel Worksheet
- Insert Worksheet Data into a Word Document

**Exercise 3**
- Create a PowerPoint Presentation from a Word Outline

- Download Clip Art from the Web
- Link Excel Data to a Table on a PowerPoint Slide

**Exercise 4**
- Save a Word File as a Web Page
- Publish a Presentation to a Web Site
- Link a Web Page and a Presentation Web Site
- Link a Web Page to an Internet Site

**Exercise 5**
- Export an Access Table to Excel
- E-mail an Excel Worksheet
- Receive an Excel Worksheet via E-mail and Save it in HTML Format
- Edit an HTML Worksheet in Excel

**Exercise 6**
- Create Queries in an Access Database
- Merge a Word Document with Access Queries
- Embed Excel Data in a Word Document
- Create Merge Envelopes using an Access Table

**Exercise 7**
- Save an Excel Worksheet as a Web Page
- Link a Word Document to an Excel Web Page
- Send a Word Document via E-mail

**Exercise 8**
- Link an E-mail Message to an Excel Worksheet
- Link an Excel Worksheet to an Access Database
- Use an Excel Worksheet as a Data Source for a Mail Merge

**Exercise 9**
- Download Clip Art from the Web
- Insert Clip Art in an Excel Worksheet
- Copy Charts from a Worksheet onto PowerPoint Slides
- Save a Presentation as a Web Site
- Link a Word Document to a Presentation Web Site

# Introduction

Microsoft Office XP is Microsoft's suite of application software. The Standard version includes Word, Excel, Outlook, and PowerPoint. The Professional version includes the above applications plus Access. This book covers Word (the word processing tool), Excel (the spreadsheet tool), PowerPoint (the presentation tool), and Access (the database tool). Because Microsoft Office is an integrated suite, the components can all be used separately or together to create professional-looking documents and to manage data.

## How We've Organized the Book

**Learning Microsoft Office XP** is made up of seven sections:

- **Basics—Included on CD** ⊘
  This short chapter introduces essential Office skills—including starting Microsoft Office, using the mouse and keyboard, screen elements, and an overview of the applications. If you are completely new to the Office suite, you should start with this lesson. All of the lessons on CD can be printed out or viewed on-screen. See page vii for details on how to access the files.

- **Word 2002**
  With Word you can create letters, memos, Web pages, newsletters, and more.

- **Excel 2002**
  Excel, Microsoft's spreadsheet component, is used to organize and calculate data, track financial data, and create charts and graphs.

- **Access 2002**
  Access is Microsoft's powerful database tool. Using Access you will learn to store, retrieve, and report on information.

- **PowerPoint 2002**
  Create dynamic on-screen presentations with PowerPoint, the presentation graphics tool.

Each chapter in **Learning Microsoft Office XP** is made up of several lessons. Lessons are comprised of short exercises designed for using Office XP in real-life business settings. Every application exercise (except for the Critical Thinking Exercises) is made up of seven key elements:

- **On the Job**. Each exercise starts with a brief description of how you would use the features of that exercise in the workplace.

- **Exercise Scenario**. The Office tools are then put into context by setting a scenario. For example, you may be a designer putting together a promotional sales flyer using Word or you may be responsible for tracking inventory for a gourmet-food store.

- **Terms**. Key terms are included and defined at the start of each exercise, so you can quickly refer back to them. The terms are then highlighted in the text.

- **Notes**. Concise notes for learning the computer concepts.

- **Procedures**. Hands-on mouse and keyboard procedures teach all necessary skills.

- **Application Exercise**. Step-by-step instructions put your skills to work.

- **On Your Own**. Each exercise concludes with a critical thinking activity that you can work through on your own. You may have to create a personal budget spreadsheet in Excel or a personal Web page in Word. You are challenged to come up with data and then additionally challenged to use the data in a document. The *On Your Own* sections can be used as additional reinforcement, for practice, or to test skill proficiency.

- In addition, each lesson ends with a **Critical Thinking Exercise**. As with the *On Your Owns*, you need to rely on your own skills to complete the task.

# Working with Data and Solution Files

As you work through the exercises in this book, you'll be creating, opening, and saving files. You should keep the following instructions in mind:

- For many of the exercises you can use the data files provided on the CD-ROM that comes with this book. The data files are used so that you can focus on the skills being introduced—not on keyboarding lengthy documents. The files are organized by application in the **Datafiles** folders on the CD-ROM.

  ✓ See **What's on the CD** for more information on the data files.

- When the application exercise includes a file name and a CD icon ☉, you can open the file provided on CD.
- The Directory of Files at the beginning of each section lists the exercise file (from the CD-ROM).

# What's on the CD ⊚

We've included on the CD:

- **Microsoft Office XP Basics** covers fundamental Office skills. If you are completely new to the Office suite, you should start with this section. The Basics lessons are provided in .pdf format. You must first install Adobe Acrobat (provided on the CD) before you can open, view, or print the files. Once Adobe Acrobat is installed, you simply double-click the file to open it. Exercises can be printed out and distributed.

- **Data files** for many of the exercises. This way you don't have to type lengthy documents from scratch.

- **Internet simulation** so that you can go to real Web sites to get information—without an Internet connection or modem. Following the steps in the book, you will experience going "online" to locate facts, data, and clip art. You will then use the information in Office documents.

- **Glossary of business and financial terms** used in the workplace, the financial arena, and *Learning Microsoft Office XP*. Key business terms help you understand the work scenarios and the data that is used to complete the exercises.

- **Touch 'N' Type Keyboarding course** was designed for those who would like to learn to type in the shortest possible time. The keyboarding skill-building drills are also ideal for those who wish to practice and improve their keyboarding. The exercises can be printed out, copied, and distributed. The files have been prepared in Adobe Acrobat format. You first need to install Adobe Acrobat (provided on the CD) before you can open the files.

- **Typing Tests with Automatic Scoring.** Use these to test typing speed and accuracy.

- **Computer Literacy Basics.** These exercises include information on computer care, computer basics, and a brief history of computers. Once Adobe Acrobat is installed, these exercises can be printed out and distributed.

# To Access the Files Included with This Book ⊚

1. Insert the *Learning Microsoft Office XP* CD in the CD-ROM drive. A menu of options should automatically appear. If it does not, perform the following steps:
   a. Click Start>Run.
   b. Type D:\CDmain.exe (where D: is the letter of your CD-ROM drive).
2. Move the mouse pointer over a menu item to display information on how to install or access the files.
3. Click a menu item to activate it.

   ✓ *IMPORTANT: Before accessing the Microsoft Office XP Basics files, you must install Acrobat Reader on your computer. (If you already have Acrobat Reader on your computer, this is not necessary.) Rest your mouse pointer on the **Install Acrobat Reader** menu item, click the left mouse button, and follow the instructions to install. Then, rest your mouse pointer on **Microsoft Office XP Basics** menu item, click your left mouse button, and follow the directions to access the files. These files can be printed out or viewed on-screen.*

# Word 2002

## Lesson 1

**Getting Started with Word 2002**
**Exercises 1-8**

## Lesson 2

**Basic Editing Skills**
**Exercises 9-14**

## Lesson 3

**Formatting Basics**
**Exercises 15-21**

## Lesson 4

**Using the Internet and E-mail; Creating Web Pages**
**Exercises 22-26**

## Lesson 5

**Creating Tables**
**Exercises 27-31**

# Directory of Data Files on CD

| Exercise # | File Name | Page # |
|---|---|---|
| 1 | N/A | N/A |
| 2 | N/A | N/A |
| 3 | N/A | N/A |
| 4 | N/A | N/A |
| 5 | N/A | N/A |
| 6 | N/A | N/A |
| 7 | N/A | N/A |
| 8 | N/A | N/A |
| 9 | 09PRESS | 49 |
| 10 | 10POLICY | 52 |
| 11 | 11POLICY | 55 |
| 12 | 12CONTEST | 62 |
| 13 | 13CONTEST, 13MEMO | 65 |
| 14 | 14CAVIAR, 14FLYER | 68 |
| 15 | 15ANNOUNCE | 72 |
| 16 | 16GRAND | 75 |
| 17 | 17FIREDRILL | 79 |
| 18 | 18PROGRAMS | 85 |
| 19 | 19COURSE | 90 |
| 20 | 20BUSINESS | 95 |
| 21 | 21TRAIN | 97 |
| 22 | 22LIST, 22RULES | 102 |
| 23 | INTERNET SIMULATION | 108 |
| 24 | 24COURSE | 113 |
| 25 | 25TRAIN, 25COURSE, INTERNET SIMULATION | 118 |
| 26 | 26SPECIALS, INTERNET SIMULATION | 122 |
| 27 | N/A | N/A |
| 28 | N/A | N/A |
| 29 | 29COOKING | 138 |
| 30 | 30BASKET | 142 |
| 31 | 31DEMOS | 145 |

# Exercise 1

Skills Covered:

◆ **Start Word** ◆ **The Word Window** ◆ **Change the Word Window**
◆ **Type in a Document** ◆ **Correct Errors** ◆ **Use Undo and Redo**
◆ **Save a New Document** ◆ **Close a Document** ◆ **Exit Word**

## On the Job

Word is the word processing application included in the Microsoft Office XP suite. You use Word to create text-based documents such as letters, memos, reports, flyers, and newsletters. The first step in mastering Word is learning how to start the program and create a document.

You are the office manager at the medical practice California Cardiology, Inc. A new doctor has recently joined the staff, and you must type up a brief biography that will be made available in the office and sent to prospective patients. In this exercise, you will start Word, create and save a document, and then exit Word.

## Terms

**Default** A standard setting or mode of operation.

**View** The way a document is displayed on screen.

**Elements** Menus, icons, and other items that are part of an on-screen interface.

**Word wrap** A feature that causes text to move automatically from the end of one line to the beginning of the next line.

**Paragraph mark (¶)** A **nonprinting** character inserted in a document to indicate where a paragraph ends.

**Nonprinting characters** Characters such as paragraph marks and tab symbols that are not printed in a document but that can be displayed on the screen.

**Undo** The command for reversing a previous action.

**Redo** The command for reversing the Undo command.

## Notes

### Start Word

■ To use Word 2002 you must first start it so it is running on your computer.

■ You use Windows to start Word.

■ When Word is running, it is displayed in a window on your screen.

■ You can start Word using the Start menu, a desktop icon, or the Office Shortcut bar.

✓ *Different methods of starting Office XP programs are covered in "Getting Started with Office XP," Exercise 1. This file is located on the CD included with this book. See page IX for information on accessing this file.*

## The Word Window

- Word opens a new, blank document using standard, or **default**, settings. Default settings control features of a new document, such as the margins, the line spacing, the character font, and the font size.

- Word starts with a new blank document open in Print Layout **view** and displays **elements** for accessing tools and menus to create, edit, format, and distribute a document.

- The following illustration identifies the default elements of the Word window. The numbers following each element correspond to the numbers next to the descriptions that follow.

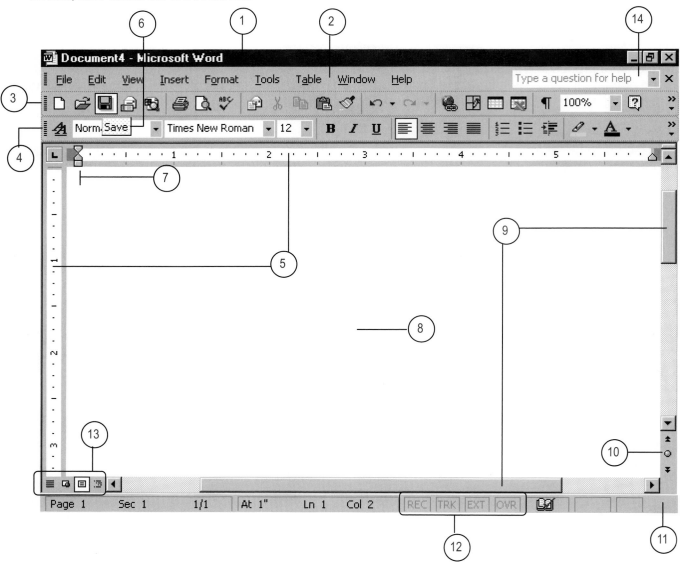

### Title bar (1)

- Displays the program and document name.

### Menu bar (2)

- Displays the names of the main menus. Select a menu name for a list of commands.

### Standard toolbar (3)

- Displays buttons for accessing common features and commands, such as saving, opening, and printing a file.

  ✓ *Toolbar buttons change according to your most recent selections. To see additional buttons, click the Toolbar Options button* 📊.

**Formatting toolbar (4)**

- Displays buttons for accessing common formatting features and commands, such as bold, italic, and centering text.

**Rulers (5)**

- The horizontal ruler measures the width of the document page; it displays information such as margins, tab stops, and indents.

- The vertical ruler measures the height of the document page.

  ✓ *The vertical ruler is displayed only in Print Layout view and Print Preview.*

**ScreenTip (6)**

- Displays the name of the element on which the mouse pointer is resting.

**Insertion point (7)**

- A blinking vertical line that displays to the right of the space where characters are inserted in a document.

**Document window (8)**

- The area where you type document text or insert graphics, tables, or other content.

**Scroll boxes (9)**

- Used with a mouse to shift the on-screen display up and down or left and right.

**Select Browse Object button (10)**

- Used to shift the on-screen display according to a selected object, such as by page, by picture, or by heading.

**Status bar (11)**

- Displays information, such as the currently displayed page, currently displayed section, how many pages are in the document, where the insertion point is located, and which mode buttons are active.

**Mode buttons (12)**

- Used to change the way Word operates to make creating and editing documents easier.

  ✓ *Active mode buttons appear bold.*

**View buttons (13)**

- Used to change to one of four available document views. These options are also available on the View menu.

**Ask a Question box (14)**

- Used to access the Help program. Type a question to display a list of topics for which help is available.

  ✓ *For more about using the Help program, refer to Exercise 4 of "Getting Started with Office XP."*

## Change the Word Window

- You can change the default settings to control which Word elements are displayed.
  - You can show or hide toolbars.
  - You can show or hide rulers.
  - You can show or hide Task Panes.
  - You can change views.

Normal view   Print Layout view

Web Layout view   Outline view

  - Normal view is used for most typing, editing, and formatting.
  - Print Layout view displays a document on-screen the way it will look when it is printed.
  - Web Layout view wraps text to fit the window, the way it would on a Web page document.
  - Outline view is used to create and edit outlines.

## Type in a Document

- By default, the insertion point is positioned at the beginning (left end) of the first line of a new document.

- You simply begin typing to insert new text.

- Characters you type are inserted to the left of the insertion point.

- **Word wrap** automatically wraps the text at the end of a line to the beginning of the next line.

- When you press the Enter key, Word inserts a **paragraph mark** and starts a new paragraph.

- After you type enough text to fill a page, Word automatically starts a new page.

## Correct Errors

- You can delete characters to the left of the insertion point by pressing the Backspace key.
- You can delete characters to the right of the insertion point by pressing the Delete key.
- You can cancel commands before you execute them by pressing the Escape key or clicking a Cancel button if available.

## Use Undo and Redo

- Use the **Undo** command to reverse a single action made in error, such as deleting the wrong word.
- The Undo command also lets you change your mind about an entire series of actions used to edit or format a document.
- Use the **Redo** command to reinstate any actions that you reversed with the Undo command.
- If the Undo command and the Undo button are dimmed and entirely gray, there are no actions that can be undone.
- If the Redo button is dimmed, there are no actions that can be redone. However, sometimes when there are no actions to redo, the Repeat command is available from the Edit menu in place of Redo. Use Repeat to repeat the most recent action.

## Save a New Document

- As mentioned, Word starts with a new blank document named *Document1* open on-screen.
  - ✓ *Subsequent new documents are named consecutively:* Document2, Document3, *etc. You learn more about creating additional new documents in Exercise 2.*
- If you want to have a file available for future use, you must save it on a removable disk or on an internal fixed disk.

- When you save a new document, you must give it a name and select the location where you want it stored.
- Word automatically adds a period and a three-character file extension to the end of the file name to identify the file type. By default, the file extension is *.doc*, which identifies a document file.
- To specify a disk for storing the document, you select the disk drive letter. Floppy disk drives are usually drives A: and B:. A hard drive is usually drive C:.
- You can store documents in a folder on your hard drive called *My Documents*, or you can select a different folder. You can also create a new folder when you save a document.

## Close a Document

- A document remains open on-screen until you close it.
- Close a document when you are finished working with it.
- If you try to close a document without saving it, Word prompts you to save it.
- You can close a document without saving it if you do not want to keep it for future use or if you are not happy with changes you have made since you last saved the document.

## Exit Word

- When you are done using Word, you exit the Word application.
- If you try to exit Word without saving your documents, Word prompts you to do so.
- If you exit Word without closing your saved documents, Word closes them automatically.

# Procedures

## Start Word

1. Click **Start** ![Start] .... Ctrl + Esc
2. Click **Programs** .................. P
3. Click **Microsoft Word** on Programs menu.

OR

1. Click **Start** ![Start] ... Ctrl + Esc
2. Click **New Office Document** ![New Office Document].
3. From the General Tab, double-click **Blank Document** ![Blank Document].

## Change the Word Window

**To show or hide toolbars:**

1. Click **View** .................. Alt + V
2. Click **Toolbars** .................... T
   - ✓ *Check mark next to toolbar name indicates that toolbar is already displayed.*
3. Click the toolbar name.

**To show or hide ruler:**

1. Click **V**iew .................... `Alt`+`V`

   ✓ *Check mark next to ruler indicates ruler is displayed.*

2. Click **R**uler .......................... `R`

**To change view:**

1. Click **V**iew ................... `Alt`+`V`
2. Click **N**ormal ...................... `N`

   OR

   Click **W**eb Layout .............. `W`

   OR

   Click **P**rint Layout ............. `P`

   OR

   Click **O**utline ...................... `O`

   OR

- Click a View button.

## Correct Errors

- Press **Backspace** `Backspace` to delete character to *left* of insertion point.
- Press **Delete** `Del` to delete character to *right* of insertion point.
- Press **Escape** `Esc` to cancel command or close dialog box.
- Click **Cancel** `Cancel` .

## Undo the Previous Action *(Ctrl+Z)*

- Click **Undo** button `↶` .

   OR

1. Click **E**dit..................... `Alt`+`E`
2. Click **U**ndo .......................... `U`

## Undo a Series of Actions *(Ctrl+Z)*

- Click **Undo** button `↶` repeatedly.

   OR

1. Click **Undo** drop-down arrow `▾` .

   ✓ *The most recent action is listed at the top of the Undo drop-down list.*

2. Click last action in the series to undo all previous actions.

## Redo the Previous Action *(Ctrl+Y)*

- Click **Redo** button `↷` .

   OR

1. Click **E**dit..................... `Alt`+`E`
2. Click **R**edo .......................... `R`

## Redo a Series of Actions *(Ctrl+Y)*

- Click **Redo** button `↷` repeatedly.

   OR

1. Click **Redo** drop-down arrow `▾` .
2. Click the last action in the series to redo all previous actions.

## Repeat the Previous Action *(Ctrl+Y or F4)*

1. Click **E**dit..................... `Alt`+`E`
2. Click **R**epeat ...................... `R`

## Save a New Document *(Ctrl+S)*

1. Click **Save** button `💾` .

   OR

   a. Click **F**ile ................ `Alt`+`F`

   b. Click **S**ave ...................... `S`

2. Click **Save in** drop-down arrow .......................... `Alt`+`I`
3. Select **drive** and **folder**.
4. Select **File name** text box...................... `Alt`+`N`
5. Type **file name**.
6. Click **Save** .................. `Alt`+`S`

**To create a new folder for storing files:**

1. Click **Save** button `💾` .

   OR

   a. Click **F**ile ............... `Alt`+`F`

   b. Click **S**ave...................... `S`

2. Click **Create New Folder** button `📁` .
3. Type **new folder name**.
4. Click **OK** .......................... Enter

   ✓ *The new folder automatically becomes the open folder.*

## Close a Document *(Ctrl+W)*

- Click **Document Close Window** button `✕` .

   OR

1. Click **F**ile ..................... `Alt`+`F`
2. Click **C**lose........................... `C`
3. Click **Y**es to save document ........................... `Y`

   OR

   Click **N**o to close without saving ................................ `N`

## Exit Word

- Click **Application Close** button `✕` .

   OR

- Double-click the **Application Control** icon `W` .

   OR

1. Click **F**ile ..................... `Alt`+`F`
2. Click E**x**it........................... `X`
3. Click **Y**es to save open documents............................ `Y`

   OR

   Click **N**o to close without saving ................................ `N`

# Exercise Directions

1. Start Word.

2. Type the first paragraph shown in Illustration A.

   ✓ Remember that you do not have to press **Enter** at the end of each line. Word wrap automatically moves the text to the next line as necessary.

3. At the end of the paragraph, press **Enter** twice to start a new paragraph and insert a blank line between the paragraphs.

4. Undo the previous action.

   ✓ When you execute the Undo command, Word reverses the action of pressing Enter twice. Sometimes Word combines actions for the purpose of Undo and Redo. In this case, it considers pressing Enter twice one action (called Typing on the Undo drop-down menu).

5. Redo the previous action.

   ✓ Word redoes the action of pressing Enter twice.

6. Type the second paragraph shown in Illustration A.

7. If you make a typing error, press Backspace to delete it, and then type the correct text.

   ✓ Word marks spelling errors with a red wavy underline, and grammatical errors with a green wavy underline. If you see these lines in the document, proofread for errors.

8. Change to Web Layout view.

9. Change to Print Layout view.

10. Change to Normal view.

11. Open the File menu.

12. Close the File menu.

13. Hide the ruler.

14. Show the ruler.

15. Hide the Formatting toolbar.

16. Show the Formatting toolbar.

17. Save the document with the name **DOCTOR**.

    ✓ Your instructor will tell you where to save the documents you create for use with this book.

18. Close the document, saving all changes if prompted.

19. Exit Word.

*Illustration A*

California Cardiology, Inc. is pleased to announce that Dr. Cynthia Ramirez has joined our practice. Dr. Ramirez received a BS degree from Stanford University in 1991 and an MD from the University of California at Los Angeles College of Medicine in 1995. She completed a residency at UCLA Medical Center and is board certified in cardiology.

We are certain that Dr. Ramirez will be a valuable addition to our practice. Her skills and experience make her highly qualified, and we are sure you will find her "bedside manner" to be professional and compassionate. Dr. Ramirez is currently accepting new patients. Please contact our office for more information or to make an appointment.

# On Your Own

1. Create a new document in Word.
2. Save the file as **OWD01**.
3. Type a brief biography about yourself, using at least two paragraphs.
4. Correct errors as necessary.
5. Practice changing from one view to another.
6. Display and hide different toolbars.
7. Close the document, saving all changes, and exit Word when you are finished.

# Exercise 2

**Skills Covered:**

◆ **Create a New Document** ◆ **Work with Show/Hide Marks**
◆ **Move the Insertion Point in a Document** ◆ **Use Click and Type**
◆ **Save Changes** ◆ **Preview an Open Document**
◆ **Print an Open Document**

## On the Job

Mastering insertion point movements in Word is necessary to enter and edit text anywhere in a document. You save changes to keep a document up-to-date as you work. When you want to have a hard copy version of a document, you must print it. Preview a document before you print it to make sure there are no errors and that it looks good on the page.

California Cardiology has decided to issue a press release announcing the hiring of a new physician. In this exercise, you will create a new document and type the press release. You will practice moving the insertion point around the document and you will align text with the click and type feature. When you have completed the press release, you will save the changes, preview the document, and then print it.

## Terms

**Insertion point** The flashing vertical line that indicates where the next action will occur in a document on-screen.

**Horizontal alignment** The position of text on a line in relation to the left and right margins.

**Hard copy** A document printed on paper.

## Notes

### Create a New Document

- As you learned in Exercise 1, when you start Word it opens and displays a new blank document called *Document1*.

- You can create additional new documents without closing and restarting Word.

- Each new document is named using consecutive numbers, so the second document is *Document2,* the third is *Document3,* and so on until you exit Word or save a file with a new name.

- In Word, you can create a new document using the New dialog box, the New Document Task Pane, or the New Blank Document button on the Standard toolbar.

  ✓ *You can also create a new Word document using Office, as described in "Getting Started with Office XP," Exercise 1.*

### Work with Show/Hide Marks

- When you type in Word you insert nonprinting characters like spaces, tabs, and paragraph marks along with printing characters like letters and numbers.

■ Displaying nonprinting characters on-screen is helpful because you see where each paragraph ends and if there are extra spaces or unwanted tab characters.

■ On-screen, the most common nonprinting characters are displayed as follows:

- Space: dot (•)

- Paragraph: paragraph symbol (¶)

- Tab: right arrow (→)

  ✓ *Other nonprinting characters include optional hyphens, and line breaks.*

## Move the Insertion Point in a Document

■ The **insertion point** indicates where text will be inserted or deleted.

■ You can move the insertion point anywhere in the existing text with keystrokes or mouse clicks.

■ Using scroll bars to shift the document view does not move the insertion point.

## Use Click and Type

■ In Print Layout view, you can use the Click and Type feature to position the insertion point anywhere in a blank document to begin typing.

  ✓ *Click and Type can only be used in Print Layout view.*

■ When Click and Type is active, the mouse pointer changes to indicate the **horizontal alignment** of the new text.

  ✓ *You learn more about horizontal alignment in Exercise 4.*

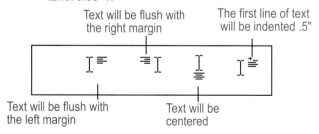

Text will be flush with the right margin

The first line of text will be indented .5"

Text will be flush with the left margin

Text will be centered

## Save Changes

■ To keep revisions permanently, you must save the document.

■ Saving frequently ensures that no work will be lost if there is a power outage or you experience computer problems.

  ✓ *The Document Recovery feature also helps insure that you won't lose your work in case of a failure. Refer to Exercise 4 of "Getting Started with Office XP" for more information.*

■ Saving replaces the previously saved version of the document with any changes.

## Preview an Open Document

■ Use Print Preview to display a document as it will look when printed.

## Print

■ Printing creates a **hard copy** version of a document.

■ Your computer must be connected to a printer in order to print.

# Procedures

## Create a New Document (Ctrl+N)

1. Start Word.
2. Click **New Blank Document** button 🗋 on the Standard toolbar.

OR

1. Start Word.
2. Click **View** .................... `Alt`+`V`
3. Click **Task Pane** .................. `K`

   ✓ *If New Document Task Pane is not displayed, select it from the Other Task Panes drop-down list.*

4. Click **Blank Document** button 🗋.

## Show or Hide Marks

- Click **Show/Hide ¶** button ¶.

OR

1. Click **Tools** .................. `Alt`+`T`
2. Click **Options** ...................... `O`
3. Click **View** tab............. `Ctrl`+`Tab`
4. Select **All** checkbox..... `Alt`+`A` in Formatting marks section.
5. Click **OK** .......................... `Enter`

## Insertion Point Movements

### To move with the mouse:

- Click mouse pointer in text where you want to position insertion point.

### To move with the keyboard:

- One character left............... `←`
- One character right............. `→`
- One line up ......................... `↑`
- One line down ..................... `↓`
- Previous word............. `Ctrl`+`←`
- Next word .................. `Ctrl`+`→`
- Up one paragraph ....... `Ctrl`+`↑`
- Down one paragraph... `Ctrl`+`↓`
- Beginning of document................. `Ctrl`+`Home`
- End of document ....... `Ctrl`+`End`
- Beginning of line............. `Home`
- End of line ......................... `End`

## Use Click and Type

1. Change to Print Layout view.
2. Click at location where you want to position insertion point.

### To enable Click and Type:

1. Click **Tools** .................. `Alt`+`T`
2. Click **Options** ...................... `O`
3. Click **Edit** tab............. `Ctrl`+`Tab`
4. Select **Enable click and type** check box............ `Alt`+`C`
5. Click **OK** .......................... `Enter`

## Save Changes (Ctrl+S)

1. Click **Save** button 🖫.

OR

   a. Click **File** ............... `Alt`+`F`
   b. Click **Save** ...................... `S`

2. Select the disk and folder where you want to save the file.
3. Enter a file name.
4. Click **Save** button  ............ `Alt`+`S`

## Preview a Document

1. Click **Print Preview** button 🔍.

OR

   a. Click **File** ............... `Alt`+`F`
   b. Click **Print Preview** ....... `V`

2. Press **Page Down** to see next page.
3. Press **Page Up** to see previous page.
4. Click **Close** `Close`.

## Print (Ctrl+P)

- Click **Print** button 🖨.

OR

1. Click **File** .................... `Alt`+`F`
2. Click **Print** .......................... `P`
3. Click **OK** .......................... `Enter`

# Exercise Directions

1. Start Word, if necessary.
2. Create a new document and save it as **PRESS**.
3. Click the Print Layout View button to change to Print Layout view if necessary.
   - ✓ Select View, Print Layout.
4. Display all nonprinting characters.
5. Use Click and Type to center the insertion point on the first line of the document.
6. Type the text shown on the first line of Illustration A.
7. Use Click and Type to move the insertion point so it is flush left on the third line of the document. You will be able to see if you have positioned the insertion point on the third line by looking at the paragraph marks on-screen. There should be one paragraph mark at the end of the first line, a second paragraph mark on the second (blank) line, and a third paragraph mark to the left of the insertion point on the third line.
   - ✓ If you press Enter twice to start a new paragraph and leave a blank line as you did in Exercise 1, the insertion point will still be centered. That's because Word carries formatting such as horizontal alignment forward from one paragraph to the next. You must use Click and Type to change the alignment to flush left.
8. Type the rest of the document shown in Illustration A.

- ✓ Depending on the default settings on your computer, Word may automatically format the Web address in the last paragraph as a hyperlink by changing the color to blue and applying an underline. If you click the hyperlink, your computer may try to log onto the Internet to locate the site. You can remove the hyperlink by right-clicking on it, then clicking *Remove Hyperlink* on the context menu.

9. Move the insertion point back to the fist sentence in the press release and delete the comma and the abbreviation **M.D.** following the name **Dr. Cynthia Ramirez**.
   - ✓ You should delete the abbreviation because you have already used the title Dr.
10. Move the insertion point between the words **a** and **staff** in the second sentence of the second paragraph.
11. Type an **n** to change the word **a** to an.
12. Type a space, then type the word **exceptional**.
13. If necessary type a space between the new word **exceptional** and the existing word **staff**.
14. Save the changes you have made to the document.
15. Display the document in Print Preview.
16. Close Print Preview.
17. Print the document.
18. Close the document, saving all changes.

Cynthia Ramirez, M.D. Joins California Cardiology, Inc.

Los Angeles, CA -- California Cardiology, Inc. is pleased to announce that Dr. Cynthia Ramirez, M.D. has joined our practice. Dr. Ramirez received a BS degree from Stanford University in 1991 and an MD from the University of California at Los Angeles College of Medicine in 1995. She completed a residency at UCLA Medical Center and is board certified in cardiology.

California Cardiology provides high-quality cardiac care to patients in the metro Los Angeles area. With the addition of Dr. Ramirez, we now have six full-time physicians supported by a staff of nurses and physician's assistants. Our offices are thoroughly *exceptional* up-to-date with the most current technologies, and we have admitting privileges at most major hospitals in L.A.

For more information about Dr. Ramirez or about California Cardiology, please call 310-555-2922, or visit us on the Web at www.ddcpub.com/calcardiology. We accept most major insurance policies.

# On Your Own

1. Create a new document.
2. Save the file as **OWD02**.
3. Draft a press release announcing that you are taking a course to learn how to use Microsoft Office XP.
4. Using Click and Type, center a headline at the top of the document.
5. Using Click and Type, move the pointer back to the flush left or first line indent position to type the rest of the press release. Include information such as your instructor's name, the textbook you are using, and when the course will be completed.
6. Save the changes, then preview the document to see how it will look when printed.
7. Print the document.
6. Close the document when you are finished, saving all changes.

# Exercise 3

## Skills Covered:

◆ **Correct Spelling as You Type** ◆ **Correct Grammar as You Type**
◆ **Check Spelling** ◆ **Check Grammar** ◆ **Use the Thesaurus**

## On the Job

A professional document should be free of spelling and grammatical errors. Word can check the spelling and grammar in a document and recommend corrections.

The marketing director has asked you to create a mission statement explaining the goals for Northwest Gear, Inc., a manufacturer of clothing for teens and young adults. In this exercise, you will type the statement, and then improve it by correcting the spelling and grammar.

## Terms

**Smart tag** A feature of Word 2002 designed to let you perform actions within Word that you would normally have to open another application to accomplish. For example, you can add a person's name and address to an Outlook contact list using a smart tag in Word.

**Thesaurus** A listing of words with synonyms and antonyms.

**Synonyms** Words with the same meaning.

**Antonyms** Words with opposite meanings.

## Notes

### Correct Spelling as You Type

- By default, Word checks spelling as you type and marks misspelled words with a red, wavy underline.

> This·is·an·example·of·a·misspelled·word.¶

- Any word not in the Word dictionary is marked as misspelled, including proper names, words with unique spellings, and many technical terms. Word will also mark double occurrences of words.

- You can ignore the wavy lines and keep typing, correct the spelling, or add the marked word to the dictionary.

- If the wavy underlines distract you from your work, you can turn off the Check spelling as you type feature.
  - ✓ *Word uses a few other underlines to mark text on-screen. For example, blue wavy underlines indicate inconsistent formatting and purple dotted lines indicate* **smart tags**. *You learn about checking for inconsistent formatting in Exercise 19.*

### Correct Grammar as You Type

- Word can also check grammar as you type, identifying errors such as punctuation, matching case or tense, sentence fragments, and run-on sentences.

- Word marks grammatical errors with a green, wavy underline.

> This·is·an·example·of·a·grammatical·errors.¶

- Word picks out grammatical errors based on one of five built-in style guides.
- The default grammar style is called Standard. You can select casual, formal, technical, or you can develop a custom style.
- As with the spelling checker, you can ignore the green wavy lines and keep typing, or correct the error.
- If the wavy underlines distract you from your work, you can turn off the Check grammar as you type feature.

## Check Spelling

- You can check the spelling in an entire document or in part of a document.
- To check the spelling in part of a document, you must first select the section you want checked.
- The spelling checker identifies any word not in the Word dictionary as misspelled, including proper names, words with unique spellings, and technical terms.
- When Word identifies a misspelled word, you can correct the spelling, ignore the spelling, or add the word to the dictionary.

*Correct spelling with Spelling Checker*

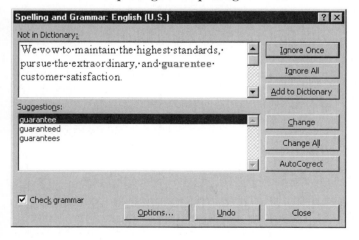

## Check Grammar

- By default, Word checks the grammar in a document at the same time that it checks the spelling.
- When Word identifies a grammatical mistake, you can accept the suggestion or ignore it.

*Correct grammar with Grammar Checker*

## Use the Thesaurus

- Use the **thesaurus** to locate **synonyms**, definitions, and **antonyms** for words typed in a document.
- A thesaurus can improve your writing by helping you eliminate repetitive use of common words and to choose more descriptive words.

*Choose synonyms with the Thesaurus*

# Procedures

## Correct Spelling as You Type

1. Right-click red, wavy underline.
2. Click correctly spelled word on context menu.
   OR
   - Click **I**gnore All ............. `I`
   - Click **A**dd to add word to dictionary ...................... `A`

## To turn off Automatic Spelling Checker:

1. Click **T**ools ................. `Alt`+`T`
2. Click **O**ptions ..................... `O`
3. Click the **Spelling & Grammar** tab ............. `Ctrl`+`Tab`
4. Deselect **Check s**p**elling as you type** check box .... `Alt`+`P`
5. Click **OK** .......................... `Enter`

## Correct Grammar as You Type

1. Right-click grammatical error marked with green, wavy underline.
2. Click **correct grammar** option on context menu.
   OR
   Click **I**gnore Once
   to hide the underline ........... `I`

## To turn Off Automatic Grammar Checker:

1. Click **T**ools ................. `Alt`+`T`
2. Click **O**ptions ..................... `O`
3. Click the **Spelling & Grammar** tab ............. `Ctrl`+`Tab`
4. Deselect **Check g**rammar as you type check box ..... `Alt`+`G`
5. Click **OK** .......................... `Enter`

## Select Grammar Style

1. Click **T**ools ................. `Alt`+`T`
2. Click **O**ptions ..................... `O`
3. Click the **Spelling & Grammar** tab ............. `Ctrl`+`Tab`
4. Click **W**riting style drop-down arrow ........ `Alt`+`W`

5. Click desired **style** .. `↕`, `Enter`
6. Click **OK** .......................... `Enter`

## Check Spelling (F7)

1. Position insertion point where you want to start checking.
   ✓ Word checks document from the insertion point forward.
   OR
   Select text you want to check.
2. Click **Spelling and Grammar** button `ABC✓`.
   OR
   a. Click **T**ools ............. `Alt`+`T`
   b. Click **S**pelling & Grammar ....................... `S`
3. Choose from the following options:
   - Click correctly spelled word in **Suggestio**n**s** list ....................... `Alt`+`N`
   - Click **C**hange ......... `Alt`+`C`
   - Click **Change A**ll to change the word everywhere in document .............. `Alt`+`L`
   - Change the misspelled word manually in the Not in Dictionary text box.
   - Click **I**gnore Once to continue without changing word ...................... `Alt`+`I`
   - Click **I**gnore All to continue without changing word and without highlighting it anywhere else in document.... `Alt`+`G`
   - Click **A**dd to Dictionary to add word to dictionary................ `Alt`+`A`
4. Repeat step 3 options for every misspelled word.
5. Click **OK** when Word completes check. ............ `Enter`

✓ *Word may prompt you to check the formatting in your document. Click* **Y**es *to check the formatting, or* **N**o *to close the prompt without checking the formatting. For more information on checking formatting, refer to Exercise 19.*

## Check Grammar (F7)

1. Position insertion point where you want to start checking.
   OR
   Select text you want to check.
2. Click **Spelling and Grammar** button `ABC✓`.
   OR
   a. Click **T**ools ............. `Alt`+`T`
   b. Click **S**pelling & Grammar ....................... `S`
3. Choose from the following options:
   - Click the correct grammar in **Suggestio**n**s** list ...... `Alt`+`N`
   - Edit the error manually in the Not in Dictionary box.
   - Click **C**hange ......... `Alt`+`C`
   - Click **I**gnore Once to continue without changing text ........................ `Alt`+`I`
   - Click **Ignore R**ule to continue without changing text and without highlighting error if it occurs anywhere else in document.... `Alt`+`G`
   - Click **Ne**x**t Sentence** to skip highlighted error and continue checking document ............... `Alt`+`X`
   - Click **E**xplain ......... `Alt`+`E` to display information about grammatical error.
4. Repeat step 3 options for every grammatical error.
5. Click **OK** when Word completes check .............. `Enter`

✓ *Word may prompt you to check the formatting in your document. Click Yes to check the formatting, or No to close the prompt without checking the formatting. For more information on checking formatting, refer to Exercise 19.*

### Use Thesaurus *(Shift+F7)*

1.  Click on the word you want to look up.
    ✓ *The insertion point should be positioned within the word.*
2.  Click **Tools** .................. `Alt`+`T`
3.  Click **Language**.................. `L`
4.  Click **Thesaurus** ................ `T`

5.  Choose from the following options:
    *   Click **Look up** to display synonyms for word highlighted in Replace with Synonym list........... `Alt`+`L`
    *   Click a word in the **Meanings list** to display synonyms for the word .............. `Alt`+`M`, `↑↓`
    *   Click **Antonyms** to display a list of antonyms for selected word.
        ✓ *The Antonyms option is not available for all words in the Thesaurus.*

6.  Click the **replacement word** you want in the **Replace with Synonym** list.......`Alt`+`S`, `↑↓`
7.  Click **Replace**............. `Alt`+`R`

### Locate a synonym as you type

1.  Right-click on the word you want to look up.
2.  Click **Synonyms** on context menu................. `Y`
3.  Click desired **synonym** on submenu................. `↑↓`, `Enter`
    OR
    Click **Thesaurus** ................ `T`
    to open the Thesaurus dialog box.

# Exercise Directions

1.  Start Word, if necessary.
2.  Create a new document.
3.  Save the file as **MISSION**.
4.  Display paragraph marks.
5.  Begin at the top of the screen and type the paragraphs shown in Illustration A, including all the circled errors.
6.  As you type, correct the spelling of the word **committed**.
7.  As you type, correct the grammar in the first sentence of the second paragraph.
8.  Check the spelling and grammar starting at the beginning of the document.
    a.  Correct the spelling of the word **clientele**.
    b.  Ignore all occurrences of the proper name **Khourie**.
    c.  Correct the spelling of the word **guarantee**.
    d.  Change the double comma in the middle of the second sentence in the second paragraph to a single comma.
    e.  Capitalize the word **we** at the beginning of the last sentence.

9.  Use the Thesaurus to replace the word **excellence** in the last sentence.
10. Display the document in Print Preview.
11. Print the document.
12. Close the document, saving all changes.

*Illustration A*

Northwest Gear, Inc. is comitted to excellence. In order to meet the needs of our clientelle, we encourage and support creativity at every level of our organization from our president, Mr. Khourie, to Bob on the loading dock. We vow to maintain the highest standards, pursue the extraordinary, and guarentee customer satisfaction.

The employees at Northwest Gear is encouraged to set personal and professional goals. Following the leadership of Mr. Khourie, we respect all employees as individuals and believe that fostering a strong community within the workplace strengthens our position in the marketplace. we are confident that our commitment to excellence will make us leaders in our industry.

# On Your Own

1. Create a new document.
2. Save the document as **OWD03**.
3. Type your own mission statement for this class in the blank document. Include information such as the goals you'd like to achieve and the things you'd like to learn.
4. Check and correct the spelling and grammar.
5. Use the Thesaurus to improve the wording of your document.
6. Print the document.
7. Save your changes, close the document, and exit Word when you are finished.

# Exercise 4

## Skills Covered:

◆ **Use AutoCorrect** ◆ **Select Text In a Document**
◆ **Replace Selected Text** ◆ **Align Text Horizontally**
◆ **Align a Document Vertically**

## On the Job

As you type a document, Word's AutoCorrect feature automatically corrects common spelling errors before you even know you've made them. You must select text in a document in order to edit it or format it. For example, changing the horizontal and vertical alignment can improve the appearance of a document, and make it easier to read.

You work in the personnel department at Perry, Hawkins, Martinez, and Klein, a large law firm based in Washington, D.C. In this exercise, your supervisor has asked you to type a memo to employees about the new Casual Friday policy.

## Terms

**AutoCorrect** A Word feature that automatically corrects common spelling errors as you type.

**Caps Lock** Keyboard key used to **toggle** uppercase letters with lowercase letters.

**Toggle** A command that turns a particular mode on and off. Also, to switch back and forth between two modes.

**Select** Mark text for editing.

**Contiguous** Next to or adjacent.

**Noncontiguous** Not next to or adjacent.

**Highlight** To apply a colored background to the text to call attention to it.

**Horizontal alignment** The position of text in relation to the left and right page margins.

**Flush** Lined up evenly along an edge.

**Vertical alignment** The position of text in relation to the top and bottom page margins.

**Selection bar** A narrow strip along the left margin of a page that automates selection of text. When the mouse pointer is in the selection area, the cursor changes to an arrow pointing up and to the right.

20

# Notes

## Use AutoCorrect

*AutoCorrect dialog box*

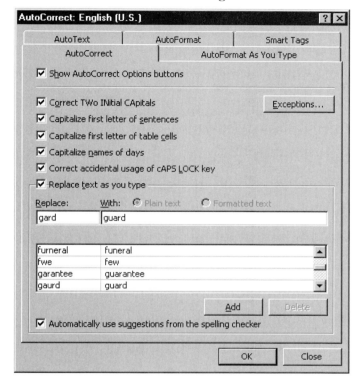

- **AutoCorrect** automatically replaces spelling errors with the correct text as soon as you press the spacebar after typing a word.
- Word comes with a built-in list of AutoCorrect entries including common typos like *adn* for *and* and *teh* for *the*.
- AutoCorrect can also replace regular characters with symbols, such as the letters *T* and *M* with the trademark symbol, ™.
- AutoCorrect also corrects capitalization errors as follows:
  - TWo INitial CApital letters are replaced with one initial capital letter.
  - The first word in a sentence is automatically capitalized.
  - The days of the week are automatically capitalized.
  - Accidental use of the cAPS LOCK feature is corrected if the **Caps Lock** key is set to ON.

- You can add words to the AutoCorrect list. For example, if you commonly misspell someone's name, you can add it to the list.
- You can also set Word to use the spelling checker dictionary to determine if a word is misspelled and to correct it automatically.
- If AutoCorrect changes text that was not incorrect, you can use Undo or the AutoCorrect Options button to reverse the change.
- If you find AutoCorrect distracting, you can disable it.

## Select Text in a Document

- You must **select** text already entered in a document in order to edit it or format it.
- You can select any amount of **contiguous** or **noncontiguous** text.
  - ✓ *You can also select nontext characters, such as symbols, nonprinting characters, such as paragraph marks, and graphics, such as pictures.*
- Selected text appears **highlighted** on screen as white characters on a black background.

*Selected text in a document*

Selected text

## Replace Selected Text

- You can replace selected text simply by typing new text.
- You can delete selected text by pressing the Delete key or the Backspace key.

## Align Text Horizontally

- **Horizontal alignment** is used to adjust the position of paragraphs in relation to the left and right margins of a page.

  ✓ *You have already used Click and Type to align text horizontally in a document.*

- There are four horizontal alignments:
  - *Left.* Text is **flush** with left margin. The text along the right side of the page is uneven (or ragged). Left is the default horizontal alignment.
  - *Right.* Text is flush with right margin. The text along the left side of the page is uneven (or ragged).
  - *Center.* Text is centered between margins.
  - *Justify.* Text is spaced so it runs evenly along both the left and right margins.

- You can use different alignments in a document.

*Text aligned in a document*

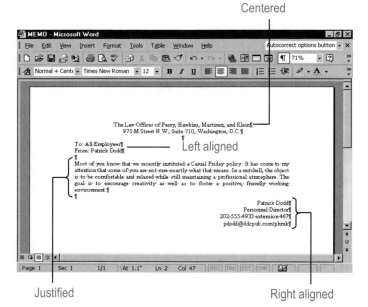

Centered

Left aligned

Justified

Right aligned

## Align a Document Vertically

- **Vertical alignment** is used to adjust the position of all text on a page in relation to the top and bottom margins.

- There are four vertical alignments:
  - *Top:* Text begins below the top margin. Top is the default vertical alignment.
  - *Center:* Text is centered between the top and bottom margins.
  - *Justified:* Paragraphs are spaced to fill the page between the top and bottom margins.
  - *Bottom:* The last line of text begins just above the bottom margin.

- Centering vertically can improve the appearance of some one-page documents, such as flyers, or invitations.

- Vertical justification improves the appearance of documents that contain nearly full pages of text.

# Procedures

## Use AutoCorrect

**Add words to the AutoCorrect list:**

1. Click **Tools** .................. `Alt`+`T`
2. Click **AutoCorrect Options** ............................ `A`
3. Click in **Replace** text box ........................ `Alt`+`R`
4. Type misspelled word to add.
5. Click in **With** text box .. `Alt`+`W`
6. Type correct word.
7. Click **Add** button

   | Add | .............. `Alt`+`A`
8. Click **OK** ........................... `Enter`

**Set AutoCorrect to correct words found in spelling checker dictionary:**

1. Click **Tools** .................. `Alt`+`T`
2. Click **AutoCorrect Options** ............................ `A`

3. Select **Automatically use suggestions from the spelling checker** check box ........................ `Alt` + `G`

### Disable AutoCorrect:

1. Click **Tools** .................... `Alt` + `T`
2. Click **AutoCorrect Options** ............................. `A`
3. Deselect **Replace text as you type** check box ............ `Alt` + `T`

   ✓ *Clicking should remove check mark; if not, click check box again.*

### Use AutoCorrect Options button:

1. Click word that was automatically corrected.

   ✓ *A small blue box is displayed below the word.*

2. Rest mouse pointer on **blue box** ⬓.

   ✓ *The AutoCorrect Options button is displayed.*

3. Click **AutoCorrect Options** button ⚡ ▾.
4. Select one of the following:
   - **Change back** ................ `H`
     to reverse the change.
   - **Stop Automatically Correcting** ..................... `A`
     to remove the word from the AutoCorrect list.
   - **Control AutoCorrect Options** ......................... `C`
     to open the AutoCorrect dialog box.

### Select Using the Keyboard

1. Position insertion point to left of first character to select.
2. Use following key combinations:
   - One character right ...................... `Shift` + `→`
   - One character left . `Shift` + `←`
   - One line up ............ `Shift` + `↑`
   - One line down ....... `Shift` + `↓`
   - To end of line ........ `Shift` + `End`
   - To beginning of line ................ `Shift` + `Home`

---

- To end of document ..... `Shift` + `Ctrl` + `End`
- To beginning of document ... `Shift` + `Ctrl` + `Home`
- Entire document ...... `Ctrl` + `A`

### Select Using the Mouse

1. Position insertion point to the left of first character to select.
2. Hold down left mouse button.
3. Drag to where you want to stop selecting.
4. Release mouse button.

### Mouse Selection Shortcuts

**One word:**
- Double-click word.

**One sentence:**
1. Press and hold **Ctrl** ............. `Ctrl`
2. Click in sentence.

**One line:**
- Click in **selection bar** to the left of the line.

   ✓ *In the selection bar, the mouse pointer changes to an arrow pointing up and to the right* ⇗.

**One paragraph:**
- Double-click in selection bar to the left of the paragraph you want to select.

**Document:**
- Triple-click in selection bar.

### Select noncontiguous blocks

1. Select first block.
2. Press and hold **Ctrl** ............. `Ctrl`
3. Select additional block(s).

### Cancel a Selection

- Click anywhere in document.
OR
- Press any arrow key ........... `↵`

---

### Replace Selected Text

1. Select text to replace.
2. Type new text.
   OR
   Press **Delete** ...................... `Del`
   to delete selected text.

### Align Horizontally

1. Position insertion point in paragraph to align.
   OR
   Select paragraphs to align.
   OR
   Position insertion point where you intend to type text.
2. Click alignment button:
   - **Center** ▤ .............. `Ctrl` + `E`
   - **Right** ▤ ............... `Ctrl` + `R`
   - **Justify** ▤ ............. `Ctrl` + `J`
   - **Left** ▤ .................. `Ctrl` + `L`

### Align Vertically

1. Click **File** ...................... `Alt` + `F`
2. Click **Page Setup** ................. `U`
3. Click **Layout** tab ......... `Alt` + `L`
4. Click **Vertical alignment** ................... `Alt` + `V`
   drop-down arrow.
5. Select **Vertical alignment** option: ..................... `↵` , `Enter`
   - **Top**
   - **Center**
   - **Justified**
   - **Bottom**
6. Click **OK** .......................... `Enter`

# Exercise Directions

1. Start Word, if necessary.
2. Create a new document and save it as **CASUAL**.
3. Display nonprinting characters, if necessary.
4. Open the AutoCorrect dialog box.
   a. Add the misspelled name **Martinex** to the AutoCorrect list; replace it with the correctly spelled **Martinez**.
   b. Add the misspelled word **personell** to the AutoCorrect list; replace it with the correctly spelled **personnel**.
   c. Add the misspelled word **casaul** to the AutoCorrect list; replace it with the correctly spelled **casual**.
   d. Be sure the *Replace text as you type* checkbox is selected, then close the dialog box.
5. Type the document shown in Illustration A.
   - Type the actual date in place of the text *Today's date*.
   - Type the circled errors exactly as shown in the illustration.
     ✓ *Notice that Word automatically corrects the errors.*
   - Press Enter twice to start new paragraphs and leave blank lines as marked on the illustration.
6. Save the document.
7. Horizontally align the text in the document as marked on the illustration.
   a. Select the lines marked for centering.
   b. Center the selected text.
   c. Select the three paragraphs marked for justification.
   d. Justify the selected paragraphs.
   e. Select the lines marked for right alignment.
   f. Right align the selected text.
8. Select the text **Personnel Director** on the *From:* line near the top of the document and replace it with the name **Patrick Dodd**.
9. Check the spelling and grammar in the document. Ignore all proper names.
10. Display the document in Print Preview.
11. Center the document vertically on the page.
12. Display the document in Print Preview again.
13. Justify the document vertically.
14. Display the document in Print Preview again.
15. Print the document.
16. Close the document, saving all changes.

# On Your Own

1. Create a new document in Word.
2. Save the file as **OWD04**.
3. Add your last name to the AutoCorrect list.
4. Add other words that you commonly misspell.
5. Type a memo to your teachers asking them to be sure to spell your name correctly. Include the misspelled version as well as the correct spelling. When AutoCorrect changes the misspelled version, use the AutoCorrect Options button to reverse the change.
6. Change the horizontal alignment of some of the text in the memo.
7. Change the vertical alignment of the document.
8. Print the document.
9. Close the document, saving all changes.

*Illustration A*

The Law Offices of Perry, Hawkins, Martinex, and Klein
975 M Street N.W., Suite 710, Washington, D.C.    } *Center*

*Enter 4x*

MEMO

*Enter 3x*

To: All Employees
From: Personell Director
Date: Today's date
Subject: Casaul Fridays

*Enter 3x*

Most of you know that we recently instituted a Casual Friday policy. It has come to my attention that some of you are not sure exactly what that means. In a nutshell, teh object is to be comfortable and relaxed while still maintaining a professional atmosphere. THe goal is to encourage creativity as well as to foster a positive, friendly working environment.    } *Justify*

*Enter 2x*

As for what constitutes appropriate attire for Casual Fridays, please use common sense. For example, do not dress for the beach. ALso, if you have a meeting with a client who is not expecting Casual friday, you should not dress for Casual Friday.

*Enter 2x*

Here are a few guidelines:

*Enter 2x*

Khakis instead of dress slacks or skirts
SWeaters instead of suit coats    } *Center*
Sneakers instead of hgih heels

*Enter 2x*

If you have any questions, feel free to contact me. I think that in a few weeks we will all be completely comfortable with the Casual Friday atmosphere.    } *Justify*

*Enter 3x*

Patrick Dodd
Personell Director
202-555-4933 extension 467    } *Right align*
pdodd@ddcpub.com/phmk

**25**

# Exercise 5

## On the Job

Write business letters as a representative of your employer to communicate with other businesses, such as clients or suppliers, or to communicate with individuals, such as prospective employees. For example, you might write a business letter to request a job quote from a supplier, or to inquire about a loan from a bank.

You are the assistant to Mr. Benjamin Boghosian, the owner of Coastline Gourmet Importers, a chain of specialty food retail stores. He has asked you to type a letter to a vendor about obtaining some Russian caviar. In this exercise, you will compose a full-block business letter regarding the caviar.

## Terms

**Full block** A style of letter in which all lines start flush with the left margin—that is, without a first-line indent.

**Modified block** A style of letter in which some lines start at the center of the page.

**Salutation** The line at the start of a letter including the greeting and the recipient's name, such as *Dear Mr. Doe.*

**Computer's clock** The clock/calendar built into your computer's main processor to keep track of the current date and time.

**Case** The specific use of upper- or lowercase letters.

## Notes

### Format a Business Letter

- There are different letter styles of business letters.
  - In a **full-block** business letter, all lines start flush with the left margin.
  - In a **modified-block** business letter, certain lines start at the center of the page.
    - ✓ *Modified-block business letters will be covered in Exercise 6.*
- The parts of a business letter are the same regardless of the style.

- Vertical spacing is achieved by inserting blank lines between letter parts.
- Refer to the illustration on page 28 to identify the parts of a business letter.
  - Return address (may be omitted if the letter is printed on letterhead stationery)
  - Date
  - Inside address (to whom and where the letter is going)
  - **Salutation**
  - Body

- Signature line
- Title line (the job title of the letter writer)
- Reference initials (the initials of the person who wrote the letter, followed by a slash, followed by the initials of the person who typed the letter)

  ✓ *Whenever you see "yo" as part of the reference initials in an exercise, type your own initials.*

- Special notations (included only when appropriate):
  - Mail service notation indicates a special delivery method. It is typed in all capital letters, two lines below the date. Typical mail service notations include *CERTIFIED MAIL, REGISTERED MAIL,* or *BY HAND.*
  - Subject notation identifies or summarizes the letter topic. The word *Subject* may be typed in all capital letters or with just an initial capital. It is placed two lines below the salutation.

    ✓ *The word* Re *(meaning* with regard to*) is sometimes used in place of the word* Subject.

  - Enclosure or attachment notation indicates whether there are other items in the envelope. It is typed two lines below the reference initials in any of the following styles: *ENC., Enc., Encl., Enclosure, Attachment.*

    ✓ *If there are multiple items, the number may be typed in parentheses following the notation.*

  - Copy notation indicates if any other people are receiving copies of the same letter. It is typed two lines below either the enclosure notation, or reference initials, whichever is last. It may be typed as Copy to:, cc:, or pc: (photocopy) with the name(s) of the recipient(s) listed after the colon.

## Insert the Date and Time in a Document

- Use the Date and Time feature to insert the current date and/or time automatically in a document.

- The inserted date and time are based on your **computer's clock**. A variety of date and time formats are available.

*The Date and Time dialog box*

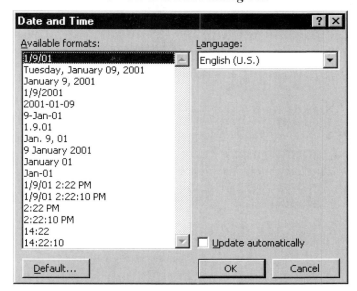

- You can set Word to update the date or time automatically whenever you save or print the document.

## Use Uppercase Mode

- Use Uppercase Mode to type all capital letters without pressing the Shift key.
- Uppercase Mode affects only letter characters.
- When Uppercase Mode is on, the Caps Lock indicator on your keyboard is lit.

## Change Case in a Document

- You can automatically change the **case** of text in a document.
- There are five case options:
  - Sentence case: First character in sentence is uppercase.
  - lowercase: All characters are lowercase.
  - UPPERCASE: All characters are uppercase.
  - Title Case: First character in each word is uppercase.
  - tOGGLE cASE: Case is reversed for all selected text.

# Procedures

## Format a Full-Block Business Letter

1. Start 2" from the top of the page........................... `Enter` **4x**

   ✓ *Press Enter four times to leave 2" of space.*

   ✓ *If you are using stationery with a printed letterhead, you may have to adjust the spacing.*

2. Insert the date.
3. Leave one blank line and type the mail service notation .......... `Enter` **2x**
4. Leave three blank lines and type the inside address ....................... `Enter` **4x**
5. Leave a blank line and type the salutation .............. `Enter` **2x**
6. Leave one blank line and type the subject notation .... `Enter` **2x**
7. Leave a blank line and type the letter body ..... `Enter` **2x**
8. Leave a blank line and type the closing .......... `Enter` **2x**
9. Leave three blank lines and type the signature line ......... `Enter` **4x**

10. Press **Enter** ...................... `Enter`
11. Type the title line .............. `Enter`

    ✓ *If you are not using letterhead stationery, type the return address information below the title line.*

12. Leave a blank line and type the reference initials. ... `Enter` **2x**
13. Leave a blank line and type the enclosure notation ........ `Enter` **2x**
14. Leave a blank line and type the copy notation ........ `Enter` **2x**

## Insert the Date and/or Time

1. Position the insertion point.
2. Click **Insert** ................. `Alt`+`I`
3. Click **Date and Time** .......... `T`
4. Click the desired format.

   ✓ *Select Update automatically check box if you want date and/or time to update when you save or print document.*

5. Click **OK** .......................... `Enter`

## Uppercase Mode

1. Press **Caps Lock** .............
2. Type text.

## To turn off Uppercase Mode:

• Press **Caps Lock** ............. `Caps`

## Change Case

1. Select text.

   OR

   Position insertion point where new text will begin.
2. Click **Format** .............. `Alt`+`O`
3. Click **Change Case** ............. `E`
4. Click the case you want:
   • **Sentence case** .............. `S`
   • **lowercase** ..................... `L`
   • **UPPERCASE** ................... `U`
   • **Title Case** ...................... `T`
   • **tOGGLE cASE** .............. `G`
5. Click **OK** .......................... `Enter`

   ✓ *You can also select text and then press Shift+F3 to toggle through sentence case, lowercase, and uppercase. Release the keys when the desired case is in effect.*

# Exercise Directions

1. Start Word, if necessary.
2. Create a new document and save it as **CAVIAR**.
3. Type the letter shown in Illustration A.
   • Press the Enter key between parts of the letter as indicated.
   • Insert the current date using the MONTH DAY, YEAR format found third from the top in the Date and Time dialog box.
   • Set the date so that it does not update automatically.
   • Use Uppercase mode to type the mail notation.

      ✓ *Word may display ScreenTips as you type certain parts of the letter (for example, CERTIFIED MAIL). Simply ignore them and continue typing.*

4. Change the text on the Subject line to title case.
5. Change all occurrences of the text **Coastline Gourmet Importers** and **Coastline Gourmet** to uppercase.

   ✓ *Do not change the text as it appears in the Web address.*

6. Check the spelling and grammar in the document.
   • Ignore all proper names.
7. Display the document in Print Preview.

   ✓ *If the document does not fit on one page, you may have inserted too many blank lines. Make sure you have nonprinting characters displayed so you can see the paragraph marks, count the marks, and delete any extras.*

8. Close the document, saving all changes.

*Illustration A*

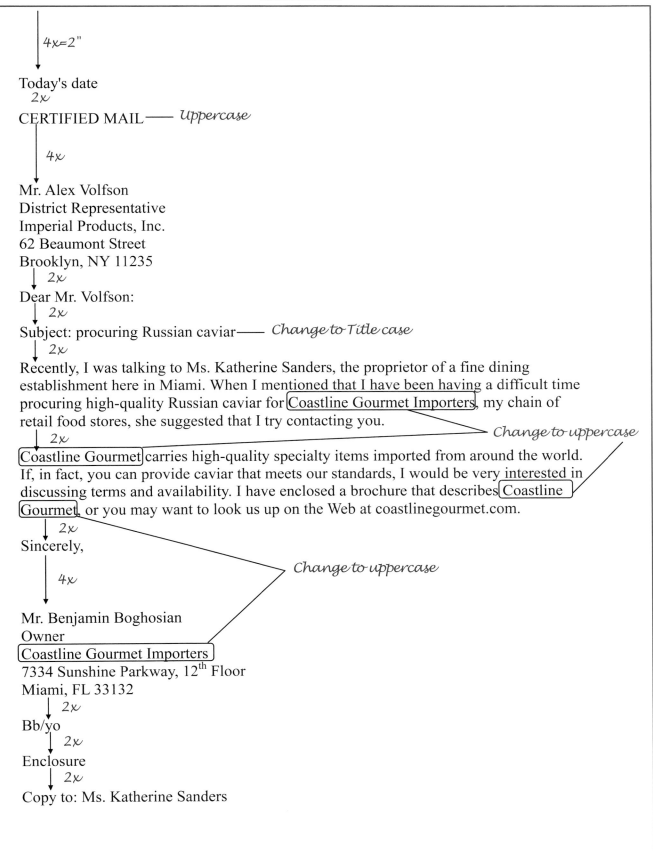

4x=2"

Today's date
   *2x*

CERTIFIED MAIL —— *Uppercase*

   *4x*

Mr. Alex Volfson
District Representative
Imperial Products, Inc.
62 Beaumont Street
Brooklyn, NY 11235
   *2x*

Dear Mr. Volfson:
   *2x*

Subject: procuring Russian caviar —— *Change to Title case*
   *2x*

Recently, I was talking to Ms. Katherine Sanders, the proprietor of a fine dining establishment here in Miami. When I mentioned that I have been having a difficult time procuring high-quality Russian caviar for Coastline Gourmet Importers, my chain of retail food stores, she suggested that I try contacting you.
   *2x*                                                          *Change to uppercase*

Coastline Gourmet carries high-quality specialty items imported from around the world. If, in fact, you can provide caviar that meets our standards, I would be very interested in discussing terms and availability. I have enclosed a brochure that describes Coastline Gourmet, or you may want to look us up on the Web at coastlinegourmet.com.
   *2x*

Sincerely,

   *4x*                                        *Change to uppercase*

Mr. Benjamin Boghosian
Owner
Coastline Gourmet Importers
7334 Sunshine Parkway, 12ᵗʰ Floor
Miami, FL 33132
   *2x*

Bb/yo
   *2x*

Enclosure
   *2x*

Copy to: Ms. Katherine Sanders

# On Your Own

1. Create a new document in Word.
2. Save the document as **OWD05**.
3. Representing your school or organization, draft a full-block business letter to a local newspaper asking them to include information about upcoming events in a calendar listing. School events might include athletic contests such as a homecoming football game, club activities, field trips, band and choir concerts, or vacation days.
4. In the letter, indicate that you have attached the necessary information and that you are sending a copy to your instructor.
5. Test different case options for different parts of the letter.
6. Save your changes, close the document, and exit Word when you are finished.

# Exercise 6

## On the Job

You use tabs to align text in a document, such as the date in a modified-block business letter. If a letter is just a bit too long to fit on a single page, use *Shrink to Fit* to automatically reduce the printed length of a document so it fits on one page.

The marketing director at Northwest Gear, Inc., a clothing manufacturer, has asked you to type a letter inviting a buyer from a chain of clothing stores to preview the new fall line. In this exercise, you compose a modified-block business letter using tabs, Shrink to Fit, and Full Screen view.

## Terms

**Tab** A location (or measurement) you use to align text.

**Font** A set of characters with a specific size and style.

## Notes

*Tab stops on the horizontal ruler*

Left tab stop   Center tab stop   Right tab stop   Decimal tab stop   Bar tab stop

### Set Tabs

- **Tabs** are used to indent a single line of text.
- Each time you press the Tab key, the insertion point advances to the next set tab stop.
- There are five types of tab stops:
  - Left: Text starts flush left with the tab stop.
  - Right: Text ends flush right with the tab stop.
  - Center: Text is centered on the tab stop.
  - Decimal: Decimal points are aligned with the tab stop.
  - Bar: A horizontal bar is displayed at the tab stop position. Text starts 1/10" to the right of the bar.

- By default, left tab stops are set every ½" on the horizontal ruler.
- You can set any type of tab stop at any point along the ruler.
- You can use the Tabs dialog box to set precise tab stops.
- You can set tabs before you type new text, for the current existing paragraph, or for selected multiple paragraphs.
- Once you set tabs, the formatting will be carried forward each time you press the Enter key to start a new paragraph.

*Tabs dialog box*

## Shrink to Fit

- Shrink to Fit automatically reduces the **font** size and spacing in a document just enough to fit the document on one less page.
- Use Shrink to Fit if the last page of a document contains only a small amo
- unt of text.
- The Shrink to Fit feature is available only in Print Preview mode.

## Full Screen View

- In any view, including Print Preview, use Full Screen view to display a document without the title bar, toolbars, ruler, scroll bars, status bar, or taskbar.
- Full Screen view lets you see more of your document on-screen at one time.

*Full Screen view*

## Format a Modified-Block Business Letter

- A modified-block style letter is set up with all lines starting flush with the left margin except the date, closing, signature, and title lines, which begin at the center point of the page.
  - ✓ *The parts of a modified-block style letter are the same as those of a full-block style letter. The special notations are used when appropriate.*
- A left tab stop set at the center point of the page enables you to position the insertion point quickly where you need it.
  - ✓ *Using a center tab stop or centered alignment centers the text; you must use a left tab stop in order to position the text to start at the center point of the page.*

# Procedures

## Set Tabs

**To set a left tab stop:**

1. Position insertion point in paragraph to format.
   OR
   Select paragraphs to format.
2. Click ruler where you want to set tab stop.

**To set a different type of tab stop:**

1. Position insertion point in paragraph to format.
   OR
   Select paragraphs to format.
2. Click the **Tab** box .
   - ✓ *Each time you click, the tab icon changes. Stop when tab stop you want is displayed.*

3. Click ruler where you want to insert new tab stop.

**To set a precise tab stop:**

1. Position insertion point in paragraph to format.
   OR
   Select paragraphs to format.
2. Click **Format** .............. `Alt`+`O`
3. Click **Tabs** ......................... `T`

4. Select type of tab:
   - **Left**.................... Alt + L
   - **Center**.................. Alt + C
   - **Right**.................... Alt + R
   - **Decimal** ............... Alt + D
   - **Bar** ...................... Alt + B
5. Click in the **Tab stop position**............. Alt + T
6. Type precise position.
7. Click **OK** ......................... Enter

**To clear a tab stop:**

1. Position insertion point in paragraph to forma.
   OR
   Select paragraphs to format.
2. Drag tab stop marker off ruler.
OR
1. Click **Format** ............... Alt + O
2. Click **Tabs** ...................... T
3. Click **Clear All** ............. Alt + A
   OR
   a. Select tab stop(s) to clear.
   b. Click **Clear** ............ Alt + E
4. Click **OK** ......................... Enter

**Format a Modified-Block Business Letter**

1. Start 2" from top of page ........................ Enter **4x**
   ✓ *Press Enter four times to leave 2" of space.*
   ✓ *If you are using stationery with a printed letterhead, you may have to adjust the spacing.*
2. Set left tab stop at 3".
3. Press **Tab** ........................... Tab
4. Insert date.
5. Leave three blank lines and type inside address ..... Enter **4x**
6. Leave a blank line and type the salutation ....... Enter **2x**
7. Leave a blank line and type the letter body...... Enter **2x**
8. Leave a blank line ........ Enter **2x**
9. Press **Tab** ........................... Tab
10. Type the closing.
11. Leave three blank lines .................. Enter **4x**
12. Press **Tab** ........................... Tab
13. Type signature line.
14. Move to next line and press **Tab** .......... Enter , Tab
15. Type title line.
16. Leave a blank line and type reference initials .. Enter **2x**

**Shrink to Fit**

1. Click **Print Preview** button.
   OR
   a. Click **File** ............... Alt + F
   b. Click **Print Preview** ........ V
2. Click **Shrink to Fit** button.
3. Click **Close** button Close.

**Full Screen View**

1. Click **View** .................. Alt + V
2. Click **Full Screen**................. U

**To display screen elements again:**

- Press **Esc**........................... Esc
OR
- Click **Close Full Screen** button Close Full Screen.

# Exercise Directions

1. Start Word, if necessary.
2. Create a new document and save it as **BUYER**.
3. Type the letter shown in Illustration A.
   ✓ *When you type the letter as shown in the illustration, it will not fit on a single page.*
   - Set a left tab stop at 3" on the ruler.
   - Position the date, closing, signature, and title at the tab stop.
   - Press the Enter key between parts of the letter as indicated.
   - Insert the current date using the MONTH DAY, YEAR format found third from the top in the Date and Time dialog box.
   - Set the date so that it does not update automatically.
4. Check the spelling and grammar and make changes as suggested.
   - Ignore all proper names.
5. Display the document in Print Preview.
6. Shrink the document to fit on a single page.
7. Display the document in Full Screen view.
8. Display the screen elements again.
9. Print the document.
10. Close the document, saving all changes.

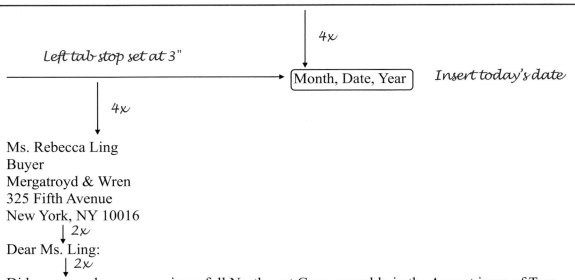

*Left tab stop set at 3"*

↓ *4x*

Month, Date, Year    *Insert today's date*

↓ *4x*

Ms. Rebecca Ling
Buyer
Mergatroyd & Wren
325 Fifth Avenue
New York, NY 10016
↓ *2x*
Dear Ms. Ling:
↓ *2x*

Did you see who was wearing a full Northwest Gear ensemble in the August issue of Teen People magazine? If you did, then you know that our clothes are currently the hottest trend among 12 to 20 year olds. And yet, Mergatroyd & Wren, one of the most popular clothing and accessory stores for teens, has yet to carry a single Northwest Gear item!
↓ *2x*

My mission, Ms. Ling, is to remedy that situation. I am sure that you agree that we should take advantage of the phenomenal overlap between your customer base and ours. Together, you and I can certainly find a way to get Northwest Gear clothing on to the sales floor at every Mergatroyd & Wren store in North America. I know your customers would be thrilled by the new inventory, and you'd be thrilled by the positive impact on your bottom line.
↓ *2x*

With that in mind, I am personally inviting you to come to Seattle (at our expense, of course) to take a sneak peak behind the scenes at Northwest Gear. Come for one day, two days, or for a week. You can tour our center of operations, meet our designers, and preview our new fall fashions. A dinner reception with our president, Mr. Khourie, will cap your visit.
↓ *2x*

In case you missed the Teen People article, I have enclosed it with this letter. I eagerly await your reply.

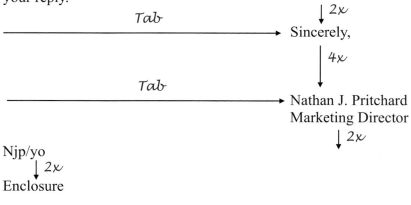

*Tab* → ↓ *2x*
Sincerely,

↓ *4x*

*Tab* → Nathan J. Pritchard
Marketing Director
↓ *2x*

Njp/yo
↓ *2x*
Enclosure

# On Your Own

1. Create a new document in Word.

2. Save the file as **OWD06**.

3. As a representative of a school organization, draft a modified-block business letter to a company that sells music CDs by mail telling the company that your organization did not receive the complete order in the last shipment.

4. List the music CDs that you ordered and indicate which titles were missing in the shipment.

5. Preview the document. Make sure it fits on one page.

6. Display the document in Full Screen view.

7. Change back to display all screen elements.

8. Print one copy of the document.

9. Close the document, saving all changes.

# Exercise 7

## Skills Covered:

◆ **Format a Personal Business Letter** ◆ **Select Fonts**
◆ **Change Font Size** ◆ **Apply Font Styles** ◆ **Apply Underlines**
◆ **Create Envelopes** ◆ **Create Labels**

## On the Job

Write personal business letters to find a job or communicate with businesses such as your bank or your insurance company. For example, you might write a personal business letter to your insurance company to ask about a claim that needs to be paid. The letter serves as a formal record of your inquiry. To send it, you need to print an accompanying envelope or label. Use fonts, font sizes, underlines, and font styles, to dress up the appearance of a document. Fonts are a basic means of applying formatting to text and characters. They can set a mood, command attention, and convey a message.

You are interested in obtaining a position as a graphic designer for Northwest Gear, Inc. In this exercise, you will create and format a personal business letter asking about job opportunities. You will also create an envelope to accompany the document. Finally, you will create return address labels and save them in a separate document.

## Terms

**Return address** The author's address, typically appearing at the very top of the letter as well as in the upper-left corner of an envelope.

**Letterhead** Paper with a company's name and address already printed on it.

**Font** A complete set of characters in a specific face, style, and size.

**Font face** The character design of a font set.

**Serif** A font that has curved or extended edges.

**Sans serif** A font that has straight edges.

**Script** A font that looks like handwriting.

**Font size** The height of an uppercase letter in a font set.

**Font style** The slant and weight of characters in a font set.

**Delivery address** The recipient's address printed on the outside of an envelope.

## Notes

### Format a Personal Business Letter

- A business letter written on behalf of an individual instead of on behalf of another business is considered a personal business letter.

- A personal business letter includes the same elements as a business letter, minus the title line and reference initials, and plus a **return address**.
    - ✓ *If the paper has a **letterhead**, omit the return address.*

- A personal business letter can be full block or modified block.
  - In full block, type the return address following the signature.
  - In modified block, type the return address above the date.
    - ✓ *For more information on the parts of a business letter, refer to Exercise 5.*

## Select Fonts

- Each **font** set includes upper- and lowercase letters, numbers, and punctuation marks.
- There are three basic categories of **font faces**:
  - **Serif** fonts are easy to read and are often used for document text.

### A Serif Font

  - **Sans serif** fonts are often used for headings.

### A Sans Serif Font

  - **Script** face fonts are often used to simulate handwriting on invitations or announcements.

### A Script Font

- The default Word font is Times New Roman, a serif font.
- The current font name is displayed in the Font box on the Formatting toolbar.

*Font box shows the font name*

- Both Office and Windows come with built-in fonts; you can install additional fonts.
- Fonts can be changed before or after you enter text in a document.
- You can set the tone of a document by putting thought into the fonts you select.
  - ✓ *More than two or three font faces makes a document look disjointed and unprofessional.*

## Change Font Size

- **Font size** is measured in points. There are 72 points in an inch.
- The default Word font size is 12 points.

- The current font size is displayed in the Font Size box on the Formatting toolbar.

*Font Size box shows the font size*

## Apply Font Styles

- The most common **font styles** are **bold** and *italic*.
- When no style is applied to a font, it is called regular.
  - ✓ *Font styles can be combined for different effects, such as bold italic.*

## Apply Underlines

- There are 17 types of underlines available in Word, which include:
  - <u>Single</u> (underlines all characters, including nonprinting characters such as spaces and tabs)
  - <u>Words</u> only
  - <u>Double</u>
  - <u>Dotted</u>
  - <u>Thick</u>
  - <u>Dash</u>
  - <u>Dot dash</u>
  - <u>Dot dot dash</u>
  - <u>Wave</u>

*The Font dialog box lets you select a font, font size, font style, and underline at the same time*

## Create Envelopes

- Word has a feature that automatically sets up an envelope for printing.
- If a letter document is open on-screen, Word picks up the inside address for the envelope's **delivery address**.
- You can print the envelope immediately or add it to the beginning of the open document and save it to print later.

## Create Labels

- Use the Label feature to create mailing labels, file folder labels, or diskette labels.

- The Label feature automatically sets up a document to print on predefined label types.
- You select the manufacturer and label type loaded in the printer.
- By default, Word creates a full page of labels using the inside address from the current document.
- You can change the default to create labels using the return address or to create a single label.

# Procedures

### Select Font

1. Select text.

   **OR**

   Position insertion point where new text will be typed.
2. Click **Font** drop-down arrow

3. Click font name......... [↓], [Enter]

   ✓ *The font list is alphabetical; however, recently used fonts are listed at the top of the list.*

   ***The Font list***

   Recently used fonts

   Alphabetical list starts here

   **OR**

1. Select text.

   **OR**

   Position insertion point where new text will be typed.

2. Click **Format** ............. [Alt]+[O]
3. Click **Font**............................ [F]
4. Click font name in **Font** list .......................... [↓]
5. Click **OK** ..........................[Enter]

### Change Font Size

1. Select text.

   **OR**

   Position insertion point where new text will be typed.
2. Click **Font Size** drop-down arrow.
3. Click font size ........... [↓], [Enter]

   ✓ *You can also type desired font size directly into Font Size box, then press Enter. You can even type half sizes, such as 10.5, 12.5, and so on.*

   **OR**

1. Select text.

   **OR**

   Position insertion point where new text will be typed.
2. Click **Format** ............... [Alt]+[O]
3. Click **Font**............................ [F]
4. Click font size in **Size list**................ [Alt]+[S], [↓]
5. Click **OK** ..........................[Enter]

### Apply Font Styles

1. Select text.

   **OR**

   Position insertion point where new text will be typed.
2. Click font style button:

   - **Bold** [B] ................ [Ctrl]+[B]
   - **Italic** [I] ............... [Ctrl]+[I]

   ✓ *To remove font styles repeat steps 1 and 2.*

   **OR**

1. Select text.

   **OR**

   Position insertion point where new text will be typed.
2. Click **Format** ............... [Alt]+[O]
3. Click **Font**.......................... [F]
4. Click font style in **Font style** list ......................... [Alt]+[Y], [↓]

   ✓ *To remove font styles click Regular.*

5. Click **OK** ..........................[Enter]

## Apply Underlines (*Ctrl+U*)

1. Select text.
   OR
   Position insertion point where new text will be typed.
2. Click **Underline** button `U` ................ `Alt`+`U`
   ✓ *Repeat steps to remove underline.*

OR

1. Select text.
   OR
   Position insertion point where new text will be typed.
2. Click **Format** .............. `Alt`+`O`
3. Click **Font** .......................... `F`
4. Click **Underline style** drop-down arrow ......... `Alt`+`U`
5. Click desired underline type.
   ✓ *Click (None) to remove underline.*
6. Click **OK** ......................... `Enter`

## Create an Envelope

1. Click **Tools** ................. `Alt`+`T`
2. Click **Letters and Mailings**. `E`
3. Click **Envelopes and Labels** ................................ `E`
4. Click **Envelopes** tab ... `Alt`+`E`
5. Type **Delivery address** ...................... `Alt`+`D`
   ✓ *If inside address is already entered, skip to step 6.*
6. Type **Return address** .......... `Alt`+`R`
   OR
   Select **Omit** check box .............................. `Alt`+`M`
   ✓ *If Omit check box is selected, you cannot type in Return address text box.*
7. Click **Print** button
   `Print` ......................... `Alt`+`P`
   OR
   Select **Add to Document** ................. `Alt`+`A`

## Create a Single Label

1. Click **Tools** ................. `Alt`+`T`
2. Click **Letters and Mailings** `E`
3. Click **Envelopes and Labels** ................................ `E`
4. Click **Labels** tab ......... `Alt`+`L`
5. Click **Single label** option button ......................... `Alt`+`N`
6. Click **Options** ..................... `O`
7. Select option from **Label products** list .............. `Alt`+`P`
8. Select option from **Product number** list ................. `Alt`+`U`
   ✓ *Make sure correct printer and tray information is selected.*
9. Click **OK** ........................... `Enter`
10. Type **label text**.
    ✓ *If inside address is already entered, skip to 11.*
11. Make sure labels are loaded in printer.
12. Click **Print** button
    `Print` ......................... `Alt`+`P`

## Create Return Address Labels

1. Click **Tools** ................. `Alt`+`T`
2. Click **Letters and Mailings** . `E`
3. Click **Envelopes and Labels** ................................ `E`
4. Click **Labels** tab ......... `Alt`+`L`
5. Select **Use return address** check box .................... `Alt`+`R`
6. Click **Options** .............. `Alt`+`O`
7. Select option from **Label products** list .............. `Alt`+`P`
8. Select option from **Product number** list ................. `Alt`+`U`
   ✓ *Make sure the correct printer and tray information is selected.*
9. Click **OK** ........................... `Enter`
   ✓ *Make sure labels are loaded in printer.*
10. Click **Print** button
    `Print` ......................... `Alt`+`P`
    OR
    a. Click **New Document** ............. `Alt`+`D`
    b. If prompted to save the return address, click **No** ... `N`
    c. Click **Save** button 💾 to save labels.

# Exercise Directions

1. Start Word, if necessary.
2. Create a new document and save it as **REQUEST**.
3. Type the letter shown in Illustration A.
   - Use the full-block format for the letter.
   - Insert today's date using the Month Date, Year format. Make sure the date will not update automatically.
   - Use the default font and font size except where marked otherwise on the illustration.
4. Check the spelling and grammar.
5. Create an envelope for the letter.
   - Use your name and address as the return address.
6. Add the envelope to the document.
   - When prompted to save the new return address as the default, choose No.
7. Preview the document.
8. Print the document.
9. Save the changes to the document.
10. Create return address labels for the document.
    a. Use the return address in the document.
    b. Create a full page of the same label.
    c. Save the label document as **LABELS**.
    ✓ *Do not save the return address as the default.*
11. Preview the new label document.
12. Print the label document.
    ✓ *You can print the labels on standard letter-sized paper if you do not have labels available.*
13. Close the label document, saving all changes.
14. Close the letter document, saving all changes.
15. Create a new document and save it as **DESIGN**.
16. Apply font styles and alignments as shown in Illustration B.
17. Close the **DESIGN** document, saving all changes.

# On Your Own

1. Create a new document in Word.
2. Save the file as **OWD07**.
3. Draft a personal business letter. For example, you might write a letter asking about summer job opportunities. If you have a job, you could write to your employer asking to take a vacation day in the coming month. You can also draft a personal letter to a company with whom you do business asking for a credit on returned merchandise, or to a college asking about application requirements. Record stores, clothing stores, or sporting goods stores are companies you might use.

✓ *If smart tag indicators are displayed, you can ignore them or turn them off. To turn them off, Click Tools, and then click AutoCorrect Options. Click the Smart Tags tab and deselect the Label text with smart tags check box. Click OK to close the dialog box and continue working.*

4. Create an envelope for your letter and attach it to the document.
5. Create your own mailing labels using the return address from your letter, and save them in a separate document with the name **OWD07-2**.
6. Check the spelling and grammar before printing the documents.
7. Save your changes, close all open documents, and exit Word when you are finished.

*Illustration A*

Your Street Address
Your City, Your State Your Postal Code

Today's date

Ms. Emily DiNapoli
Vice President
Northwest Gear, Inc.
2749 Mission Street
Seattle, WA 98122

Dear Ms. DiNapoli:

I am writing to inquire about job opportunities in graphic design at Northwest Gear, Inc. Currently, I am employed as a sales associate at the Mergatroyd & Wren store in downtown Seattle. However, design is my true passion.

While studying graphic design at a local university, I worked as an assistant to a Web designer. I gained valuable experience working with other designers, creating designs of my own, and meeting deadlines. Now that I have a degree in graphic design, I would like to obtain a full-time position in design. Working at Northwest Gear would be a dream come true. I've enclosed a sample flyer that I did for a local CD shop.

In addition to my degree and experience, I believe that I have talent and style. Being young, I also have a good idea of the types of clothes that appeal to teens. I would be happy to meet you and show you my portfolio at any time.

I look forward to hearing from you soon.

Sincerely,

Your Name

Enc.

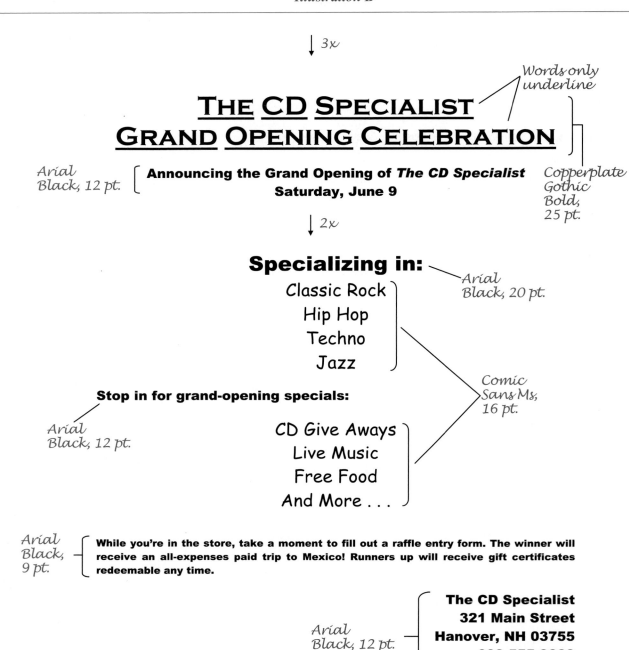

# Exercise 8

## ◆ Critical Thinking

You are a party planner interested in developing a joint catering service venture with Coastline Gourmet Importers. In this exercise, you will start by creating a business letter proposing the idea to the owner of Coastline Gourmet. Next, you will create an envelope for the letter along with return address labels. Finally, you will create a flyer about the proposed service that you can attach to the letter. You will use alignments and font formatting to make the flyer visually exciting.

## Exercise Directions

1. Start Word, if necessary.
2. Create a new document and save it as **PROPOSAL**.
3. Display nonprinting characters.
4. Make sure AutoCorrect is on.
5. Type the letter in Illustration A exactly as shown, including all circled errors.
6. Insert the date in the Month Date, Year format so that it does not update automatically.
7. Correct spelling and grammatical errors.
   - Add your name to the dictionary, if necessary.
   - Ignore all proper names.
   - Correct all other spelling errors that AutoCorrect did not automatically change.
8. Use the Thesaurus to find an appropriate replacement for the word **simply**.
9. Save the changes you have made to the document.
10. Display the document in Print Preview.
11. Display the document in Full Screen view.
12. Return the document to Normal view.
13. Create an envelope for the letter and add it to the document. Omit the return address.
14. Print the document.
15. Close the document, saving all changes.
16. Create return address mailing labels for your party planning business using the following information:

**Your Name**
**Party Planner**
**P.O. Box 765**
**Miami, FL 33132**

17. Save the labels document with the name **RETURN**.
18. Display the **RETURN** document in Print Preview, and then print it.
    - ✓ If you do not have labels available, print it on regular paper.
19. Close the **RETURN** document, saving all changes.
20. Create a new document.
21. Save the document as **FLYER**.
22. Display nonprinting characters.
23. Type the document shown in Illustration B, using the specified alignments, font formatting, and tabs.
24. Check the spelling and grammar in the document.
25. Display the document in Print Preview.
26. If the document is longer than one page, shrink it to fit; if it is shorter than one page, adjust the vertical alignment to improve the appearance, as necessary.
27. Print the document.
28. Close the document, saving all changes.

[Today's date]  *Insert date in month, date, year format*

Mr. Benjamin Boghosian
Owner
Coastline Gourmet Importers
7334 Sunshine Parkway, 12th Floor
Miami, FL 33132

Dear Mr. Boghosian:

Have you ever considered expanding your business? I have! As a party planner in [the the] Miami area[,,] I spend a great deal of time on the look out for reliable caterers. I finally realized that it would be [alot] easier to simply provide the service myself!

However; I am smart enough to know that I would benefit from a partner such as yourself. I think that together you and I have the [knowldege], contacts, and resources to develop a [sucessful] catering service. My experience [as a party planners], and your access to fine quality specialty foods make us [uniqely] positioned to pursue such a venture.

[I has] attached a flyer detailing my ideas for the new business. [PLease] call me to discuss the [possibbillities].

Sincerely,



Your Name
Party Planner

Attachment

*Illustration B*

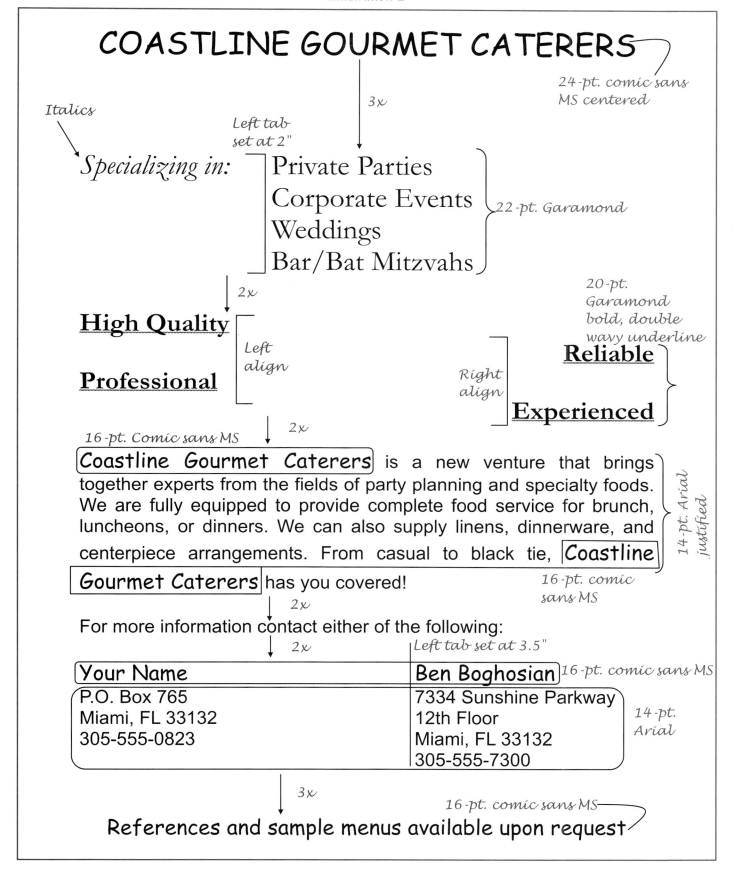

# COASTLINE GOURMET CATERERS

*24-pt. comic sans MS centered*

*3x*

*Italics*

*Left tab set at 2"*

*Specializing in:*

Private Parties
Corporate Events
Weddings
Bar/Bat Mitzvahs

*22-pt. Garamond*

*2x*

**High Quality**

*Left align*

**Professional**

*20-pt. Garamond bold, double wavy underline*

**Reliable**

*Right align*

**Experienced**

*16-pt. Comic sans MS*

*2x*

Coastline Gourmet Caterers is a new venture that brings together experts from the fields of party planning and specialty foods. We are fully equipped to provide complete food service for brunch, luncheons, or dinners. We can also supply linens, dinnerware, and centerpiece arrangements. From casual to black tie, Coastline

*14-pt. Arial justified*

Gourmet Caterers has you covered!

*16-pt. comic sans MS*

*2x*

For more information contact either of the following:

*2x*

*Left tab set at 3.5"*

Your Name

Ben Boghosian

*16-pt. comic sans MS*

P.O. Box 765
Miami, FL 33132
305-555-0823

7334 Sunshine Parkway
12th Floor
Miami, FL 33132
305-555-7300

*14-pt. Arial*

*3x*

*16-pt. comic sans MS*

References and sample menus available upon request

# Exercise 9

◆ **Use Proofreaders' Marks** ◆ **Open a Recently Saved Document**
◆ **Open a Document not Recently Saved** ◆ **Insert and Edit Text**
◆ **Use Overtype Mode** ◆ **Save a Document with a New Name**

## On the Job

When you are ready to revise or improve a document that you've already created and saved—open it again in Word. Use the Save As command to save a copy of the document with a new name or in a new location. For example, you might need to write a letter that is similar to one you wrote earlier. Instead of starting from scratch, you can open the original letter, save it as a new document, then edit it.

As the office manager for California Cardiology, you have decided that you need to revise the press release that you wrote earlier regarding the new physician who has joined the practice. In this exercise, you will open the press release document and save it with a new name. You will then revise the document and save the changes. Finally, you will print the document.

## Terms

**Proofreaders' marks** Symbols written on a printed document by a copyeditor or proofreader to indicate where revisions are required.

**Places Bar** A strip of buttons on the left side of certain dialog boxes used to open common folders quickly.

**Insert mode** The method of operation used for inserting new text within existing text in a document. Insert mode is the default.

**Overtype mode** The method of operation used to replace existing text in a document with new text.

## Notes

### Proofreaders' Marks

- Often, you may need to revise a Word document based on a marked-up printed copy of the document. **Proofreaders' marks** on printed documents are written symbols that indicate where to make revisions.

- Following is a list of common proofreaders' marks:
  - ∿∿∿∿ indicates text to be bold.
  - ∧ indicates where new text should be inserted.
  - ⸹ indicates text to be deleted.

- ⌗ indicates where a new paragraph should be inserted.
- ≡ indicates that a letter should be capitalized.
- _____ or (ital) indicates text to be italicized.
- (highlight) indicates text to highlight.
- ][ indicates text to center.
  - ✓ There are many other common proofreading symbols. You can find a list in Webster's Collegiate Dictionary, or The Chicago Manual of Style.

## Open a Recently Saved Document

- To revise a document that has been saved and closed, open it in Word.

- The four most recently used documents are listed at the bottom of the File menu and at the top of the New Document Task Pane.

  ✓ *The listed file names may also include the complete path to the file, which means the folder and/or disk where the file is stored. Since you can have a file with the same name stored in different locations, be sure you select the one you really want to open.*

*Open saved documents from the File menu*

Recently opened files

*Open saved documents from the New Document Task Pane*

Recently opened files

- Click on a document to open it.

## Open a Document not Recently Saved

- Any document stored on disk can be opened from Word, no matter when it was last used.

- Use the Open dialog box to locate files that you want to open.

*Open dialog box*

Current folder

File list

Places Bar

## Insert and Edit Text

- By default, you insert new text in a document in **Insert mode**. Existing text moves to the right as you type to make room for new text.

- You can insert text anywhere in a document.

- You can also insert nonprinting characters, including paragraph marks to start a new paragraph, tabs, and spaces.

## Use Overtype Mode

- To replace text as you type, use **Overtype mode**.

- In Overtype mode, existing characters do not shift right to make room for new characters. Instead, new characters replace existing characters as you type, deleting existing characters.

- Most editing should be done in Insert mode, so you do not accidentally type over text that you need.

## Save a Document with a New Name

- The Save As feature lets you save a copy of a document in a different location or with a different file name.
- Use the Save As command to leave the original document unchanged while you edit the new copy.

*Save As dialog box*

# Procedures

## Open a Recently Saved Document

1. Click **File**...................... Alt+F
2. Click document name at bottom of menu.

OR

1. Click **View**.................... Alt+V
2. Click **Task Pane** .................. K

   ✓ *If the New Document Task Pane is not displayed, select it from the Other Task Panes drop-down list.*

3. Click document name at top of Task Pane.

## Open a Document not Recently Saved *(Ctrl+O)*

1. Click **Open** button 📂.

   OR

   a. Click **File** ............... Alt+F
   b. Click **Open** ..................... O

2. Click **Look in** drop-down arrow ........................... Alt+I
3. Select drive or folder.

   ✓ *If necessary double-click folder name.*

   OR

   Click folder in Places Bar to open it.

4. Double-click document name.

   OR

   a. Click document name.
   b. Click **Open** ..................... O

## Insert Text

1. Position insertion point to right of character where you want to insert new text.
2. Type new text.

## Overtype mode

1. Position insertion point to left of first character you want to replace.
2. Press **Insert** key................. Ins

OR

Double-click **OVR** indicator OVR on Status bar.

   ✓ *OVR indicator appears in bold when active.*

3. Type new text.

**To turn off Overtype mode:**

- Press **Insert** key again........ Ins

OR

- Double-click **OVR** indicator OVR again.

   ✓ *OVR indicator appears dimmed when inactive.*

## Save a Document with a New Name

1. Click **File** .................... Alt+F
2. Click **Save As**...................... A
3. Type new file name.
4. Select new drive and/or folder.
5. Click **Save** button

    .............. Alt+S

## Exercise Directions

1. Start Word, if necessary.
2. Open ⌨**PRESS** or open 💿**09PRESS**.
   - ✓ *If necessary, ask your instructor where this file is located.*
3. Save the file as **NEWPRESS**.
4. Make the revisions as indicated by the proofreaders' marks in Illustration A.
   a. Insert new text as marked.
   b. Replace text as marked.
   c. Apply font styles as marked.

5. Check the spelling and grammar.
6. Print the document.
7. Close the document, saving all changes.

*Illustration A*

*ital*

Cynthia Ramirez, M.D. Joins California Cardiology, Inc.

*Bold*

Los Angeles, CA -- California Cardiology, Inc. is pleased to announce that Dr. Cynthia Ramirez has joined our practice. Dr. Ramirez received a BS degree from Stanford University in 1991 and an MD from the University of California at Los Angeles College of Medicine in 1995. She completed a residency at UCLA Medical Center and is board certified in cardiology. *Dr. Ramirez is fluent in Spanish. In her spare time she enjoys skiing, biking, and hiking.*
California Cardiology provides high-quality cardiac care to patients in the metro Los Angeles area. With the addition of Dr. Ramirez, we now have six *ten* full-time physicians supported by an exceptional staff of nurses and physician's assistants. Our offices are thoroughly up-to-date with the most current technologies, and we have admitting privileges at most major *numerous* hospitals in L.A.

For more information about Dr. Ramirez or about California Cardiology, please call 310-555-2922, or visit us on the Web at www.ddcpub.com/calcardiology. We accept most major insurance policies.

## On Your Own

1. Open ⌨**OWD06**, the document you created in the On Your Own section of Exercise 6, or open 💿**09LETTER**.
2. Save the file as **OWD09**.

3. Make revisions to the document using Insert mode and Overtype mode.
4. Print the document.
5. Close the document, saving all changes.

# Exercise 10

## Skills Covered:

◆ **Move Text** ◆ **Use Cut and Paste**
◆ **Use the Clipboard** ◆ **Use Drag-and-Drop Editing**
◆ **Move a Paragraph**

## On the Job

Move text to rearrange a document quickly without retyping existing information. You can move any amount of text, from a single character to an entire page.

The employees at the law firm of Perry, Hawkins, Martinez, and Klein have been asking a lot of questions regarding "Casual Fridays." The personnel director has asked you to edit a document that lists guidelines for the new policy. In this exercise, you will open the existing document, edit and format the text, and rearrange the guidelines into a more suitable order.

## Terms

**Cut** To delete a selection from its original location and move it to the Clipboard.

**Paste** To insert a selection from the Clipboard into a document.

**Clipboard** A temporary storage area that can hold up to 24 selections at a time.

**Drag-and-drop editing** The action of using a mouse to drag a selection from its original location and drop it in a new location.

## Notes

### Move Text

- While editing, you may decide you need to move text that is already typed in a document to a new location.

- Word's move commands can save you from deleting and retyping text.

- Be sure to consider nonprinting characters when you select text to move:
  - Select the space following a word or sentence to move along with text.
  - Select the paragraph mark following a paragraph or line to move paragraph formatting with text.

- Use Undo to reverse a move that you made unintentionally.

✓ *When you paste text into a new location, Word may display the Paste Options button, which allows you to select the way formatting is pasted along with the text. For now, ignore the Paste Options button. It is explained in Exercise 15. You can turn off the display of the Paste Options button if you want. Click Tools, Options, Edit. Deselect the Show Paste Options button check box, then click OK.*

### Use Cut and Paste

- Use the **Cut** and **Paste** commands to move text in a document.

- The Cut command deletes selected text from its original location and moves it to the **Clipboard**.

- The Paste command copies the selection from the Clipboard to the insertion point location.

- Up to 24 selections can remain in the Clipboard at one time.
- You can access the Cut and Paste commands from the Edit menu, from the Standard toolbar, from a shortcut menu, or with keyboard shortcuts.

### Use the Clipboard

- Use the Clipboard Task Pane to access selections for pasting.
- The last 24 items cut or copied are displayed in the Clipboard.
- You can paste or delete one or all of the items.
- You can turn the following Clipboard options off or on:
  - Show Office Clipboard Automatically. Sets the Clipboard Task Pane to open automatically when you cut or copy a selection.
  - Collect Without Showing Office Clipboard. Sets the Clipboard Task Pane so it does not open automatically when you cut or copy data.
  - Show Office Clipboard Icon on Taskbar. Displays a Clipboard icon at the right end of the Taskbar if there are selections on the Clipboard. Double-click the icon to open the Task Pane.
  - Show Status Near Taskbar When Copying. Displays a ScreenTip with the number of items on the Clipboard when you cut or copy a selection.

*Clipboard Task Pane*

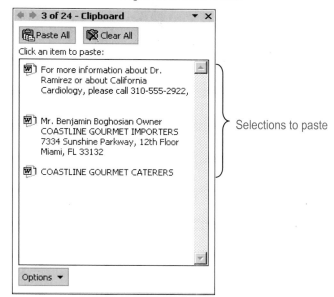

Selections to paste

### Use Drag-and-Drop Editing

- Use **drag-and-drop editing** to move text with the mouse.
- Drag-and-drop editing is convenient when you can see the text to move and the new location on the screen at the same time.

### Move a Paragraph

- You can quickly move an entire paragraph up or down in a document.

## Procedures

**Move Text**
1. Select text to move.
2. Press **F2** key ....................... `F2`
3. Position insertion point at new location.
4. Press **Enter** ...................... `Enter`

**Use Cut and Paste to Move Text** *(Ctrl+X, Cltr+V)*
1. Select text to move.
2. Click **Cut** button ✂.
   OR
   a. Click **Edit** ............... `Alt`+`E`
   b. Click **Cut** ....................... `T`

OR
   a. Right-click selection.
   b. Click **Cut** ....................... `T`
3. Position insertion point in new location.
4. Click **Paste** button 📋.
   OR
   a. Click **Edit** ............... `Alt`+`E`
   b. Click **Paste** .................... `P`
   OR
   a. Right-click new location.
   b. Click **Paste** .................... `P`

**Paste a Selection from the Clipboard Task Pane**
1. Click **View** .................. `Alt`+`V`
2. Click **Task Pane** .................. `K`
3. Click **Other Task Panes** drop-down arrow `New Document ▼`.
4. Click **Clipboard**.
5. Click item to paste.
   OR
   Click **Paste All** button
   `📋 Paste All` to paste all selections from the Clipboard.

**Set Clipboard Options**
1. Display Clipboard Task Pane.

2. Click **Options** drop-down button `Options ▼`.

3. Click desired options:
   - **Show Office Clipboard** **Automatically**...............[A]
   - **Collect Without Showing** **Office Clipboard** ..........[C]
   - **Show Office Clipboard** **Icon on Taskbar**............[T]
   - **Show Status Near** **Taskbar When** **Copying**........................[S]

   ✓ *A check mark indicates the option is selected.*

### Delete Selections from the Clipboard

1. Right-click selection to delete.
2. Click **Delete**..........................[D] on context menu
   OR
   Click **Clear All** button `Clear All` to delete all selections from the Clipboard.

### Use Drag-and-Drop Editing to Move Text

1. Select text to move.
2. Move mouse pointer anywhere over selected text and click, continuing to hold down the left mouse button.
3. Drag selection to new location.

✓ *As you drag, the mouse pointer changes to a box with a dotted shadow attached to an arrow; selection does not move until you drop it in step 4.*

4. Release mouse button when insertion point is in new location.

### Move a Paragraph

1. Position insertion point anywhere within paragraph to move.
2. Press .................[Alt]+[Shift]+[↑]
   OR
   Press .................[Alt]+[Shift]+[↓]
3. Repeat step 2 until paragraph is in desired location.

# Exercise Directions

1. Start Word, if necessary.
2. Open 💿 **10POLICY**.
3. Save the file as **POLICY**.
4. Revise the document so it resembles the document shown in Illustration A.
   - Apply alignments as marked.
   - Apply fonts, font sizes, and font styles as marked.
   - Insert blank lines by pressing the Enter key as marked.
   - Move text to rearrange the document as marked.

5. Check the spelling and grammar in the document.
6. Display the document in Print Preview.
7. Print the document.
8. Close the document, saving all changes.

# On Your Own

1. Create a new document in Word.
2. Save the file as **OWD10**.
3. Create a list of things you have accomplished in the past year. For each item in the list, describe what you accomplished, how you accomplished it, and when it was done.

4. Rearrange the listed items using cut-and-paste and drag-and-drop techniques. For example, you might want to arrange the list by importance of what you accomplished or by date.
5. Print the document.
6. Close the document, saving all changes.

*Illustration A*

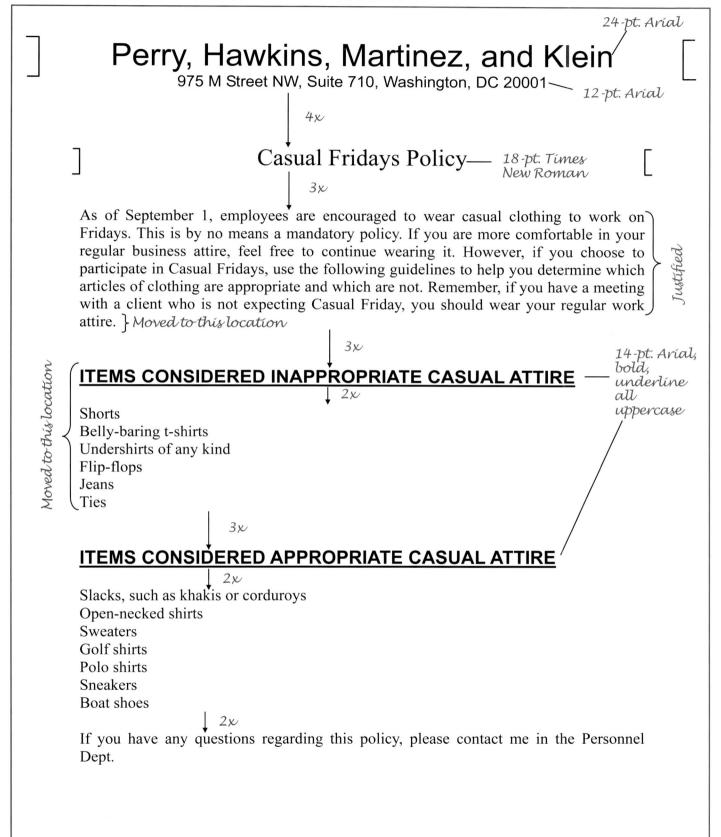

# Perry, Hawkins, Martinez, and Klein

*24-pt. Arial*

975 M Street NW, Suite 710, Washington, DC 20001 *12-pt. Arial*

*4x*

## Casual Fridays Policy *18-pt. Times New Roman*

*3x*

As of September 1, employees are encouraged to wear casual clothing to work on Fridays. This is by no means a mandatory policy. If you are more comfortable in your regular business attire, feel free to continue wearing it. However, if you choose to participate in Casual Fridays, use the following guidelines to help you determine which articles of clothing are appropriate and which are not. Remember, if you have a meeting with a client who is not expecting Casual Friday, you should wear your regular work attire. } *Moved to this location*

*Justified*

*3x*

## ITEMS CONSIDERED INAPPROPRIATE CASUAL ATTIRE

*14-pt. Arial, bold, underline all uppercase*

*2x*

*Moved to this location*

Shorts
Belly-baring t-shirts
Undershirts of any kind
Flip-flops
Jeans
Ties

*3x*

## ITEMS CONSIDERED APPROPRIATE CASUAL ATTIRE

*2x*

Slacks, such as khakis or corduroys
Open-necked shirts
Sweaters
Golf shirts
Polo shirts
Sneakers
Boat shoes

*2x*

If you have any questions regarding this policy, please contact me in the Personnel Dept.

# Exercise 11

### ◆ Use Copy and Paste
### ◆ Use the Drag-and-Drop Feature to Copy

## On the Job

Copy or move text from one location to another to speed up your work and avoid repetitive typing. You can copy or move any amount of text, from a single character to an entire document.

The personnel director of Perry, Hawkins, Martinez, and Klein wants you to enhance the Casual Fridays policy document. In this exercise, you will revise the guidelines using some of the editing and formatting techniques you have learned so far in this book.

## Terms

**Copy** To create a duplicate of a selection and move it to the Clipboard.

## Notes

### Use Copy and Paste

- Use the Copy and Paste feature to copy existing text from one location in a document and paste it to another location.

- The **Copy** command stores a duplicate of selected text on the Clipboard, leaving the original selection unchanged.

- The Paste command pastes the selection from the Clipboard to the insertion point location.

- You can access the Copy and Paste commands from the Edit menu, the Standard toolbar, from a shortcut menu, or with keyboard shortcuts.

- You can store up to 24 selections on the Clipboard at one time.

- Use the Clipboard Task Pane to choose which selection to paste into the document.

  ✓ *The same Clipboard used for moving is used for copying. For more information, refer to Exercise 10.*

### Use the Drag-and-Drop Feature to Copy

- Use drag-and-drop editing to copy text with the mouse.

- The Drag-and-Drop feature is convenient when you can see the text to copy and the new location on the screen at the same time.

# Procedures

## Use Copy and Paste
*(Ctrl+C, Ctrl+V)*

1. Select the text to copy.
2. Click **Copy** button [icon].
   OR
   a. Click **Edit**............... [Alt]+[E]
   b. Click **Copy** ................... [C]
   OR
   a. Right-click selection.
   b. Click **Copy** ................... [C]
3. Position insertion point in new location.
4. Click **Paste** button [icon].
   OR
   a. Click **Edit**............... [Alt]+[E]
   b. Click **Paste**................... [P]
   OR
   a. Right-click new location.
   b. Click **Paste**................... [P]

## Paste a Selection from the Clipboard Task Pane

1. Click **View** ................... [Alt]+[V]
2. Click **Task Pane**.................. [K]
3. Click **Other Task Panes** drop-down arrow `New Document ▾`.
4. Click **Clipboard**.
5. Click item to paste.
   OR
   Click **Paste All** button
   [Paste All icon] to paste all selections from the Clipboard.
   ✓ *The actions for pasting a copied item from the Task Pane are the same as for pasting a cut item. For more information on using the Clipboard Task Pane, refer to Exercise 10.*

## Use Drag-and-Drop to Copy Text

1. Select text to copy.
2. Move mouse pointer anywhere over selected text and click, continuing to hold down the left mouse button.
3. Press and hold the **Ctrl** key...................................... [Ctrl]
4. Drag selection to new location [icon].
   ✓ *As you drag, the mouse pointer changes to a box with a dotted shadow and a plus sign attached to an arrow; the selection does not move until you drop it in step 5.*
5. Release mouse button.
6. Release the **Ctrl** key .......... [Ctrl]

# Exercise Directions

1. Start Word, if necessary.
2. Open 📁**POLICY** or open 💿**11POLICY**.
3. Save the file as **POLICY**.
4. Use the following steps to revise the document so it looks like the one in Illustration A.
5. Delete blank lines above and below the headline **Casual Fridays Policy**.
6. Copy the second sentence of the document to the beginning of the last paragraph, and format it bold.
7. Insert the sentence at the end of the last paragraph.
8. Start a new paragraph at the end of the document, leaving one blank line.
9. Type the heading **Dos**; apply Words only underlining.
10. Copy the list of appropriate attire to the new location under the heading **Dos**.

11. Set a Left tab stop at 4" on the horizontal ruler for all lines from the heading **Dos** to the end of the document.
12. Position the insertion point at the end of the word **Dos**, press Tab, and type the heading **Don'ts**, underlined.
    • One by one, copy the items from the list of inappropriate attire under the heading **Don'ts**. Use the tab stop to align them.
    • Copy the text to the Clipboard being sure not to copy the paragraph mark with it.
    • Position insertion point at the end of the current line, press Tab, paste the item at the tab stop location.
13. Check the spelling and grammar in the document.
14. Display the document in Print Preview. It should look similar to the one in the Illustration.
    ✓ *If necessary, use Shrink to Fit to fit the document on a single page.*
15. Print the document.
16. Close the document, saving all changes.

# Perry, Hawkins, Martinez, and Klein

975 M Street NW, Suite 710, Washington, DC 20001

*2x*

## Casual Fridays Policy

*2x*

As of September 1, employees are encouraged to wear casual clothing to work on Fridays. This is by no means a mandatory policy. If you are more comfortable in your regular business attire, feel free to continue wearing it. However, if you choose to participate in Casual Fridays, use the following guidelines to help you determine which articles of clothing are appropriate and which are not. Remember, if you have a meeting with a client who is not expecting Casual Friday, you should wear your regular work attire.

*Copy sentence*

## ITEMS CONSIDERED INAPPROPRIATE CASUAL ATTIRE

Shorts
Belly-baring t-shirts
Undershirts of any kind
Flip-flops
Jeans
Ties

## ITEMS CONSIDERED APPROPRIATE CASUAL ATTIRE

Slacks, such as khakis or corduroys
Open-necked shirts
Sweaters
Golf shirts
Polo shirts
Sneakers
Boat shoes

**This is by no means a mandatory policy**. If you have any questions regarding this policy, please contact me in the Personnel Dept. Use the following for quick reference:

*2x*

*Copy items*

*Copy list*

| Dos | Don'ts |
|---|---|
| Slacks, such as khakis or corduroys | Shorts |
| Open-necked shirts | Belly-baring t-shirts |
| Sweaters | Undershirts of any kind |
| Golf shirts | Flip-flops |
| Polo shirts | Jeans |
| Sneakers | Ties |
| Boat shoes | |

*Set left tab stop at 4" on horizontal ruler*

# On Your Own

1. Create a new document in Word.

2. Save the file as **OWD11**.

3. Create a letter in which you apply for an officer's position of a group or organization to which you might belong. For example, the group could be a school club. The officer's position could be secretary, treasurer, or president. Mention that you have accomplished many things in the past year.

4. Open the document ⌨**OWD10**, the list of your personal accomplishments for the past year, which you created in the On Your Own section of Exercise 10, or open ⊙**11LIST**.

5. Save the file as **OWD11-2**.

6. Copy some of the items from **OWD11-2** to the **OWD11** document.

   • First, copy an item from **OWD11-2** to the Clipboard. Next position the insertion point in the **OWD11** document. Finally, paste the item from the Clipboard into the **OWD11** document.

7. Complete the letter.

8. Display the document in Print Preview. Make editing or formatting changes as necessary.

9. Print the document.

10. Close the document, saving all changes.

# Exercise 12

## Skills Covered:

◆ **Open a Document as Read-Only** ◆ **Open a Document from Windows**
◆ **Document Properties** ◆ **File Types**
◆ **Use Basic Search to Find a File**

## On the Job

Word offers many options for opening a document. For example, open a document as read-only when you do not want to allow changes made to the original file. (You must save the file with a new name in order to save changes.) You can use Windows features to open a document and start Word at the same time, and you can use Word to open files created with different word processing programs. You can even locate and open a file when you don't know the file name. And you can use document properties to identify important information about a file, such as the name of the author and the main topic.

Northwest Gear, Inc., a maker of clothes for teenagers, is sponsoring an essay contest. The marketing director stored a text file with the information you need to create a press release on your computer without telling you the folder location. In this exercise, you will search for the text file, open it, and save it as a Word document. You will apply formatting to the document and add document properties. You will then close the file and open it again as read-only.

## Terms

**Read-only**  A mode of operation in which revisions cannot be saved in the original document.

**Document Properties**  Categories of information about a document.

**Keywords**  Important words found in a document. Keywords can be used to classify a document.

**File type**  The format in which the file is stored. Usually, the file type corresponds to the program used to create the file.

**File extension**  A dot followed by three or four characters at the end of a file name, used to indicate the file type. For example, a *.doc* file extension indicates a Word document file.

**File icon**  The icon used to represent a file in a file list, such as Windows Explorer or Word's Open dialog box.

**Compatible file type**  A file type that Word can open, even though it was created and saved using a different program.

# Notes

## Open a Document as Read-Only

■ Opening a document as **read-only** is a safeguard against accidentally making changes.

■ Word prompts you to use Save As to save revisions made to a document opened as read-only in a new document with a different file name.

■ The words *Read-Only* appear in the title bar of a document opened as read-only.

## Open a Document from Windows

■ Use the Windows Start Menu to open a document and start Word at the same time.

  • Click Documents on the Start menu to select from a list of recently used files.

  • Locate and open any document using Windows Explorer.

  ✓ *You can also open a Word document using the Open Office Document dialog box accessed from the Windows Start menu or from the Office Shortcut Bar. See "Getting Started with Office XP", Exercise 1 for more information.*

## Document Properties

■ With the **Document Properties** feature you can save information that is unique to a particular document.

■ Document Properties lets you enter information in five categories.

■ Three of the more useful categories are:

  • General properties: Include the type of document, its size, its location, when it was created, last accessed, and last modified.

    ♦ Use General properties to check file storage and access information.

  • Summary properties: Include a document title, subject, author, **keywords**, and comments.

    ♦ Use Summary properties to save summary information with a document.

  • Statistics properties: Include the number of pages, paragraphs, lines, words, characters, and bytes in the document.

    ♦ Use Statistics properties to create documents of a specific length or word count.

■ You can set Word to display the Properties dialog box automatically each time you save a document.

*The Summary page of the Properties dialog box*

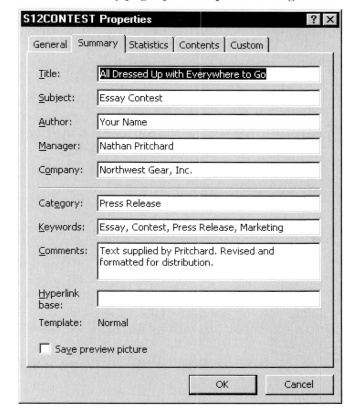

## File Types

■ Files are saved in different **file types**, depending on the application used to create, save, and open the file.

■ In Windows and Windows applications, file types can be identified by the **file extension** and by the **file icon**.

■ Word 2002 can open documents saved in **compatible file types**. For example, Word can open text files, Web page files, and files created with other versions of Word.

■ You can save a compatible file in its original file type or as a Word document file.

■ Some common file types include the following:

  • Word document files     .doc

  • Word template files     .dot

- Text files                  .txt
- Web pages             .htm
- Excel workbooks       .xls
- Access databases      .mdb
- PowerPoint presentations    .ppt

## Use Basic Search to Find a File

■ Word has a Search feature that can help you find a file stored anywhere on your computer system, even if you can't remember the file name.

■ Use a basic search to locate a file that contains specified text in its title, contents, or properties.

■ Enter text in the Search text box to locate files containing that text. The text may be in the body of the file, or in the document properties.

- Word finds files containing various forms of the search text. For example, if you enter *run*, Word finds documents containing *run*, *running*, or *ran*.

- You can use wildcard characters in the search text.

  - \* represents one or more characters.
  - ? represents any single character.

■ Before starting a search, select the disks or folders to search, as well as the types of files to search for.

- If you know the folder to search, type it in the Search in box.

- Alternatively, select the check box beside the folder(s) to search.

■ In the *Results should be* box, select the types of files to find:

- Anything. Finds all file types.

- Office Files. Finds all files created with Office programs. You can select the specific program type.

- Outlook Items. Finds only files created with Microsoft Outlook.

- Web Pages. Finds only Web page files.

■ You can search using the Search Task Pane, or by opening the Search dialog box from the Open dialog box. Both methods offer you the same options.

*Search Task Pane*

■ Word displays files matching your criteria in the Search Results list.

*Search Results in Task Pane*

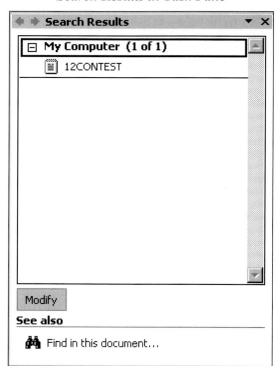

# Procedures

### Open a Document as Read-Only *(Ctrl+O)*

1. Click **Open** button 📂.
   OR
   a. Click **File** ................ `Alt`+`F`
   b. Click **Open** ..................... `O`
2. Click document name.
3. Click **Open** drop-down arrow
   [📂 Open ▾].
4. Click **Open Read-Only** ....... `R`

### Open a Word Document from the Documents Menu

1. Click **Start** button
   [🎬 Start] .................. `Ctrl`+`Esc`
2. Select **Documents** ............. `D`
3. Click document name.

### Open a Word Document From Windows Explorer

1. Right-click **Start**
   button [🎬 Start].
2. Click **Explore** ...................... `X`
3. Select drive where folder/file is located.
4. Open folder.
5. Double-click document name that you want to open.

### Use Document Properties

1. Click **File** .................... `Alt`+`F`
2. Click **Properties** ................... `I`
3. Select desired tab ....... `Ctrl`+`Tab`
   For example:
   • Click **Summary** tab and type summary information.
   • Click **Statistics** tab to see statistical information.
   • Click **General** tab to see file storage and access information.
4. Click **OK** .......................... `Enter`

### Automatically Display Properties Dialog Box

1. Click **Tools** ................. `Alt`+`T`
2. Click **Options** ..................... `O`
3. Click **Save** tab ........... `Ctrl`+`Tab`
4. Select **Prompt for document properties** check box... `Alt`+`I`
5. Click **OK** .......................... `Enter`

### Open a Compatible File Type *(Ctrl+O)*

1. Click **File** ..................... `Alt`+`F`
2. Click **Open** ......................... `O`
3. Click the **Look in** drop-down arrow ......... `Alt`+`I`
4. Select the disk or folder.
   ✓ Alternatively, click the folder you want to open in the Places Bar.
5. Click the **Files of type** drop-down arrow ......... `Alt`+`T`
6. Click the file type.
7. Click the desired file name.
8. Click **Open** ................. `Alt`+`O`
   ✓ If the File Conversion dialog box is displayed, click OK.

### Save a Compatible File *(Ctrl+S)*

1. Open the compatible file.
2. Click **File** ..................... `Alt`+`F`
3. Click **Save** ......................... `S`
4. Click **Yes** ........................... `Y`
   to save the file in its original format.
   OR
   Click **No** ............................ `N`
   to save the file as a Word document.

### Save a Compatible File as a New File in Word Format

1. Open the compatible file.
2. Click **File** ..................... `Alt`+`F`
3. Click **Save As** ..................... `A`
4. Click the **Save as type** drop-down arrow ......... `Alt`+`T`

5. Click **Word document (*.doc)**.
6. Click the **File name** text box ...................... `Alt`+`N`
7. Type the new file name.
8. Click **Save** ................. `Alt`+`S`

### Search for Files from the Search Task Pane

1. Click **View** .................. `Alt`+`V`
2. Click **Task Pane** ................... `K`
3. Click **Other Task Panes** drop-down arrow
   [New Document ▾] ....... `Ctrl`+`↓`
4. Click **Search** ............. `↓`, `Enter`
5. Type search text in **Search text** box.
6. If necessary, delete existing text first.
7. Click **Search in**: drop-down arrow.
8. Select folders as follows:
   • Click **plus sign** to expand list ................................. `+`
   • Click check box to select folder .............. `Space`
9. Click **Results should be:** drop-down arrow .... `Tab`, `Space`
10. Click **plus sign** to expand list ...................................... `+`
11. Click desired file type(s) ............. `↑`, `↓`, `Space`
12. Click **Search** button [Search].
13. Click file to open.
    OR
    Click **Modify** button [Modify] to display Basic Search Task Pane again.
    ✓ To interrupt a search before it is complete, click the Stop button [Stop].

## Search for Files from the Open Dialog Box

1. Click **F**ile ..................... `Alt`+`F`
2. Click **O**pen ...................... `O`
3. Click the **Look in** drop-down arrow ........................ `Alt`+`I`
4. Select the disk or folder.
   - ✓ *Alternatively, click the folder you want to open in the Places Look in bar.*
5. Click **Tools** drop-down arrow `Tools ▾` ............. `Alt`+`L`
6. Click **S**earch ...................... `S`
7. Click **Basic** tab, if necessary ............... `Ctrl`+`Tab`
8. Type search text in **Search text** box.
   - ✓ *If necessary, delete existing text first.*
9. Click **Search in:** drop-down arrow ......................... `Alt`+`I`
10. Select folders as follows:
    - Click **plus sign** to expand list .................... `+`
    - Click check box to select folder ............. `Space`, `Enter`
11. Click **Results should be:** drop-down arrow ......... `Alt`+`B`
12. Click **plus sign** to expand list ....................................... `+`
13. Click desired file type(s) ... `↑`, `↓`, `Space`, `Enter`
14. Click **Search** ............... `Alt`+`S`
15. Double-click file to open.
    OR
    Click file to open.
16. Click **OK** ......................... `Enter`
17. Word displays Open dialog box.
18. Click **O**pen ................. `Alt`+`O`

# Exercise Directions

- ✓ *Before beginning this exercise, make sure that the* 💿**12CONTEST** *file is stored somewhere on your computer. Ask your instructor for more information.*

1. Start Word, if necessary.
2. Search your computer for the file about the essay contest using the following steps:
   a. Open the Search Task Pane or the Search dialog box.
   b. Enter the Search text **Essay Contest**.
   c. Select the folder(s) to search. For example, if the file is stored locally, choose to search drive C, or My Computer. If the file is stored on a network, choose the network drive. The more you can narrow down the location, the faster the search will be.
   d. Select Word Files in the Files Should be list.
   e. Start the search.
3. Open the document from the Search Results list.
4. Save the file as **CONTEST**.
5. Using the Document Properties dialog box, check the number of words in the document.
6. Enter the following summary information:
   Title: **All Dressed Up with Everywhere to Go**
   Subject: **Essay Contest**
   Author: **Your name**
   Manager: **Nathan Pritchard**
   Company: **Northwest Gear, Inc.**
   Category: **Press Release**
   Keywords: **Essay, Contest, Press Release, Marketing**
   Comments: **Text supplied by Pritchard. Revised and formatted for distribution**.
7. Check the spelling and grammar in the document.
8. Display the document in Print Preview.
9. Print the document.
10. Close the document.
11. Open the document as read-only.
12. Change the headline to **All Dressed Up with Everywhere to Go**.
13. Save the changes.
    - ✓ *Word will display the Save As dialog box.*
14. Save the document in plain text format, with the name **CONTEST2**.
15. Close the document, saving all changes. If prompted, remember to save the file in text format, not Word format.
16. Open the **CONTEST2.TXT** document in Word. The text file should look similar to the one in the illustration.
17. Close the file, saving all changes.

*Illustration A*

All Dressed Up with Everywhere to Go

Seattle, WA – Northwest Gear, Inc., a maker of clothing for teenagers, has announced that it is sponsoring an essay contest. Prizes include scholarship money, trips, computers, and gift certificates.

The topic of the essay contest is "All Dressed Up with Everywhere to Go." According to Northwest's Marketing Director, Nathan Pritchard, the object of the contest is to get teens thinking about the opportunities available to them in the 21st century.

"We live in an exciting time. We want to encourage teens to explore their own potential," said Mr. Pritchard.

The rules for the contest are as follows:

Students aged 12 through 18 are eligible.
Essays must be between 1,000 and 1,500 words.
Essays may be typed or handwritten.
Original copies will not be returned, and will become the property of Northwest Gear, Inc.
All entries must be postmarked by March 1. Winners will be announced on June 1.

The essays will be judged based on originality, creativity, grammar, and spelling. The judges will be employees of Northwest Gear, Inc.

For more information, contact Mr. Pritchard at 206-555-3922, or consult the company's Web site: northwestgear.com.

# On Your Own

1. Search for the **OWD11**, the file you created in the On Your Own section of Exercise 11, or search for 💿 **12LETTER**.

2. Open the file as read-only.

3. Check the number of words in the document.

4. Note the file size, date created, and date last modified.

5. Enter document properties, including Title, Subject, Manager, Company, Category, Keywords, and Comments.

6. Try saving the document.

7. Save the file as **OWD12**.

8. Save the file in text format as **OWD12-2**.

9. Print the file.

10. Close the document, saving all changes.

# Exercise 13

## Skills Covered:
◆ **Preview a Closed Document**
◆ **Print Files without Opening Them**

## On the Job

Preview a document before opening it or printing it to make sure it is the correct file. Print files without opening them to save time or to print more than one document at once.

As the assistant to the marketing director at Northwest Gear, Inc., you have been asked to find employees willing to serve as judges for the essay contest. In this exercise, you will preview, open, and revise the press release about the contest. Then you will create a memo to employees. Finally, you will print both documents.

## Notes

### Preview a Closed Document

- By default, Word displays a list of files in the Open dialog box.
- You can change the display in the dialog box to show a preview of the document selected in the file list.
- Previewing is useful for making sure a document is the one you want before you open it or print it.
- Most documents are too large to be displayed completely in the dialog box; use the scroll arrows in the preview area to scroll up and down.
- If you don't want to display a preview, you can set the Open dialog box to display large or small file icons, the default file list, file details, such as size, type, and date last saved, or document properties.

*Preview a document in the Open dialog box*

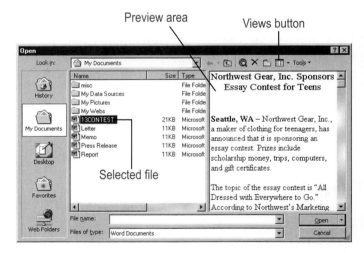

### Print Files without Opening Them

- To save time, you can print a document from the Open dialog box without opening it.
- Print without opening when you are certain the document is ready for printing.
  - ✓ *You can also print a document without opening it from the Open Office dialog box or from Windows Explorer.*

■ You can select more than one file at a time for printing in the Open dialog box.

■ Selecting multiple files for printing sends them all to the printer, where they will be printed one after the other.

■ All selected files must be in the same folder.

# Procedures

**Preview a Closed Document**

1. Click **File** ..................... Alt+F
2. Click **Open** ......................... O
3. Click **Views** button drop-down arrow ⊞▼.
4. Click **Preview** ...................... V
5. Click document name to preview.

   ✓ *If necessary, select drive and/or folder to locate document.*

**To turn Preview off:**

1. Click **File** ..................... Alt+F
2. Click **Open** ......................... O
3. Click **Views** button drop-down arrow ⊞▼.

4. Select another view:

   ● Click **Large Icons** ⊞ ....G
   ● Click **Small Icons** ⊞.....M
   ● Click **List** ⊞ ...............L
   ● Click **Details** ⊞ ...........D
   ● Click **Properties** ⊞ .....R

   ✓ *Or click the Views button repeatedly to cycle through the Views options.*

**Print a File without Opening It**

1. Click **File**..................... Alt+F
2. Click **Open**......................... O

   ✓ *If necessary, select drive and/or folder to locate document.*

3. Click **Tools** button Tools▼ ......................... Alt+L
4. Click **Print**.......................... P

**Print Multiple Files**

1. Click **File**..................... Alt+F
2. Click **Open**......................... O
3. Click the first document name.
4. Press and hold **Ctrl**............. Ctrl
5. Click each additional document name.
6. Click **Tools** button Tools▼ ......................... Alt+L
7. Click **Print**........................... P

# Exercise Directions

1. Start Word, if necessary.

2. In the Open dialog box, preview ⌨**CONTEST**, the document you created in Exercise 12, or preview ⊙**13CONTEST**.

3. This should be a press release announcing the essay contest sponsored by Northwest Gear, Inc.

4. Change the Open dialog box to display document properties instead of the preview.

5. Open the document and save it as **PRESS**.

6. Make revisions as indicated in Illustration A.

7. Check the spelling and grammar in the document.

8. Close the document, saving all changes.

9. Create a new document and type the memo shown in Illustration B, or open ⊙**13MEMO**.

10. Save the document as **MEMO**, then close it.

11. Preview the document **MEMO** in the Open dialog box.

12. Print both the **PRESS** and **MEMO** documents without opening them.

~~Northwest Gear, Inc. Sponsors Essay Contest for Teens~~

**Seattle, WA** – Northwest Gear, Inc., a maker of clothing for teenagers, has announced that it is sponsoring an essay contest. Prizes include scholarship money, trips, computers, and gift certificates. ∧ *on the topic of "All Dressed Up with Everywhere to Go."*

~~The topic of the essay contest is "All Dressed Up with Everywhere to Go."~~ According to Northwest's Marketing Director, Nathan Pritchard, the object of the contest is to get teens thinking about the opportunities available to them in the 21st century.

*Northwest Gear selected the topic because*

"We live in an exciting time. We want to encourage teens to explore their own potential," said Mr. Pritchard.

The rules for the contest are as follows:

Students aged 12 through 18 are eligible.
Essays must be between 1,000 and 1,500 words.
Essays may be typed or handwritten.
Original copies will not be returned, and will become the property of Northwest Gear, Inc.
All entries must be postmarked by March 1. Winners will be announced on June 1.

The essays will be judged based on originality, creativity, grammar, and spelling. The judges will be employees of Northwest Gear, Inc.

For more information, contact Mr. Pritchard at 206-555-3922, or consult the company's Web site: northwestgear.com.

*Illustration B*

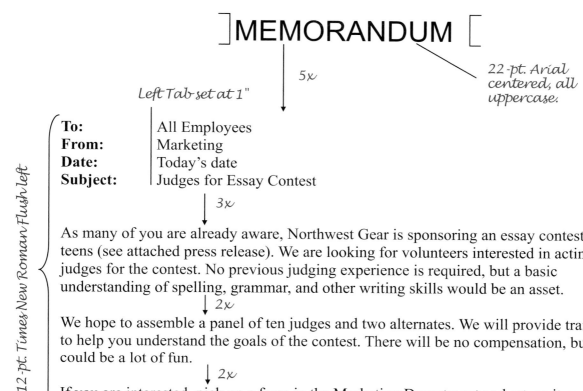

# ]MEMORANDUM [

*22-pt. Arial centered, all uppercase.*

*5x*

*Left Tab set at 1"*

*12-pt. Times New Roman flush left*

| | |
|---|---|
| **To:** | All Employees |
| **From:** | Marketing |
| **Date:** | Today's date |
| **Subject:** | Judges for Essay Contest |

*3x*

As many of you are already aware, Northwest Gear is sponsoring an essay contest for teens (see attached press release). We are looking for volunteers interested in acting as judges for the contest. No previous judging experience is required, but a basic understanding of spelling, grammar, and other writing skills would be an asset.

*2x*

We hope to assemble a panel of ten judges and two alternates. We will provide training to help you understand the goals of the contest. There will be no compensation, but it could be a lot of fun.

*2x*

If you are interested, pick up a form in the Marketing Department and return it as soon as possible. The form is also available on the company Intranet.

## On Your Own

1. Start Word.
2. Preview some of the documents that you have created for the On Your Own sections of previous exercises, or preview ⊙ **13LETTER**, ⊙ **13MISSION** and ⊙ **13LIST**.
3. Display file properties instead of the preview.
4. Display the preview again.
5. Print at least two of the documents without opening them.
6. When you are finished, exit Word.

# Exercise 14

The owner of Coastline Gourmet Importers has received a new lead on someone who may be able to help him procure Russian caviar. In this exercise, you will search for and open the existing letter to Mr. Volfson regarding the caviar. You will save it with a new name, revise it using the techniques you have learned so far, and add document properties. Finally, you will preview and print the new letter.

## Exercise Directions

1. Start Word, if necessary.

2. Open 🖮**CAVIAR** or 💿**14CAVIAR** as read-only.

3. Save the file as **CAVIAR**.

4. Insert, delete, and replace text as marked on Illustration A.

5. Copy and move text as marked on the illustration.

6. Apply formatting as marked on the illustration.

7. Enter Document Properties summary information as follows:
   Title: **Romanov Brothers**
   Subject: **Russian Caviar**
   Company: **Coastline Gourmet**
   Author: **Your name**
   Category: **Letter**
   Keywords: **Caviar, Russian, Romanov**.
   Comments: **Letter of inquiry regarding importing caviar**.

8. Check the spelling and grammar.

9. Save the changes.

10. Close the document.

11. Use a basic search to locate and open 💿**14FLYER**.

12. Save the document as **FLYER** in Rich Text Format.
    ✓ *Rich Text Format preserves some of the font formatting that Plain Text format does not preserve. It adds an .rtf file extension to the file name.*

13. Close the document.

14. Preview the **CAVIAR** and **FLYER** documents without opening them.
    ✓ *Remember, to display the FLYER document in the Open dialog box you will have to select All Files to display all file types.*

15. Print both the **CAVIAR** and **FLYER** documents without opening them.

16. Exit Word.

*Illustration A*

~~Today's date~~ *Replace with today's date*

~~CERTIFIED MAIL~~ *Delete mail notation and extra blank lines*

Mr. Alex Volfson
District Representative
Imperial Products, Inc.
62 Beaumont Street
Brooklyn, NY 11235

*Mr. Boris Kolchenko*
*Proprietor*
*Romanov Brothers Food Company*
*1922 Beacon Street*
*Boston, MA 02115*

*Replace with new inside name and address. Format company name in bold.*

Dear Mr. ~~Volfson~~ *Kolchenko* :

Subject: Procuring Russian Caviar

*Mr. Jake Pierson of the Fine Foods Emporium in Boca Raton, Florida.*
Recently, I was talking to ~~Ms. Katherine Sanders, the proprietor of a fine dining establishment here in Miami.~~ When I mentioned that I have been having a difficult time procuring high-quality Russian caviar for COASTLINE GOURMET IMPORTERS, my chain of retail food stores, she suggested that I try contacting you.

COASTLINE GOURMET carries high-quality specialty items imported from around the world. If, in fact, you can provide caviar that meets our standards, I would be very interested in discussing terms and availability. I have enclosed a brochure that describes ~~COASTLINE GOURMET~~ *the new catering service,* or you may want to look us up on the Web at coastlinegourmet.com.

*We have also recently started a catering service.*

Sincerely,

Mr. Benjamin Boghosian
Owner
COASTLINE GOURMET IMPORTERS
7334 Sunshine Parkway, 12th Floor
Miami, FL 33132

Bb/yo

Enclosure

Copy to: ~~Ms. Katharine Sanders~~ *Mr. Jake Pierson*

# Exercise 15

## Skills Covered:

◆ **Apply Font and Text Effects** ◆ **Font Color**
◆ **Highlight Text** ◆ **Format Painter**

## On the Job

You can enhance text using font effects, text effects, and colors. You can highlight text to change the color around the text without changing the font color. Highlighting is useful for calling attention to text and for making text stand out on the page. Use the Format Painter to quickly copy formatting from one location to another. The Format Painter saves you time and makes it easy to duplicate formatting throughout a document.

You have been asked to design a document advertising the essay contest for Northwest Gear, Inc. If the company approves of the document, it will be made available at retail stores and posted as a Web page on the company Web site. In this exercise, you will create the document using font effects, text effects, and color. You will also highlight text, and use the Format Painter to copy formatting.

## Terms

**Text effects** Effects used to animate text on-screen.

**Font effects** Formatting features used to enhance or emphasize text.

**Highlight formatting** Applying a color background to selected text.

## Notes

### Apply Font and Text Effects

- Font and **text effects** are used to enhance and emphasize text in a document.
- Word includes numerous **font effects** for enhancing and emphasizing text, including the ones available in the Font dialog box:
  - ~~Strikethrough~~
  - ~~Double strikethrough~~
  - Superscript
  - Subscript
  - Shadow
  - Outline
  - Emboss
  - Engrave
  - Sᴍᴀʟʟ ᴄᴀᴘs
  - ALL CAPS

✓ *Hidden is also an option in the Effects area of the font dialog box. Hidden text is not displayed on-screen or printed unless you select to display it.*

- Text effects are animations used in documents that will be viewed on-screen. They cannot be printed.
- Select font and text effects in the Font dialog box.

*The Font dialog box*

## Font Color

■ Use color to enhance text in documents that will be viewed on-screen or printed on a color printer.

■ You can change the color of an underline independently from the color of the font.

## Highlight Text

■ Highlighting calls attention to text by placing a color background on the text just like using a highlighter pen on paper.

■ Yellow is the default highlight color, but you can change the color of **highlight formatting**.

✓ *Color highlighting will print in color when printed on a color printer and print in gray when printed on a black and white printer.*

## Format Painter

■ Use the Format Painter to copy formatting from existing formatted text to existing unformatted text.

# Procedures

## Apply Font Effects

1. Select text.
   OR
   Position insertion point where new text will be typed.
2. Click **Format** .............. `Alt`+`O`
3. Click **Font** ........................... `F`
4. Select check box for desired effect(s).
   ✓ *Clear check mark to remove effect.*
5. Click **OK** ........................... `Enter`
   ✓ *Select text and press Ctrl+Spacebar to remove all character formatting.*

## Apply Text Effects

1. Select text.
   OR
   Position insertion point where new text will be typed.
2. Click **Format** .............. `Alt`+`O`
3. Click **Font** ........................ `F`
4. Click **Text Effects** page tab ..................... `Alt`+`X`
5. Click desired **Animation** ...... `Alt`+`A`, `↑`/`↓`
   ✓ *View a sample of the effect in the Preview area.*
6. Click **OK** ........................... `Enter`

## Apply Font Color

1. Select text.
   OR
   Position insertion point where new text will be typed.
2. Click **Format** .............. `Alt`+`O`
3. Click **Font** ........................ `F`
4. Click **Font color** drop-down arrow ......... `Alt`+`C`
5. Click desired **color** .. `↕↕`, `Enter`
   ✓ *Click Auto to select default color.*
6. Click **OK** ........................... `Enter`
   OR
1. Select text.
   OR
   Position insertion point where new text will be typed.
2. Click **Font Color** button drop-down arrow `A ▾`
3. Click desired color.

## Apply Color to Underlines

1. Select underlined text.
   OR
   Position insertion point where new underlined text will be typed.
2. Click **Format** .............. `Alt`+`O`
3. Click **Font** ........................ `F`
4. Click **Underline color** drop-down arrow ......... `Alt`+`I`
5. Click desired **color**.
   ✓ *Click Auto to select default color.*
6. Click **OK** ........................... `Enter`

## Apply Highlights

**Highlight existing text:**

1. Select text.
2. Click **Highlight** button `✐`.
   ✓ *Repeat steps to remove highlight.*
   OR
1. Click **Highlight** button `✐`.
   ✓ *Mouse pointer changes to look like an I-beam with a pen attached to it.*
2. Drag across text to highlight.
3. Click **Highlight** button `✐` again to turn off Highlight feature.

**Change highlight color:**

1. Click **Highlight** button drop-down arrow `✐ ▾`
2. Click new color.
   ✓ *Click None to select the automatic background color.*

## Copy Formatting

**Copy formatting once;**

1. Select formatted text.
2. Click **Format Painter** button .
   ✓ *The mouse pointer looks like an I-beam with a paintbrush:*
   `⬛I`
3. Select text to format.
   ✓ *Click a word to quickly copy the formatting to that word.*

**Copy formatting repeatedly:**

1. Select formatted text.
2. Double-click **Format Painter** button ✐.
3. Select text to format.
4. Repeat step 3 until all text is formatted.
5. Click **Format Painter** button ✐ to turn off Format Painter.

# Exercise Directions

1. Start Word, if necessary.
2. Open 💿 **15ANNOUNCE**.
3. Save the document as **ANNOUNCE**.
4. Apply the formatting shown in the illustration.
   a. Change the font and font size as marked.
   ✓ *If the specified font is not available on your computer, select a different font.*
   b. Set horizontal alignments as marked.
   c. Apply font and text effects as marked.
   d. Change font color as marked.
   e. Apply highlighting as marked.
   ✓ *Use the Format Painter to copy formatting whenever possible.*
5. Check the spelling and grammar.
6. Display the document in Print Preview. It should look similar to the illustration.
   ✓ *The animated effects do not appear in Print Preview or in a printed document.*
   ✓ *If the document is longer or shorter than the one shown, check to see if you inadvertently formatted the blank lines between paragraphs. In the illustration, all blank lines have the default 12-pt. Times New Roman formatting.*
7. Save the changes.
8. Print the document.
9. Close the document, saving all changes.

# On Your Own

1. Create an invitation to an event such as a birthday party, graduation, or meeting.
2. Save the document as **OWD15**.
3. Format the document using the techniques you have learned so far, including fonts, alignment options, and font effects.
4. Change the font color for some text.
5. Try some text effects.
6. Try different underline styles.
7. Copy the formatting from one location to another.
8. Preview the document and print it.
9. Save your changes, close the document, and exit Word.

*Illustration A*

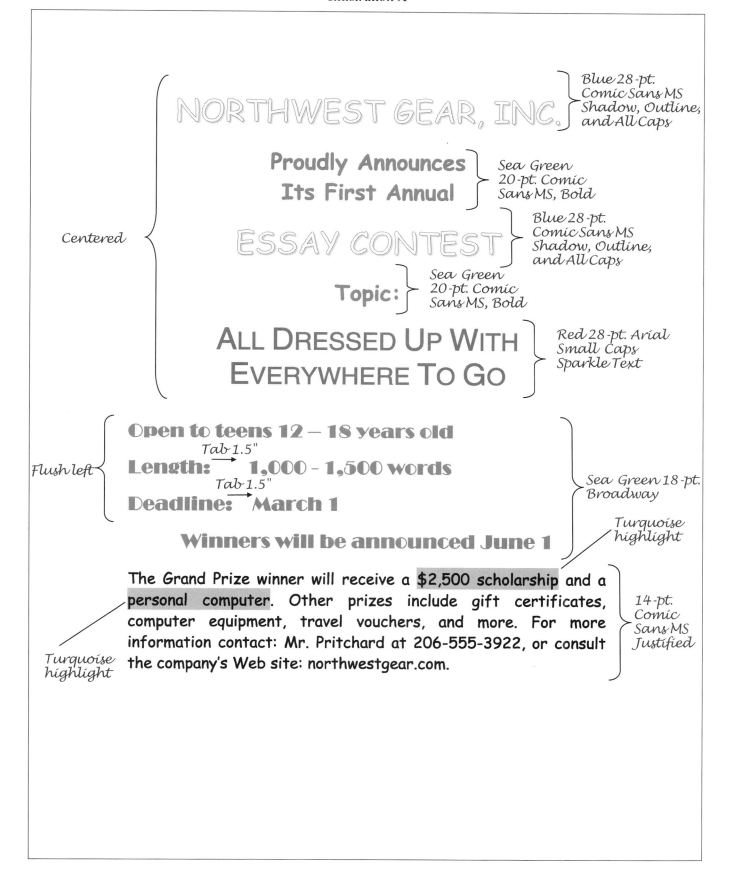

NORTHWEST GEAR, INC.

Blue 28-pt. Comic Sans MS Shadow, Outline, and All Caps

Proudly Announces
Its First Annual

Sea Green 20-pt. Comic Sans MS, Bold

ESSAY CONTEST

Blue 28-pt. Comic Sans MS Shadow, Outline, and All Caps

Topic:

Sea Green 20-pt. Comic Sans MS, Bold

Centered

ALL DRESSED UP WITH EVERYWHERE TO GO

Red 28-pt. Arial Small Caps Sparkle Text

Open to teens 12 – 18 years old

Tab-1.5"

Length:    1,000 – 1,500 words

Tab-1.5"

Deadline:    March 1

Flush left

Winners will be announced June 1

Sea Green 18-pt. Broadway

Turquoise highlight

The Grand Prize winner will receive a $2,500 scholarship and a personal computer. Other prizes include gift certificates, computer equipment, travel vouchers, and more. For more information contact: Mr. Pritchard at 206-555-3922, or consult the company's Web site: northwestgear.com.

14-pt. Comic Sans MS Justified

Turquoise highlight

# Exercise 16

### ◆ Use Symbols

## On the Job

Use symbols to supplement the standard characters available on the keyboard and to add visual interest to documents. For example, you can insert shapes such as hearts and stars into documents as borders or separators.

The owner of Coastline Gourmet Importers has asked you to create a flyer announcing the grand opening of a new store. In this exercise, you will create the flyer using the formatting techniques you have learned so far. You will also insert symbols to enhance the flyer.

## Terms

**Symbol** Shapes, mathematical and scientific notations, currency signs, and other visual elements you can insert in documents by using the Symbol dialog box.

## Notes

### Use Symbols

- **Symbols** are characters that cannot be typed from the keyboard, such as hearts, stars, and other shapes, as well as foreign alphabet characters.

- Symbols can be selected, edited, and formatted in a document just like regular text characters.

- Several symbol fonts come with Office XP and others are available through vendors and shareware.

- Many regular character fonts also include some symbol characters.

- You select a font, then select the desired symbol in the Symbol dialog box.

- You can also select from a list of recently used symbols.

- When you insert symbols, the symbol font formatting is applied to the character. You can change the font style and effects just as you can for regular text characters.

Current font  *Symbol dialog box*     Selected symbol

Recently used symbols

# Procedures

**Insert Symbols**

1. Position insertion point where you want to insert a symbol.
2. Click **Insert**.................. `Alt`+`I`
3. Click **Symbol**. ..................... `S`
4. Click **Font** drop-down arrow................. `Alt`+`F`
5. Select any symbol **font**.............. `↓`, `Enter`
6. Click desired **symbol**...................... `Tab`, `→`
7. Click **Insert**.................. `Alt`+`I`

   ✓ *Repeat the steps to insert additional symbols without closing the Symbol dialog box.*

8. Click **Close**......................... `Esc`

# Exercise Directions

1. Start Word, if necessary.
2. Open ⊙**16GRAND**.
3. Save the document as **GRAND**.
4. Format the text as marked in the illustration.
   a. Use a serif font for the entire document. (Perpetua is used in Illustration A.)
   b. Apply font sizes, colors, and effects as shown.
      ✓ *Be careful not to change the font size and formatting of the blank lines in the document. They should remain at 12-point Times New Roman.*
   c. Apply alignments as shown.

5. Use the Wingdings font to insert symbols as marked in the illustration.
   ✓ *Leave spaces between each snowflake symbol. Adjust the font size and formatting of symbol characters the same way you adjust the font size and formatting of text characters.*
   ✓ *Hint: Use Copy and Paste to copy a symbol from one location to another, or use the Repeat command (Ctrl+Y) to repeat the insertion. Use the Format Painter to copy formatting.*

6. Display the document in Print Preview. It should look similar to the illustration.
7. Print the document.
8. Close the document, saving the changes.

# On Your Own

1. Open the document **OWD15**, the document you created in exercise 15, or open ⊙**16INVITE**.
2. Save the document as **OWD16**.
3. Use symbols to enhance the document. For example, use symbols as separators between words or paragraphs, or use them to decorate or emphasize the document.

4. Try different symbol fonts.
5. Try changing the font size for a symbol inserted in a document.
6. Try repeating a symbol to create a line across the page.
7. Preview and print the document.
8. Close the document, saving all changes

Grand Opening  *26-pt., red*

# COASTLINE GOURMET IMPORTERS

*34-pt., red,*
*Engrave,*
*Small Caps*

Announces  *18-pt., red*

The Grand Opening of its Newest Retail Outlet  *20-pt.*
*Turquoise*

*Centered*

❋ ❋ ❋ ❋ ❋ ❋ ❋ ❋ ❋ ❋ ❋ ❋ ❋ ❋ ❋ ❋  *Wingdings*
*Symbol (#175)*

# 16509 NORTHEAST 26TH AVENUE

# NORTH MIAMI BEACH, FL 33160

*34-pt., red,*
*Engrave*
*Small Caps*

❋ ❋ ❋ ❋ ❋ ❋ ❋ ❋ ❋ ❋ ❋ ❋ ❋ ❋ ❋ ❋  *Wingdings*
*Symbol (#175)*

Stop in to share our grand opening celebration
Saturday, April 13 and Sunday, April 14  *24-pt. black*

*Wingdings*
*Symbol (#70)*

→ ☞ →  PRODUCT SAMPLES

*Left tab 1"*  → ☞ →  DEMONSTRATIONS

*34-pt., red,*
*Engrave*
*Small Caps*

→ ☞ →  AND MORE…

*Left tab 2"*

Coastline Gourmet Importers is well known as a  *24-pt.*
specialty food store featuring items imported  *Justified*
from around the world.

# Exercise 17

## On the Job

Lists are an effective way to present items of information. Use a bulleted list when the items do not have to be in any particular order, like a grocery list or a list of objectives. Use a numbered list when the order of the items is important, such as directions or instructions. Use Sort to organize a list into alphabetical or numerical order.

As a personnel assistant at Electron Consumer Industries, Inc., a manufacturer of computer electronics, you have been asked to issue a memo about a change in emergency procedures. In this exercise, you will edit and format a memo document using a bulleted list and a numbered list. You will also sort the bulleted list into alphabetical order.

## Terms

**Bullet** A dot or symbol that marks an important line of information or designates items in a list.

**Sort** To organize items into a specified order.

## Notes

### Bulleted Lists

- Use **bullets** to mark lists when the order of items does not matter.
- Word has seven built-in bullet symbols, but uses a simple black dot by default.
- A variety of bullet styles are available in the Bullets and Numbering dialog box, or you can create a customized bullet using a symbol.
- Word automatically carries bullet formatting forward to new paragraphs in a list.

*Select a bullet style in the Bullets and Numbering dialog box*

77

## Numbered Lists

- Use numbers to mark lists when the order of items matters, such as directions or how-to steps.
- Word automatically renumbers a list when you add or delete items.
- Word comes with seven numbering styles, but the default numbering style is an Arabic numeral followed by a period.
- You can select a different number style in the Bullets and Numbering dialog box.
- Word automatically carries number formatting forward to new paragraphs in a list.

*Select a number style in the Bullets and Numbering dialog box*

## Sort

- Word can automatically **sort** items into alphabetical, numerical, or chronological order.
- A sort can be ascending (A to Z or 0 to 9) or descending (Z to A or 9 to 0).
- The default sort order is alphabetical ascending.
- Although the Sort command is on the Table menu, sorting is available for arranging lists, paragraphs, or rows in regular text as well as a table.

*Options for a default sort*

# Procedures

### Create Bulleted List

**Use the default bullet:**

1. Position insertion point where you want to start list.
   OR
   Select paragraphs you want in the list.
2. Click **Bullets** button 📋.

**Select a different bullet style:**

1. Position insertion point where you want to start list.
   OR
   Select paragraphs you want in the list.

2. Click **Format** ............... `Alt`+`O`
3. Click **Bullets and Numbering** ........................ `N`
4. Click **Bulleted** page tab.............................. `Alt`+`B`
5. Click desired Bullet style .... `↕`
6. Click **OK** ........................... `Enter`

**Customize bullet:**

1. Position insertion point where you want to start list.
   OR
   Select paragraphs you want in list.

2. Click **Format** ............... `Alt`+`O`
3. Click **Bullets and Numbering** ........................ `N`
4. Click **Bulleted** page tab .............................. `Alt`+`B`
5. Click desired **Bullet style** ...................... `↓` `↑` `→` `←`
6. Click **Customize** ......... `Alt`+`T`
7. Click desired **Bullet character** ......... `Alt`+`U`, `→` `←`

## Use a symbol as a bullet:

1. Position insertion point where you want to start list.
   OR
   Select paragraphs you want in list.
2. Click **Format** ............... [Alt]+[O]
3. Click **Bullets and Numbering** ........................ [N]
4. Click **Bulleted** page tab ............................ [Alt]+[B]
5. Click desired **Bullet style** .................... [↓][↑][→][←]
6. Click **Customize** ........ [Alt]+[T]
7. Click **Character** .................. [C]
8. Click desired symbol .......... [Tab], [↓][↑][→][←]
9. Click **OK** ............................ [Enter]
10. Click **OK** .......................... [Enter]

## Turn off bullets:

- Click **Bullets** button [≡]
  ✓ *To remove existing bullets, select bulleted list then click Bullets button.*

## Create Numbered List

### Use default number style:

1. Position insertion point where you want to start list.
   OR
   Select paragraphs you want in list.
2. Click **Numbering** button [≡].

### Select different number style:

1. Position insertion point where you want to start list.
   OR
   Select paragraphs you want in list.
2. Click **Format** ............... [Alt]+[O]
3. Click **Bullets and Numbering** ........................ [N]
4. Click **Numbered** page tab ............................ [Alt]+[N]
5. Click **Number style** ........... [↕]
6. Click **OK** .......................... [Enter]

### Turn off numbering:

- Click **Numbering** button [≡].
  ✓ *To remove numbers, select numbered list, then click Numbering button.*

## Sort a List

### Use default sort order:

1. Select the paragraphs you want sorted.
2. Click **Table** ................. [Alt]+[A]
3. Click **Sort** ...........................[S]
4. Click **OK** .......................... [Enter]

### Use a numerical or chronological sort:

1. Select the paragraphs you want sorted.
2. Click **Table** ................. [Alt]+[A]
3. Click **Sort** ...........................[S]
4. Click **Type** drop-down arrow .......................... [Alt]+[Y]
5. Click **Number** ........... [↓], [Enter]
   OR
   Click **Date** ................. [↓], [Enter]
6. Click **OK** .......................... [Enter]

### Reverse the sort order:

1. Select the paragraphs you want sorted.
2. Click **Table** ................. [Alt]+[A]
3. Click **Sort** ...........................[S]
4. Click **Descending** ....... [Alt]+[D]
5. Click **OK** .......................... [Enter]

# Exercise Directions

1. Start Word, if necessary.
2. Open 💿 **17FIREDRILL**.
3. Save the document as **FIREDRIL**.
4. Edit and format the document as shown in Illustration A.
   a. Set fonts, font sizes, and alignments as shown.
   b. Insert symbols as shown.
   c. Use the default bullet style to turn the five guidelines into a bulleted list.
   d. Select a different bullet style.
   e. Use the default number style to turn the four steps for evacuation into a numbered list.
   f. Select a different number style.
   g. Change back to the default number style.
   h. Sort the bulleted list into ascending alphabetical order.
5. Check the spelling and grammar.
6. Display the document in Print Preview. It should look similar to the one in the Illustration, depending on the bullet and number styles you selected.
7. Print the document.
8. Close the document, saving all changes.

**Electron Consumer Industries, Inc.**

*22 pts.*

*Arial Black*

**8740 S. Crawford Rd. ✦ Chicago, IL 60619**

**Phone: (312) 555-7700 ✦ Fax: (312) 555-7800 ✦ e-mail: electron@ddcpub.com**

*16 pts.*

*Insert Wingdings Symbol*

*8 pts.*

*Left Tab 1"*

**Memo To:** → All employees

**From:** → Your name

**Date:** → Today's date

**Subject:** → Emergency procedures

Recently, we invited professionals in the field of emergency evacuations to evaluate our emergency procedure policies. While most of our policies received high marks, we have made some changes to our fire emergency procedure. Please review the following information, and then post this memo within clear sight of your desk. We will have a drill sometime in the near future.

*Numbered list*

1. Alarm sounds.
2. Proceed calmly to one of the fire exits.
3. Walk out of the building.
4. Convene with your department in the designated meeting area.

Adhere to the following guidelines:

*Bulleted list in alphabetical order*

➢ Avoid the elevators.
➢ Do not ignore the alarm.
➢ Leave personal belongings behind.
➢ Use the closest fire exit.
➢ Walk! Do not run.

If you have any questions about the new procedures, please contact me in the Personnel Department at ext. 344. Thank you for your cooperation.

# On Your Own

1. Create a new document in Word.

2. Save the file as **OWD17**.

3. Type a bulleted list of five things you'd like to accomplish in the next year. These can be goals for school, work, or personal development. Examples might include earning a better grade in math, completing a project on the job, or getting in better shape by exercising and eating right.

4. Sort the list in alphabetical order.

5. Type a numbered list that includes at least five steps describing how you expect to accomplish one of the items in the bulleted list.

6. Change the sort order of the bulleted list to descending order.

7. Save your changes, close the document, and exit Word.

# Exercise 18

## Skills Covered:

◆ **Line Spacing** ◆ **Paragraph Spacing** ◆ **Indent Text**

## On the Job

Format documents using the right amount of space between lines, paragraphs, and words to make the pages look better and the text easier to read. Use indents to call attention to a paragraph, to achieve a particular visual effect, or to leave white space along the margins for notes or illustrations.

Coastline Gourmet is instituting a few new programs in response to a marketing survey. In this exercise, you will format a document explaining the new programs using line and paragraph spacing and indents. You will also use other formatting techniques, such as font formatting, alignments, and tabs.

## Terms

**Line spacing**  The amount of white space between lines of text in a paragraph.

**Leading**  Line spacing measured in points.

**Paragraph spacing**  The amount of white space between paragraphs.

**Indent**  A temporary left and/or right margin for lines or paragraphs.

## Notes

### Line Spacing

- **Line spacing** sets the amount of vertical space between lines. By default, line spacing in Word is set to single space. Line spacing can be measured in either lines (single, double, etc.) or in points.

- When line spacing is measured in points, it is called **leading** (pronounced *ledding*).

  By default, Word uses leading that is 120% of the current font size. For a 10-point font, that means 12-point leading. This paragraph is formatted with the default leading for a 12-point font (14.4 pts.).

  Increase leading to make text easier to read. In this paragraph, the font is still 12 points, but the leading has been increased to exactly 16 points.

  Decrease leading to fit more lines on a page. In this paragraph, the leading has been set to exactly 10 points, while the font size is still 12 points. Keep in mind that decreasing leading makes text harder to read.

- Line spacing measured in lines can be set to single spaced, 1.5 spaced, or double spaced.

## Paragraph Spacing

- **Paragraph spacing** affects space before or after paragraphs.

- Amount of space can be specified in lines or in points. The default is points.

- Use increased paragraph spacing in place of extra returns or blank lines.

## Indent Text

- There are five types of **indents**:
  - *Left* indents text from the left margin.
  - *Right* indents text from the right margin.
  - *Double* indents text from both the left and right margins.
  - First line indents just the first line of a paragraph from the left margin.
  - *Hanging* indents all lines but the first line from the left margin.

- Indent markers on the horizontal ruler show where current indents are set.

*Indents in a document*

# Procedures

## Set Line Spacing
*(Ctrl+1, Ctrl+2, Ctrl+5)*

1. Position insertion point where text will be typed.
   OR
   Position insertion point in paragraph to change.
   OR
   Select paragraphs to change.
2. Click **Format** .............. `Alt`+`O`
3. Click **Paragraph** .................. `P`
4. Click **Indents and Spacing** page tab ..................... `Alt`+`I`
5. Click **Line spacing** ...... `Alt`+`N`
6. Select a **line spacing** option: ..................... `↓`, `Enter`
   - Single
   - 1.5 lines
   - Double
   OR
   a. Select **leading** option: ................ `↓`, `Enter`
      - **At least** to set a minimum leading.
      - **Exactly** to set an exact leading.
      - **Multiple** to specify a percentage by which to increase leading.
   b. Click **At** box ............ `Alt`+`A`
   c. Type value in points.
7. Click **OK** .......................... `Enter`

## Set Paragraph Spacing

1. Position insertion point where text will be typed.
   OR
   Position insertion point in paragraph to change.
   OR
   Select paragraphs to change.
2. Click **Format** .............. `Alt`+`O`
3. Click **Paragraph** .................. `P`
   ✓ *To open the Paragraph dialog box quickly, right-click paragraph to format, then click Paragraph.*

4. Click **Indents and Spacing** page tab........ `Alt`+`I`
5. Click **Before** text box .. `Alt`+`B`
   OR
   Click **After** text box ..... `Alt`+`E`
6. Type amount of space to leave.
   ✓ *Type li after value to specify lines.*
7. Click **OK** .......................... `Enter`

## Indent Text

### Quickly Indent from the left:

1. Position insertion point where text will be typed.
   OR
   Position insertion point in paragraph to change.
   OR
   Select paragraphs to change.
2. Click **Increase Indent** button.
   OR
   Click **Decrease Indent** button.
   OR
   Drag **Left-indent** marker on ruler.

### Indent from the left and/or right:

1. Position insertion point where text will be typed.
   OR
   Position insertion point in paragraph to change.
   OR
   Select paragraphs to change.
2. Drag **Left-indent** marker on ruler.
3. Drag **Right-indent** marker on ruler.

### Set Precise left and/or right indents:

1. Click **Format** .............. `Alt`+`O`
2. Click **Paragraph** .................. `P`
3. Click **Indents and Spacing** page tab........ `Alt`+`I`
4. Click **Left** text box ....... `Alt`+`L`
5. Type distance from left margin.
6. Click **Right** text box..... `Alt`+`R`
7. Type distance from right margin.
8. Click **OK** .......................... `Enter`

### Indent first line only *(Tab)*:

1. Position insertion point where text will be typed.
   OR
   Position insertion point in paragraph to change.
   OR
   Select paragraphs to change.
2. Drag **First Line indent** marker.
   OR
   a. Click **Format** .......... `Alt`+`O`
   b. Click **Paragraph** ............ `P`
   c. Click **Indents and Spacing** page tab ................ `Alt`+`I`
   d. Click **Special** drop-down arrow ........... `Alt`+`S`
   e. Click **First line** ..... `↓`, `Enter`
   f. Click **By** text box .... `Alt`+`Y`
   g. Type amount to indent.
   h. Click **OK** ..................... `Enter`

### Hanging indent *(Ctrl+T)*:

1. Position insertion point where text will be typed.
   OR
   Position insertion point in paragraph to change.
   OR
   Select paragraphs to change.
2. Drag **Hanging indent** marker.
   OR
   a. Click **Format** .......... `Alt`+`O`
   b. Click **Paragraph** ............ `P`
   c. Click **Indents and Spacing** page tab ................ `Alt`+`I`
   d. Click **Special** drop-down arrow ..................... `Alt`+`S`
   e. Click **Hanging** ...... `↓`, `Enter`
   f. Click **By** text box .... `Alt`+`Y`
   g. Type amount to indent.
   h. Click **OK** ..................... `Enter`

# Exercise Directions

1. Start Word, if necessary.

2. Open 💿 **18PROGRAMS**.

3. Save the document as **PROGRAMS**.

4. Follow steps 5 through 9 to achieve the results shown in the illustration.

5. Remember, you can use the Format Painter to copy formatting from one paragraph to another.

6. Apply font formatting as shown.

   ✓ *Unless otherwise specified, all text is 12-point sans serif. (Arial is used in Illustration A.)*

7. Insert symbols as marked in the illustration.

8. Set alignments and tabs as marked in the illustration.

   ✓ *Unless otherwise noted, all paragraphs are justified.*

9. Set line spacing, paragraph spacing, and indents as shown in the illustration.

10. Check spelling and grammar.

11. Display the document in Print Preview. It should look similar to the illustration.

12. Print the document.

13. Close the document, saving all changes.

# On Your Own

1. Create a new document in Word.

2. Save the file as **OWD18**.

3. Think of some documents that could benefit from line spacing, paragraph spacing, and indent formatting. For example, many instructors require reports and papers to be double spaced. First drafts of documents that will be read by others should be double spaced so reviewers can jot notes or make corrections. A resume can be set up neatly using spacing and indent features, as can a reference list.

4. Create a resume describing your school experience, outside activities such as clubs or athletic teams, and any work experience.

5. Use spacing and indent features to format the resume.

6. Use alignments and font formatting to enhance the text and to call attention to important items.

7. Use lists and symbols if appropriate.

8. Save your changes, close the document, and exit Word.

Flush left

## Coastline Gourmet Importers

28-pt. Harlow Solid Italic Underlined

7334 Sunshine Parkway ♻12ᵗʰ Floor Miami, FL 33132 — 10-pt. Arial

Phone: (305) 555-7300 ♻ Fax: (305) 555-7301 ♻ e-mail: coastlinegourmet@ddcpub.com — 8-pt. Arial

Insert Wingdings Symbol

Leave 24 pts. of space after

Contact: → Marissa Hernandez

Left Tab 1" → Ext. 245 — Leave 24 pts. of space after

Double-spaced

First line indent .5"

→ Coastline Gourmet Importers recently conducted a marketing survey in an attempt to determine how best to boost sales. The results of the survey have been compiled, and the key point can be summarized in a few lines:

6 pts. of space before; 6 pts. of space after

Indent 1.5" from left and right

Set leading to at least 12 pts.

"Coastline Gourmet Importers faces challenges from numerous other retail stores in the Southern Florida area. To boost sales, Coastline Gourmet must make every effort to bring more customers into each store, and to keep them in the store for a longer period of time in order to maximize buying potential."

10-pt. Arial

6 pts. of space before; 0 pts. of space after

Indent 3" from left

Survey Results

10-pt. Arial 0 pts. before 18 pts. after

In response to the survey results, the company has decided to implement the following programs in selected stores. If the programs are successful, the company will expand them into all stores.

Same as first paragraph above

Hanging indent set at 1.5"

**Product demos**. Coastline Gourmet will invite customers to attend demonstrations for using small appliances and utensils such as espresso and cappuccino machines, pasta makers, and food processors.

**Cooking classes**. Coastline Gourmet will sponsor hands-on cooking classes in which customers can learn how to make simple, yet elegant dishes such as salads, appetizers, and desserts.

**Singles parties**. Coastline Gourmet will invite customers to meet and mingle while sampling some of the imported cheeses, crackers, and sweets. Door prizes will be offered, and shopping will be encouraged.

6 pts. of space before; 6 pts of space after

Set leading to exactly 16 pts.

# Exercise 19

◆ **Apply Styles** ◆ **Create a Style** ◆ **Edit a Style**
◆ **Reapply Direct Formatting** ◆ **Check Formatting**
◆ **Select Paste Formatting Options** ◆ **Clear Formatting**

## On the Job

Word provides many ways to apply and remove formatting in documents. Use styles to apply a collection of formatting settings to characters or paragraphs. Styles help ensure continuity in formatting throughout a document. You can also set Word to check for formatting inconsistencies in much the same way it checks for spelling and grammatical errors.

Murray Hill Marketing, an advertising and public relations firm, has contracted with a training company to provide computer training for employees. You have been asked to prepare a document listing the courses that will be available for the first three months of the year. In this exercise, you will use styles and direct formatting to apply consistent formatting to the document.

## Terms

**Style** A collection of formatting settings that can be applied to characters or paragraphs.

**Style sheet** A list of available styles.

**Direct formatting** Individual font or paragraph formatting settings applied directly to text, as opposed to a collection of settings applied with a style.

## Notes

### Apply Styles

- **Styles** make it easy to apply a collection of formatting settings to characters or paragraphs all at once.
- Word includes built-in styles for formatting body text, headings, lists, and other parts of documents.
- Different Word templates have different **style sheets** depending on formatting required for the document. For example, the default Normal template uses only five styles, while the Resume template includes 25 styles.

*The Style list for the Normal template style sheet*

- You can apply a style to existing text, or select a style before you type new text.
- You can select a style from the drop-down style list or from the Styles and Formatting Task Pane.

*Styles and Formatting Task Pane*

## Create a Style

- You can create new styles for formatting your documents.
- Styles can contain font and/or paragraph formatting.
- Style names should be short and descriptive.
- The style will be added to the style sheet for the current document.

## Edit a Style

- You can modify an existing style.
- When you modify a style that has already been applied to text in the document, the formatted text automatically changes to the new style.
- If you modify a style and give it a new name, it becomes a new style; the original style remains unchanged.

## Reapply Direct Formatting

- You can also use the Styles and Formatting Task Pane to apply **direct formatting** that you have already used in a document to selected text.
- This feature is similar to the Format Painter, but you do not have to scroll through the document from the formatted text to the text you want to format.

## Check Formatting

- Use Word's Format Checker to insure consistent formatting throughout a document.
- As with the spelling checker and the grammar checker, you can have Word check formatting while you work. Word underlines formatting inconsistencies with a wavy blue underline.

*Use the Format Checker*

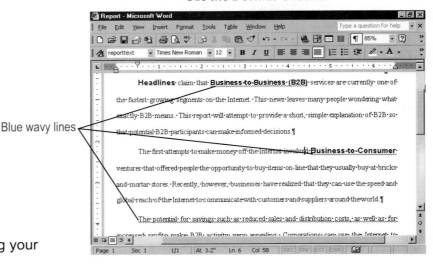

Blue wavy lines

- You can ignore the blue lines and keep typing, or correct the error.
- The automatic format checker is off by default; you must turn it on to use it.
- If the wavy underlines distract you from your work, you can turn off the automatic formatting checker.
- You can also have Word check the formatting immediately after you check the spelling and grammar in a document.

## Select Paste Formatting Options

- When you use the Clipboard to paste text from one location to another, Word automatically displays the Paste Options button.
- Click the Paste Options button to display a list of options for formatting the text in the new location.

*The Paste Options button*

## Clear Formatting

- You can quickly remove all formatting from selected text. This returns text to the default font.

- Clearing the formatting from text removes both direct formatting and styles.

  ✓ *To quickly remove direct character formatting from selected text, press Ctrl+Spacebar; to remove direct paragraph formatting, press Ctrl+Q.*

- You can clear formatting using the Style list, or the Styles and Formatting Task Pane.

- After you clear the formatting, text is displayed in the default normal style for the current document. For the default document, that means single spaced 12-point Times New Roman, flush left.

# Procedures

### Apply a Style

1. Click in the paragraph.
   OR
   Select the text.
2. Click the **Style** drop-down arrow `Normal ▾` on the Formatting toolbar.
3. Select style to apply..............`↑`, `↓`, `Enter`

### Apply a Style Using the Task Pane

1. Click in the paragraph.
   OR
   Select the text.
2. Click the **Styles and Formatting** button
   on the Formatting toolbar
   OR
   a. Click **Format**.......... `Alt`+`O`
   b. Click **Styles and Formatting** ................... `S`
3. Click style to apply in **Pick formatting to apply** list.
   ✓ *If necessary, scroll through the list to find the desired formatting.*

### Create a Style

1. Format text or paragraph.
2. Click in the **Style** box `Normal ▾` on the Formatting toolbar.
3. Type style name.
4. Press **Enter**......................`Enter`

### Edit a Style

1. Change formatting of text or paragraph formatted with the style.
2. Click in **Style** box `Normal ▾` on the Formatting toolbar.
3. Press **Enter**......................`Enter`
4. Click **Update the style to reflect recent changes?** ................. `Alt`+`U`
5. Click **OK** ..........................`Enter`

### Reapply Direct Formatting

1. Select text to format.
2. Click the **Styles and Formatting** button
   on the Formatting toolbar.
   OR
   a. Click **Format**.......... `Alt`+`O`
   b. Click **Styles and Formatting** ................... `S`
3. Click style to apply in **Pick formatting to apply** list.
   ✓ *If necessary, scroll through the list to find the desired formatting.*

### Turn on Automatic Format Checking

1. Click **Tools**.................. `Alt`+`T`
2. Click **Options**..................... `O`
3. Click the **Edit** tab........`Ctrl`+`Tab`
4. Select **Mark formatting inconsistencies** check box ................... `Alt`+`F`
5. Click **OK** ..........................`Enter`

### Check Formatting as You Type

1. Right-click formatting inconsistency marked with blue, wavy underline.
2. Click desired correct formatting option on context menu.
   OR
   Click **Ignore Once** to hide this occurrence...................`I`
   OR
   Click **Ignore Rule** to hide all occurrences...................`U`

### Check Formatting

1. Run Spelling and Grammar checker.
   ✓ *Refer to Exercise 3 for information on checking the spelling and grammar in a document.*
2. When check is complete, click **Check Formatting**.
3. Choose from the following options:
   - Click **Change**......... `Alt`+`C` to accept the recommended formatting.
   - Click **Ignore** to continue without changing formatting.............. `Alt`+`I`
   - Click **Ignore Rule** to continue without changing formatting and without highlighting inconsistency if it occurs anywhere else in document .............. `Alt`+`G`

## Select Paste Formatting Options

1. Paste text at new location.
   - ✓ *Refer to Exercises 10 and 11 for information on pasting.*
2. Click **Paste Options** button 📋.
3. Select one of the following:
   - **Keep Source Formatting** .................. Ⓚ
     to maintain formatting from original location.
   - **Match Destination Formatting** .................. Ⓓ
     to apply existing formatting to new text.
   - **Keep Text Only** ............. Ⓣ
     to remove all applied formatting.

- **Apply Styles or Formatting** ..................... Ⓐ
  to open Styles and Formatting Task Pane.

**If Paste Options button is not displayed:**

1. Click **Tools** .................. `Alt`+`T`
2. Click **Options** ...................... `O`
3. Click the **Edit** tab ........ `Ctrl`+`Tab`
4. Select **Show Paste Options buttons** check box ...... `Alt`+`O`
5. Click **OK** ........................... `Enter`

## Clear Formatting

1. Select text.
2. Click the **Style** drop-down arrow `Normal ▾` on the Formatting toolbar.
   OR

Click the **Styles and Formatting** button 🄰 on the Formatting toolbar.
OR
a. Click **Format** .......... `Alt`+`O`
b. Click **Styles and Formatting** ................... Ⓢ

3. Select **Clear Formatting**......... `↑`, `↓`, `Enter`
   - ✓ *Clear Formatting is usually found at the top of the drop-down style list or at the top of the Formatting to Apply list.*

# Exercise Directions

1. Start Word, if necessary.
2. Open 💿**19COURSE**.
3. Save the document as **COURSE**.
4. Apply the Heading 1 style to the company name.
5. Apply the Heading 3 style to the names of the months.
6. Increase the font size of the company name to 26 points, center it, and increase the amount of space after it to 12 points.
7. Modify the Heading 1 style to include the changes.
8. Apply the new Heading 1 style to the text **Training Schedule**.
9. Insert Wingding symbols to separate the parts of the company address, then format the address as follows:
   a. Increase the font size to 14 points.
   b. Center the line horizontally.
   c. Apply italics.
   d. Add 6 points of space before and after the line.
10. Reapply the formatting you have just applied to the company address to the names of the three courses.

11. Format the paragraph describing the Word 1 course as follows:
    a. Change the font to 14-point Arial.
    b. Justify the alignment.
    c. Indent the paragraph 1" from both the left and the right.
    d. Leave 12 points of space before and after the paragraph.
12. Create a style named *Course* based on the formatting of the course description.
13. Apply the *Course* style to the paragraphs describing the Word 2 and Word 3 courses.
14. Add a new line to the end of the document.
15. Clear all formatting from the new line, then type: **For more information, call:**
16. Copy the phone number from the company address line near the top of the document and paste it at the end of the new last line of the document.
17. Select to paste only the text, without any formatting.
18. Complete the line by typing **ext. 343** after the pasted phone number.
19. Set Word to automatically check formatting.

20. Format the text **Training Schedule** in 13-point bold Arial, then move the insertion point to a different location in the document. The format checker should display a wavy blue underline under the text Training Schedule.

21. Right-click the wavy blue underline to see what Word suggests.

22. Ignore the rule, then reapply the Heading 1 style to the text.

23. Check the spelling, grammar, and formatting in the document.

24. Display the document in Print Preview. It should look similar to the one in the illustration.

25. Print the document.

26. Close the file saving all changes.

# On Your Own

1. Start Word and open **OWD18**, the document you created in the On Your Own section of Exercise 18, or open ☉ **19RESUME**.

2. Save the document as **OWD19**.

3. Clear all formatting from the document.

4. Use styles to format the document. You can use existing styles, modify existing styles, or create new styles.

5. Apply some direct formatting for emphasis, then reapply the formatting to other text in the document.

6. If you want, try pasting text and selecting different Paste Options for formatting.

7. Check the spelling, grammar, and formatting in the document.

8. Close the document, saving all changes.

# Murray Hill Marketing, LLC *Heading 1*

*285 Madison Avenue ✦ New York, NY 10016 ✦ 212-555-4444*    *14-pt. Italics, centered, 6 pts. before, 6 pts. after*

*Heading 1* ## Training Schedule

*Heading 3* {

**January**

*Microsoft Word 1*    *Same as address*

This introductory course will cover the basics of using Microsoft Word to create common business documents. By the end of the course you will know how to: create and print text-based documents such as letters and envelopes, and apply formatting.

**February**

*Microsoft Word 2*    *Same as address*

A continuation of the Word I course, this introductory level class will delve into some of the more intriguing features of Microsoft Word. By the end of the course you will know how to conduct a mail merge, set up a document in columns, include headers and footers, and insert pictures.

**March**

*Microsoft Word 3*    *Same as address*

This final course in the Microsoft Word series covers the advanced features. By the end of this course you will know how to work with tables, create and modify outlines, use e-mail and Internet features in Word, and share documents with other users.

*Course*

For more information call: 212-555-4444, ext. 343.    *Normal*

# Exercise 20

## On the Job

Format a one-page report so that it is attractive and professional. Set margins to meet expected requirements and to improve the document's appearance and readability. For example, leave a wider margin in a report if you expect a reader to make notes or comments; leave a narrower margin to fit more text on a page.

Regency General, Inc. has realized that many people are not sure what *business-to-business*—"B2B"— means. In this exercise, you are responsible for formatting a one-page report explaining how business-to-business services work. The report can be included in marketing packets given to prospective clients.

## Terms

**Gutter** Space added to the margin to leave room for binding.

**Margins** The amount of white space between the text and the edge of the page on all four sides.

**Section** In Word, a segment of a document defined by a section break. A section may have different page formatting from the rest of the document.

**Portrait orientation** The default position for displaying and printing text horizontally across the shorter side of a page.

**Landscape orientation** Rotating document text so it displays and prints horizontally across the longer side of a page.

## Notes

### Format a One-Page Report

■ Traditionally, a one-page report is set up as follows:

- Text starts 1" or 2" from the top of the page.
- Text is justified.
- Lines are double spaced.
- First-line indents are .5" or 1".
- The report title is centered and all uppercase.
- Spacing following the title ranges from ¾" (54 pts.) to 1" (72 pts.).
- Unbound reports have left and right margins of 1".

- A **gutter** on bound reports makes the left margin wider than the right margin.
  - ✓ *Use the Mirror margins option to set gutter width on inside margin of each page.*

### Set Margins

■ **Margins** are measured in inches.

■ Default margins are 1.25" on the left and right and 1" on the top and bottom.

■ Margin settings affect an entire document, or the current **section**.
  - ✓ *To set margins for a paragraph that are different from the page margins, use indents as described in Exercise 18.*

- On the rulers, areas outside the margins are shaded gray, while areas inside the margins are white.
  - ✓ *To see both vertical and horizontal rulers, use Print Layout view.*
- Light gray bars mark the margins on the rulers.

## Set Page Orientation

- There are two page orientations available:
  - **Portrait**
  - **Landscape**

- Portrait is the default orientation, and is used for most documents, including letters, memos, and reports.
- Use landscape orientation to display a document across the wider length of the page. For example, if a document contains a table that is wider than the standard 8.5" page, Word will split it across two pages. When you change to landscape orientation, the table may fit on the 11" page.

# Procedures

### Set Margins in Print Layout View

1. Move the mouse pointer over the margin marker on the ruler.
   - ✓ *The mouse pointer changes to a double-headed arrow, and the ScreenTip identifies the margin.*
2. Drag the margin marker to a new location.
   - ✓ *Press and hold the Alt key while you drag to see the margin width.*

### Set Margins in any View

1. Click **File** .................... `Alt`+`F`
2. Click **Page Setup** ............... `U`
3. Click **Margins** tab ........ `Alt`+`M`
4. Click **Top** text box ....... `Alt`+`T`
5. Type top margin width.
6. Click **Bottom** text box ............................. `Alt`+`B`
7. Type bottom margin width.
8. Click **Left** text box ....... `Alt`+`F`
9. Type left margin width.
10. Click **Right** text box ............................. `Alt`+`H`
11. Type right margin width.
12. Click the **Apply to** drop-down arrow .......................... `Alt`+`Y`
13. Select **This point forward**.
    OR
    Select **Whole document**.
14. Click **OK** .......................... `Enter`

### Set Page Orientation

1. Click **File** .................... `Alt`+`F`
2. Click **Page Setup** ............... `U`
3. Click **Margins** tab.
4. Click **Portrait** ..................... `P`
   OR
   Click **Landscape** ............... `S`
5. Click **OK** .......................... `Enter`

# Exercise Directions

1. Start Word, if necessary.
2. Open ☙ **20BUSINESS**.
3. Save the document as **BUSINESS**.
4. Change the margins to 1" on all sides of the page.
5. Format the report as shown in the illustration.
6. Use a 16-point sans serif font in all uppercase for the title. (Arial is used in the illustration.)
7. Center the title and leave 54-points of space after it.
8. Use a 12-point serif font for the body text. (Times New Roman is used in the illustration.)
9. Justify and double-space all body text paragraphs.
10. Leave 6 points of space before and after each paragraph.
11. Indent the first line of each body text paragraph by .5".
12. If the document extends onto a second page, change the top and bottom margins to .75".
13. Check the spelling and grammar.
14. Change the page orientation to Landscape.
15. Display the document in Print Preview.
16. Print the document.
17. Change the page orientation back to Portrait.
18. Print the document.
19. Close the document, saving all changes.

# On Your Own

1. Create a new document in Word.
2. Save the file as **OWD20**.
3. In the third person, draft a one-page report about yourself. For example, draft a document that you could include in a directory for an organization of which you are a member. Think of the *About the Author* paragraphs found in books and magazines, or the *About the Performers* paragraphs found in a theater program.
4. Double space the report.
5. Use correct document formatting for a one-page report.
6. Use other formatting effects, including fonts, lists, and symbols.
7. Check the spelling and grammar, then print the document.
8. Save your changes and close the document.

1"

# BUSINESS-TO-BUSINESS: MAKING THE INTERNET WORK

*16-pt. Arial Centered*

*54 pts.*

Headlines claim that Business-to-Business (B2B) services are currently one of the fastest growing segments on the Internet. This news leaves many people wondering what exactly B2B means. This report will attempt to provide a short, simple explanation of B2B so that potential B2B participants can make informed decisions.

1"

The first attempts to make money off the Internet involved Business-to-Consumer ventures that offered people the opportunity to buy items on-line that they usually buy at "bricks–and–mortar" stores. Recently, however, businesses have realized that they can use the speed and global reach of the Internet to communicate with customers and suppliers around the world.

The potential for savings such as reduced sales and distribution costs, as well as for increased profits make B2B activity very appealing. Corporations can use the Internet to communicate more effectively with their current strategic partners, but they can also use it to locate new partners. This increase in competition promotes additional savings in terms of lower prices and better service.

1"

One obstacle in achieving B2B Internet interaction has been locating and implementing the links between companies. As a result, a new order of Internet service company has emerged. These companies specialize in providing the hardware, software, and consulting services that help businesses locate and communicate with suppliers, customers, strategic partners, and distributors. By assuming the responsibility for maintaining databases and tracking orders and shipments, this new segment of Internet service companies is making it possible for corporations of all sizes to successfully implement B2B ventures on-line.

1"

*Double spaced 12-pt. Times New Roman, Justified .5" 1ˢᵗ line indent, 6 pts. Before, 6 pts. after*

# Exercise 21

◆ **Critical Thinking**

You are responsible for preparing a document for Murray Hill Marketing employees who are participating in the in-house training program. In this exercise, you will format the document using font formatting, symbols, lists, line and paragraph spacing, indents, styles, and margins.

## Directions

1. Start Word, if necessary.
2. Open ⊙ **21TRAIN**.
3. Save the file as **TRAIN**.
4. Set the margins to 1" on all sides.
5. Format the title with a 20-point blue, sans serif font in all uppercase letters, centered, with 48 points of space after.
6. Apply the Heading 3 style to the headings **Introduction**, **Come Prepared**, and **Behavior in Class**.
7. Modify the Heading 3 style so it is a 16-point plum colored, sans serif font, small caps, with a solid underline. Apply 12 points of space before and after.
8. Insert an appropriate Wingding symbol at the beginning of each heading.
9. Format the remaining Normal text in a 14-point serif font with a leading of exactly 17 points. Justify the alignment.
10. Format the three items in the list under the heading **Introduction** as a numbered list, using letters instead of numbers.

11. Apply a different color highlight to each item in the list.
12. Change the indents of the list so the left indent is .5" and the hanging indent is .5".
13. Create two bulleted lists under the heading **Come Prepared** (refer to the illustration) using an appropriate Wingding symbol as a bullet.
14. Sort all three lists into descending alphabetical order.
15. Emphasize the text **come prepared** at the end of first sentence under the heading **Come Prepared** by applying font formatting and color.
16. Reapply the formatting you applied in step 15 to the text **maintain a professional attitude** in the last paragraph.
17. Check the spelling, grammar, and formatting in the document.
18. Display the document in Print Preview. It should look similar to the one in the illustration.
19. Print the document.
20. Close the document, saving all changes.

# WHAT TO EXPECT FROM IN-HOUSE TRAINING

## ▢INTRODUCTION

In-house training courses are offered to insure that employees have the opportunity to stay current in their selected fields, or to provide instruction that the employer requires. In general, you can expect the following from most in-house training courses:

A.   Hands-on training
B.   Focused content
C.   Experienced teachers

## ▢COME PREPARED

One of the most important things you can do to insure your success in any in-house training course is to *come prepared*. If there is any homework or outside reading to complete, be sure it is done on time. Also, there are a few basic items you should always bring to class:

- Pencil
- Pen
- Notebook

In addition, there may be items that are specific to the course as well as optional items. For example:

- Water bottle
- Pencil sharpener
- Calculator

## ▢BEHAVIOR IN CLASS

Keep in mind that although in-house training classes may feel like a day off, you are still at work. You should *maintain a professional attitude* at all times. The other members of the class are your co-workers, who you will see every day. The information you are learning is designed to enhance your job performance. With that said, you should make every effort to be relaxed, to have fun, and to get as much as possible out of the course. If you pay attention, ask questions, and complete the assignments, you will find that in-house training is a positive, enjoyable experience.

# Exercise 22

Skills Covered:

◆ **Send E-Mail from Word**
◆ **Attach a Word Document to an E-Mail Message**
◆ **Send a Word Document as E-Mail**
◆ **Receive E-Mail Messages in Outlook or Outlook Express**

## On the Job

E-mail is suitable for jotting quick notes such as an appointment confirmation. You can create and format e-mail messages and then send the messages via Outlook or Outlook Express directly from Word. When you need to communicate in more depth, you can attach a Word document to the message, or simply send a document as the message itself. You can exchange e-mail messages via the Internet or an intranet with anyone who has an e-mail account, including coworkers located down the hall, in a different state, or halfway around the world. To receive e-mail, you can use Outlook or Outlook Express.

As the assistant to the marketing director at Northwest Gear, you have been compiling a list of employees willing to be judges for an essay contest. In this exercise, you will use e-mail to communicate with the marketing director about the contest. First, you will create and send a brief e-mail message about the list of judges. Then, you will follow up with a second message to which you will attach the list of prospective judges. You will then send a copy of a memo you plan to distribute to the prospective judges. Finally, you will launch Outlook Express and check to see if you have received any e-mail messages.

## Terms

**E-mail (electronic mail)** A method of sending information from one computer to another across the Internet or intranet.

**HTML (Hypertext Markup Language)** A universal file format used for files displayed on the World Wide Web.

**Internet** A global network of computers.

**Intranet** A network of computers within a business or organization.

**Mail service provider** A company that maintains and controls e-mail accounts.

**Outlook** A personal information management program that includes e-mail features that comes with the Office suite.

**Outlook Express** An e-mail program that is included as part of the Microsoft Internet Explorer Web browser.

**E-mail address** The string of characters that identifies the name and location of an e-mail user.

**To** Mail notation that indicates to whom an e-mail message is addressed.

**Cc (carbon copy)** Mail notation that indicates to whom you are sending a copy of the message.

**Subject** The title of an e-mail message.

**Message window** The area in an e-mail message where the message body is typed.

**Online** Actively connected to the Internet.

**Attachment** A document attached to an e-mail message and sent in its original file format.

**Offline** Not connected to the Internet.

# Notes

## Send E-mail from Word

- You can create and send **e-mail** messages directly from Word.

- You can edit and format the messages with Word's editing and formatting features, including the spelling and grammar checkers, and AutoCorrect.

- Messages created in Word are sent in **HTML** format so they can be read by almost all e-mail applications.

- To send e-mail messages you must have the following:
  - A connection to the **Internet** or to an **intranet**.
  - An account with a **mail service provider**.
  - An e-mail program such as **Outlook** or **Outlook Express**.
  - ✓ *To exchange e-mail, the e-mail program must be correctly configured with your e-mail account information.*

- To send an e-mail message you must know the recipient's **e-mail address**.

- E-mail messages have four basic parts:
  - The recipient's address is entered in the **To**: text box.
  - The addresses of other people receiving copies of the message are entered in the **Cc**: text box.
  - A title for the message is entered in the **Subject** text box.
  - The body of the message is typed in the **message window**.

- When you send the message, Word automatically accesses the Internet using your Internet connection settings.

- The Internet connection remains **online** in the background until you disconnect.

## Attach a Word Document to an E-mail Message

- You can attach a Word document to an e-mail message.

- The original document remains stored on your computer, and a copy is transmitted as the **attachment**.

- An attached message is sent in its original file format.

- The message recipient can open the attached Word document on his or her computer in Word, or in another application that is compatible with Word.

## Send a Word Document as E-mail

- You can send an entire Word document as an e-mail message without attaching it to another message.

- Word adds an Introduction text box to the message header when you send a Word document as e-mail. This text box gives you more room to enter information about the document.

- The original document remains stored on your computer, and a copy is transmitted as e-mail.

- The transmitted document is sent in HTML format so it retains its original formatting when opened in the recipient's e-mail application.

  - ✓ *If you don't want to send or attach an entire document, you can paste a selection from the document into the e-mail message. Simply copy the text from the Word document, make the message window active, and then paste the text into the message.*

*E-mail created in Word*

## Receive E-mail Messages in Outlook or Outlook Express

■ To receive electronic mail (e-mail) messages with Microsoft Outlook or Outlook Express, you must have a connection to the Internet or to an intranet and an account with a mail service provider.

  ✓ *To exchange e-mail, Outlook or Outlook Express must be correctly configured with your e-mail account information.*

■ When you connect to the Internet, the e-mail application downloads new messages into a folder called *Inbox*.

■ You can read the downloaded messages at any time.

■ You can read downloaded messages **offline**.

■ Messages remain in the Inbox until you move them or delete them.

■ You can save e-mail messages in HTML format to open in Word.

  ✓ *See Exercise 24 for information on opening HTML documents in Word.*

# Procedures

### Send an E-mail Message from Word

1. Click **E-mail** button .

  ✓ *Use a ScreenTip to identify the button; it looks a lot like the E-mail button used to send a document as e-mail.*

  OR

  a. Click **File** ................ Alt + F

  b. Click **New** ...................... N

  c. Click **Blank E-mail Message** icon E-mail Message in Task Pane.

2. Fill in **To:** information: type recipient's address

3. Press **Tab** ......................... Tab

4. Fill in **Cc:** information: type additional recipients' addresses.

5. Press **Tab** ......................... Tab

6. Fill in **Subject** information: type subject title.

7. Press **Tab** ......................... Tab

8. Type and format **message text**.

9. Click **Send** button

   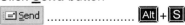 ...................... Alt + S

  ✓ *Log on to transmit message as necessary.*

  ✓ *If you change your mind about sending the message, simply click the **New E-Mail Message** button again. Word removes the message heading.*

### Attach a Word Document to an E-mail Message

1. Compose an e-mail message.

2. Click **Insert File** button.

3. Select **file to attach**.

  ✓ *Select disk or folder from Look in drop-down list, then double-click folder name to locate file.*

4. Click In**s**ert ................. Alt + S

  ✓ *Word adds a new text box to the message heading called Attach: and enters the document name.*

5. Click **Send** button ............. Alt + S

  OR

1. Open or create the document to attach.

2. Click **File** .................... Alt + F

3. Highlight **Send To** ............... D

4. Click **Mail Recipient (as Attachment)** ............... A

5. Compose e-mail message.

  ✓ *By default, Word enters the document name in the Attach text box.*

6. Click **Send** button ............. Alt + S

### Send an Existing Word Document as E-mail

1. Open document to send.

2. Click **E-Mail** button.

  OR

  a. Click **File** ................ Alt + F

  b. Select **Send To** .............. D

  c. Click **Mail Recipient** ....... M

3. Fill in **To:** information: type recipient's address.

4. Press **Tab** ......................... Tab

5. Fill in **Cc:** information: type additional recipients' addresses.

6. Press **Tab** ......................... Tab

7. Fill in **Subject** information: type subject title.

  ✓ *By default, Word enters the document name in the Subject text box. You can edit it if necessary.*

8. Press **Tab** ......................... Tab

9. Fill in **Introduction** information type introductory text.

10. Click **Send a Copy**

   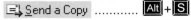 ............ Alt + S

  ✓ *If you change your mind about sending the document as e-mail, simply click the **E-Mail** button again. Word removes the message heading and displays the document.*

## Receive E-mail Messages in Outlook or Outlook Express

**In Outlook:**

1. Click **Start** 🏁 Start ..... `Ctrl`+`Esc`
2. Click **Programs** .................. `P`
3. Select **Microsoft Outlook**.
   - ✓ Outlook may automatically connect to your mail service provider and download new messages. Enter account name and password if prompted.
4. Click **Send/Receive** button 📧 Send/Receive ... `Alt`+`C`
   - ✓ You may read messages online, or disconnect from Internet to read messages offline.
5. Click **Inbox** folder.
6. With Preview Pane displayed, click message to open and read.
   - ✓ To open the message in its own window, double-click it.

**In Outlook Express:**

1. Click **Start** 🏁 Start ..... `Ctrl`+`Esc`
2. Click **Programs** .................. `P`
3. Select **Outlook Express**.
   - ✓ Outlook Express may automatically connect to your mail service provider and download new messages. Enter account name and password if prompted.
4. Click **Send/Recv** button  Send/Recv .
5. Click **Inbox** folder.
6. With Preview Pane displayed, click message to read.
   - ✓ To open the message in its own window, double-click it.

**Disconnect Outlook Express from the Internet**

1. Click **File** .................... `Alt`+`F`
2. Click **Work Offline** ............. `W`
3. Click **Yes** ........................... `Y`

**Disconnect Outlook from the Internet**

1. Click **File** .................... `Alt`+`F`
2. Click **Work Offline** ............. `K`
3. Click **Yes** ........................... `Y`

# Exercise Directions

- ✓ If you do not have access to the Internet, you may still complete the steps in this exercise. However, when you try to send the e-mail, you will receive an error message.

1. Start Word, if necessary.
2. Compose an e-mail message as follows:
   a. Enter the address:
      **northwestgear@ddcpub.com**
   b. Enter the subject: **Essay Judges**
   c. Enter the message: **Boss, I just want to let you know I have just about completed the list of employees interested in judging the essay contest. As soon as I type it up, I'll send it to you. Thanks**.
3. Send the message.
   - • Enter your user name and password if prompted.
4. Open the document 💿 **22LIST**.
5. Save the document as **LIST**.
6. Sort the names listed in the document alphabetically in ascending order.
7. Apply a numbered list format to the names.
8. Change paragraph formatting to leave 6 pts. of space before and after each paragraph.
9. Check the spelling and grammar in the document.
10. Save the file and close it.
11. Compose another e-mail message as follows:
    a. Enter the address:
       **northwestgear@ddcpub.com**
       - ✓ Don't be surprised if Word automatically completes the address as you type it!
    b. Enter the subject: **List of Judges**
    c. Enter the message: **Boss, I've attached the list of potential judges. Let me know if there's anyone you think we should omit. I'll send you a copy of the memo I plan to distribute to the people on the list. Thanks, again.**
12. Attach the document **LIST** to the e-mail message. The message should look similar to the one in Illustration A.
13. Send the message.
14. Open the document 💿 **22RULES**.
15. Save the document as **RULES**.

16. Prepare to send the **RULES** document as e-mail by creating an e-mail message and entering the following message heading information:

    a. Enter the address: **northwestgear@ddcpub.com**

    b. Enter the subject: **Memo About Judging Rules**

    c. Enter the introduction: **As promised, here's a copy of the memo I plan to send to the employees interested in judging the essay contest. Let me know what you think.**

17. The message should look similar to the one in Illustration B.

18. Send the document.

19. Close all open documents, saving all changes.

20. Launch Outlook Express.

    ✓ *If Outlook Express is not installed on your computer, use Outlook, or any other mail program.*

21. Check for new messages.

    ✓ *The northwestgear@ddcpub.com site is set to automatically return messages to you.*

22. Disconnect from the Internet.

23. Read the new message(s) offline, then exit Outlook Express.

*Illustration A*

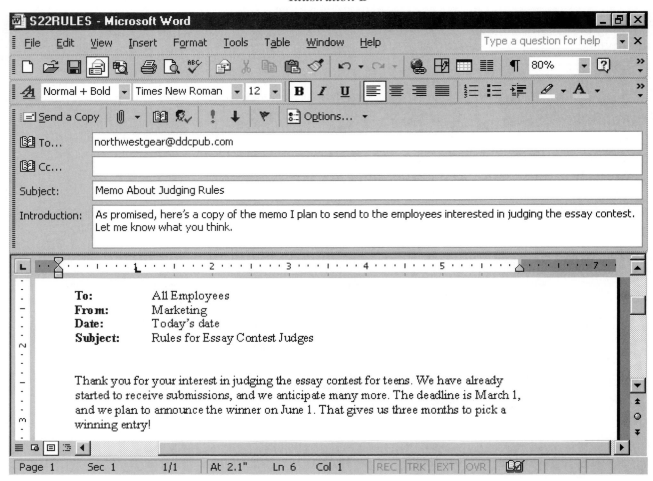

# On Your Own

1. Look up and record e-mail addresses for friends, coworkers, and companies.

2. Send an e-mail message to a friend or coworker and ask him or her to send one back to you.

3. Create a new document and save it as **OWD22**.

4. Type a letter to someone else whose e-mail address you have. For example, type a letter to a teacher requesting a missed homework assignment, or to your employer.

5. Attach the document to an e-mail message and send it.

6. Check your e-mail to see if you received a reply.

7. When you are finished, close all open documents, and exit all open applications.

# Exercise 23

## On the Job

Log on to the Internet to access information on any subject and to communicate with other people. Use Word's Internet features to make using the Internet easy and familiar.

Your supervisor at Murray Hill marketing is going to meet a client in Cleveland, Ohio. She is interested in visiting the Rock and Roll Hall of Fame while she is there and has asked you to locate some basic information, such as what exhibits will be there, what the hours are, and how much it costs. In this exercise, you will use the Internet to locate the Rock and Roll Hall of Fame site. You will add the site to your Favorites folder, and save the page that has the information you need locally so you can read it offline in Word.

## Terms

**Modem** A hardware device that controls communication connections between computers.

**Internet** A worldwide network of computers.

**World Wide Web** A system for finding information on the Internet through the use of linked documents.

**Internet Service Provider (ISP)** A company that provides access to the Internet for a fee.

**Web browser** Software that makes it easy to locate and view information stored on the Internet. Common browsers include Internet Explorer and Netscape Navigator.

**Shareware** Software that can be downloaded from the Internet for free or for a nominal fee.

**Web site** A set of linked Web pages.

**Web page** A document stored on the World Wide Web.

**Uniform Resource Locator (URL)** A Web site's address on the Internet.

**Hyperlinks or links** Text or graphics in a document set up to provide a direct connection with a destination location or document. When you click a hyperlink, the destination displays.

## Notes

### Internet Basics

■ Anyone with a computer, a **modem**, communications software, and a standard phone line can access the **Internet** and the **World Wide Web**.

■ For a fee, **Internet Service Providers (ISP)** provide you with an e-mail account, **Web browser** software, and Internet access.

■ Office XP comes with the Internet Explorer Web browser, although your computer may be set up to use a different browser.

✓ *This exercise assumes you are using Internet Explorer. If your computer is set up to use a different browser, ask your instructor for directions.*

■ Some things available via the Internet and the World Wide Web include e-mail communication, product information and support, reference material, shopping, stock quotes, travel arrangements, real estate information, **shareware,** and games.

## Use Internet Features in Word

■ If you have a connection to the Internet and Web browser software, you can use Word's Web toolbar to access the Internet.

*The Web toolbar*

■ Word remains running while you use the Internet, so you can go back and forth from Word to the Internet sites that you have opened on your browser.

■ To locate a **Web site**, **Web page**, or document, you enter its Internet address, or **Uniform Resource Locator (URL)**, in the Address field on the Web toolbar.

■ If you don't know the URL of a site, you can search the Web for the site you want using an Internet search engine.

■ Most sites provide **hyperlinks**, also called **links,** to related pages or sites. Text links are usually a different color and underlined to stand out from the surrounding text. Graphics may also be links.

■ When the mouse pointer rests on a link, the pointer changes to a hand with a pointing finger, and a ScreenTip shows the destination.

■ Word tracks the Web sites you have visited during the current Internet session so you can move back and forth through them.

## Save a Web Page Locally

■ You use your browser's Save As command to save a Web page on your computer.

■ Once you save a Web page, you can access it while you are working offline.

■ When you save a Web page you can select from four file types:
  • Web page, complete. This saves all of the associated files needed to display the Web page, including graphics in a separate folder in the same location as the HTML file.
  • Web Archive. Saves a snapshot of the current Web page in a single file.
  • Web Page, HTML only. Saves the information on the Web page but does not save the associated files.
  • Text Only. Saves the information in plain text format.

■ If you don't need to save an entire Web page, you can paste selected information into a Word document.

■ You can also use your browser to print a Web page.

## The Favorites Folder

■ Use the Favorites folder on your computer to store the URLs of Web sites you like to access frequently.

■ You can also add locally stored files and folders to your Favorites folder.

■ The easiest way to add a URL to the Favorites folder is by using your Web browser.

■ Access the Favorites folder from Word or from Windows when you want to go directly to one of your favorite sites.

*The Favorites Folder*

# Procedures

## Use Internet Features in Word

**To display the Web toolbar:**

1. Click **View** .................. Alt + V
2. Select **Toolbars** .................. T
3. Click **Web** ............ ↑ , ↓ Enter

OR

Right-click on any toolbar and select **Web**.

✓ *Be sure to select the Web toolbar, and not the Web Tools toolbar.*

**To search the Web:**

✓ *You must have an Internet connection and an account with an ISP in order to search the Web.*

1. Click **Search the Web** button Q.

OR

a. Click **Go** Go ▼ ........ Alt + G
b. Click **Search the Web** ... W

✓ *The default search site will vary depending on ISP. Common Search sites include Yahoo!, AltaVista, and Excite.*

2. Type search topic in Search text box.
3. Click **Search** button.

✓ *The name on the search button (Find It, Go Get It, etc.) will vary depending on the search site.*

4. Click a hyperlink on the Search Results page to go to that site.

**To go to a specific URL:**

1. Type URL in Address drop-down list box on Web toolbar
2. Press **Enter** ....................... Enter

OR

1. Click **Go** Go ▼ ............ Alt + G
2. Click **Open Hyperlink** 🖰 .. O

3. Type the URL in the **A**ddress list box.
4. Click **OK** ............................. Enter

**To go to a previously visited URL:**

1. Click Address list drop-down arrow on Web toolbar.
2. Click URL.

**To use a hyperlink:**

1. Move mouse pointer to touch link.
2. Click left mouse button.

**To display the previously displayed page or document:**

- Click **Back** button ⇐ Back on the Browser's toolbar.

OR

- Click **Back** button ⇐ on Web toolbar

OR

1. Click **Go** Go ▼ ............ Alt + G on the Web toolbar.
2. Click **Back** ........................... B

**To display the next Web page:**

- Click **Forward** button ⇒ Forward on the Browser's toolbar.

✓ *If the Back or Forward button is dimmed on the toolbar, there is no page to go to.*

OR

- Click **Forward** button ⇒ on Web toolbar

OR

1. Click **Go** Go ▼ ............ Alt + G on the Web toolbar.
2. Click **Forward** ..................... F

**Save a Web page locally:**

1. Open Web page in browser.
2. Click **File** ..................... Alt + F
3. Click **Save As** ..................... A
4. Type file name.

5. Select disk or folder.
6. Click **Save as type** ............. T drop-down arrow.
7. Click desired file type.
8. Click **Save** .................. Alt + S

## The Favorites Folder

**To use Internet Explorer to add a site to your Favorites folder:**

1. Open Internet site to add to Favorites.
2. Click **F**avorites ........... Alt + A
3. Click **A**dd to Favorites........ A
4. Type site name if necessary................... Alt + N

✓ *Your browser automatically enters a site name; you can edit it if you want.*

5. Click **OK** ........................... Enter

**To use Word to add a file to your Favorites folder:**

1. Open file to add to Favorites.
2. Click **Favorites** button Favorites ▼ provided..... Alt + S on Web toolbar.
3. Click **A**dd to Favorites........ A

✓ *The Add to Favorites dialog box is similar to the Save As dialog box.*

4. Type a name.
5. Click **Add** 🖫 Add ......... Enter

**To go to a site from your Favorites folder:**

1. Click **Favorites** button Favorites ▼ .................. Alt + S
2. Click site name.

✓ *If necessary, Word starts your Web browser to connect to the Internet and display the site.*

# Exercise Directions

✓ *Use the Internet simulation provided on the CD that accompanies this book to complete this exercise.*

1. Start Word, if necessary.

2. Display the Web toolbar.

3. On the Address line, type the following and press Enter:
   **D:/Internet/Word/Ex23/altavista.htm**

   ✓ *If you've copied the Internet simulation files to your hard drive or your CD-ROM drive is not D:, substitute the correct drive letter for D.*

4. In the Search text box type **What is the address of the Rock and Roll Hall of Fame**.

   ✓ *The simulation uses the search site AltaVista. If you are using a live Internet connection instead of the simulation, the results of the search will vary depending on the search site used.*

5. Click the **Search** button.

6. Scroll down the search results page, and click the number 1 link.

7. A Welcome page for the Rock and Roll Hall of Fame opens in your browser.

8. Click the **Back** button to return to the search results page.

9. Click the **Forward** button.

10. Click the enter link on the Welcome page.

11. Use your Web browser to add the Rock and Roll Hall of Fame Home Page to your Favorites folder.

12. Scroll down the page and click the explore link under the heading **Calendar**.

13. Click the March link.

14. Scroll through the page to see what events are scheduled in March.

15. Click the visitor information link.

16. Save the Visitor Information page in Web archive format with the name **VISITOR**.

17. Close the Internet simulation by clicking the Close button ⊠.

18. Open the **VISITOR** document in Word. It should look similar to the one in the Illustration.

    ✓ *If the document is not listed in the Open dialog box, change the list to display all file types.*

19. Use Word to add the **VISITOR** document to your Favorites folder.

20. Close the document, saving all changes.

*Illustration A*

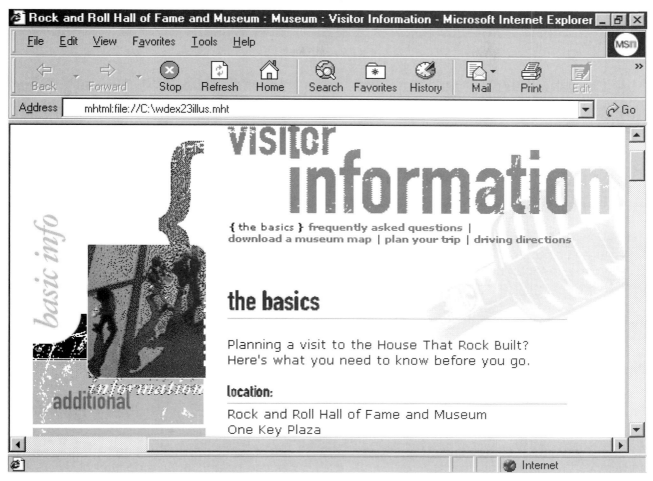

## On Your Own

1. If you have access to the Internet, use it to locate a Web site about something that interests you. For example, search for information about your hometown, a sports team that you follow, or a writer, musician, or artist you admire.

2. When you find a site you like, add it to your Favorites folder.

3. Save one of the pages you find as a Web archive document so you can spend more time reading it offline. Save it as **OWD23**.

4. Disconnect from the Internet.

5. In Word, open **OWD23** or open ⊙ **23WEB**.

6. Read the document in Word.

7. Close the document and exit Word.

# Exercise 24

## Skills Covered:

◆ **Create a Web Page Document in Word** ◆ **Use Web Layout View**
◆ **Use Web Page Titles** ◆ **Apply a Background** ◆ **Apply a Theme**
◆ **Preview a Web Page** ◆ **Open an HTML Document in Word**

## On the Job

Documents on the World Wide Web are created in HTML format. With Word, you can easily save documents in HTML format. You can save existing documents in HTML format, and you can use all of Word's features and tools to edit and format HTML documents. When you complete a document in HTML format, you can store it on a **Web server**, so everyone with access to the Web can access the document.

You have been asked to post the in-house training course schedule for Murray Hill Marketing on the company's intranet. In this exercise, you will open the existing training course document, format it with color, a theme, and a background, and then save it as a Web page. You will view it in your browser, close it, and then open it again to make some additional changes. Finally, you will print it.

## Terms

**Web server** A computer connected to the Internet used to store Web page documents.

**HTML** Hypertext Markup Language. It is the file format used for files accessed on the World Wide Web.

**htm** An extension given to files saved in HTML format.

**Background** The color, pattern, or fill displayed on the page behind data in a document.

**Fill effect** A texture, shading, picture, or pattern used as a background.

**Theme** A unified set of design elements and colors that can be applied to a document.

**Web bullets** Graphics files inserted as bullet markers.

**Graphics lines** Graphics files inserted as horizontal rules or dividers.

**Graphics object** A picture, chart, shape, or other element that can be inserted into a Word document.

**Clip art** Picture files that can be inserted into a document.

## Notes

### Create a Web Page Document in Word

- You can save an existing Word document in **HTML** format. Word preserves the formatting in the new document.

- You can also create a new blank Web page document.

- When you save a Web page document, Word abbreviates the file extension to **htm**.

■ Word automatically creates a folder to store graphics files such as bullets, lines, and pictures that are associated with the Web page. The folder has the same name as the file, followed by an underscore and the word *files*, like this: *Filename_files*

   ✓ *Use caution when moving or renaming the graphics files or the folder they are stored in. The graphics files are linked to the HTML document; if they are not available, the page will display without graphics elements.*

*The Save As Web Page dialog box*

## Use Web Layout View

■ Web Layout view displays documents in Word as they will look on the Web.

■ Word automatically switches to Web Layout view when you save a document as a Web page, when you create a new Web page document, or when you open an existing Web page document.

■ You can also switch to Web Layout view using the View menu or the View buttons.

■ Web Layout view lets you edit a document for viewing on screen, instead of for printing on a page.

■ Features of Web Layout view include:
   • Wordwrapping to fit the window, not a page.
   • Graphics positioned as they would be in a Web browser.
   • Backgrounds (if there are any) displayed as they would be in a browser.

## Use Web Page Titles

■ Web page titles are displayed in the Web browser title bar.

■ By default, Word uses the file name or the first line of document text as the Web page title.

■ You can set or change the page title name from the Save As dialog box.

## Apply a Background

■ By default, Word documents—including HTML documents—have a plain white **background**.

■ Add visual interest or create an effect by applying a color, pattern, **fill effect,** or picture to a document background.

■ You should coordinate backgrounds for pages in a Web site to establish continuity.

## Apply a Theme

■ Word comes with built-in **themes** you can use to format any Word document.

■ Each theme includes a background, font formatting, and graphics elements such as **Web bullets** and **graphics lines**.

■ You can select a theme to apply consistent formatting to a document.

■ Themes can be used with any Word document, but they are particularly useful for formatting Web pages.

## Preview a Web Page

■ Use Web Page Preview to see how a Word document will look in a Web browser.

■ You can display regular Word documents or HTML documents in Web Page Preview.

■ When you preview a Web page document, Word opens the document in your default browser.

■ You cannot edit a document in Web Page Preview.

## Open an HTML Document in Word

■ You open an HTML document in Word the same way you open a regular Word document.

■ The document displays in Web Layout view.

■ When you save the document, it remains in HTML format.

   ✓ *By default, if you try to open an HTML document from Windows, the document displays in your Web browser, not in Word.*

# Procedures

## Save a Document as a Web Page

1. Open the document.
2. Click **File**.................... `Alt`+`F`
3. Click **Save as Web Page** .... `G`
4. Type file name.
   - ✓ *If necessary, open the folder, disk, or server where the file will be stored.*
5. Click **Save**
   `💾 Save` ............... `Alt`+`S`

## Create a New Blank Web Page Document

1. Click **File**.................... `Alt`+`F`
2. Click **New** .......................... `N`
3. Click **Blank Web Page** in New Document Task Pane.
4. Click **File**.................... `Alt`+`F`
5. Click **Save as** ...................... `A`
6. Type file name.
   - ✓ *If necessary, open the folder, disk, or server where the file will be stored.*
7. Click **Save**
   `💾 Save` ............... `Alt`+`S`

## Change to Web Layout View

- Open Web page document in Word.

OR

- Click **Web Layout View** button `🔲`.

OR

1. Click **View** ................. `Alt`+`V`
2. Click **Web Layout** .............. `W`

## Set a Web Page Title to a Saved Web Page

1. Click **File** ..................... `Alt`+`F`
2. Click **Save As**...................... `A`
3. Click **Change Title** button
   `Change Title...` ............... `Alt`+`C`
4. Type new title.
5. Click **OK**
6. Click **Save**
   `💾 Save` ............... `Alt`+`S`

## Apply a Background

1. Open file to format.
2. Click **Format** .............. `Alt`+`O`
3. Click **Background**.............. `K`
4. Click desired color.
   OR
   a. Click **Fill Effects** ............ `F`
   b. Click desired page tab............... `Ctrl`+`Tab`
   c. Select desired **effect**.
   d. Click **OK** ..................... `Enter`

## Apply a Theme

1. Open file to format.
2. Click **Format** .............. `Alt`+`O`
3. Click **Theme**....................... `H`
4. Select desired **Theme**........... `Alt`+`T`, `↑`, `↓`
5. Click **OK** .......................... `Enter`
   - ✓ *Not all themes are installed automatically; if a theme you select is not installed, use the Setup disk to install it, or select a different theme.*

## Use Web Page Preview

1. Click **File** ..................... `Alt`+`F`
2. Click **Web Page Preview**.... `B`

## Close Web Page Preview

1. Click **File** ..................... `Alt`+`F`
2. Click **Close**........................ `C`

## Open an HTML Document in Word

1. Click **File** ..................... `Alt`+`F`
2. Click **Open** ......................... `O`
3. Click **file name**.
   - ✓ *If necessary, open the folder or disk where the file is stored.*
4. Click **Open** ................. `Alt`+`O`

# Exercise Directions

1. Start Word, if necessary.
2. Open ⌨**COURSE** or open 💿**24COURSE**.
3. Save the file as **COURSE**.
4. Use the following steps to format the document as shown in the illustration.
5. Apply the Pixel Theme to the document.
6. Highlight each of the three months/course/course descriptions by using a different font color. Change the **January** information to Blue, the **February** information to Red, and the **March** information to Green.
7. Change the month names to bullet items.
8. Apply the Newsprint Texture fill effect background to the document.
9. Save the document as a Web page with the name **COURSE2** and the Web page title MHM Training Schedule.
10. Display it in Web Page Preview.
11. Close Web Page Preview.
12. Close the file, saving all changes.
13. Open the **COURSE2** document in Word.
14. Change the color of the font for the first three lines to Plum.
15. Change the color of the font for the last line in the document to Plum.
16. Display the document in Web Page Preview again. It should look similar to the one in the illustration.
17. Close Web Page Preview.
18. Check the spelling and grammar in the document.
19. Print the document.
20. Close the file, saving all changes.

# On Your Own

1. Create a new document in Word.
2. Save the file as **OWD24**.
3. Use this document to create your own personal Web page. You should include your name and other information about yourself—what you like to do, who your favorite musicians and sports teams are, where you go to school or where you work.
4. Add some other information you think will be interesting: favorite sayings, upcoming events in your life, or fun things your family or friends plan to do.
5. Save the document as a Web page in HTML format with the name **OWD24-2**.
6. Applying formatting to improve the appearance of your Web page. For example, change the font formatting, apply a theme or background, create lists, and so on.
7. View the document in Web Layout view.
8. Use Web Page Preview to look at your new Web page in your browser software.
9. Close Web Page Preview.
10. Close the document and exit Word.

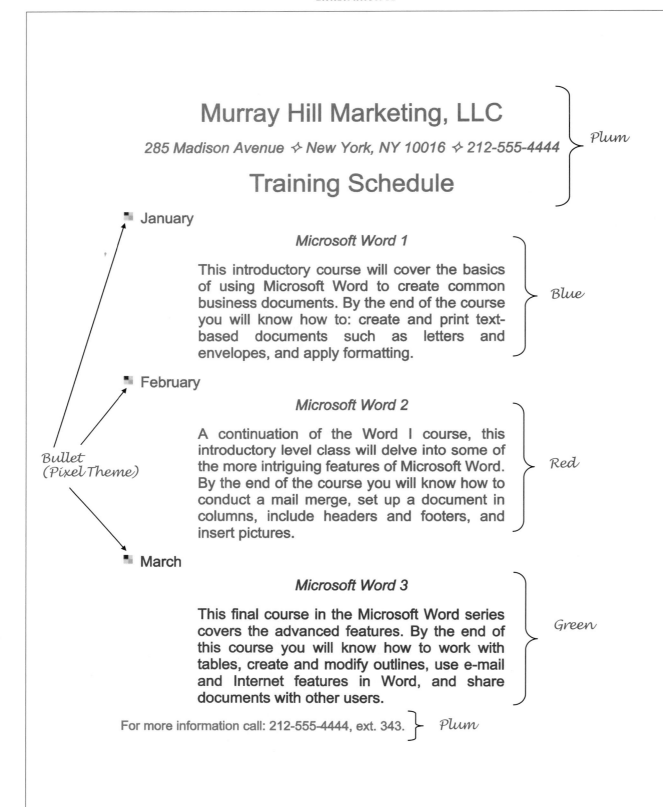

# Murray Hill Marketing, LLC

*285 Madison Avenue ✧ New York, NY 10016 ✧ 212-555-4444*

## Training Schedule

} *Plum*

■ January

### *Microsoft Word 1*

This introductory course will cover the basics of using Microsoft Word to create common business documents. By the end of the course you will know how to: create and print text-based documents such as letters and envelopes, and apply formatting.

} *Blue*

■ February

### *Microsoft Word 2*

A continuation of the Word I course, this introductory level class will delve into some of the more intriguing features of Microsoft Word. By the end of the course you will know how to conduct a mail merge, set up a document in columns, include headers and footers, and insert pictures.

} *Red*

■ March

### *Microsoft Word 3*

This final course in the Microsoft Word series covers the advanced features. By the end of this course you will know how to work with tables, create and modify outlines, use e-mail and Internet features in Word, and share documents with other users.

} *Green*

For more information call: 212-555-4444, ext. 343. } *Plum*

*Bullet (Pixel Theme)*

# Exercise 25

## ◆ Create Hyperlinks

## On the Job

Create a hyperlink to connect related documents to each other, to connect a Word document to a Web site, or to connect one location in a document to another location in the same document. For example, create hyperlinks from a report topic to an Internet site where more information can be found. Hyperlinks let you expand the boundaries among documents and among computers because, in effect, you can link to information stored anywhere on the Internet.

You have created a Web page document listing training courses for Murray Hill Marketing. In this exercise, you will insert hyperlinks to help readers navigate through the Web page. You will also link the Web page to a Word document describing what employees should expect from in-house training, and to a Web site that provides more information about Microsoft Office products.

## Terms

**Hyperlink**  Text or graphics linked to a destination file or location. Click the link to jump to the destination.

**Hypertext**  Text formatted as a hyperlink.

**Hyperlink destination**  The location displayed when the hyperlink is clicked.

**Hyperlink source**  The document where the hyperlink is inserted.

**Bookmark**  A nonprinting character that you insert and name so that you can quickly find a particular location in a document.

## Notes

### Create Hyperlinks

- **Hyperlinks** can be used to link locations within a single document, to link two documents, or to link a document to an e-mail address.

- Hyperlinks can be created in any Word document, including HTML files.

- A **hyperlink destination** does not have to be in the same file format as the **hyperlink source** document. For example, you can link a Word document file to an HTML file or to an Excel file, and the like.

- The hyperlink destination can be a file stored on your computer, on your company intranet, or a site on the Internet.

- When you click a hyperlink to an e-mail address, Word starts your e-mail program and displays a new e-mail message. The address and subject are filled in with the hyperlink information.

- You can create a hyperlink within a document for moving to the top of the document, to a specific heading, or to a **bookmark**.

*The Insert Hyperlink dialog box*

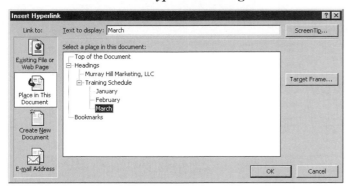

- By default, in Word documents (including those saved in HTML) you must press Ctrl and click the hyperlink in order to go to the hyperlink destination.

- You can change the setting so that you don't have to press Ctrl.

- You can edit and format hyperlink text the same way you edit and format regular text.

  ✓ *If you change the setting so that you don't have to press Ctrl to follow a hyperlink, you must select the hyperlink before you can edit it or format it.*

- You can change a hyperlink destination.

- You can remove a hyperlink completely.

# Procedures

## Insert a Hyperlink within a Document

1. Position insertion point where you want to insert hyperlink.
   **OR**
   Select text to change to a hyperlink.

2. Click **Insert Hyperlink** button 🖳 .
   **OR**
   a. Click **Insert**............. `Alt`+`I`
   b. Click **Hyperlink**.............. `I`

3. Click **Place in this document** in Link to bar .......................... `Alt`+`A`

4. In the **Select a place in this document list**, click hyperlink destination ............ `Alt`+`C`, `↓`

   ✓ *If necessary click the expand symbol + to expand the list to show additional headings and/or bookmarks.*

5. Click **OK** .......................... `Enter`

   ✓ *If existing text is not selected, Word uses the destination name as the hyperlink text.*

## Insert a Hyperlink to a Different Document

1. Position insertion point where you want to insert hyperlink.
   **OR**
   Select text to change to a hyperlink.

2. Click **Insert Hyperlink** button 🖳 .
   **OR**
   a. Click **Insert**............. `Alt`+`I`
   b. Click **Hyperlink**.............. `I`

3. Click **Existing File or Web Page** in the Link to bar................... `Alt`+`X`

4. In the **Address** text box, type the hyperlink destination file name .. `Alt`+`E`, *type file name*

   ✓ *Word automatically completes the file name as you type based on recently used file names; stop typing to accept the entry or keep typing to enter the name you want.*

   **OR**

   a. Click **Current Folder** in the Look in bar ............. `Alt`+`U` to display a list of files stored in the current folder

   b. Click the file name in the list of files.

   **OR**

   a. Click **Browsed Pages** to display a list of recently viewed Web pages ..................... `Alt`+`B`

   b. Locate and click file name.

   c. Click **OK** ..................... `Enter`

   **OR**

   a. Click **Recent Files** . `Alt`+`C` to display a list of recently used files.

   b. Click the file name in the list of files.

5. Edit **Text to display** ........... `Alt`+`T`

   ✓ *Word displays this text as the hyperlink in the document.*

6. Click **OK** .......................... `Enter`

## Insert a Hyperlink to a Web Page

1. Position insertion point where you want to insert the hyperlink.
   **OR**
   Select text to change to a hyperlink.

2. Click **Insert Hyperlink** button 🖳 .
   **OR**
   a. Click **Insert**............. `Alt`+`I`
   b. Click **Hyperlink**.............. `I`

3. Click **Existing File or Web Page** in Link to bar ...... `Alt`+`X`

4. In the **Address** text box, type the hyperlink destination URL ............ `Alt`+`E`, *type URL*

   ✓ *Word automatically completes the URL as you type based on other URLs you have typed in the past. Stop typing to accept the entry, or keep typing to enter the URL you want.*

   OR

   a. Click **Browsed Pages**..................... `Alt`+`B`
      to display a list of Web pages you have recently accessed.

   b. Click the URL or site name you want in the list of files.

5. Edit **Text to display** ........................ `Alt`+`T`

   ✓ *Type the text you want displayed for the hyperlink. Word displays this text as the hyperlink.*

6. Click **OK** ............................ `Enter`

## Insert a Hyperlink to an E-Mail Address

1. Position insertion point where you want to insert the hyperlink.
   OR
   Select text to change to a hyperlink.

2. Click **Insert Hyperlink** button 🌐.
   OR

   a. Click **Insert** ............ `Alt`+`I`

   b. Click **Hyperlink**.............. `I`

3. Click **E-mail Address** in Link to in bar............ `Alt`+`M`

4. In the **E-mail address** text box, type the e-mail address ..................... `Alt`+`E`, *type address*

   ✓ *This address will be inserted in the to line of the e-mail message.*

   OR

   a. Click the address in the **Recently** used e-mail addresses list....... `Alt`+`C`, `↑↓`, `Enter`

   b. In the **Subject** text box, type the text you want displayed in the e-mail Subject text box. ......... `Alt`+`U`, *type text*

5. Click **OK** ............................ `Enter`

## Remove a Hyperlink

1. Right-click hyperlink text.

2. Click **Remove Hyperlink**..... `R`

   ✓ *This removes hyperlink, not the text.*

## Change a Hyperlink Destination

1. Right-click hyperlink text.

2. Click **Edit Hyperlink**............ `H`

3. Select new destination.

4. Click **OK** ........................... `Enter`

## Set Word to Follow Hyperlink On Click

1. Click **Tools**................. `Alt`+`T`

2. Click **Options**...................... `O`

3. Click **Edit** tab............... `Ctrl`+`Tab`

4. Deselect **Use CTRL+Click to follow hyperlink** check box ............................ `H`

5. Click **OK** ........................... `Enter`

## Select a Hyperlink

1. Right-click hyperlink text.

2. Click **Select Hyperlink** ........ `S`

# Exercise Directions

✓ *Use the Internet simulation provided on the CD that accompanies this book to complete this exercise.*

1. Start Word, if necessary.

2. Open ⌨**TRAIN** or open 💿**25TRAIN**.

3. Save the file as **TRAIN**.

4. Insert a new line at the top of the document and clear all formatting from it.

5. Type the text **Return**, and then press **Enter**.

6. Display the document in Print Preview.

7. If the document extends on to two pages, use the Shrink to Fit command to fit it on one page.

8. Close Print Preview, and then close the document, saving all changes.

9. Open the file ⌨**COURSE2** or open 💿**25COURSE**.

   ✓ *Remember, this is an HTML document. If you try to open it from Windows, it will open in your browser, not in Word.*

10. Save the file as **COURSE3**.

11. Edit and format the document using the following steps.

    ✓ *Refer to Illustration A to see the completed document.*

12. Position the insertion point at the end of the heading **Training Schedule** and press **Enter**.

13. Type **January** and press **Enter**.

14. Type **February** and press **Enter**.

15. Type **March** and press **Enter** twice.

16. Type the following: **Questions?** and press **Enter** twice.

17. Type **Click here to read about in-house training** and press **Enter**.

18. Type **Click here to learn more about Microsoft Office**.

19. Insert a hyperlink from the text **January** that you typed in step 13 to the heading **January**.

20. Insert a hyperlink from the text **February** that you typed in step 14 to the heading **February**.

21. Insert a hyperlink from the text **March** that you typed in step 15 to the heading **March**.

22. At the end of each course description paragraph, press **Enter** and type **Back to Top**.

23. Insert hyperlinks from each occurrence of **Back to Top** to the top of the document.

24. Insert a hyperlink from the text you typed in step 17 to the **TRAIN** document.

25. Insert a hyperlink from the text you typed in step 18 to the URL **D:/Internet/Word/Ex25/microsoft.htm**

    ✓ *If you've copied the Internet simulation files to your hard drive or your CD-ROM drive is not D:, substitute the correct drive letter for D.*

    ✓ *If you have an Internet connection, point the hyperlink to the URL www.microsoft.com/office/ instead.*

26. Increase the font size of all hyperlink text to 16 points.

27. Test the hyperlinks to navigate through the **COURSE3** document.

    ✓ *Use the hyperlinks to go to each month heading, then to return to the top of the document.*

28. Test the hyperlink to go to the **TRAIN** document.

29. Insert a hyperlink from the text **Return** at the top of the **TRAIN** document, back to the **COURSE3** document.

30. Test the hyperlink to return to the **COURSE3** document.

31. Test the hyperlink to go to the Microsoft Office Web site.

    ✓ *You may be prompted to sign on to your ISP.*

32. Click the Back button on your browser's toolbar to return to the **COURSE3** document.

33. Disconnect from the Internet, if necessary.

34. Close all open documents, saving all changes.

*Illustration A (Page 1 of 2)*

# Murray Hill Marketing, LLC

*285 Madison Avenue ✧ New York, NY 10016 ✧ 212-555-4444*

## Training Schedule

January ——————— *Hyperlink to heading January*
February ——————— *Hyperlink to heading February*
March ——————— *Hyperlink to heading March*

### Questions?

Click here to read about in-house training. ——————— *Hyperlink to TRAIN.DOC*
Click here to learn more about Microsoft Office.

*Hyperlink to www.microsoft.com\office\*

◼ January

### Microsoft Word 1

This introductory course will cover the basics of using Microsoft Word to create common business documents. By the end of the course you will know how to: create and print text-based documents such as letters and envelopes, and apply formatting.

Back to top. ——————— *Hyperlink to top of document*

◼ February

### Microsoft Word 2

A continuation of the Word I course, this introductory level class will delve into some of the more intriguing features of Microsoft Word. By the end of the course you will know how to conduct a mail merge, set up a document in columns, include headers and footers, and insert pictures.

Back to Top ——— *Hyperlink to top of document*

■ March

*Microsoft Word 3*

This final course in the Microsoft Word series covers the advanced features. By the end of this course you will know how to work with tables, create and modify outlines, use e-mail and Internet features in Word, and share documents with other users.

Back to Top ——— *Hyperlink to top of document*

For more information call: 212-555-4444, ext. 343.

# On Your Own

1. Open the document **OWD20**, your personal Web page, or open ☄ **25WEB**.

2. Save the file as **OWD25**.

3. Think of ways you can link the Web page to documents you have created in the On Your Own sections of previous exercises. For example, you could link the Web page to the list of things you'd like to accomplish, to your resume, or to the announcement of the upcoming event.

4. Open the document **OWD19**, your resume, or open ☄ **25RESUME**.

5. Save the file as **OWD25-2**.

6. Create a hyperlink from **OWD25** to **OWD25-2**. You can create new hyperlink text, or use text that is already entered in the document.

7. Create a link back to the Web page from the resume.

8. Open the document **OWD17**, your list of personal goals, or open ☄ **25GOALS**.

9. Save the file as **OWD25-3**.

10. Create a hyperlink from **OWD25** to **OWD25-3**. Again, you can create new hyperlink text, or use text that is already entered in the document.

11. Create a link back to the Web page from the list of goals.

12. If you have access to the Internet, try linking your Web page to a Web site that you like.

13. Test the links.

14. Save your changes to all documents, then close the documents.

# Exercise 26

## ◆ Critical Thinking

You have been hired to develop a Web site for Coastline Gourmet Importers. In this exercise, you will use e-mail to communicate with your supervisor. You will also browse the Internet looking at gourmet food sites, and save a Web page that you like. You will create and format a Web page document, and you will insert hyperlinks linking the Web page to a regular Word document.

## Exercise Directions

1. Start Word, if necessary.
2. Create a new e-mail message with the following header information:
   To: **coastlinegourmet@ddcpub.com**
   Subject: **Company Web page**
   Message text: **Dear Mr. Boghosian, I am delighted that you asked me to design the company Web site. Look for future e-mail including sample page designs. Thanks**.
3. Send the message.
4. Start the browser of your choice.
   ✓ *If you don't have Internet access, choose to work offline.*
5. On the address line of your browser, type the following and press Enter:
   **D:/Internet/Word/Ex26/ harryanddavid.htm**
   ✓ *If necessary, substitute the correct drive letter for D.*
6. Go back to Word.
7. Display the Web toolbar.
8. On the Address line, type the following and press Enter:
   **D:/Internet/Word/Ex26/cardullos.htm**
9. Go back to Word.
10. On the Address line, type the following and press Enter:
    **D:/Internet/Word/Ex26/altavista.htm**
11. Type **gourmet food** in the search text box and click the **Search** button.
12. Scroll down and click the link to GourmetUSA.

✓ *The simulation uses the Altavista search engine. If you are using a different search engine, the results may vary. The URL is www.freshcaviar.com.*

13. Save the Web page in Web archive format with the name **GOURMET**.
14. Close Internet Explorer.
15. Create a new e-mail message with the following header information:
    To: **coastlinegourmet@ddcpub.com**
    Subject: **Company Web page**
    Message text: **Dear Mr. Boghosian, I've been browsing the Web looking at gourmet food site home pages. What do you think of the attached page? Thanks**.
16. Attach the **GOURMET** file to the message and send it.
17. Create a new blank Web page document in Word.
18. Save the file as **WEBCOAST**, with the page title **COASTLINE GOURMET HOME PAGE**.
19. Apply the Edge theme to the document.
20. Type and format the document shown in Illustration A.
21. Check the spelling and grammar in the document.
22. Display the file in Web Page Preview. It should look similar to the one in the illustration.
23. Open the file ⊚ **26SPECIALS**.
24. Save the file as **SPECIALS**.

25. At the beginning of the line of text beginning **Coastline Importers is running**... type **Return to Home Page**, and then press **Enter** twice.

26. Insert a hyperlink from the text **Return to Home Page** to the **WEBCOAST** document.

27. At the end of the document, following the phone number, type the following sentence. **Or, click here to request information via e-mail**.

28. Select the new sentence and insert a hyperlink to *coastlinegourmet@ddcpub.com,* with the subject **Info about special programs**.

29. Test the *Return to Home Page* hyperlink.

30. Insert a hyperlink from the text **Special Programs** to the **SPECIALS** document.

31. Test the hyperlink.

32. Close the **SPECIALS** document, saving all changes.

33. Send a copy of the **WEBCOAST** document as an e-mail using the following message header information:

    To: **coastlinegourmet@ddcpub.com**

    Subject: Company Web page

    Introduction: **Here's my first stab at a Home Page. Click the link to see a document stored on the company intranet**.

34. Send the document.

35. Disconnect from the Internet, if necessary.

36. Close the **WEBCOAST** document, saving all changes.

*Illustration A*

# Exercise 27

◆ **Create a Table** ◆ **Enter Data in a Table** ◆ **Select in a Table**
◆ **Change Table Structure** ◆ **Format a Table**

## On the Job

Create tables to organize data into columns and rows. Any information that needs to be presented in side-by-side columns can be set up in a table. For example, a price list, an invoice, and a resume are all types of documents for which you should use a table. The table format lets you align information side by side and across the page so the information is easy to read.

Murray Hill Marketing is offering the staff training courses. In this exercise, you will create a memo that includes a list of courses being offered. You will set up the course list in a table.

## Terms

**Table** A grid comprised of horizontal rows and vertical columns into which you can enter data.

**Column** A vertical series of cells in a table.

**Row** A horizontal series of cells in a table.

**Column markers** Markers on the horizontal ruler that indicate column dividers.

**Dividers** The lines that indicate the edges of cells in a table. Dividers do not print, although they are indicated on-screen by either gridlines or borders.

**Border** A line drawn around the edges of an element, such as a table or a table cell. Borders can also be drawn around paragraphs and pages.

**Cell** The rectangular area at the intersection of a column and a row in a table, into which you enter data or graphics.

**Gridlines** Nonprinting lines that can be displayed around cells in a table.

**End of row/cell marks** Nonprinting characters used to mark the end of a cell or a row in a table.

## Notes

### Create a Table

- **Tables** are easier to use than tabbed columns when setting up and organizing data in **columns** and **rows**.
- You can create a table in any Word document; they are frequently used to align data on Web page documents.
- You select the number of columns and rows you want in the table.

- Word creates the table at the insertion point location.
- By default, Word sizes the columns equally across the width of the page.
- **Column markers** on the horizontal ruler show the location of the right **divider** of each column.
- By default, Word places a ½-pt. **border** around all **cells** in a table.

*A table with four columns and four rows*

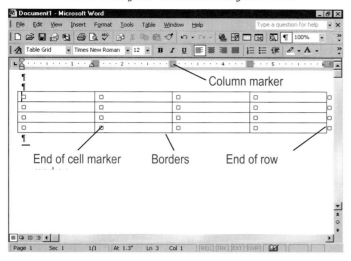

- Tables have three unique nonprinting elements:
  - **Gridlines**
  - **End of cell markers**
  - **End of row markers**

## Enter Data in a Table

- You enter data in the cells of a table.
- Row height increases automatically to accommodate as much data as you type.
- Column width does not change automatically. Text wraps at the right margin of a cell the same way it wraps at the right margin of a page.
- To move from cell to cell you press Tab, or click in another cell with the mouse.
- When you press Enter in a cell, Word starts a new paragraph within the cell.
- You can edit and format text within a cell the same way you do outside a table.

## Select in a Table

- As with other Word features, you must select table components before you can affect them with commands.
- You select text within a cell using the standard selection commands.
- You can select one or more columns, one or more rows, one or more cells, or the entire table.
- Selected table components appear highlighted.

## Change Table Structure

- Change a table's structure by inserting and deleting columns, rows, or cells.
- You can insert components anywhere in a table.
- **You** can delete any component.
  - ✓ *Data entered in a deleted column or row is deleted as well.*
- You choose which way to shift existing cells when cells are inserted or deleted.

## Format a Table

- You can format text within a table using standard Word formatting techniques. For example, use font formatting, alignments, spacing, indents, and tabs to enhance text in a table.
- You can apply formatting to selected text, or to selected cells, columns, or rows.
- Use Table AutoFormat to quickly apply formatting effects to an existing table.
- AutoFormat styles include border lines, shading, color, fonts, and other formatting.

*Table AutoFormat dialog box*

- AutoFormat overrides existing formatting. Therefore, you should apply AutoFormat first, then apply additional formatting as needed.

# Procedures

## Create a Table

### To use the toolbar button:

1. Position insertion point.
2. Click **Insert Table** button ⊞.
3. Drag the mouse pointer across the grid to select desired number of columns and rows.
4. Release the mouse button.

### To use menu commands:

1. Position the insertion point.
2. Click **T̲able** ................. `Alt` + `A`
3. Select **I̲nsert** ........................ `I`
4. Click **T̲able** ........................ `T`
5. Type **number of c̲olumns** ...................... `Alt` + `C`
6. Press **Tab** ........................ `Tab`
7. Type **number of r̲ows** ........................... `Alt` + `R`
8. Click **OK** ........................ `Enter`

### To show/hide gridlines:

1. Click **T̲able** ................. `Alt` + `A`
2. Click **Show G̲ridlines** ......... `G`
   OR
   Click **Hide G̲ridlines** ........... `G`

   ✓ *The default border is not hidden when you select to hide gridlines.*

## To move the insertion point in a table:

### With the mouse

- Click mouse pointer where you want to position insertion point.

### With the keyboard

- One cell left ................ `Shift` + `Tab`
- One cell right ...................... `Tab`
- One cell up ........................... `↑`
- One cell down ...................... `↓`
- First cell in column ...... `Alt` + `Page Up`
- Last cell in column ...... `Alt` + `Page Down`
- First cell in row ........ `Alt` + `Home`
- Last cell in row .......... `Alt` + `End`

## Enter Data in a Table

1. Click in desired cell.
2. Type data.
3. Press **Tab** ........................... `Tab`
4. Type data in next cell.
5. Repeat until all data is entered.

## Select in a Table

1. Position insertion point within table component to select.

   ✓ *For example, click in cell if selecting cell; click anywhere in row if selecting row, etc.*

2. Click **T̲able** ................. `Alt` + `A`
3. Select **Sele̲ct** ...................... `C`
4. Click one of the following:
   - **T̲able** ........................... `T`
   - **C̲olumn** ...................... `C`
   - **R̲ow** ............................ `R`
   - **C̲ell** ............................ `E`

## Select Adjacent Components

1. Select first component.
2. Press and hold **Shift** .......... `Shift`
3. Click in last component to select.

   ✓ *This method enables you to select adjacent columns, adjacent rows, or adjacent cells.*

## Change Table Structure

### Insert columns or rows:

1. Position insertion point within table.

   ✓ *To insert more than one component, select as many as you want to insert. For example, to insert two columns, select two columns.*

2. Click **T̲able** ................. `Alt` + `A`
3. Click **I̲nsert** ........................ `I`
4. Click one of the following:
   - **Columns to the L̲eft** ...... `L`
   - **Columns to the R̲ight** ... `R`
   - **Rows A̲bove** .................. `A`
   - **Rows B̲elow** .................. `B`
   - **C̲ells** ........................... `E`

   ✓ *Select option for shifting existing cells to make room for new cells, then click OK.*

### Delete entire table, columns, rows, or cells:

1. Select or click in the row or column to delete.
2. Click **T̲able** ................. `Alt` + `A`
3. Select **D̲elete** ...................... `D`
4. Click one of the following:
   - **T̲able** ........................... `T`
   - **C̲olumns** ...................... `C`
   - **R̲ows** ........................... `R`
   - **C̲ells** ........................... `E`

   ✓ *Select option for shifting existing cells to fill in deleted cell area, then click OK.*

## Apply AutoFormat

1. Click **T̲able** ................. `Alt` + `A`
2. Click **Table AutoF̲ormat** ..... `F`
3. Select table style .. `Alt` + `T`, `↓`
4. Click **A̲pply** .... `Alt` + `A` or `Enter`

## Format Text in a Table

1. Select text or cell(s) to format.
2. Apply formatting as with regular document text.

# Exercise Directions

1. Start Word, if necessary.
2. Create a new document.
3. Save the file as **SCHEDULE**.
4. Move the insertion point to the last line of the document.
5. Type the document shown in Illustration A.
   - Create the table as follows:
   a. Insert a table with three columns and four rows.
   b. Enter the data as shown.
      - ✓ *To enter an en dash between the times, simply type a space, a hyphen, and a space. By default, AutoFormat automatically replaces the hyphen and spaces with an en dash after the second number is typed.*
6. Select the last two rows.
7. Insert two new rows above the selected rows.
8. Enter the following data in the new rows:
   **Advanced Word Conference**
   **Room A        8:30 – 11:45**

   **Excel for Beginners Conference**
   **Room B      1:30 – 3:30**
9. Insert a new column to the left of the Time Column.

10. Enter the following data in the new column:
    **Days**
    **Tuesday, Thursday**
    **Monday, Wednesday**
    **Tuesday, Wednesday**
    **Monday, Thursday**
    **Friday**
11. Delete the row for the Beginner's Word course.
12. Apply the Table Contemporary AutoFormat to the table.
13. Apply italics to all of the course names.
    - ✓ *Select the text, then apply the formatting.*
14. Check the spelling and grammar in the document.
15. Preview the document. It should look similar to the one in Illustration B.
16. Save the changes and print the document
17. Close the document and exit Word.

# On Your Own

1. Think of documents that would benefit from table formatting. Some examples include a weekly schedule, meeting agenda, travel itinerary, sales report, telephone/address list, and roster.
2. Create a new document in Word.
3. Save the file as **OWD27**.
4. Use a table to set up the document as a telephone list. The list could include friends, family members, or members of a club or organization to which you belong.

5. Use at least three columns—one for the first name, one for the last name and one for the telephone number. You may use more columns if you want to include mailing addresses, e-mail addresses, cell phone numbers, or other information.
6. Include at least eight names in the list.
7. Apply an AutoFormat to the table. If you are not satisfied with the results, try a different AutoFormat.
8. Check the spelling and grammar in the document, then print it.
9. Close the document, saving all changes.

*Illustration A*

MEMO


To:          All Employees
From:        Your Name
Date:        Today's date
Subject:     Training Schedule

Here is the schedule of courses being offered next week. If you haven't signed up, see me
immediately.

*Insert column*

| Course Name | Location | Time |
|---|---|---|
| Word for Beginners | Conference Room A | 8:30 – 11:45 |
| Advanced Excel | Conference Room B | 8:30 – 11:45 |
| Introduction to the Internet | Media Lab | 1:30 – 3:30 |

*Insert two
new rows*

*Illustration B*

MEMO


To:         All Employees
From:       Your Name
Date:       Today's date
Subject:    Training Schedule

Here is the schedule of courses being offered next week. If you haven't signed up, see me immediately.

| Course Name | Location | Days | Time |
|---|---|---|---|
| *Advanced Word* | Conference Room A | Monday, Wednesday | 8:30 – 11:45 |
| *Excel for Beginners* | Conference Room B | Tuesday, Wednesday | 1:30 – 3:30 |
| *Advanced Excel* | Conference Room B | Monday, Thursday | 8:30 – 11:45 |
| *Introduction to the Internet* | Media Lab | Friday | 1:30 – 3:30 |

# Exercise 28

## Skills Covered:
◆ **Set Alignments within Table Cells** ◆ **Align Table on the Page**
◆ **Column Width and Row Height**

## On the Job

Use alignment options and tabs to make tables easy to read. Numbers are usually aligned flush right in a cell, while text can be flush left, centered, justified, or rotated to appear vertical. You can vertically align data in a cell as well. Decimal tabs are especially useful in tables for aligning dollar values. Other ways to improve the appearance of a table include aligning the table horizontally on the page, and adjusting column width and row height.

Northwest Gear, Inc. is offering employees special savings on selected items from its inventory. In this exercise, you will create a memo that includes information about the available items. You will use alignment options to set up the data in the table. You will also set row heights and column widths, and you will align the table horizontally on the page.

## Terms

**Column width** The width of a column in a table, measured in inches.

**Row height** The height of a row in a table, measured in inches.

## Notes

### Set Alignments within Table Cells

- You can set horizontal alignment within a cell the same way you set alignment in a document by using paragraph formatting and tabs.

- In a table, numbers are usually right aligned, and text is either left aligned or centered.

- All tab stops can be used within a table cell, but the most useful is the decimal tab stop.

- Decimal tab stops automatically align numbers such as dollar values within a cell or a column.

- You can vertically align data at the top of the cell, centered in the cell, or at the bottom of the cell. The default is at the top.

*Text aligned in a table*

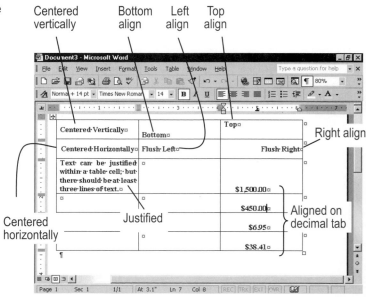

**130**

## Align Table on the Page

- You can left align, right align, or center a table on the page.

*Table tab of the Table Properties dialog box*

## Column Width and Row Height

- By default, Word creates columns of equal **column width**, sized so the table extends from the left margin to the right margin.

- Rows are sized according to the line spacing on the line where the table is inserted.

- By default, **row height** automatically increases to accommodate lines of text typed in a cell.

- You can drag column dividers to increase or decrease column width.

✓ *Press and hold the Alt key as you drag to see the column width measurements displayed on the ruler.*

- In Print Layout view, you can drag row dividers to increase or decrease row height.

✓ *You cannot drag row dividers in Normal view.*

- You can set precise measurements for columns, rows, cells, and entire tables in the Table Properties dialog box.

*Column tab of the Table Properties dialog box*

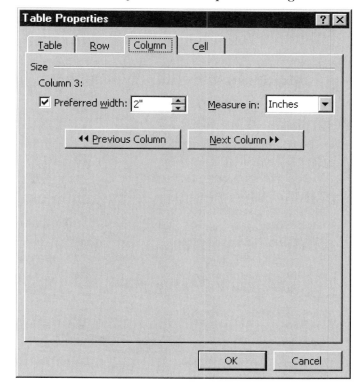

# Procedures

## Set Alignments within Table Cells

**To change horizontal alignment:**

1. Position insertion point in cell.
   OR
   Select component to format.
2. Click desired alignment button on Formatting toolbar:
   - **Align Left** ≣ .
   - **Center** ≣ .
   - **Align Right** ≣ .
   - **Justify** ≣ .

**To set tabs in a cell:**

1. Position insertion point in cell.
   OR
   Select component(s) to format.
2. Click Tab box at left end of horizontal ruler to select tab stop type.
3. Click desired position on horizontal ruler.
   - ✓ For more information on tabs, refer to exercise 6.

**To advance insertion point one tab stop within a cell:**

- Press .......................... Ctrl + Tab

**To change vertical alignment:**

1. Position insertion point in cell.
   OR
   Select component to format.
2. Click **Table** .................. Alt + A
3. Click **Table Properties** ........ R
4. Click the **Cell** tab ........ Alt + E
5. Click desired Vertical Alignment option:
   - **Top** ⬜ ................. Alt + P
   - **Center** ⬜ ............ Alt + C
   - **Bottom** ⬜ ............ Alt + B
6. Click **OK** .......................... Enter

## Align Table Horizontally in Document

1. Select **table**.

2. Click desired alignment button on Formatting toolbar:
   - **Center** ≣ .
   - **Align Right** ≣ .
   - **Align Left** ≣ .

   OR

1. Click anywhere in table.
2. Click **Table** .................. Alt + A
3. Click **Table Properties** ........ R
4. Click the **Table** tab ...... Alt + T
5. Click desired Alignment option:
   - **Left** ⊞ ................. Alt + L
   - **Center** ⊞ ........... Alt + C
   - **Right** ⊞ .............. Alt + H
6. Click **OK** .......................... Enter

## Change Column Width

1. Position mouse pointer on column divider.
   - ✓ Pointer changes to a double-vertical line with arrows pointing left and right.
2. Click and drag divider left or right.
   - ✓ Press Alt at the same time that you drag the divider to see the width displayed on the horizontal ruler.

   OR

   a. Click in column.
   b. Click **Table** ............. Alt + A
   c. Click **Table Properties** .. R
   d. Click **Column** tab ... Alt + U
   e. Select **Preferred Width** check box .... Alt + W
   f. Press **Tab** ...................... Tab
   g. Type column width.
   h. Click **OK** ..................... Enter
      OR
      Click **Next Column**
      [ Next Column ▶▶ ] ... Alt + N

   OR

   Click **Previous Column**
   [ ◀◀ Previous Column ] ... Alt + P

   i. Repeat steps e – h to set additional column widths.
   j. Click **OK** ...................... Enter

## Change Row Height

1. Click **Print Layout View** button ⊟ .
2. Position mouse pointer on row divider.
   - ✓ Pointer changes to a double-horizontal line with arrows pointing up and down.
3. Click and drag divider up or down.
   - ✓ Press Alt at the same time that you drag the divider to see the height displayed on the vertical ruler.

   OR

   a. Click in row.
   b. Click **Table** ............. Alt + A
   c. Click **Table Properties** ... R
   d. Click **Row** tab ........ Alt + R
   e. Select **Specify Height** check box .............. Alt + S
   f. Press **Tab** ...................... Tab
   g. Type row height in inches.
      - ✓ Select Exactly in Row height is box to fix row height at specified size.

   OR

   Click **Next Row**
   [ Next Row ▼ ] ... Alt + N

   OR

   Click **Previous Row**
   [ ▲ Previous Row ] ... Alt + P

   h. Repeat steps e – h to set additional row heights.
   i. Click **OK** ..................... Enter

# Exercise Directions

1. Start Word, if necessary.
2. Create a new document.
3. Save the file as **SALE**.
4. Use the following steps to create the document shown in Illustration A.
5. Type the memo text.
6. Create a table with five columns and eight rows and enter the data as shown.

   ✓ *You can enter the data before setting alignments in step 7, or after.*

7. Set alignment as follows:

   a. Align the data in the first column flush right horizontally and on the top vertically.

   b. Align the data in columns 2, 3, 4, and 5 flush left horizontally and on the bottom vertically.

   c. Center the data in the first row horizontally and vertically.

   d. Set a left tab within column 4 at approximately .7" and use it to align the sizes (press Ctrl+Tab to move the insertion point to the tab stop).

   ✓ *To see the location of the tab, insert the tab stop, then press and hold the Alt key as you drag the tab stop marker.*

   e. Use a decimal tab to align the prices in the fifth column.

   ✓ *Try to set the tab stop at about .5" to match the illustration. Also, notice that the numbers align automatically as soon as you set the tab.*

8. Make the text in the first row bold.
9. Set preferred column widths as follows:
   - Column 1: .8"
   - Column 2: .7"
   - Column 3: 1.25"
   - Column 4: 1.5"
   - Column 5: .6"
10. Set all rows to be at least .5" high.
11. Center the entire table horizontally on the page.
12. Check the spelling and grammar.
13. Display the document in Print Preview. It should look similar to the one in Illustration A.

    ✓ *If necessary, adjust the column widths so your document looks like the illustration.*

14. Print the document.
15. Close the document, saving all changes.

# On Your Own

1. Create a new document in Word.
2. Save the file as **OWD28**.
3. Use a table to set up the document as a weekly schedule. The schedule might include your classes, things you do at work, afternoon or evening activities, or activities you do on the weekends
4. Set up the table so that times are listed in the first column and the days of the week are listed in the first row.
5. Set the first row to exactly .25" high.
6. Set the first column to exactly .5" wide and set the remaining columns to 1" wide.
7. If necessary, adjust other columns and rows by dragging the table dividers.
8. Use different alignments in the table. For example, center the names of the days but right-align the times.
9. Center the table on the page.
10. Save the changes, close the document, and exit Word.

↓ *4x*

MEMO

↓ *4x*

*Tab to 1"*

To: → All employees
From: (Your name) — *Type your name*
Date: (Today's date) — *Insert today's date*
Subject: Special Pricing on Selected Items

↓ *3x*

We are pleased to announce that we are making some of our most popular items available to you at special discounted prices.

↓*2x*

You may order the items on the company Intranet, or pick up an order form from the receptionist in the Fulfillment department.

↓*2x*

| | Item No. | Description | Sizes | | Price |
|---|---|---|---|---|---|
| Clothing | R-242V | Fleece Vest | Men: M, L, XL<br>Women: S, L | | $12.99 |
| | S-966X | Hiker's convertible pants | Men: 29 – 38<br>Women: 6, 10, 12 | | $15.99 |
| | R-244P | Fleece Pullover | Men: S, M, L<br>Women: S, M, L | | $15.99 |
| | R-246L | Fleece Pants | Men: S, M, L<br>Women: S, M, L | | $16.99 |
| Accessories | A-567H | Baseball cap | | | $5.99 |
| | G-459C | Daypack | | | $10.99 |
| | B-980L | Web belt | S, M, L | | $4.99 |

# Exercise 29

## Skills Covered:

◆ **Tables and Borders Toolbar**
◆ **Draw a Table** ◆ **Move and Resize Tables**
◆ **Merge and Split Cells** ◆ **Rotate Text** ◆ **Wrap Text**

## On the Job

Word's Draw Table tool gives you great flexibility to organize tables the way you want them, not necessarily in rigid columns and rows. You can lay out the table cells exactly as you want them in order to organize text and data. You can then move and resize the table, if necessary, merge and split cells, and rotate the text to achieve the exact effect you need.

Your supervisor at Coastline Gourmet Importers has asked you to design a flyer announcing a series of cooking classes. In this exercise, you will open and format a document describing the classes. You will then create a table listing the schedule of classes, and integrate it into the flyer.

## Terms

**Merge** Combine multiple adjacent cells together to create one large cell.

**Split** Divide one cell into multiple cells, either vertically to create columns or horizontally to create rows.

## Notes

*Tables and Borders toolbar*

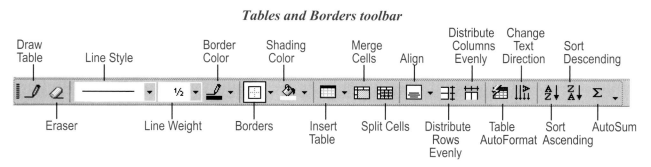

## Tables and Borders Toolbar

■ Use the buttons on the Tables and Borders toolbar to create and format tables.

✓ *If the toolbar is in your way while working, move it or dock it across the top of the document window.*

## Draw a Table

■ Word's Draw Table feature lets you create tables with uneven or irregular columns and rows.

*A table drawn with uneven columns and rows*

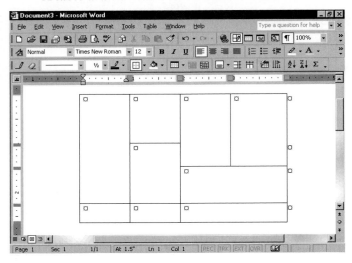

*Table anchor and sizing handle*

- You must use Print Layout view to draw a table.
- When you draw a table, the mouse pointer functions as a pencil.

- You drag the pointer to draw lines vertically or horizontally to create cell dividers.
  - ✓ *Word creates straight lines at 90 degree angles to existing cell dividers, even if you do not drag in a straight line.*
- You can draw a diagonal line across a cell as a visual element or border, not to split the cell diagonally.
- New cells can be drawn anywhere. Rows and columns do not have to extend across the entire table.
- You can combine the Insert Table command with the Draw Table command to customize any table.

## Move and Resize Tables

- You can drag the table anchor to move the table anywhere on the page.
- You can drag the sizing handle to change the table size.

## Merge and Split Cells

- You can **merge** horizontally adjacent cells or vertically adjacent cells.
- You can use the eraser tool to erase dividers between cells, thus merging the cells.
  - ✓ *If you erase a divider on the outer edge of the table, you simply erase the border line, not the divider itself.*
- Merging is useful for creating a heading row across a table.
- **Split** a cell to insert dividers to create additional columns or rows.

## Rotate Text

- Rotate text direction within a cell so text runs from left to right, from top to bottom, or from bottom to top.

*Rotate text in a table*

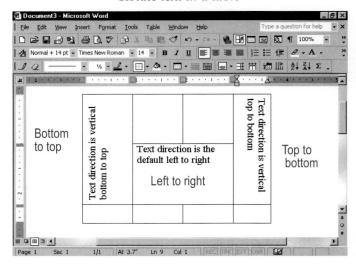

## Wrap Text

- By default, tables are inserted on a blank line above or below existing text.

- You can set Word to wrap text around the table.
- Wrapping text around a table integrates the table object into the text so text appears above, below, and on either side of the table.

# Procedures

### Display Tables and Borders Toolbar

- Click **Tables and Borders** button  on the Standard toolbar.

OR

1. Click **View** .................. Alt + V
2. Click **Toolbars** .................... T
3. Click **Tables and Borders**.

OR

1. Right-click any toolbar.
2. Click **Tables and Borders**.

### Draw a Table

1. Click **Table** .................. Alt + A
2. Click **Draw Table** ................ W

   OR

   Click **Draw Table** button 🖉 on Tables and Borders toolbar.

   ✓ The mouse pointer resembles a pencil.

3. Click where you want to position upper-left corner of the table.
4. Drag diagonally down and to the right.
5. Release mouse button where you want to position lower-right corner of the table.

   ✓ This draws one cell.

6. Click and drag mouse pointer to draw horizontal borders and vertical borders.

   ✓ As you drag, Word displays a dotted line where the border will be. Once you drag far enough, Word completes the line when you release the mouse button.

7. Press **Esc** ........................... Esc
   to turn off Draw Table.

   OR

   Click **Draw Table** button 🖉.

### Move a Table

1. Rest mouse pointer on table so handles are displayed.
2. Click and drag table anchor to new location.

   ✓ A dotted outline moves with the mouse pointer to show new location.

3. Release mouse button to drop table in new location

### Resize a Table

1. Rest mouse pointer on table so handles are displayed.
2. Click and drag sizing handle to increase or decrease table size.

   ✓ A dotted outline moves with the mouse pointer to show new size.

3. Release mouse button to resize table.

### Merge Cells

1. Select cells to merge.
2. Click **Merge Cells** button ▦ on Tables and Borders toolbar.

   OR

   a. Click **Table** ............. Alt + A
   b. Click **Merge Cells** .......... M

### Merge Cells and Erase Table Dividers

1. Click **Eraser** button ⌀ on Tables and Borders toolbar.
2. Drag over borders to erase.

### Split a Cell

1. Select cell to split.
2. Click **Split Cells** button ▦ on Tables and Borders toolbar.

   OR

   a. Click **Table** ............. Alt + A
   b. Click **Split Cells** ............ P

3. Enter **Number of columns** to create ........... Alt + C, number
4. Enter **Number of rows** to create ........... Alt + R, number
5. Click **OK** ......................... Enter

### Rotate Text

1. Click in cell to format.

   OR

   Select components to format.

2. Click **Change Text Direction** button ⼞ on Tables and Borders toolbar.

   ✓ Click the button to toggle through the three available directions.

### Wrap Text

1. Click in table.
2. Click **Table** .................. Alt + A
3. Click **Table Properties** ........ R
4. Click **Table** ........................ T
5. Click **Around** ............... Alt + A
6. Click **OK** ......................... Enter

# Exercise Directions

1. Start Word, if necessary.
2. Open 💿 **29COOKING**.
3. Save the file as **COOKING**.
4. On the first line of the document, use the Draw Table tool to draw a cell approximately 4" wide and 4" high.
   - ✓ *Use the rulers as guides to measure the height and width of cells as you draw, but don't worry if the table components are not sized exactly.*
5. Create three columns by drawing vertical lines through the cell. Try to size the columns as follows:
   Column 1: 1" wide
   Columns 2 and 3: 1.5" wide
6. Leave the first column intact, and create five rows across the second and third columns as follows:
   Row 1: .5" high
   Rows 2, 3, and 4: 1" high
   Row 5: .5" high
7. Merge the cells in the top row of the right two columns, and then merge the corresponding cells in the bottom row.
8. Leaving the top and bottom rows intact, use the Split Cells tool to create three rows within each of the cells in the third column (refer to Illustration A to see the desired result).
9. Enter the text in the table as shown in Illustration A, using the following formatting and alignments to achieve the desired result:

   a. Column 1 (program name): 26-pt. serif, rotated so it runs from bottom to top, centered horizontally and vertically.
   b. Row 1 (table title): 16-pt. serif, centered horizontally and vertically.
   c. Dates: 12-pt. serif, aligned left, and centered vertically.
   d. Menus: 12-pt. serif, aligned left horizontally, and aligned with the cell bottom vertically.
   e. Bottom row: 10-pt. serif, centered horizontally, and aligned with the cell bottom vertically.
10. Format the text that is not in the table in a 14-point sans serif font (Comic Sans MS is used in the illustration).
11. Center the first three lines of text below the table.
12. Leave 30 points of space after the third line.
13. Leave 6 points of space after the three paragraphs of text in the document.
14. Set text to wrap around the table.
15. Position the table flush right on the page, with its top at about 2" on the vertical ruler.
16. Resize the table to decrease its height to about 3.5".
17. Check the spelling and grammar in the document.
18. Display the document in Print Preview. It should look similar to the one in the illustration.
19. Print the document.
20. Close the document, saving all changes.

# On Your Own

1. Create a new document in Word.
2. Save the file as **OWD29**.
3. Type a personal business letter to an employer or to your parents explaining why you need a raise. Write at least two paragraphs about why you deserve the raise and what you plan to do with the additional funds. Include information about how you spend the money you receive now.
4. To illustrate your point, draw a table in the letter and list items that you have purchased in the past two weeks. For example, include CDs, books, meals, movie tickets, and other expenses. The table should have at least three columns—for the date, the item, and the cost. List at least four items.
5. Merge a row across the top of the table and type in a title.
6. Try rotating text in some of the cells.
7. Use different alignments in the table cells.
8. Set the text in the letter to wrap around the table.
9. Try moving and resizing the table to improve the appearance of the letter.
10. When you are satisfied with the appearance of the table and the letter, check the spelling and grammar and print the document.
11. Close the document, saving all changes.

*Illustration A*

Cooking with Coastline
A new series of cooking classes sponsored by
Coastline Gourmet Importers

Cooking with Coastline is a series of hands-on cooking classes designed to introduce customers to a complete dinner menu. Each two-hour class will cover preparation of an appetizer, an entrée, and a dessert. Some classes will have themes, such as Valentine's Day, and St. Patrick's Day.

Classes will also include information such as shopping tips, selecting the right beverage, and how to set the table.

| Cooking with Coastline | Scheduled Dates and Menus | |
|---|---|---|
| | January 23 | Antipasto |
| | | Pasta Primavera |
| | | Crème Brulee |
| | February 11 | Oysters on the half shell |
| | | Rosemary Lamb Chops |
| | | Chocolate Fondue |
| | March 16 | Baked Potato Skins |
| | | Corned Beef and Cabbage |
| | | Apple Crisp |
| | Space is limited. Reservations are required. | |

The first series of classes will begin in January. The classes will be held at our flagship store in Miami Beach.

Space is limited, so please make your reservations early.

Coastline Gourmet Importers
7334 Sunshine Parkway
12th Floor
Miami, FL 33132
305.555.7300
coastlinegourmet@ddcpub.com

# Exercise 30

## On the Job

Perform basic calculations in tables to total values in a column or row. If the values change, you can update the result without redoing the math. At the same time, you can format the calculation results with one of Word's built-in number formats. Sorting rows helps you keep your tables in order, while cell borders and shading let you dress up your tables to make them look good as well as to highlight important information.

Coastline Gourmet is offering a special gift basket for Valentine's Day. In this exercise, you will create a document to advertise the gift basket. You will use a table to organize the information and to calculate costs. You will format the table using cell borders and shading.

## Terms

**Spreadsheet** An application, such as Microsoft's Excel 2002, used for setting up mathematical calculations.

**Function** A built-in **formula** for performing calculations, such as addition, in a table.

**Formula** A mathematical equation.

**Field** A placeholder used to insert information that changes, such as the date, the time, a page number, or the results of a calculation.

**Line style** The appearance of a line.

**Line weight** The thickness of a line.

**Shading** A color or pattern used to fill the background of a cell.

## Notes

### Calculate in a Table

- Word tables include basic **spreadsheet functions** so you can perform calculations on data entered in tables.

- By default, Word assumes you want to add the values entered in the column above the current cell, or in the row beside the current cell.

- Word enters the calculation result in a **field**, so it can be updated if the values in the table change.

- For anything other than basic calculations, use an Excel worksheet, not a Word table.

*The Formula dialog box set up to total the column*

## Number Formats

- When you set up a calculation in a table, you can select a number format to use for the result.
- Number formats include dollar signs, commas, percent signs, and decimal points.

*Number formats*

## Cell Borders and Shading

- By default, Word applies a ½-pt. black solid line border around all table cells.
- Use the Tables and Borders toolbar buttons to change the borders and shading of table cells.
- You can select borders and shading before you draw new cells, or apply them to selected cells.

- • Select a different **line style**.
- • Select a different **line weight**.
- • Change the border color.
- • Erase or add border lines.
- • Add color or **shading**.
- Selected border and shading formatting remains in effect until new formatting is selected.
  - ✓ *When table borders are removed, you can see table cells on-screen by displaying gridlines.*

## Sort Rows

- Sort rows in a table the same way you sort lists or paragraphs.
  - ✓ *See Word, Exercise 17.*
- Rows can be sorted according to the data in any column.
- For example, in a table of names and addresses, rows can be sorted alphabetically by name or by city, or numerically by ZIP Code.
- Word rearranges the rows in the table but does not rearrange the columns.

# Procedures

### Total Values in a Column or Row

1. Click in cell where you want the total to be displayed.
2. Click **Table** .................. Alt + A
3. Click **Formula** ..................... O
   - ✓ *By default, Word enters the formula for totaling the values in the cells in the column above or the row to the left.*
4. Click **Number format** .. Alt + N
5. Click desired format ..... ↑, ↓
6. Click **OK** ........................... Enter

### Update the Total

1. Select the text in the cell where the total is displayed.
2. Press **F9** .............................. F9

- ✓ *You must update the total each time one of the values used in the formula is changed. The total is not updated automatically.*

### Sort Rows

1. Select the data in the column by which you want to sort.
2. Click **Sort Ascending** button to sort from A to Z or from 0 to 9.
   OR
   Sort **Descending** button to sort from Z to A or from 9 to 0.
   - ✓ *If the sort should not include the first row, click Table, Sort and select the My list has Header row option button, then click OK.*

OR

1. Click **Table** .................. Alt + A
2. Click **Sort** ........................... S
3. Click **Sort by** .............. Alt + S
4. Click desired column.
5. Click **Type** ................. Alt + Y
6. Click either:
   - • **Text**
   - • **Number**
   - • **Date**
7. Click either:
   - • **Ascending** ............. Alt + A
   - • **Descending** ........... Alt + D
   - ✓ *If the sort should not include the first row, make sure the My list has Header row option button is selected.*
8. Click **OK** ........................... Enter

## Sort by Multiple Columns

1. Click **Table** .................. Alt + A
2. Click **Sort** ......................... S
3. Click **Sort by** .............. Alt + S
4. Click desired column.
5. Click **Type** .................. Alt + Y
6. Click either:
   - **Text**
   - **Number**
   - **Date**
7. Click either:
   - **Ascending** ............. Alt + A
   - **Descending** ........... Alt + D
8. Click **Then by** .............. Alt + T
9. Click desired column.
10. Click **Type** .................. Alt + P
11. Click either:
    - **Text**
    - **Number**
    - **Date**
12. Click either:
    - **Ascending** ............. Alt + C
    - **Descending** ........... Alt + N
13. Click **Then by** .............. Alt + B
14. Click desired column.
15. Click **Type** .................. Alt + E
16. Click either:
    - **Text**
    - **Number**
    - **Date**
17. Click either:
    - **Ascending** ............. Alt + I
    - **Descending** ........... Alt + G
    - ✓ *If the sort should not include the first row, make sure the My list has Header row option button is selected.*
18. Click **OK** ......................... Enter

## Apply Cell Borders

1. Select cell(s) to format.
2. Click **Borders** drop-down arrow ▦ ▾.
3. Click Border style.
   - ✓ *Border buttons are toggles— click on to display border, click off to hide border.*

## Select Line Style

1. Click **Line Style** drop-down arrow ▭ ▾.
2. Click desired line style.
   - ✓ *Click No Border to remove border lines.*
3. Click on a border line to apply the style.

## Select Line Weight

1. Click **Line Weight** drop-down arrow ¼ ▾.
2. Click desired line weight.
3. Click on a border line to apply the style.

## Select Line Color

1. Click **Border Color** button 🖊.
2. Click desired color.
3. Click on a border line to apply the style.

## Select Cell Shading

1. Click in cell to shade.
2. Click **Shading Color** drop-down arrow 🎨 ▾.
3. Click desired color.
4. Click **No Fill** to remove shading or color.

# Exercise Directions

1. Start Word, if necessary.
2. Open ⊙ **30BASKET**.
3. Save the file as **BASKET**.
4. Move the insertion point to the last line of the document.
5. Use either the Draw Table tool or the Insert Table command to create a table with two columns and five rows.
6. Enter the data shown in Illustration A.
7. Align all dollar values with a decimal tab.
8. Preview the document. It should look similar to the one in Illustration A.
9. Sort the rows in descending order according to the values in the Price column.
   - ✓ *Remember not to sort the header row.*
10. Insert a new row at the end of the table.
11. In the first cell in the new row, type **Total**.
12. In the last cell of the new row, insert a formula to calculate the total cost.
    - ✓ *Select the currency format showing two decimal places.*
13. Insert a row above the total.
14. In the left column, type **1 bottle sparkling white grape juice**.
15. In the right column type **$4.59**.
16. Update the calculation result.
17. Apply the Table Grid 8 AutoFormat to the table.
18. Apply a dark blue double-line border around all of the cells in the bottom row.
    - ✓ *If you have trouble seeing the change on-screen, try zooming in to a higher magnification.*

19. Remove the borders between columns in the bottom row.

✓ *Do not merge the cells. Just remove the printing border lines.*

20. Apply a 12.5% gray shading to all of the cells in the bottom row.

✓ *ScreenTips display the % Gray Shading.*

21. Resize the table so it is approximately 4" wide by 3½" high.

22. Set column 1 to be approximately 2.5" wide and column 2 to be approximately 1.5" wide

23. Vertically center the text in the bottom row.

24. Center the table horizontally on the page.

25. Check the spelling and grammar.

26. Preview the document. It should look similar to the one in Illustration B.

27. Print the document.

28. Close the document, saving all changes.

*Illustration A*

# Coastline Gourmet
## $49.99 Gift Basket Valentine's Day Special

This specially priced package includes all of the items listed below, artfully arranged in a delightful wicker basket and wrapped in red cellophane with a bow. Attached to the handle is a Mylar heart-shaped balloon, and your own personalized card.

| Basket includes: | Regularly priced: |
|---|---|
| 8 oz. box of premium chocolate | $12.99 |
| Teddy bear | $9.99 |
| 1 dozen red roses | $32.99 |
| 1 dozen chocolate chip cookies | $14.99 |

# Coastline Gourmet

## $49.99 Gift Basket Valentine's Day Special

This specially priced package includes all of the items listed below, artfully arranged in a delightful wicker basket and wrapped in red cellophane with a bow. Attached to the handle are a Mylar heart-shaped balloon and your own personalized card.

| Basket includes: | Regularly priced: |
|---|---|
| 1 dozen red roses | $32.99 |
| 1 dozen chocolate chip cookies | $14.99 |
| 8 oz. box of premium chocolate | $12.99 |
| Teddy bear | $9.99 |
| 1 bottle sparkling white grape juice | $4.59 |
| Total | $ 75.55 |

# On Your Own

1. Open the document **OWD29**, the letter asking for a raise that you wrote in the On Your Own section of Exercise 29, or open 💿 **30RAISE**.

2. Save the file as **OWD30**.

3. Sort the rows in the table into descending numerical order, according to the amount of the expenses.

4. Add a row to the bottom of the table.

5. Label the row **Total**.

6. Calculate the total amount of expenses in the table. Make sure the result is displayed in dollar format.

7. Change one or more of the values in the table.

8. Update the calculation.

9. Format the table using cell borders and shading. For example, use borders and shading to highlight the cell in which the total is displayed.

10. Check the spelling and grammar, then print the document.

11. Close the document, saving all changes.

# Exercise 31

## ◆ Critical Thinking

Coastline Gourmet has been collecting demographic information about customers who come into its stores. In this exercise, you will create a memo to the marketing director listing some of the interesting demographics in table form.

## Exercise Directions

1. Start Word, if necessary.

2. Open ⊙ **31DEMOS**.

3. Save the document as **DEMOS**.

4. Complete the memo heading information as follows, tabbing in to the 1" mark to enter the data:

   **To:       Marketing Director**
   **From:     your own name**
   **Date:     Today's date**
   **Subject: Customer Demographics**

5. Between the first two paragraphs of the memo, insert a table with three columns and seven rows.

6. Set all columns to be 1" wide and all rows to be .25" high.

7. Enter the following data:

   | Age | 18 – 25 | 5% |
   |---|---|---|
   | | 26 – 35 | 22% |
   | | 36 – 45 | 23% |
   | | 46 – 55 | 28% |
   | | 55 + | 22% |
   | Gender | Male | 54% |
   | | Female | 46% |

8. Vertically align all data on the bottom.

9. Left align the data in columns 1 and 2.

10. Right align the data in column 3.

11. Insert a new row at the top of the table.

12. Merge the cells in the new row.

13. In the new row, type the table title: **CUSTOMER DEMOGRAPHICS**.

14. Center the table title horizontally and vertically.

15. Insert another blank row above the row labeled **Gender**.

16. Apply the Table Contemporary AutoFormat to the table.

17. Apply a single line ¾-pt. outside border to the entire table.

18. Between the second and third paragraphs of the memo, insert a table with two columns and five rows.

19. Set column 1 to be 1.5" wide and column 2 to be .5" wide.

20. Set all rows to be .25" high.

21. Enter the following data:

    | Naples | 42 |
    |---|---|
    | Miami Beach | 36 |
    | Fort Lauderdale | 47 |
    | Fort Meyers | 8 |
    | North Miami | 21 |

22. Align column 2 flush right.

23. Delete the cells containing the label and data for Fort Meyers, shifting the cells up.

24. Insert a blank row at the bottom of the table.

25. In the blank cell at the bottom of column 1, type **Total**, and right align it.

26. In the blank cell at the bottom of column 2, insert a formula to calculate the total number of respondents.

27. Sort the rows in ascending alphabetical order by city.

28. Insert a new column at the left side of the table.

29. Merge the cells in the first column.

30. Type **Respondents by Store** in column 1.
31. Rotate the text in column 1 so it reads from the bottom of the table to the top, and center it vertically.
32. Apply a 1-pt. Indigo border around the inside and outside of all cells in the table.
33. Apply a 10% gray shading to column 1.
34. Apply a 20% gray shading to rows 1, 3, and 5. Reduce the width of the column as necessary.
35. Center the table on the page.
36. Change the number of respondents in the North Miami store to **24**.
37. Update the result of the calculation.
38. Check the spelling and grammar in the document.
39. Display the document in Print Preview. It should look similar to the illustration.
40. Print the document.
41. Close the document, saving all changes.

*Illustration A*

MEMO

To:          Marketing Director
From:        Your Name
Date:         Today's date
Subject:     Customer Demographics

I thought you might like a preview of the customer demographic data we have been collecting. I find the age breakdowns quite interesting. Based on what we know of spending patterns, I think we should pursue promotions that will attract some younger consumers.

| CUSTOMER DEMOGRAPHICS | | |
|---|---|---|
| Age | 18 – 25 | 5% |
| | 26 – 35 | 22% |
| | 36 – 45 | 23% |
| | 46 – 55 | 28% |
| | 55 + | 22% |
| | | |
| Gender | Male | 54% |
| | Female | 46% |

Customers were surprisingly eager to fill out our questionnaire, as you can see from the numbers in the table below.

| Respondents by Store | Fort Lauderdale | 47 |
|---|---|---|
| | Miami Beach | 36 |
| | Naples | 42 |
| | North Miami | 24 |
| | Total | 149 |

We should have the complete report by the end of next week. We'll meet then to go over the results.

# Excel 2002

## Lesson 1

**Getting Started with Excel 2002**
**Exercises 1-6**

## Lesson 2

**Working with Formulas and Formatting**
**Exercises 7-12**

## Lesson 3

**Working with Functions, Formulas, and Charts**
**Exercises 13-19**

# Directory of Data Files on CD

| Exercise # | File Name | Page # |
|---|---|---|
| 1 | N/A | N/A |
| 2 | N/A | N/A |
| 3 | 03DEMOS, 03PLAYSETS | 165 |
| 4 | 04OVERDUE | 171 |
| 5 | 05OVERDUE | 173 |
| 6 | 06CHANG, 06CGIORDER | 176 |
| 7 | 07DBQUOTE | 180 |
| 8 | 08CASHTOPS | 184 |
| 9 | 09CASHTOPS | 188 |
| 10 | 10DRUGINV | 192 |
| 11 | 11ORGANIC | 196 |
| 12 | 12OVERDUE | 198 |
| 13 | 13COMPETE | 204 |
| 14 | 14CHIPSALES | 208 |
| 15 | 15NWGNEW | 212 |
| 16 | 16CGISALES | 218 |
| 17 | 17NWGNEW | 224 |
| 18 | 18COMPETE | 229 |
| 19 | 19SALESCONT | 231 |

# Exercise 1

### Skills Covered:

◆ **Start Excel** ◆ **The Excel Window** ◆ **Excel Menu and Toolbars**
◆ **Explore the Worksheet Using the Mouse and Keyboard**
◆ **Change Between Worksheets** ◆ **The View Menu** ◆ **Exit Excel**

## On the Job

When you want to analyze business, personal, or financial data and create reports in a table format consisting of rows and columns, use the Microsoft Excel spreadsheet application in the Office suite.

You've just been hired as a legal aide for Perry, Hawkins, Martinez, and Klein, and you've enrolled yourself in a class to learn to use Excel. In this exercise, you will start Excel, familiarize yourself with the Excel window, change your view of the worksheet, and practice moving around the worksheet using the mouse and the keyboard.

## Terms

**Workbook** An Excel file with one or more worksheets.

**Worksheet** The work area for entering and calculating data made up of columns and rows separated by gridlines (light gray lines). Also called a *spreadsheet.*

**Cell** A cell is the intersection of a column and a row on a worksheet. You enter data into cells to create a worksheet.

**Active cell** The active cell contains the cell pointer—a dark outline around the cell.

**Formula bar** As you enter data into a cell, it simultaneously appears in the Formula bar, which is located above the worksheet frame.

**Cell reference** The location of a cell in a worksheet identified by its column letter and row number. This is also known as the cell's *address.*

**Scroll** A way to view locations on the worksheet without changing the active cell.

**Sheet tabs** Tabs that appear at the bottom of the workbook window, which display the name of each worksheet.

**Tab scrolling buttons** Buttons that appear just to the left of the sheet tabs, which allow you to scroll hidden tabs into view.

## Notes

### Start Excel

■ Start Excel using the Start menu.

### The Excel Window

■ When the program starts up, the Microsoft Excel window displays an empty **workbook** with three worksheets.

● A **worksheet** contains rows and columns that intersect to form **cells**.

✓ *You may see the New Workbook Task Pane briefly on the right-hand side of the Excel window when you first start the program. You use this Task Pane to create new workbooks and open existing ones. You'll learn more about this Task Pane in Exercise 2.*

■ A black border appears around the **active cell**.

■ The name box, located on the left side of the **Formula bar**, displays the cell reference (also known as the address) of the active cell (its column letter and row number).

*Name box*

Name box        Active /cell        Formula bar

■ To help you identify the **cell reference** for the active cell, Excel highlights its column label (above the worksheet) and row number (to the left of the worksheet).

✓ *Notice, for example, that the active cell shown in the Name box figure is surrounded by a dark outline. The active cell's address or cell reference, A1, appears in the Name box just to the left of the Formula bar. Notice also that the column label A, and the row label 1, are highlighted in blue gray in order to make it easier for you to decipher the address of the current cell.*

■ You can change the active cell using the mouse or the keyboard.

## Excel Menu and Toolbars

■ The menu bar, Standard toolbar, Formatting toolbar, formula bar, and Ask a Question box appear at the top of the workbook window while the status bar appears at the bottom.

■ The Standard and Formatting toolbars share one row but you can use the View, Toolbars, Customize command, Options tab to change this option.

■ The menu bar, toolbars (except for the Formula bar), and the Ask a Question box are similar to those used in Word and are covered in Exercise 1 of the Word section of this text.

*Excel window*

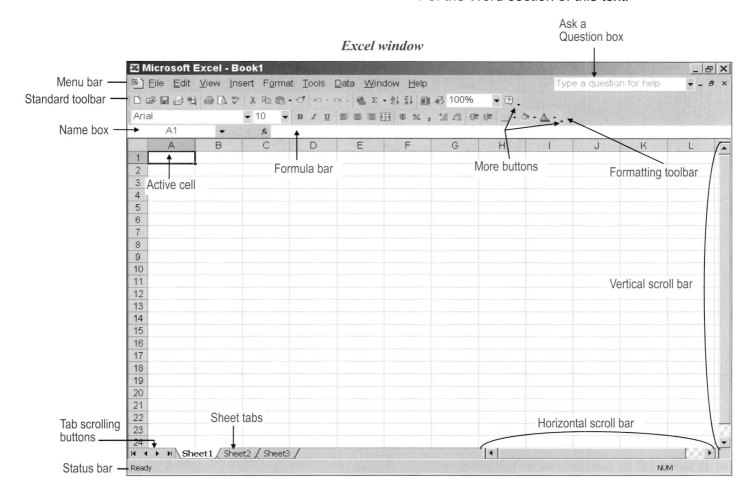

## Explore the Worksheet Using the Mouse and Keyboard

- Since the workbook window displays only a part of a worksheet, you **scroll** through the worksheet to view another location.

- Use the mouse or keyboard to scroll to different locations in a worksheet without changing the active cell.

- With the mouse, you can scroll using the horizontal or vertical scroll bars.

- With the keyboard, you can scroll by pressing specific keys or key combinations.

- There are 256 columns and 65,536 rows available in a worksheet, but you don't need to fill the entire worksheet in order to use it—just type data into the cells you need.

*Active cell in bottom-left corner of worksheet*

*Active cell in bottom-right corner of worksheet*

## Change Between Worksheets

- Normally, each workbook comes with three worksheets. You can add or delete worksheets as needed.

  ✓ *You'll learn how to add and remove worksheets in Exercise 11.*

- You can enter related data on different worksheets within the same workbook.

  ✓ *For example, you can enter January, February, and March sales data on different worksheets within the same workbook.*

- Change between worksheets using the **sheet tabs** located at the bottom of the Excel window.

  ✓ *If a particular worksheet tab is not visible, use the **tab scrolling buttons** to display it.*

## The View Menu

- To view or hide the Formula bar, Status bar, or Task Pane, select or deselect them from the View menu.

  ✓ *When you click the View menu several options are hidden. Wait a few seconds for the menu to expand automatically, or click the arrows at the bottom of the menu.*

- The Toolbar command from the View menu displays a submenu with a list of available toolbars.

*Available toolbars*

- If you need to expand the worksheet to fill the screen, choose Full Screen. The menu bar is still displayed for commands and a Close Full Screen dialog box appears in order to return to the default view.

- The Zoom command magnifies cells in a worksheet by choosing from a list of magnification options or setting a specific zoom percentage from 10%–400%.

  ✓ *You can also change the Zoom by selecting the Zoom level you want from the Zoom button, located on the Standard toolbar.*

*Zoom button on the Standard toolbar*

*Zoom dialog box*

## Exit Excel

- When your worksheet is complete and you want to close the Excel application, use the Exit command from the File menu.

# Procedures

### Start Excel

1. Click **Start** [Start] ... [Ctrl]+[Esc]
2. Select **Programs** ................ [P]
3. Click **Microsoft Excel 2002** .................. [↓], [Enter]

### Change Active Cell Using Keyboard

- One cell right ...................... [→]
- One cell left ........................ [←]
- One cell down .................... [↓]
- One cell up ........................ [↑]
- One screen up ................... [Page Up]
- One screen down ............... [Page Down]
- One screen right ........ [Alt]+[Page Down]
- One screen left .......... [Alt]+[Page Up]
- First cell in current row.... [Home]
- First cell in worksheet ................ [Ctrl]+[Home]
- Last used cell in worksheet .................. [Ctrl]+[End]

### Change Active Cell Using Mouse

- Click desired cell.

### Change Active Cell Using Go To (Ctrl+G)

1. Press **F5** .............................. [F5]
   OR
   a. Click **Edit** .............. [Alt]+[E]
   b. Click **Go To** ................... [G]
   
   ✓ *Go To list box displays last four references that you accessed.*

2. Type cell reference in **Reference** text box.
3. Click **OK** ........................... [Enter]

### Change Active Cell Using Name Box

1. Click in Name box.
2. Type cell reference.
3. Press **Enter** ...................... [Enter]

### Scroll Using Mouse

**To scroll one row up or down:**

- Click up or down scroll arrow, located at the top or bottom of the vertical scroll bar.

**To scroll one column left or right:**

- Click left or right scroll arrow, located at either end of the horizontal scroll bar.

**To scroll one screen right or left:**

- Click horizontal scroll bar to right or left of scroll box.

**To scroll one screen up or down:**

- Click vertical scroll bar above or below scroll box.

**To scroll to beginning rows:**

- Drag vertical scroll box to top of scroll bar.

**To scroll to beginning columns:**

- Drag horizontal scroll box to extreme left of scroll bar.

**To scroll to last row containing data:**

- Press Ctrl and drag vertical scroll box to bottom of scroll bar.

### Change to a Different Worksheet

- Click the tab of the worksheet you want to display.

## Customize View of Standard and Formatting Toolbars

1. Click **View** ................... Alt + V
2. Click **Toolbars** ................... T
   OR
   Right-click on toolbar.
3. Click **Customize** ................. C
4. Click **Options** tab ....... Ctrl + Tab
   ✓ Press Ctrl+Tab until Options page displays.
5. Select **Show Standard and Formatting toolbars on two rows** check box............. Alt + S
   ✓ Removes check mark from option.
6. Click **Close** button
   Close ............................. Enter

## Display or Hide Task Pane

1. Click **View** ................... Alt + V
2. Click **Task Pane** ................. K
   ✓ The New Workbook task pane appears by default. You can scroll to recently displayed task panes by clicking the left or right arrows.

## Display or Hide Formula Bar

1. Click **View** ................... Alt + V
2. Click **Formula Bar** .............. F

## Display or Hide Status Bar

1. Click **View** ................... Alt + V
2. Click **Status Bar**................. S

## Display or Hide Toolbar

1. Click **View** ................... Alt + V
2. Click **Toolbars** ................... T
3. Select toolbar name ............ ↓
4. Click toolbar name ..........Enter

## Set Zoom Percentage

1. Click **View** ................... Alt + V
2. Click **Zoom**......................... Z
3. Set percentage.............. ↓ ↑
4. Click **OK** ..........................Enter

## Set Zoom Percentage with Zoom Button

1. Click arrow on Zoom button.
2. Select Zoom level.
   ✓ You can also type the zoom percentage you want to use in the box on the Zoom button, and press **Enter**.

## Exit Excel

1. Click **File** ................... Alt + F
2. Click **Exit**........................... X
   OR
   Click **Application Close** button X.

# Exercise Directions

1. Follow these steps to start Excel from the taskbar.
   a. Click Start.
   b. Select Programs, Microsoft Excel 2002.
2. Move the active cell pointer to cell A1 using the keyboard:
   a. Press the down arrow key four times until cell A5 is highlighted.
   b. Press the right arrow key twice until cell C5 is highlighted.
   ✓ View the cell references in the name box.
3. Click cell B3 to make it the active cell.
   ✓ View the cell reference in the name box.
4. Point to the horizontal scroll bar and click the right scroll arrow.
   ✓ The worksheet moves right by one column but the active cell does not change.
5. Point to the horizontal scroll bar and click to the left of the scroll box.
   ✓ The worksheet moves left by one screen but the active cell does not change.

6. Point to the horizontal scroll bar, then drag the scroll box all the way to the right.
   ✓ The view of the worksheet has changed again but the active cell does not change.
7. Click the down scroll arrow on the vertical scroll bar.
   ✓ The worksheet moves down two rows but the active cell does not change.
8. Press F5 to activate the Go To command.
9. In the Reference text box, type **M41**.
10. Click OK.
   ✓ The active cell changes to M41.
11. Click in the name box to change the active cell to the following, pressing Enter after each new cell address:
    • M1200 (Row 1200, column M)
    • A65536 (Bottom left of worksheet)
    • IV65536 (Bottom right of worksheet)
    • A1 (Home)
12. Click the tab for Sheet 2 to display it.
13. Click the tab for Sheet 1 to redisplay it.

14. Rest the mouse pointer on each visible button on the Standard and Formatting toolbars until the ScreenTip appears.

   ✓ *A ScreenTip appears under the button with the name of the button.*

15. Click the More Buttons button next to the Microsoft Excel Help button, located on the Standard toolbar.

   ✓ *The More Buttons menu appears, displaying the hidden buttons from both toolbars.*

16. Point to the Zoom button and click its down arrow.

   ✓ *The Zoom menu appears.*

17. Select 200% from the Zoom menu.

   ✓ *The Zoom changes to 200%, so cells appear much larger. Also, the Zoom button is added to the Standard toolbar.*

18. Select View, Zoom to display the Zoom dialog box.

19. Select 100%, then click OK.

   ✓ *Cells are restored to their normal size as you return to 100% magnification.*

20. Click View, Status Bar to remove the Status bar from the screen.

21. Click View, Status Bar to restore the Status bar to the screen.

22. Click View, Toolbars, Drawing to display the Drawing toolbar.

23. Right-click the Drawing toolbar and select Drawing from the menu that appears to remove the Drawing toolbar.

24. Click the Close button ☒ to exit Excel.

# On Your Own

1. Use the New Office Document command on the Start menu to start Excel and create a new workbook document.

2. Click cell G7.

   ✓ *View the cell reference in the name box.*

3. Move the active cell pointer to cell D21 using the keyboard.

4. Click below the scroll box in the vertical scroll bar.

   ✓ *The worksheet moves down one screen but the active cell does not change.*

5. Drag the scroll box all the way to the top of the vertical scroll bar.

   ✓ *The view of the worksheet changes but the active cell does not change.*

6. Use the horizontal scroll bar to scroll one screen to the right.

7. Use the horizontal scroll bar to scroll one screen to the left.

8. Change to Sheet 3.

9. Use the Go To command to make V20 the active cell.

10. Use the Name box to make AA1000 the active cell.

11. Make A1 the active cell.

12. Return to Sheet 1.

13. Display the Standard and Formatting toolbars in two rows.

14. Hide the Formula bar.

15. Redisplay the Formula bar.

16. Change the View, Toolbar, Customize options so that the Standard and Formatting toolbars will once again appear on the same row.

17. Change the Zoom percentage to 155%.

18. Return the Zoom percentage to 100%.

19. Exit Excel without saving the current workbook document.

# Exercise 2

## Skills Covered:

◆ **Create a New (Blank) Workbook**
◆ **Create a Workbook from a Template**
◆ **Enter Labels** ◆ **Make Simple Corrections** ◆ **Undo and Redo**
◆ **Delete (Clear) Cell Contents** ◆ **Save a Workbook**
◆ **Document Recovery** ◆ **Close a Workbook**

## On the Job

To create your first worksheet, you begin by entering the column and row titles (labels) for a report. Next, you enter the numeric data, using the row and column labels to help you enter each amount into the correct cell. As you enter data, you may make a few mistakes and then find out how easy it is to correct them. Finally, you save your workbook before exiting Excel so that the entries are not lost.

You are an invoice clerk for California Cardiology, Inc., and it is your job to send overdue notices to insurance companies that have not made payments on their patients' behalf. You'll create a report that lists overdue amounts for the Healthcare HMO and then complete the report in a later exercise.

## Terms

**Blank workbook** The Excel default workbook contains three worksheet tabs or sheets.

**Template** A workbook with certain labels, formulas, and formatting preset, saving you time in creating commonly used forms, such as invoices or purchase orders.

**Label** Text in the first row or column of a spreadsheet that identifies the type of data contained there.

**Defaults** The standard settings Excel uses in its software, such as column width or number of pages in a workbook.

**Undo** The command used to reverse one or a series of editing actions.

**Redo** The command used to redo an action you have undone.

## Notes

### Create a New (Blank) Workbook

- Excel displays a **blank workbook** when you open the Excel application.
- A blank workbook initially contains three blank worksheets into which you can enter data.
- When you need to create a new, blank workbook, click the New button on the Standard toolbar, or select that option from the New Workbook task pane.

*Create new workbooks using the Task Pane*

```
New
  [] Blank Workbook
New from existing workbook
  [] Choose workbook...
New from template
     Timecard
     Sales Invoice
  [] General Templates...
  [] Templates on my Web Sites...
  [] Templates on Microsoft.com
```

## Create a Workbook from a Template

■ To save time when creating a new workbook from scratch, select an Excel **template** from the New Workbook Task Pane.

■ Excel provides a small number of templates for use in creating common forms, such as balance sheets, sales invoices, expense statements, and time cards. There's even a template for comparing loans.

   ✓ *If a template for the type of report you want to create is not available, you can base your new workbook on a copy of an existing workbook by selecting that option from the Task Pane. You can also go on the Internet and select a template from Microsoft's Web site by clicking **Templates on Microsoft.com**.*

■ When you select a template for a new workbook, a lot of the work is already done for you, including most of the formatting, formulas, and layout design.

■ After the new workbook is created from the template, simply enter your data.

   ✓ *For example, enter your company's name and address where indicated, then type the actual data for the report (such as the individual items you want to appear on an invoice).*

## Enter Labels

■ The first character entered into a cell determines the status of a cell.

■ If you enter an alphabetical character or a symbol (` ~! # % ^ & *( ) _ \ | { } ; : ' " < > ,?) as the first character in a cell, you are entering a **label**.

■ A label generally represents text data, such as the labels: Blue, Sally Smith, Ohio, or Above Average.

■ The **default** width of each cell is 8.43 characters wide in the standard font (Arial, 10 point); therefore, a label longer than the cell width will display fully only if the cell to the right is blank, or if the column is made wider to accommodate the long entry.

■ Excel supports up to 32,000 characters in a cell entry.

■ As you type a label into a cell, it appears in the cell and the Formula bar.

■ To enter the label in the cell, type the text, and then do any of the following to finalize the entry: press the Enter key, an arrow key, or the Tab key, click another cell, or click the Enter button (the green check mark) on the Formula bar.

■ A label automatically aligns to the left of the cell, making it a left-justified entry.

*Entry in cell and Formula bar*

## Make Simple Corrections

■ As you type data into a cell, if you notice a mistake before you press Enter (or any of the other keys that finalize an entry), you can press the Backspace key to erase characters to the left of the insertion point.

■ Before you finalize an entry, you can press the Escape key or click the Cancel button (the red X) on the Formula bar to cancel it.

■ After you enter data, you can make the cell active (by clicking it, pressing an arrow key, etc.) and then type a new entry to replace the old one.

■ You can also double-click a cell in which the entry has been finalized to enable cell editing and then make changes to only part of the entry.

## Undo and Redo

■ Use the **Undo** command from the Edit menu or the Undo button on the Standard toolbar to reverse any editing action.

■ With the Undo command, you can reverse up to 16 previous editing actions.

■ The Undo command names the last editing action to be reversed.

■ You can also redo (reinstate any action you've undone in error) up to 16 reversed actions using the **Redo** command.

## Delete (Clear) Cell Contents

■ Press the Escape key or click the Cancel box on the Formula bar to clear a cell's contents before finalizing any cell entry.

■ To erase a single cell entry or a range of cell entries after you enter data, use the Clear, Contents command from the Edit menu or the Delete key on the keyboard.

## Save a Workbook

- After entering data into a workbook, you must save it, or that data will be lost when you exit Excel.

- A workbook may be saved on a hard drive or a removable disk for future use. A saved workbook is referred to as a file.

- You must provide a name for the file when you save it. File names should be descriptive, with a limit of 255 characters for the name, drive, and path.

- A file name may contain letters, numbers, and spaces, but not \ / : * ? " < > or | .

- Excel automatically adds a period and a file type extension (usually .xls) to the end of a file name when you save it.

*Save As command*

- Workbooks are saved in the My Documents folder by default, although you may select another location if you like. You can even create new folders in which to store your workbooks.

- Data can also be saved in other formats, such as Lotus 1-2-3 or older versions of Excel.

  ✓ *You might want to save data in a different format in order to share that data with someone who uses a different version of Excel, or a different spreadsheet program, such as Lotus 1-2-3.*

- Once you've saved a workbook, you need only click the Save button to resave any changes made since the last save action. You will not need to reenter the file name.

## Document Recovery

- Even after saving your workbook data in a file, you must periodically resave it in order to avoid accidental loss of new data you are entering in an open workbook.

- You can lose changes that you have not yet saved if Excel locks up for some reason (refuses to respond), or you suddenly lose power.

- To avoid accidental loss of data, click the Save button periodically to resave new changes.

- If you forget to resave a workbook, your data may not be lost if Excel has saved it for you using its AutoRecovery feature.

- By default, AutoRecovery automatically saves changes made to a file every 10 minutes. You can have AutoRecovery save changes more often or turn it off completely if you want.

*Document Recovery Task Pane*

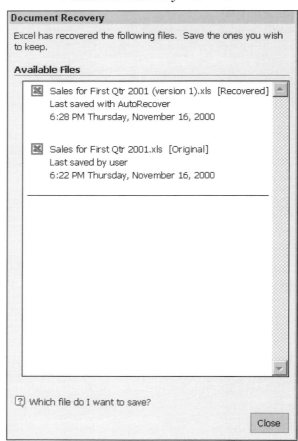

- If AutoRecovery is on and Excel is restarted after a power loss or program crash, the Document Recovery task pane will automatically appear.

- Manually saved workbooks are listed as [Original], while versions created by AutoRecovery are listed as [Recovered].

- Use the Document Recovery Task Pane to view each version of a workbook and to select the version you want to save.

  ✓ *AutoRecovery is not a perfect process, so don't be tempted to select that version of a workbook after a crash. Review each version listed and select the one that contains the most complete version of your document. To avoid critical data loss, your best bet is to manually save open workbooks as often as you can.*

## Close a Workbook

- Save a workbook before you close it or you will lose the current data or updated entries that you made.

- If you attempt to close a workbook or close Excel before saving, you will be prompted to save the changes.

- If you have more than one file open, Excel allows you to close and save all of the files before you exit the program.

# Procedures

### Create a New, Blank Workbook (Ctrl+N)

- Click **New** button [ ].

OR

1. Click **File** ..................... Alt + F
2. Click **New** ............................. N
3. Click **Blank Workbook** in the New Workbook Task Pane.

### Create a New Workbook from a Template

1. Click **File** ..................... Alt + F
2. Click **New** ............................. N
3. Click **General Templates**.

   ✓ *If you have a connection to the Internet, you can download additional templates from Microsoft's Web site by clicking Templates on Microsoft.com.*

4. Click the **Spreadsheet Solutions** tab .............. Ctrl + Tab
5. Double-click the desired template.

   ✓ *Some of these templates may not be installed, in which case, you'll need to insert the Office CD-ROM when prompted.*

### Enter Labels

1. Click cell for data entry. ..... [ ]
2. Type label text.
3. Press **Enter** ..................... Enter
   OR

   Press any arrow key to enter label and move to next cell.

OR

Click **Enter** button ✓ on Formula bar.

### Correct Data while Typing

1. Type character(s) in cell.
2. Press **Backspace** key .. Backspace to erase characters to left of insertion point.

### To cancel all characters while typing:

- Press **Escape** key ............. Esc
OR
- Click **Cancel** button ✕ on Formula bar.

### Replace Cell Contents in Typeover Mode

1. Click cell with data to be replaced.
2. Type new data.

### Enable Cell Editing

1. Select cell.
2. Click in Formula bar.
   OR
   Double-click cell.
3. Make correction.
4. Press **Enter** ..................... Enter

   ✓ *To replace an entry with something else, simply select the cell and type the new entry.*

### Undo Last Action (Ctrl+Z)

- Click **Undo** button [ ].
OR

1. Click **Edit** ..................... Alt + E
2. Click **Undo** action name ...... U

### Redo Last Reversed Action (Ctrl+Z)

- Click **Redo** button [ ].
OR
1. Click **Edit** ..................... Alt + E
2. Click **Redo** action name ...... R

### Undo Multiple Actions

1. Click **Undo** arrow [ ].
2. Drag through actions to undo, and then click.

   ✓ *You can only undo consecutive actions, beginning with the action at the top of the list.*

### Delete (Clear) Cell Contents

1. Select desired cell(s).
2. Press **Delete** key............... Del
   OR
   a. Click **Edit** .............. Alt + E
   b. Click **Clear** ..................... A
   c. Click **Contents** .............. C

### Save Workbook (Ctrl+S)

1. Click **File** ..................... Alt + F
2. Click **Save** ........................... S
OR

- Click **Save** button [ ].
3. Type name in **File name** text box......................... Alt + N

4. Click **Save** **in**
   drop-down arrow.......... `Alt`+`I`

5. Select drive and folder in which to save workbook.

   ✓ *You can skip steps 4 and 5 and click a folder on the Places bar, such as My Documents.*

6. Click **Save** ...................... `Enter`

   ✓ *To save the workbook in a different file format such as Lotus 1-2-3, select that format from the **Save as type** list before you click Save.*

## Recover a Workbook

✓ *After a program crash, or power outage, the Document Recovery Task Pane automatically appears.*

1. In the Document Recovery Task Pane, click the entry for any version of the workbook you're looking to recover.

   ✓ *The contents of that version of the workbook appears.*

2. Select another version of the same workbook to view it.

3. Once you've decided on the version you wish to keep, close all other versions of the workbook (if open).

4. In the Document Recovery list, point to the entry for the workbook version you want to save.

   ✓ *An outline surrounds the entry you point to, and a drop-down list arrow appears to the right.*

5. Click the arrow on the drop-down list and select **Save As**.............................. `S`

6. If needed, change the file name to match the workbook's original file name.

   ✓ *If you selected one of the [Recovered] versions of the workbook, the file name will not be the same as the original file name, so you'll need to edit it slightly to make it match.*

7. Click **Save** ...................... `Enter`

8. Click **Yes** to save changes.. `Y`

### Close Workbook

1. Click **File** ..................... `Alt`+`F`

2. Click **Close** ........................ `C`

3. Click **Yes** to save changes.. `Y`
   OR
   Click **No** to cancel changes... `N`

### Exit Excel and Save Files

1. Click **File** ..................... `Alt`+`F`

2. Click **Exit** ........................ `X`

3. Click **Yes to All** to save all changes ......................... `A`
   OR
   Click **No** to exit without saving changes .................. `N`

# Exercise Directions

1. Start Excel, if necessary.

2. Save the file as **OVERDUE**.

3. Using the arrow keys, or by clicking, move the active cell pointer to cell B3.

4. Type **California Cardiology, Inc.** and press Enter.

5. Go to cell B5.

6. Type **Healthcare HMO**, but do *not* press Enter.

7. Press Backspace to erase characters as needed, and change the entry to read, **Healthman HMO**, and then click the Enter button on the Formula bar.

   ✓ *The Cancel and Enter buttons are to the left of the formula bar.*

8. Go to cell B7.

9. Type **Invoice Number**, but instead of pressing Enter, cancel the entry by clicking the Cancel box or pressing the Escape key.

10. Type **Patient** in cell B7 instead.

11. Enter the rest of the data as shown in Illustration A.

12. Correct any errors using Backspace, or if the entry has been finalized, by retyping it. You can also try in-cell editing if you like, by double-clicking a cell and editing its contents.

13. Go to cell B11.

14. Erase the entry by pressing Delete.

15. Undo the erasure by clicking Undo, and the entry reappears.

16. Click Redo to redo the erasure so that cell B11 is empty.

17. Close the file and exit Excel, saving all changes.

*Illustration A*

| | A | B | C | D | E |
|---|---|---|---|---|---|
| 1 | | | | | |
| 2 | | | | | |
| 3 | | California Cardiology, Inc. | | | |
| 4 | | | | | |
| 5 | | Healthman HMO | | | |
| 6 | | | | | |
| 7 | | Patient | Amount | Invoice Number | |
| 8 | | J. Thomas Wilson | | | |
| 9 | | Carlos Riveria | | | |
| 10 | | Alice Thomson | | | |
| 11 | | Ricky Valdez | | | |
| 12 | | | | | |

# On Your Own

1. Create a new workbook using the template Timecard.

   ✓ *After you select the General Templates link in the New Workbook Task Pane, the Templates dialog box is displayed. You'll find the Time Card template on the Spreadsheet Solutions tab.*

2. Save the file as **OXL02**.

3. Enter your information in the Employee section.

   ✓ *Your employee number is 12345, and you're an Invoice Clerk working in the Accounting Department under Ms. Shaledra Gamble.*

4. The pay period begins 5/8/01 and ends 5/14/01.

5. Enter your hours on different rows, as shown.

6. Save the changes, close the file, and exit Excel.

*Illustration B*

| Account Description | Account Code | M | T | W | Th | F |
|---|---|---|---|---|---|---|
| Regular Hours | REG | 8.00 | 8.00 | 8.00 | | |
| Sick Time | SICK | | | | 8.00 | |
| Holiday | HOL | | | | | 8.00 |

# Exercise 3

◆ **Open Files** ◆ **Change from Workbook to Workbook**
◆ **Arrange Workbooks** ◆ **AutoComplete** ◆ **Pick From List**
◆ **AutoCorrect** ◆ **Spell Check**

## On the Job

When you've saved and closed a workbook, if you need to view it again or make changes, you must open it first. After opening several workbooks, you may want to arrange them on-screen so you can view their contents at the same time. When entering data, take advantage of the many time-saving features Excel offers: Excel's AutoComplete feature, for example, automatically completes certain entries based on previous entries that you've made. AutoCorrect automatically corrects common spelling errors as you type, while the spelling checker checks your worksheet for any additional errors.

You're a marketing manager for a mid-sized advertising and PR firm, and you've recently been assigned the Penguin Play Sets account. To increase public awareness of these high quality play sets, you've decided to arrange for a series of demonstrations at various children's shows, home shows, and festivals. In this exercise, you'll use Excel to create a worksheet that tracks upcoming demos.

## Terms

**AutoComplete** A feature used to complete an entry based on previous entries made in the column containing the active cell.

**Pick From List** A shortcut used to insert repeated information.

**AutoCorrect** A feature used to automate the correction of common typing errors.

**Spelling checker** A tool used to assist you in finding and correcting typographical or spelling errors.

## Notes

### Open Files

- When you have saved and closed a workbook you can open it from the same drive, folder, and file name you used during the save process.

- In the Open dialog box, click the Look in text box arrow to display a drop-down list with the drives or folders.

- If the location of the workbook is shown on the Places bar, click its icon to display that location's contents.

✓ *You can customize the Places bar with buttons that point to the folders you use often, making it easier to open and save files to them.*

- Click the Views button in the Open dialog box to preview a file, change the list to display file details, or display the properties of a file.

- You can access a recently used file more quickly by clicking its file name from the list displayed at the top of the New Workbook Task Pane, or at the bottom of the File menu.

- A newly opened workbook becomes the active workbook and hides any other open workbook.

*Workbooks listed on the New Workbook Task Pane*

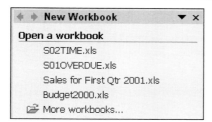

- You can arrange workbooks in four ways:
  - Tiled: arranges windows in small, even rectangles to fill the screen.
  - Horizontal: arranges windows one on top of the other.
  - Vertical: arranges windows side by side.
  - Cascade: creates a stack of windows with only the title bar in view.

*Arrange Windows dialog box*

Places bar          *Open dialog box*

## Change from Workbook to Workbook

- When more than one workbook is open, use the Window menu to change to a different workbook by selecting it from the displayed list of names.

*Window menu displays list of open files*

- You can also change between workbooks by clicking a workbook's button on the Windows taskbar.

*Windows taskbar*

## Arrange Workbooks

- Arrange workbooks on-screen if you want to view their contents simultaneously.

## AutoComplete

- When you need to repeat a label that has already been typed in the same column, the **AutoComplete** feature allows you to enter the label automatically.

*AutoComplete a label entry*

## Pick From List

- If several labels are entered in a list and the next items to be typed are repeated information, click the right mouse button to display the **Pick From List** command on the shortcut menu.

*List of labels for next entry in column*

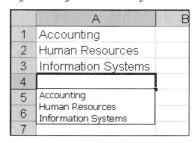

✓ *The cells in the list and the cell to be typed must be contiguous and in the same column.*

## AutoCorrect

- If you type a word incorrectly and it is in the **AutoCorrect** list, Excel automatically changes the word as you type.

- You can add words to the AutoCorrect list that you often type incorrectly.

- AutoCorrect automatically capitalizes the first letter of a sentence and names of days of the week, corrects incorrectly capitalized letters in the first two positions in a word, and undoes accidental use of the Caps Lock key.

- When certain autocorrections are made, you're given an option to remove the corrections by clicking the arrow on the AutoCorrect button that appears, and selecting the action you want to take.

*AutoCorrect Button*

*AutoCorrect dialog box*

## Spell Check

- To check the spelling of text in a worksheet and obtain replacement word suggestions, use the **spelling checker** feature.

# Procedures

## Open Recent Workbook

1. Click **File**...................... Alt + F
2. Click the workbook you want to open from the list at the bottom of the menu.

## Open Workbook *(Ctrl+O)*

1. Click **Open** button ⎙.
   OR
   a. Click **View** .............. Alt + V
   b. Click **Task Pane**............. K
   c. Click the workbook you want to open, or if it is not listed in the task pane, click **More Workbooks**.
2. If the workbook you want to open is not listed in the current folder, perform one of the following:
   a. Click **Look in**.......... Alt + I
   b. Select desired drive................. ↑↓ , Enter

   OR
   Double-click folder name .............. Tab , ↑↓ , Enter
   OR
   Click the appropriate button on the Places bar.
3. Click the file you want to open.
4. Click **Open** ...................... Enter

## Change to Different Open Workbook

1. Click **Window**.............. Alt + W
2. Click workbook name in list at bottom of menu ...... ↑↓ , Enter
   OR
   - Click anywhere in open workbook window.
   OR
   - Click workbook's button on Window's taskbar.

## Arrange Open Workbooks

1. Click **Window**.............. Alt + W
2. Click **Arrange**...................... A

3. Select from four options:
   - **Tiled**...................... Alt + T
   - **Horizontal**............. Alt + O
   - **Vertical** .................. Alt + V
   - **Cascade** ................ Alt + C
4. Click **OK** ......................... Enter

## AutoComplete

1. Type part of label.
   ✓ *Repetitive text is highlighted as you type label.*
2. Press **Enter**...................... Enter
   ✓ *Just continue typing if you do not want to repeat label.*

## Pick From List

1. Right-click cell to receive entry.
2. Click **Pick From List**........... K
3. Click desired text.

## Create AutoCorrect Replacement

1. Click **Tools** ................. `Alt`+`T`
2. Click **AutoCorrect Options** ........................... `A`
3. Click **Replace** ............. `Alt`+`R`
4. Type misspelled word.
5. Click **With** ................... `Alt`+`W`
6. Type replacement characters.
7. Click **Add** ............................ `A`
8. Click **OK** ......................... `Enter`

## Check Spelling *(F7)*

1. Select a cell.
   - ✓ *If you don't start the spell check from the beginning of the worksheet, Excel completes the spell check then displays "Do you want to continue checking at the beginning of the sheet?"*

2. Click **Spelling** button `ABC✓`.
   OR
   a. Click **Tools** ............. `Alt`+`T`
   b. Click **Spelling** ............... `S`

3. To change the spelling of a word:
   - Click correctly spelled word in **Suggestions** list .......................... `Alt`+`N`
   OR
   - Change the misspelled word manually in the **Not in Dictionary:** text box ................. `Alt`+`D`

4. Select an option:
   - Click **Change** ......... `Alt`+`C`

   - Click **Change All** to change the word everywhere in document ............... `Alt`+`L`
   - Click **Ignore Once** to continue without changing word ...................... `Alt`+`I`
   - Click **Ignore All** to continue without changing word and without highlighting it anywhere else in document.... `Alt`+`G`
   - Click **Add to Dictionary** to add word to dictionary .............. `Alt`+`A`

5. Repeat steps 3 and 4 for every misspelled word.
6. Click **OK** when Excel completes check. ............ `Enter`

# Exercise Directions

1. Start Excel, if necessary.
2. Open ⊙ **03DEMOS**.
3. Save the file as **DEMOS**.
4. Open ⊙ **03PLAYSETS**.
5. Using the Windows, Arrange command, arrange the two workbooks on-screen in a tiled fashion.
6. Arrange the workbooks again, this time horizontally.
7. Click within the window of the **DEMOS** workbook to activate it.
   - ✓ *Notice that the title bar of the active workbook's window is dark blue, while the inactive workbook's title bar is gray.*
8. Maximize the **DEMOS** workbook.
   - ✓ *The 03PLAYSETS workbook is no longer visible.*
9. Change to the **03PLAYSETS** workbook by clicking its button on the taskbar.
10. Close **03PLAYSETS**.

11. Double-click cell E10 to enable cell editing, then type **(r)** at the end of the entry, after **Princess Playhouse**.
    - ✓ *After you press Enter to finalize the entry, notice that AutoCorrect has changed Princess Playhouse (r) to Princess Playhouse®.*
12. Type the data as shown in Illustration A.
    a. As you type the names of the play sets for Haywood and Lyton, use the AutoComplete feature to speed up the process.
    b. Use the Pick From List feature to enter the play sets for Claymore.
13. Click cell B3.
14. Use the spelling checker to check your worksheet.
    a. At the first error, select **play sets** from the Suggestions list, then click Change All to change playsets to play sets throughout.
    b. Click Ignore All to ignore the error for Lyton.
    c. Click Yes to continue the spell check at the beginning of the worksheet.
15. Close the **DEMOS** workbook, saving all changes.

*Illustration A*

| Date | Event | City | Playsets We'll Demo |
|---|---|---|---|
| 7/14/2001 | Kids Day | Chicago | Mountain Climber ® |
| | | | King of the Hill ® |
| | | | Princess Playhouse ® |
| 7/21/2001 | Haywood Home Show | Haywood | King of the Hill ® |
| | | | King's Castle ® |
| 7/21/2001 | Children's Fair | Lyton | Mountain Climber ® |
| | | | Princess Playhouse ® |
| 7/21/2001 | Claymore Kids Carnival | Claymore | King of the Hill ® |
| | | | Princess Playhouse ® |
| | | | Mountain Climber ® |
| | | | King's Castle ® |

# On Your Own

1. Start Excel, if necessary.

2. Open ✪ **03TEACHERS**.

3. Start a new workbook, and save the file as **OXL03**.

   ✓ *Here you'll create a report to track homework assignments. You'll start by entering information about each assignment—in later lessons, you'll add the dates when the assignments are due and make other adjustments.*

4. Type a title for the report in row 2.

5. Label column A: **ASSIGNMENTS**.

6. Label column C: **SUBJECT**.

7. Label column E: **ASSIGNED BY**.

8. In column A, type a list of assignments, such as a book report, term paper, chapters to read, or a topic report (such as a report on China).

9. In column C, type the name of the class in which the assignment was given. If you repeat names, use AutoComplete and Pick From List to complete the entries.

10. Arrange the two open workbooks vertically.

11. Using the list of teachers in **03TEACHERS**, type the name of the teacher who assigned each homework assignment.

12. Close **03TEACHERS** and maximize the **OXL03** window.

13. Type your school's Web address in cell G2, like this: **www.coolschool.org**.

    ✓ *If your school doesn't have a Web site, make up an appropriate Web address.*

    ✓ *Notice that AutoCorrect automatically creates a hyperlink from the entry by underlining it and making it blue. If you click this link, Internet Explorer starts, and displays the Web address. You don't want this to happen, so you'll change the link back into ordinary text.*

14. Revert the Web address back to simple text by moving the active cell pointer to cell F2 (use the arrow keys and do not click the cell). Click the AutoCorrect button that appears in the left-hand corner of the cell when you point to it, and select the Undo Hyperlink option.

15. Spell check the workbook.

16. Close the workbook, saving all changes.

# Exercise 4

## On the Job

Because Excel allows you to work with numbers so easily, numeric values are one of the most common Excel entry types. After typing numbers and labels into a worksheet, you can improve its appearance by changing the alignment of data and the widths of columns. If entering a series of labels (such as Monday, Tuesday, Wednesday) or values (such as 1, 2, 3), use Excel's AutoFill feature to save data-entry time and reduce errors.

As the invoice clerk for California Cardiology, Inc., you started a report that listed overdue amounts for the Healthman HMO. In this exercise, you'll add invoice numbers, dates, and amounts to the report.

## Terms

**Value** A number entered in the worksheet.

**Numeric label** A number entered in the worksheet as a label, not as a value—such as the year 2002 used as a column label.

**Label prefix** An apostrophe (') used to indicate that a number is really a label and not a value.

**Series** A list of sequential numbers, dates, times, or text.

**Standard column width** The default number of characters that display in a column based on the default font.

## Notes

### Numeric Labels and Values

■ A cell contains a **value** when its first character begins with either a number or one of the following symbols (+, −, =, $).

■ Type the value, and then do one of the following to enter it into the cell:

• Press the Enter key.

• Press an arrow key.

• Click the Enter box on the Formula bar.

• Click another cell.

■ If you enter a value that contains more than 11 digits into a cell that uses the default format, Excel will display the number in scientific notation.

✓ *For example, the entry 123,456,789,012 is displayed as 1.234567E11.*

✓ *To display the number in a different format, apply the number format you want to use, as explained in Exercise 8.*

■ If you see pound signs displayed in a cell instead of a number, simply widen the column to display the value.

✓ *If a number is displayed in scientific notation, widen the column and apply a different format to the cell as explained in Exercise 8.*

- A **numeric label**, such as a Social Security number, is a number that will not be used in calculation.

- Begin the entry of a numeric label with an apostrophe (') as a **label prefix** to indicate that the number should be treated as a label (text) and not as a value.

- Although the label prefix (') is shown on the Formula bar, it is not displayed on the worksheet or printed.

- When you enter a value with an apostrophe, Excel displays a green triangle in the upper left-hand corner of the cell. Select the cell again, and an error button appears. Click the button and confirm that the number is really a label (Ignore Error), or that the value was entered in error and should be treated as a number (Convert to Number).

*Error button appears after you enter a numeric label*

| | A | B | C | D | E |
|---|---|---|---|---|---|
| 1 | Text | | Error button | | |
| 2 | 1200 | | | | |
| 3 | 2001 | ◇ ▾ | | | |
| 4 | | Number Stored as Text | | | |
| 5 | | Convert to Number | | | |
| 6 | | Help on this error | | | |
| 7 | | | | | |
| 8 | | Ignore Error | | | |
| 9 | | Edit in Formula Bar | | | |
| 10 | | Error Checking Options... | | | |
| 11 | | Show Formula Auditing Toolbar | | | |
| 12 | | | | | |

## Enter Dates

- You can enter a date using one of these date formats:
  - mm/dd/yy, as in 1/14/02 or 01/14/02
  - mm/dd, as in 3/14
  - dd-mmm-yy, as in 14-Jan-02
  - dd-mmm, as in 14-Jan
    - ✓ *The current year is assumed.*
  - mmm-yy, as in Jan-02
    - ✓ *The first day of the month is assumed.*

- After entering a date, you can change its display to suit your needs.
  - ✓ *For example, you can change the date 1/14/02 to display as January 14, 2002.*

- To enter time, follow a number with **a** or **p** to indicate AM or PM, like this:

  **10:43 p**

- You can enter a date and time in the same cell, like this:

  **10/16/99 2:31 p**

## Create a Series

- A series is a sequence of numbers (such as 1, 2, 3), dates (such as 10/21/02, 10/22/02, 10/23/02), times (such as 2:30, 2:45, 3:00) or text (such as January, February, March).

- To enter a series based on the active cell, drag the fill handle, a small square in lower-right corner of the active cell that turns into a plus sign (+), over the range of cells you want to fill with the series.
  - ✓ *For example, type January into a cell, then drag the fill handle down or to the left to create the series January, February, March, and so on.*

*Drag the fill handle of the active cell to create a series*

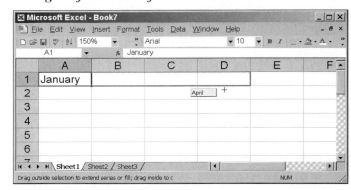

  - ✓ *A SmartTag appears under the mouse pointer, displaying the values of the series you're creating. The series values appear in the cells after you release the mouse button.*

- To create an incremental series (i.e., 1, 3, 5, 7), enter the data for the first and second cells of a series, select the two cells, then drag the fill handle for the selection over the range of cells to fill.

- You can also use the fill handle to copy formatting (such as bold, italics, and so on) from one cell to adjacent cells, and not its value.

## Data Alignment

■ When a label is typed in a cell, it automatically aligns to the left of the cell. Values are automatically right aligned.

■ To improve the appearance of a worksheet, you can change the alignment of column labels, row labels, and other data.

### *Example of how data is aligned in cells*

|   | A | B |
|---|------|----------------------------------------------------|
| 1 | Text | Text is aligned to the left |
| 2 | 1200 | Values are aligned to the right |
| 3 | 2001 | Numeric labels entered with an apostrophe are aligned left |

■ To align data, use the alignment buttons on the Formatting toolbar or choose other alignment options through the Format Cells dialog box.

### *Format Cells dialog box*

### *Alignment buttons on Formatting toolbar*

■ To center a label across the columns use the Merge and Center button on the Formatting toolbar.

✓ You most often use this option to center a worksheet title within a range of cells. The Merge and Center button actually merges the selected cells into one large cell and then centers the data in the newly merged cell.

✓ To get Merge and Center to work properly, enter the data into the first cell in a range, then select adjacent cells to the right.

## Change Column Width

■ The default Excel workbook is set for a **standard column width** (80 pixels or 8.43 characters in the standard font of Arial, 10 point).

■ You can change (widen or narrow) the column widths individually so that text or values fit the longest entry or be arranged more neatly on the page.

■ Changing column width changes the width of an entire column or a group of columns—not the width of a single cell.

■ You can quickly adjust a column to fit the longest entry in that column, or you can set the column to any width you like.

■ You can also shrink text to fit in a cell (the Shrink to fit option on the Alignment tab of the Format Cells dialog box), regardless of its width. (The text size readjusts automatically if the column width is changed.)

# Procedures

### Enter Numeric Label

✓ A number entered as a numeric label is left aligned and cannot be calculated.

1. Select cell............................
2. Type **apostrophe**................ 
3. Type number.
4. Press **Enter**....................... Enter

✓ If a green triangle appears in a the cell, select it again to display the error button, then click its down arrow and select the option **Ignore Error** from its list.

✓ You can select multiple cells prior to choosing Ignore Error.

### Enter Value

✓ A number entered as a value is right-aligned and can be calculated.

1. Select cell........................... 
2. Type number.
   ✓ Start the entry with a number from zero to nine, a decimal point, or a dollar sign ($). Enclose a negative number in parentheses() or precede it with a minus sign (-).

3. Press **Enter** .....................
   - ✓ *If Excel displays pound signs (######), the column needs to be widened. Double-click the right border of the column heading to display the value.*

## Create a Series Using Mouse

1. Enter the value to copy in active cell.
2. Select the cell, and then point to its fill handle.
   - ✓ *The mouse changes to* **+**.
3. Drag the fill handle down, up, left, or right to copy the value.
4. Click arrow on AutoFill button and select an option:
   - ✓ *If you don't select an option from the AutoFill button, then the range is filled with a series as explained below. Also, the button disappears after you enter data into any other cell.*
   - ✓ *You can select multiple cells at once, and choose the same option for all of them.*
   - **Copy Cells**
     - ✓ *Copies the contents of the first cell into the fill range.*
   - **Fill Series**
     - ✓ *Increases the value in the first cell by one to fill each cell in the fill range.*
   - **Copy Formatting Only**
     - ✓ *Copies the formatting of the first cell, but not its value.*
   - **Fill Without Formatting**
     - ✓ *Same as Fill Series option, but this does not copy the formatting of the first cell to the cells in the fill range.*
   - **Fill Days**
     - ✓ *Fills cells in the range with dates one day apart.*
   - **Fill Weekdays**
     - ✓ *Fills cells in the range with dates one day apart, skipping over dates that fall on weekends.*
   - **Fill Months**
     - ✓ *Fills cells in the range with dates one month apart.*
   - **Fill Years**
     - ✓ *Fills cells in the range with dates one year apart.*

## Create an Incremental Series Using Mouse

1. Enter first and second data in adjacent cells.
   - ✓ *The text can be numbers, dates, or times, such as 2:45 and 3:00.*
2. Select the two cells containing series data.
3. Point to fill handle.
4. Drag fill handle down, up, left, or right.
   - ✓ *Using the two cells as a sample, cells in the range are filled with values that increase or decrease by that same amount.*
   - ✓ *If desired, click the arrow on the AutoFill button that appears and select an option as explained in the previous procedure. However, if you select any of the date options, the dates in the fill range will still be incremented based on the two sample cells.*

## Align Entry Using Formatting Toolbar

1. Select cell(s) containing label(s)...............................
2. Click **Align Left** button .
   OR
   Click **Center** button .
   OR
   Click **Align Right** button ▤.

## Merge and Center Entry Using Formatting Toolbar

1. Drag across the cell with entry and adjacent cells to select them.
2. Click **Merge and Center** button ▦.
   - ✓ *Data is centered within the selected range. If you want, you can left- or right-align data within the merged cell by clicking the Align Left or Align Right buttons on the Formatting toolbar.*
   - ✓ *To unmerge the cells (and create separate cells again), click the **Merge and Center** button to turn it off.*

## Align Labels Using Format Cells Dialog Box

1. Select cell(s) containing label(s)............................... ↨
2. Click **Format** .............. Alt + O
3. Click **Cells** .......................... E
4. Click **Alignment** tab .... Ctrl + Tab
5. Click **Horizontal** ......... Alt + H
6. Click **Left (Indent)** ..... L, Enter
   OR
   Click **Center** .............. C, Enter
   OR
   Click **Right** ................ R, Enter
   - ✓ *You can also select two lesser used options: **Fill** (repeats data in cell to fill cell completely, regardless of its width) or **Justify** (adds spaces between characters as needed to fill the cell completely).*
7. Click **OK** ..........................

## Change Column Width Using Menu

1. Select any cell in column to change.
2. Click **Format** .............. Alt + O
3. Click **Column** ..................... C
4. Click **Width** ...................... W
5. Type number (0-255) in Column Width text box.
   - ✓ *This value represents the number of characters wide you want the column to be, using the standard font.*
6. Click **OK** .......................... Enter

## Change Column Width Using Mouse

1. Point to right border of column heading to be sized.
2. Pointer becomes **↔**.
3. Drag **↔** left or right to desired width.
   - ✓ *Excel displays column width above and to the right of the mouse pointer as you drag.*

## Set Column Width to Fit Longest Entry

- Double-click right border of column heading.

OR

1. Select column to size ............ [↔], [Ctrl]+[Space]
2. Click **Format** ............... [Alt]+[O]
3. Click **Column**. .................... [C]
4. Click **AutoFit Selection** ...... [A]

## Set Standard Column Width

✓ This command will adjust column widths that have not been previously changed in a worksheet.

1. Click **Format** ............... [Alt]+[O]
2. Click **Column**. .................... [C]
3. Click **Standard Width** ......... [S]
4. Type new number (0-255) ........in Standard Column Width text box.

   ✓ This number represents number of characters to be displayed in cell using the standard font.

5. Click **OK** .......................... [Enter]

# Exercise Directions

1. Start Excel, if necessary.
2. Open ⌨**OVERDUE** or 💿**04OVERDUE**.
3. Save the file as **OVERDUE**.
4. Enter the values in columns C and D as shown in Illustration A.

   ✓ Make sure the invoice numbers in column D are entered as numeric labels.

   ✓ Select Ignore Error from the Error button list for each entry in column D.

5. Enter the label **Date Due** and the date shown in cell E8.
6. Copy the date in cell E8 to cells E9 and E10 by dragging its fill handle.

   ✓ Select the option, Copy Cells from the AutoFill button menu.

7. Set the width of column D to fit the longest entry.
8. Change column B to a width of 16.0.
9. Drag across cells B3, C3, D3, and E3 to select them, then merge and center the worksheet title as shown in Illustration A.
10. Center the **Amount**, **Invoice Number**, and **Date Due** column labels.
11. Spell check the worksheet.
12. Close the workbook, saving all changes.

*Illustration A*

| | A | B | C | D | E | F |
|---|---|---|---|---|---|---|
| 1 | | | | | | |
| 2 | | | | | | |
| 3 | | | California Cardiology, Inc. | | | |
| 4 | | | | | | |
| 5 | | Healthman HMO | | | | |
| 6 | | | | | | |
| 7 | | Patient | Amount | Invoice Number | Date Due | |
| 8 | | J. Thomas Wilson | 2147.48 | 2145801 | 4/21/2001 | |
| 9 | | Carlos Riveria | 375.97 | 2189357 | 4/21/2001 | |
| 10 | | Alice Thomson | 1281.72 | 2049462 | 4/21/2001 | |

# On Your Own

1. Open a new workbook in Excel and save it as **OXL04**.

2. Create a worksheet to track inventory. For example, you might want to track your CD collection, or your books. For a business, club, or organization, you might want to track office supplies or equipment.

3. In row 1, type a title for your inventory report.

4. Enter the following labels as column headings starting in column A:

   **ITEM**
   **DESCRIPTION**
   **COST**

5. In the rows below each column heading, enter the appropriate data for at least five items.

   ✓ *If you enter numeric labels, be sure to include the label prefix (').*

6. Adjust the column width so you can read all of the data entered in the report.

7. Center the column heading labels.

8. Right align all number values.

9. Left align all text (except the column headings).

10. Merge the cells in row 1 and center the report title over the worksheet.

11. Save the worksheet, close the file, and exit Excel.

# Exercise 5

## On the Job

One of the benefits of Excel is its ability to create formulas within a worksheet that perform calculations. When you make a change to a cell that is referenced in a formula, Excel performs the recalculation, and the formula result is automatically updated to reflect the change.

As the invoice clerk for California Cardiology, Inc., you're glad that the invoice for Healthman HMO is almost ready. However, you know that there are still a few things you need to do to the report before you print it, such as adding formulas to calculate the total invoice amount and late fees.

## Terms

**Formula**  An instruction Excel uses to calculate a number.

**Mathematical operators**  Symbols used in mathematical operations: **+** for addition, **-** for subtraction, **\*** for multiplication, **/** for division, and **^** for exponentiation.

**Order of mathematical operations**  The order in which Excel performs the calculations specified in a formula.

## Notes

### Enter a Formula

- A **formula** is a worksheet instruction that performs a calculation.

- You enter a formula in the cell where the answer should display.

- As you type a formula, it displays in the cell and in the Formula bar.

- After you enter a formula into the cell, the answer displays in the cell while the formula appears in the formula bar.

- When creating formulas, you use cell references, values, and **mathematical operators**.

  ✓ *A formula can also contain Excel's predefined "functions," which are covered in Exercise 13.*

- The following are standard mathematical operators used in formulas:

    +    Addition
    -    Subtraction
    \*    Multiplication
    /    Division
    ^    Exponentiation

- The equal sign (=) must be typed at the beginning of a formula. For example, the formula =B2+B4+B6 adds the values in these cell locations together.

- When you make a change to a value in a cell that is referenced in a formula, the answer in the formula cell automatically changes.

- The **order of mathematical operations** is important to remember when creating formulas.
  - When calculating a formula, Excel performs operations enclosed in parentheses first.
  - Exponential calculations have the next priority.
  - Moving left to right within the formula, multiplication and division operations are then calculated before the addition and subtraction operations.

- When typing a percentage as a value in a formula, you can enter it with the percent symbol or as a decimal.
- Excel automatically provides assistance in correcting common mistakes in a formula (for example, omitting a parenthesis).

# Procedures

**Enter Formula Using Mathematical Operators**

1. Click cell where answer should display....................
2. Press **Equal** `=` ..................
3. Type formula.
   - ✓ *Example: =(C2+C10)/2*
4. Press **Enter**......................Enter
   - ✓ *Instead of typing a cell reference into a formula, you can simply click the appropriate cell.*

# Exercise Directions

1. Start Excel, if necessary.
2. Open ⌨OVERDUE or 💿05OVERDUE.
3. Save the file as **OVERDUE**.
4. In cells B12, B13, B14, and B16, type the labels shown in Illustration A.
5. Right align the labels entered in step 4.
6. In cell C12, type a formula to calculate the total amount that Healthman owes you: **=C8+C9+C10**
   - ✓ *Click the cells in the formula instead of typing their addresses. For example, type = then click cell C8. Type + then click C9. Type another + and click C10.*
7. In cell C13, calculate a 2% late fee by entering this formula: **=C12*2%**

8. In cell C14, calculate the current amount due, (the old total plus the 2% late fee) by entering this formula: **=C12+C13**
9. In cell C16, type the new amount that will be due if the current amount is not paid on time (the current amount plus another 2%): **=C14+(C14*2%)**
   - ✓ *In this formula, you must use parentheses to get the correct answer. If you type =C14+C14*2%, then Excel will add cell C14 to cell C14, then take that total times 2%. If you didn't want to use parentheses, you could type this formula instead: =C14*102%.*
10. Spell check the workbook.
11. Close the file, saving all changes.

*Illustration A*

|  | A | B | C | D | E | F |
|---|---|---|---|---|---|---|
| 3 |  | California Cardiology, Inc. | | | | |
| 4 |  |  |  |  |  |  |
| 5 |  | Healthman HMO |  |  |  |  |
| 6 |  |  |  |  |  |  |
| 7 |  | Patient | Amount | Invoice Number | Date Due |  |
| 8 |  | J. Thomas Wilson | 2147.48 | 2145801 | 4/21/2001 |  |
| 9 |  | Carlos Riveria | 375.97 | 2189357 | 4/21/2001 |  |
| 10 |  | Alice Thomson | 1281.72 | 2049462 | 4/21/2001 |  |
| 11 |  |  |  |  |  |  |
| 12 |  | Overdue amount: | 3805.17 |  |  |  |
| 13 |  | Late charge: | 76.1034 |  |  |  |
| 14 |  | Current amount due: | 3881.273 |  |  |  |
| 15 |  |  |  |  |  |  |
| 16 | Amount due if paid after 5/16: | | 3958.899 |  |  |  |
| 17 |  |  |  |  |  |  |

# On Your Own

1. Start Excel, if necessary.

2. Start a new workbook in Excel and save it as **OXL05**.

   ✓ *As the treasurer of the Art Club, you'll use Excel to set up a worksheet for tracking the total weekly candy sales for your current fundraiser.*

3. Enter a title for the worksheet in row 2.

4. Label the columns as follows:
   **Member Name**
   **Candy**
   **Price**
   **Number Sold**
   **Total Sales**

5. Type sales data for the first member, using multiple rows to list each type of candy sold by that person.

   ✓ *For example, the first row might be: Jane Brown, Milk chocolate candy bars, price 1.50, 10 sold. The next line might be: Tamika Brown, Toffee bars, price 2.25, 17 sold.*

   ✓ *Enter at least three people, with each person selling at least two types of candy. In the Member Name column, use the fill handle to copy the person's name to additional rows as needed.*

6. In the Total Sales column for the first item, enter a formula that multiples the value in the Price column by the value in the Number Sold column.

7. Repeat step 6 for each item.

8. Below the last item in the Total Sales column, enter a formula that adds the total sales for each item to compute a grand total for the week.

9. To the left of the cell that contains the grand total, type the label **Weekly Total**.

10. Adjust the width of columns so you can read all of the data.

11. Spell check the worksheet.

12. Close the worksheet, saving all changes.

# Exercise 6

### ◆ Critical Thinking

You are the owner of a store in the Coastline Gourmet Importers food chain, and it's time to order some seafood from one of your best suppliers, Chang Lo Lee Oriental Seafood. Luckily, Coastline has supplied you with a template you can use to create your order form. All you need to do is to enter the items you want, the number of cases for each item, and the cost per case (which you'll look up in an Excel workbook you created using Chang Lo Lee's current price list).

## Exercise Directions

1. Start Excel, if necessary.

2. Open 💿 **06CHANG**.

3. Start a workbook using the template 💿 **06CGIORDER**.

   ✓ *This template file is included with the data files. You will need to copy the file to the \Program Files\Microsoft Office\Templates folder. After you've copied the file, you'll see this template listed with the other General Templates.*

4. Save the file as **CHANGLEE**.

   ✓ *To save the template as an Excel workbook, select **Microsoft Excel Workbook** from the Save as type drop-down list. Otherwise, the file will remain a template.*

5. In cell B9, type the name of the supplier you're ordering from: **Chang Lo Lee Seafood**.

6. In cell B10, type their Web site address: **www.changlolee.com**.

   ✓ *Notice how AutoComplete creates an Internet link with your entry, underlining the text and making it blue.*

7. Enter particulars for this order in the **Item** and **No. of Cases** columns, as shown in Illustration A.

8. Arrange the two open workbooks horizontally.

9. Using the prices listed in **06CHANG**, enter appropriate data in the **Cost per Case** column of the **CHANGLEE** workbook for each item ordered.

10. Close **06CHANG**.

11. In cell E13, type a formula that calculates the total cost for the order of Mongolian Barbequed Shrimp.

    ✓ *Take the number of cases times the cost per case.*

12. In column E, type similar formulas that compute the total cost of the remaining items.

13. In cell E24, type a formula that calculates the total for the order.

    ✓ *Add cells E13, E14, E15, E16, and E17 together.*

    ✓ *Your worksheet should now look like the one in Illustration B.*

14. Spell check the workbook.

    ✓ *Be sure to correct the spelling of Florida.*

15. Close the workbook, saving all changes.

*Illustration A*

| Item | No. of Cases |
|---|---|
| Mongolian Barbequed Shrimp | 6 |
| Crab Meat AA | 10 |
| Sesame Crab Claw | 2 |
| Squid Paste | 7 |
| Sea Bass Sushi | 11 |

*Illustration B*

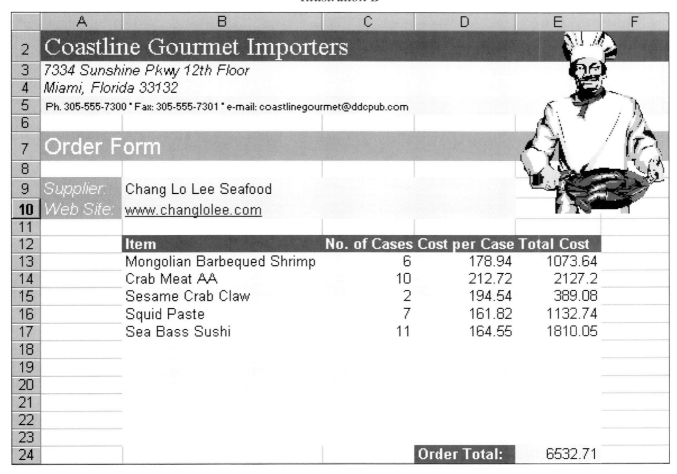

|  | A | B | C | D | E | F |
|---|---|---|---|---|---|---|
| 2 | Coastline Gourmet Importers | | | | | |
| 3 | 7334 Sunshine Pkwy 12th Floor | | | | | |
| 4 | Miami, Florida 33132 | | | | | |
| 5 | Ph. 305-555-7300 * Fax: 305-555-7301 * e-mail: coastlinegourmet@ddcpub.com | | | | | |
| 6 | | | | | | |
| 7 | Order Form | | | | | |
| 8 | | | | | | |
| 9 | Supplier: | Chang Lo Lee Seafood | | | | |
| 10 | Web Site: | www.changlolee.com | | | | |
| 11 | | | | | | |
| 12 | | Item | No. of Cases | Cost per Case | Total Cost | |
| 13 | | Mongolian Barbequed Shrimp | 6 | 178.94 | 1073.64 | |
| 14 | | Crab Meat AA | 10 | 212.72 | 2127.2 | |
| 15 | | Sesame Crab Claw | 2 | 194.54 | 389.08 | |
| 16 | | Squid Paste | 7 | 161.82 | 1132.74 | |
| 17 | | Sea Bass Sushi | 11 | 164.55 | 1810.05 | |
| 18 | | | | | | |
| 19 | | | | | | |
| 20 | | | | | | |
| 21 | | | | | | |
| 22 | | | | | | |
| 23 | | | | | | |
| 24 | | | | Order Total: | 6532.71 | |

# Exercise 7

## On the Job

Select a group of cells (a range) to copy, move, or erase them, or to quickly apply the same formatting throughout the range. You can also perform calculations on cell ranges—creating sums and averages, for example.

You're a salesperson with Regency General, Inc., a Web company that offers Internet-based database and inventory management services to other companies. Baylor Furniture is interested in putting their inventory online and offering Web-based sales to the general public, so they've asked for a price quote. In this exercise, you'll use Excel to make some final adjustments to the quote before you send a copy to your manager for her approval.

## Terms

**Range**  A block of cells in an Excel worksheet.

**Contiguous range**  A block of adjacent cells in a worksheet.

**Noncontiguous range**  A block of cells in a worksheet that is not necessarily adjacent to each other.

## Notes

### Use Ranges

- A **range** is an area made up of two or more cells.

- When you select cells A1, A2, and A3, for example, the range is indicated as A1:A3.

- The range A1:C5 is defined as a block of cells that includes all the cells in columns A through C in rows one through five.

- A range of cells can be **contiguous** (all cells are adjacent to each other) or **noncontiguous** (not all cells are adjacent to each other).

- When a range is selected, the active cell is displayed normally, but the rest of the cells appear highlighted, as shown.

*Selected range of contiguous cells*

|   | A | B | C |
|---|---|---|---|
| 1 | 123 | 287 | 142 |
| 2 | 415 | 794 | 835 |
| 3 | 189 | 688 | 974 |

*Selected range of noncontiguous cells*

|   | A | B | C |
|---|---|---|---|
| 1 | 123 | 287 | 142 |
| 2 | 415 | 794 | 835 |
| 3 | 189 | 688 | 974 |

## Range Entry Using Collapse Button

■ When you need to enter cell addresses or ranges in a dialog box, you may click the Collapse button on the right side of the text box to return to the worksheet temporarily and select the range.

■ After selecting the range, click the Collapse button to return to the dialog box to finalize your selections.

*Example of text box with Collapse button*

Collapse button

# Procedures

### Use Keyboard to Select Range of Cells

**To select range of adjacent cells:**

1. Press arrow key(s)............. [↑↓] to move to first cell of range.
2. Press **Shift + arrow** key........................... [Shift] + [↑↓]

**To select entire column containing active cell:**

- Press **Ctrl + Spacebar**..... [Ctrl] + [Space]

**To select entire row containing active cell:**

- Press **Shift + Spacebar** .. [Shift] + [Space]

**To select adjacent rows:**

1. Press arrow keys.............. [↑↓] to move to cell in first row to select.
2. Press and hold down **Shift**................ [Shift], then press **spacebar**..... [Space], to select first row.
3. While still pressing **Shift**, press up or down arrow key........ [↕] to select additional adjacent rows.

### To select worksheet from top-left cell to bottom-right cell:

1. Press arrow keys ............. [↑↓] to move to first cell in selection.
2. Press and hold down **Ctrl**, then press and hold down **Shift**, then press and release **End**....... [Ctrl] + [Shift] + [End]
3. Release **Ctrl** and **Shift** keys.

### Use Mouse to Select Range of Cells

**To select range of adjacent cells:**

- Click and drag across cells.

**To select noncontiguous cells and ranges:**

- Click and drag across first selection of cells.
- Press and hold **Ctrl** as you click additional cells, and/or drag over additional ranges.

**To select entire row:**

- Click row heading.

**To select entire column:**

- Click column heading.

**To select adjacent rows:**

- Click and drag across row headings.

### To select adjacent columns:

- Click and drag across column headings.

**To select noncontiguous rows:**

1. Click row heading.
2. Press and hold down **Ctrl** key and click additional row headings.

**To select noncontiguous columns:**

1. Click column heading.
2. Press and hold down **Ctrl** key and click additional column headings.

### Range Entry Using Collapse Button

1. Click **Collapse** button 📑 at right of text box.

   ✓ *The dialog box collapses to provide a better view of the worksheet.*

2. Select desired cell(s) by following either the keyboard or mouse method described here.

3. Press **Enter**...................... [Enter]

   OR

   Click **Collapse** button 📑.

   ✓ *The dialog box returns to normal size and the text box displays the cell reference(s). Continue making selections within the dialog box as needed.*

# Exercise Directions

1. Start Excel, if necessary.
2. Open ⊙**07DBQUOTE**.
3. Save the file as **DBQUOTE**.
4. Select the range D13:F19. (See Illustration A.)
5. Center-align the data in the range by clicking the Center button on the Formatting toolbar.
6. Select the range B8:B10.
7. Press Ctrl, and click cell E10 to create a non-contiguous selection. See Illustration A below.
8. Right-align the selected cells by clicking the Align Right button on the Formatting toolbar.
9. Click the heading for column G to select the entire column.
10. Erase the contents of column G by pressing Delete.
11. Spell check the workbook.
12. Close the workbook, saving all changes.

*Illustration A*

| | A | B | C | D | E | F | G |
|---|---|---|---|---|---|---|---|
| 1 | | | | | | | |
| 2 | | | | | | | |
| 3 | | | Regency General, Inc. | | | | |
| 4 | | | | | | | |
| 5 | | | Monthly Price Quote | | | | |
| 6 | | | | | | | |
| 7 | | | | | | | |
| 8 | | Name: | Baylor Furniture | | | | |
| 9 | | Address: | 2143 Grand Ave. Austin, TX 73309 | | | | |
| 10 | | Phone: | 512-555-7989 | | Fax: | 512-555-7941 | |
| 11 | | | | | | | |
| 12 | | | | | | | |
| 13 | | | Service | Price per Unit | No. of Units | Total | |
| 14 | | | Database server | $ 0.50 | 1505 | $ 752.50 | |
| 15 | | | Remote administration | $ 0.35 | 1505 | $ 526.75 | |
| 16 | | | Shopping cart | $ 0.15 | 1505 | $ 225.75 | |
| 17 | | | Credit verification | $ 0.09 | 1505 | $ 135.45 | |
| 18 | | | Real-time inventory | $ 0.27 | 1505 | $ 406.35 | |
| 19 | | | Search-enabled | $ 0.05 | 1505 | $ 75.25 | |
| 20 | | | | | | $ 2,046.80 | |
| 21 | | | | | | | |
| 22 | | | | | | | |

# On Your Own

1. Open the file named **OXL05** that you created in the On Your Own section of Exercise 5, or open the file ⊙**07CANDY**.
2. Save the file as **OXL07**.
3. Select the range of cells containing the column labels (Member Name, etc.), and change the cell alignment to center.
4. Select the range of cells containing the member names and candy names, and change the cell alignment to right.
5. Select the columns that contain the **Price**, **Number Sold**, and **Totals Sales** labels, and set the column widths to exactly 10.5.
6. Spell check the workbook.
7. Close the workbook, saving all changes.

# Exercise 8

◆ **Format Data** ◆ **Fonts and Font Size**
◆ **Number Formats** ◆ **Percent Format** ◆ **Comma Format**
◆ **Currency** ◆ **Add Color to Cells**

## On the Job

When you change the appearance of worksheet data by applying various formats, you also make that data more attractive and readable.

As the manager of the local Northwest Gear store, you've been asked by your regional office to track the sales fluctuations for a new item, a sleeveless cashmere sweater. You've entered the raw data, and in this exercise, you will format the worksheet using various number formats. You'll make font and font size changes as well and apply color to enhance the appearance of the report.

## Terms

**Format** To apply attributes to cell data to change the appearance of the worksheet.

**Font** The typeface or design of the text.

**Font size** The measurement of the typeface in points ($1/72$ of an inch).

**Number format** A format that controls how numerical data is displayed, including the use of commas, dollar signs (or other symbols), and the number of decimal places.

**Percent format** A style that displays decimal numbers as a percentage.

**Comma format** A style that displays numbers with a thousands separator (,).

**Currency format** A style that displays dollar signs ($) immediately preceding the number and includes a thousands separator (,).

**Accounting format** A style that vertically aligns with dollar signs ($), thousands separators (,), and decimal points.

**Fill** A color that fills a cell, appearing behind the data.

**Pattern** A secondary color added to the background of a cell in a pattern.

## Notes

### Format Data

■ **Format** data by selecting it and clicking the appropriate button on the Formatting toolbar or by choosing options from the Format Cells dialog box.

### Fonts and Font Size

■ A **font** is a set of characters with a specific design and name.

■ The **font size** of a set of characters is based on its average height in points. One point is equal to 1/72 of an inch.

- Change the font and font size of your data to improve its appearance and to make it more readable.

- You can apply special effects—such as bold, italics, or underline—to any font you select.

- You make font, font size, and special effects changes through the Formatting toolbar or the Format Cells dialog box.

*Font and font size changes from Formatting toolbar*

| Arial | ▼ | 10 | ▼ | **B** | *I* | U |
|---|---|---|---|---|---|---|

| E10 | ▼ | fx | |
|---|---|---|---|

|  | A | B | C | D |
|---|---|---|---|---|
| 1 | **2001 BUDGET** | | | |
| 2 | | January | February | March |
| 3 | *Income* | 5654 | 6102 | 4987 |
| 4 | *Expenses* | 3102 | 3254 | 2795 |

- The way in which your data appears after making font and font size changes is dependent on your monitor and printer.

  ✓ *If your monitor cannot display a particular font, it will choose a similar font to replace it with. However, when you print the data out, the actual font you picked may be used. To avoid this discrepancy between what you see on-screen and what is printed, use Windows TrueType fonts whenever possible.*

- Windows TrueType fonts are "true" to their on-screen appearance—what you see is what you will get when your data is printed.

  ✓ *TrueType fonts are identified with a small TT in front of their name in the Font drop-down list on the Formatting toolbar.*

- When you change the size of a font, Excel automatically adjusts the row height but does not adjust the column width.

- By default, data appears in Arial 10-point font. You can change the standard (default) font and font size if you want, or you can apply different fonts and font sizes to selected data.

## Number Formats

- When formatting numerical data, you may want to change more than just the font and font size— you may want to also apply a **number format**.

- The number format determines the number of decimal places and the position of zeros (if any) before/after the decimal point. Number formats also place various symbols such as dollar signs or percentage signs with formatted numbers. You can also add dollar signs and commas with the number format you select.

- Changing the format of a cell does not affect the actual value stored there or used in calculations—it affects only the way in which that value is displayed.

- You can quickly apply Currency, Percent, or Comma format to numerical data using the buttons on the Formatting toolbar.

- You can also increase or decrease the number of decimal places displayed in a number with buttons on the Formatting toolbar.

- To apply other number formats, or to adjust the settings used by default with Currency, Percent, or Comma format, use the Number tab of the Format Cells dialog box.

*Number tab of Format Cells dialog box*

## Percent Format

- To change data entered as decimals (such as .75) into percentages (75%), use the **percent format**.

## Comma Format

- If you want to make large numbers easier to read, use the **comma format** to include commas in the number, as in 2,345,945.98.

## Currency

- The currency and accounting formats may be used for formatting money values.

- **Currency format** displays numbers with currency symbols: dollar signs, commas, and decimals. For example, $21,456.83.

- **Accounting format** displays numbers in a style similar to currency format, but the dollar signs are aligned to the far left of the cell, with additional spaces inserted between the dollar sign and the first digit, depending on the column width. For example, $ 21,456.83.

  ✓ *When you use the Currency button on the Formatting toolbar to apply a number format, you're really applying Accounting format.*

## Add Color to Cells

- To focus attention on particular areas of the worksheet, such as the column or row labels or important totals, fill the cell background with color. You can add color to your data as well.

- You can add color (called a **fill**) to a cell with the Fill Color button on the Formatting toolbar. Add color to the text in a cell with the Font Color button.

- With the Format Cells dialog box, you can select from a wider variety of color fills. You can also include a **pattern**.

*Color or pattern added to cells*

| 2001 Budget | | | |
|---|---|---|---|
| | **January** | **February** | **March** |
| **Income** | 5654 | 6102 | 4987 |
| **Expenses** | 3102 | 3254 | 2795 |

# Procedures

### Change Font Using Font Box

1. Select cells or characters in cells to format.
2. Click **Font** list box arrow `Arial ▼`.
3. Select font ............. 🔾↓, Enter

### Change Font Size Using Font Size Box

1. Select cells or characters in cells to format.
2. Click **Font Size** list box arrow `10 ▼`.
3. Select number in list ...................... 🔾↓, Enter
   OR
   a. Click **Font Size** box `10 ▼`.
   b. Type desired number.
   c. Press **Enter** ................ Enter

### Percentage Number Format

1. Select cell(s) to format.
2. Click **Percent Style** button `%`.
   OR
   a. Click **Format** .......... Alt+O

   b. Click **Cells** ..................... E
   c. Select **Number** tab .......... Ctrl+Tab
   d. Click **Percentage** in **Category** list box ........... Alt+C, 🔾↓
   e. Click **Decimal places** ..... Alt+D
   f. Set number of places.
   g. Click **OK** ..................... Enter

### Comma Number Format

1. Select cell(s) to format.
2. Click **Comma Style** button `,`.
   OR
   a. Click **Format** .......... Alt+O
   b. Click **Cells** ..................... E
   c. Select **Number** tab ... Ctrl+Tab
   d. Click **Number** in **Category** list box ........... Alt+C, 🔾↓
   e. Click **Decimal places** ..... Alt+D
   f. Set number of places.

   g. Click **Use 1000 Separator** ..... Alt+U
   h. Click **OK** ..................... Enter

### Currency Number Format

1. Select cells(s) to format.
2. Click **Format** .............. Alt+O
3. Click **Cells** ..................... E
4. Select **Number** tab ..... Ctrl+Tab
5. From the **Category** list box click **Currency** ............ Alt+C, 🔾↓
6. Set decimal places and choose currency symbol.
7. Click **OK** ......................... Enter

### Accounting Number Format

1. Select cell(s) to format.
2. Click **Format** .............. Alt+O
3. Click **Cells** ........................... E
4. Select **Number** tab ..... Ctrl+Tab
5. From the **Category** list box click **Accounting** ....... Alt+C, 🔾↓
6. Click **Decimal places** .. Alt+D

7. Set number of places.
   - ✓ *You can choose a symbol other than the US dollar and specify how negative numbers display in the cell.*
8. Click **OK** .......................... `Enter`
   - ✓ *If you prefer, you can click the Currency Style button* `$` *on the Formatting toolbar.*

## Increase or Decrease Decimal Places

1. Select cell(s) to format.
2. Click **Increase Decimal** `+.0 .00` or **Decrease Decimal** `.00 +.0` buttons on the Formatting toolbar.

### Add a Color Fill

1. Select cell(s) to format.
2. Click the arrow on the **Fill Color** button `▼` and select a color.
   - ✓ *You can also add a fill by choosing Format, Cells, clicking the Patterns tab and selecting a color.*
   - ✓ *Add a pattern to a fill by selecting its color from the Pattern list on the Patterns tab of the Format Cells dialog box. Be sure to choose a pattern for the second color from the top of the Pattern list.*

### Add Text Color

1. Select cell(s) to format.
2. Click the arrow on the **Font Color** button `A ▼` and select a color.
   - ✓ *You can also add a color to text by choosing Format, Cells, clicking the Font tab and selecting a color from the Color list.*

# Exercise Directions

1. Start Excel, if necessary.
2. Open 🔘 **08CASHTOPS**.
3. Save the file as **CASHTOPS**.
4. Select the ranges B14:C19 and E14:E19.
5. Using the Comma Style button, format the data for two decimal places.
6. Click the Currency Style button to apply Accounting format to the selection.
7. Click the Decrease Decimal button twice to remove the decimal places.
8. Select the ranges D14:D19 and F14:F19.
9. Click the Percent Style button to apply the Percent format.
10. Click the Increase Decimal button three times to display three decimal places.
11. Apply these fonts to the following cells or ranges:
    - ✓ *If you don't have these exact same fonts, choose ones of your own, using Illustration A as an example.*
    a. A2: Chilada ICG Dos, 20 point
    b. A3:A5: Andy, 12 point
    c. A9: Chilada ICG Dos, 18 point
    d. A10: Andy, 14 point
    e. A14:A19: Andy 12 point, italic
    f. B13:F13: Andy 14 point

12. Apply the following color fills:
    a. A9:C9: Tan
    b. A10:C10: Pale Blue
    c. B13:F13: Aqua
    d. A14:A19: Red
13. Select the range A14:A19, and change its text color to white.
14. Widen any columns, if necessary. See Illustration A.
15. Spell check the workbook.
16. Close the workbook, saving all changes.

*Illustration A*

## On Your Own

1. Open the file 📖**OXL07** that you created in the On Your Own section of Exercise 7, or open 💿**08CANDY**.

2. Save the file as **OXL08**.

3. Apply the Comma format to the data in the Price and Total Sales columns.

4. Apply the Currency format with no decimal places to the data instead.

5. Finally, apply the Accounting format with two decimal places to the same data in the Price and Total Sales columns.

6. Change the font for all the data in B5:F12 to Verdana, and increase the font size to 11 points.

7. Increase the font size of the title to 18 points, and apply bold and italics effects. Select the cells that contain the title and fill them with yellow.

8. Increase the font size of the column labels to 14 points. Apply a light yellow color fill. Change the text color to green. Apply these same changes to cell E13.

9. Adjust the width of columns as necessary so that you can see all of the data in the worksheet.

10. Spell check the workbook.

11. Close the workbook, saving all changes.

# Exercise 9

## Skills Covered:

**◆ Copy and Paste Data ◆ Relative Reference**
**◆ Absolute Reference ◆ Preview and Print a Worksheet**

## On the Job

Excel provides many shortcuts to save you time as you enter data and write formulas in your worksheets. For example, you can use the copy and paste features to reuse data and formulas in the same worksheet, in another worksheet, or in another workbook. The **AutoFill** handle bypasses the copy and paste features and allows you to copy data to adjacent cells. When you complete a report, you can preview and print a hard copy.

The worksheet you designed to track cashmere sweater sales was complete—that is, until the regional office called to tell you to add January sales data as well. In addition, they want you to add totals by month, a grand total, and the percentage of grand total sales by month. Luckily, all you need to do is create a few formulas and copy them throughout the worksheet.

## Terms

**AutoFill** A method used to copy data from a cell or range of cells to an adjacent cell or range of cells by dragging the fill handle.

**Clipboard** A feature of Windows that holds data or graphics that you have cut or copied ready to be pasted into any document.

**Fill handle** Dragging this handle, located in the lower-right corner of the active cell, will copy cell contents, formatting, or a formula to adjacent cells.

**Relative cell reference** A cell address expressed in relation to another cell in a formula. For example, rather than naming a cell such as A3, a relative cell reference might identify a range of cells to the left of the cell containing the formula.

**Absolute cell reference** A cell address, such as E14, referenced in a formula that does not change based on the location of the formula.

**Print Preview** A feature used to display a document as it will appear when printed.

## Notes

### Copy and Paste Data

- Copying data involves two actions: copying and pasting.
  - When you copy data, the copy is placed on the **Clipboard**.
  - When you paste data, that data is copied from the Clipboard to the new location.

- Worksheet data (labels, values, and formulas) may be copied to another cell, a range of cells, another worksheet, or another workbook. Excel data can also be copied to documents created in other programs, such as Word.

- To copy a range of data to a new location, use the Copy and Paste buttons on the Standard toolbar or the Copy and Paste commands from the Edit menu.

- If the cells to which you want to copy data are adjacent to the original cell, you can use the **fill handle** to copy the data.
  - ✓ *In Exercise 4, you learned how to use the fill handle to create a series. Here, you'll learn to use the fill handle to copy labels, values, and formulas to adjacent cells instead of creating a series.*

- When you copy data, its format is copied as well, and overrides any format in the destination cell.
  - ✓ *You can override this and copy just the data without copying its formatting.*

- If data exists in the destination cell, that data will be overwritten.

## Relative Reference

- When you copy a formula to another cell, Excel uses **relative cell referencing** to change the formula to reflect its new location.
  - ✓ *For example, the formula =B4+B5 written in column B becomes =C4+C5 when copied to column C or =D4+D5 when copied to column D, etc.*

## Absolute Reference

- Usually, you want the cell addresses in the original formula to change when you copy it. Sometimes, you don't want it to change, so you need to create an **absolute cell reference**.

- Absolute cell references do not change when a formula is copied.

- To make a cell reference absolute, enter a dollar sign ($) before both the column letter and row number of that cell in the formula.
  - ✓ *For example, the formula =$B$4+$B$5 written in column B remains =$B$4+$B$5 when copied to column C. The cell addresses do not adjust based on the new formula location.*

- Sometimes, you may wish to copy a formula's result, and not the actual formula.
  - ✓ *For example, if cell B10 contains the formula =B2-B3 with a result of $1200, and you copy that formula to cell C10, the formula will change to =C2-C3. The result of this copied formula would be based on the contents of cells C2 and C3. However, if all you want to do is to show the result, $1200, in another location of the worksheet, copy the value of cell B10 instead of its formula.*

## Preview and Print a Worksheet

- You may print the selected worksheet(s), an entire workbook, or a selected data range.

- Use the Print command from the File menu to access the print options in the Print dialog box.

- To view the output before you print, use the **Print Preview** command, which appears on the File menu, in the Print dialog box, and as a button on the Standard toolbar.

*Print dialog box*

# Procedures

## Copy Data *(Ctrl+C)*

1. Select cell(s) to copy.
2. Click **Edit**..................... Alt +E
3. Click **Copy**........................... C
   OR
   Click **Copy** button.
   - ✓ *A moving line (marquee) surrounds selected cell(s).*

4. Select cell(s) to receive data.
   - ✓ *Click upper-left cell of destination range or select entire range of cells to receive data on current worksheet, another worksheet, or another workbook.*

## Paste Data *(Ctrl+V)*

1. Click **Edit**..................... Alt +E
2. Click **Paste**........................... P
   OR

Click **Paste** button .

- ✓ *Press **Escape** key to remove marquee that surrounds original selected cell(s).*

- ✓ *If you paste formatting along with data and you don't want to do that, click the Paste Options button that appears and select the desired option.*

## Paste Formula Result

1. Click arrow on **Paste** button
   ![Paste icon].
2. Select **Values**.

## Copy Formula Using AutoFill

1. Select cell(s) to copy.
2. Point to fill handle.
   - ✓ *Mouse shape changes to crosshair.*
3. Drag fill handle across or down to adjacent cells to fill them.

## Print Worksheet *(Ctrl+P)*

1. Select sheet(s) to print.
   - ✓ *To print a range of data instead of an entire sheet, select that range now.*
2. Click **File** ..................... `Alt`+`F`
3. Click **Print** ........................... `P`
4. Select appropriate print options.

OR

- Click **Print** button ![Print icon].
   - ✓ *When you click the Print button on the Standard toolbar, the active worksheet is sent directly to the printer without displaying the Print dialog box.*

## Print Preview a Worksheet

1. Click **File** ..................... `Alt`+`F`
2. Click **Print Preview**............. `V`

   OR

   Click **Print Preview** button
   ![Preview icon] on the toolbar.
3. Select options from the Print Preview toolbar.
4. Click **Close** button ![Close button] to close Print Preview.

# Exercise Directions

1. Start Excel, if necessary.
2. Open ⌨**CASHTOPS** or open 💿**09CASHTOPS**.
3. Save the file as **CASHTOPS**.
4. Select the range E13:F19.
5. Using the fill handle, copy the selection to the range G13:H19.
   - ✓ *Ignore the AutoFill Options box that appears.*
6. Change the data in column G to match the data shown in Illustration A.
7. In cell A21, type **Totals**.
   - ✓ *Notice that the formatting from cell A20 is copied automatically to cell A21. Excel repeats formatting from adjacent cells, on the assumption that's what you'll want nine times out of ten. You can, of course, modify this automatic formatting when needed to suit your own taste.*
8. Enter a formula in cell B21 that totals the sales for October.
9. Use the Copy and Paste buttons to copy this formula to cells C21, E21, and G21.
10. In cell A22, type **Grand Total**.
11. In cell B22, create a formula that totals the sales for October through January.

12. In cell A23, type **% of Grand Total**.
13. Type this formula in cell B23: **=B21/B22**.
14. Use the Copy and Paste buttons to copy this formula to cells C23, E23, and G23.
15. You've created an error because the relative cell addresses changed, and now Excel thinks you want to divide by zero. Change the original formula in cell B23 to read: **=B21/$B$22**.
    - ✓ *This change will cause each month's total to be divided by the grand total in cell B22, instead of some empty cell.*
16. Copy the formula again to cells C23, E23, and G23.
    - ✓ *Notice that this time, there is no error, because all the formulas divide that month's total by the grand total in cell B23.*
17. Apply Percent format, 3 decimal places, to cells B23, C23, E23 and G23.
18. Widen any columns as necessary.
19. Spell check the worksheet.
20. Preview the worksheet.
21. Print two copies of the completed worksheet.
    - ✓ *Each copy of the worksheet will print on two pages.*
22. Close the workbook, saving all changes.

*Illustration A*

| 13 | | October | November | % Inc./Dec. | December | % Inc./Dec. | January | % Inc./Dec. |
|---|---|---|---|---|---|---|---|---|
| 14 | Red | $ 2,415 | $ 2,694 | 11.553% | $ 2,421 | -10.134% | $ 2,018 | -16.646% |
| 15 | Lt. Blue | $ 3,108 | $ 3,278 | 5.470% | $ 4,386 | 33.801% | $ 4,187 | -4.537% |
| 16 | Brown | $ 978 | $ 1,105 | 12.986% | $ 1,098 | -0.633% | $ 955 | -13.024% |
| 17 | Burnt Umber | $ 1,027 | $ 1,594 | 55.209% | $ 1,655 | 3.827% | $ 1,459 | -11.843% |
| 18 | Burgundy | $ 2,374 | $ 3,497 | 47.304% | $ 4,297 | 22.877% | $ 4,299 | 0.047% |
| 19 | Cyan | $ 2,156 | $ 3,387 | 57.096% | $ 4,092 | 20.815% | $ 3,975 | -2.859% |
| 20 | | | | | | | | |
| 21 | Totals | $ 12,058 | $ 15,555 | | $ 17,949 | | $ 16,893 | |
| 22 | Grand Total | $ 62,455 | | | | | | |
| 23 | % of Grand Total | 19.307% | 24.906% | | 28.739% | | 27.048% | |

# On Your Own

1. Open a new workbook in Excel.

2. Save the file as **OXL09**.

3. Imagine that you are general manager of CD Mania, a chain of music stores. Set up a worksheet showing the monthly sales for three stores in the first three months of the year.

4. In row 1, type a title for the worksheet.

5. Labels columns for: **Store**, **Jan**, **Feb**, and **Mar**.

6. List data for three different stores in the rows below the column labels. You can make up names for the stores, and sales totals.

   ✓ *For example, Store 1 might have had sales of $21,548 in January, $27,943 in February, and $25,418 in March.*

7. Apply the Accounting format, 2 decimal places, to the sales data.

8. In the row below the data for the third store, enter the label **Totals**.

9. In the Totals row for the Jan column, enter a formula to add the January sales for all three stores.

10. Copy the formula to the Totals row for Feb and Mar.

11. Add a column for the April sales data. Label the column **Apr**.

12. Copy the data for each store from the Jan column into the April column.

13. Copy the Totals formula from the Mar column to the Apr column.

14. Adjust the width of the columns so you can read all of the data in the worksheet.

15. Apply formatting such as font, font size, fill color, and text color changes to improve the appearance of the worksheet.

16. Spell check the workbook.

17. Preview then print the file.

18. Close the workbook, saving all changes.

# Exercise 10

## Skills Covered:
### ◆ Insert and Delete Columns and Rows
### ◆ Move Data (Cut/Paste) ◆ Drag-and-Drop Editing

## On the Job

After you create a worksheet, you may want to rearrange data or add additional information. For example, you may need to insert additional rows to a section of your worksheet because new employees have joined a department. With Excel's editing features, you can easily add, delete, and rearrange entire rows and columns. You can also move or drag and drop sections of the worksheet with ease.

As the head nurse at California Cardiology, Inc., it's your job to keep track of all the supplies, including the in-office pharmacy. You've designed a worksheet to help you perform a weekly inventory of the pharmacy. It still needs some work, but with Excel's powerful tools for inserting, deleting, and moving data, you'll be able to make changes quickly.

## Terms

**Cut** The command used to remove data from a cell or range of cells and place it on the Clipboard.

**Paste** The command used to place data from the Clipboard to a location on the worksheet.

**Drag-and-drop feature** A method used to move or copy the contents of a range of cells by dragging the border of a selection from one location in a worksheet and dropping it in another location.

## Notes

### Insert and Delete Columns and Rows

- You can insert or delete columns or rows when necessary to change the arrangement of the data on the worksheet.

- When you insert column(s) into a worksheet, existing columns shift their position to the right.

  ✓ For example, if you select column C and then insert two columns, the data that was in column C is shifted to the right, and becomes column E.

- Likewise, if you insert row(s) into a worksheet, existing rows are shifted down to accommodate the newly inserted row(s).

  ✓ For example, if you select row 8 and insert two rows, the data that was in row 8 is shifted down to row 10.

- When you delete a column or row, existing columns and rows shift their positions to close the gap.

  ✓ Any data in the rows or columns you select for deletion is erased.

  ✓ Data in existing columns is shifted back to the left to fill the gap left by deleted columns.

  ✓ In a similar manner, data in existing rows is shifted up to fill any gaps.

- Instead of deleting columns or rows, you can hide them temporarily and then redisplay them as needed.

  ✓ You might do this, for example, to hide data from a coworker who's not authorized to view it.

### Move Data (Cut/Paste)

- To move data from one location to another, you "cut" it out of the worksheet, then "paste" it in its new location.

- When you cut data from a location, it is temporarily stored on the Clipboard. That data is then copied from the Clipboard to the new location when you paste.

- If data already exists in the location you wish to paste to, Excel overwrites it.
  - Instead of overwriting data with the Paste command, you can insert the cut cells and have Excel shift cells with existing data down or to the right.

- To move data from one place in the worksheet to another, use the **Cut** and **Paste** commands from the Edit menu or the buttons on the Standard toolbar.

- When you move data, its format is moved as well.
  - ✓ You can override this and move just the data.

## Drag-and-Drop Editing

- The **drag-and-drop feature** allows you to use the mouse to copy or move a range of cells simply by dragging them.

- The drag-and-drop process works like this: first, you select a range to copy or move, then you use the border surrounding the range to drag the data to a different location. When you release the mouse button, the data is "dropped" there.
  - ✓ An outline of the selection appears as you drag it to its new location on the worksheet.
  - ✓ Drag and drop normally moves data, but you can copy data instead by simply holding down the Ctrl key as you drag.

*Example of drag-and-drop editing*

- Insert, delete, move, and copy operations may affect formulas, so you should check the formulas after you have made changes to be sure that they are correct.

- When a drag-and-drop action does not move data correctly, use the Undo feature to undo it.

# Procedures

## Insert Columns/Rows with Menu

1. Select as many adjacent columns or rows you need to insert.
   - ✓ Drag across column letters or row numbers to select entire column(s) or row(s).
2. Click **Insert**.................. `Alt`+`I`
3. Click **Columns** .................... `C`
   OR
   Click **Rows**........................... `R`
   - ✓ New columns are inserted to the left of selected columns. New rows are inserted above selected rows.

## Insert Columns/Rows with Mouse

1. Select as many adjacent columns or rows you need to insert.
   - ✓ Drag across column letters or row numbers to select entire column(s) or row(s).
2. Right-click selection.
3. Click **Insert**.......................... `I`

## Delete Columns/Rows with Menu

1. Select column(s) or row(s) to be removed.
2. Click **Edit**.................... `Alt`+`E`
3. Click **Delete**......................... `D`

## Delete Columns/Rows with Mouse

1. Select column(s) or row(s) to be removed.
2. Right-click selection.
3. Click **Delete**......................... `D`

## Hide Columns or Rows

1. Select the columns or rows you wish to hide.
2. Click **Format** .............. `Alt`+`F`
3. Click **Column** ...................... `C`
   OR
   Click **Row**........................... `R`
4. Click **Hide**............................ `H`

## Unhide Columns or Rows

1. Select surrounding columns or rows.
2. Click **Format** ........................ `F`
3. Click **Column** ...................... `C`
   OR
   Click **Row** ........................... `R`
4. Click **Unhide** ....................... `U`

## Cut Data *(Ctrl+X)*

1. Select cell(s) to move.
2. Click **Edit**.................... `Alt`+`E`
3. Click **Cut** ............................. `T`
   OR
   Click **Cut** button .
   - ✓ A moving line (marquee) surrounds selected cell(s).
4. Select cell(s) to accept data.
   - ✓ You only need to select the top left cell of destination range. You can also move data to another worksheet or another workbook.

### Paste Data *(Ctrl+V)*

1. Click **Edit**..................... Alt + E
2. Click **Paste** ......................... P

   OR

   Click **Paste** button

   ✓ *If you paste formatting along with data and you don't want to do that, click the Paste Options button that appears and select the desired option.*

### Insert Data between Cells

1. Click **Insert**................. Alt + I
2. Click **Cells** ......................... E
3. Click **Shift cells right**.......... I

   OR

   **Shift cells down**................. D
4. Click **OK** ......................... Enter

### Move Selection with Drag-and-Drop Editing

1. Select cell or range of cells to move.
2. Move mouse pointer to border of selection.

---

**To move selection to destination cells and *overwrite* existing data:**

a. Drag selection outline to new location.
b. Release mouse button.
c. Click **OK**. ..................... Enter

**To move selection to destination cells and *insert* between existing data:**

a. Press **Shift** while dragging selection outline to column or row gridline.............. Shift

   ✓ *If you drag outline to column gridline, existing data shifts right. If you drag outline to a row gridline, existing data shifts down.*

b. Release mouse button and then Shift key.

### Copy Selection with Drag-and-Drop Editing

1. Select cell or range of cells to copy.
2. Move mouse pointer to border of selection.

---

**To copy selection to destination cells and *overwrite* existing data:**

a. Press **Ctrl** while dragging selection outline to column or row gridline ............... Ctrl
b. Release **Ctrl** key, then mouse button.

**To copy selection to destination cells and *insert* between existing data:**

a. Press **Ctrl+Shift** and drag selection outline to column or row gridline ....... Ctrl + Shift

   ✓ *If you drag the outline to column gridline, existing cells shift right. If you drag outline to row gridline, existing cells shift down.*

b. Release mouse button, then **Ctrl** and **Shift** keys.

---

# Exercise Directions

1. Start Excel, if necessary.
2. Open ⊙ **10DRUGINV**.
3. Save the file as **DRUGINV**.
4. Type today's date in cell C5.
5. Insert two columns between columns E and F. Label the columns **Additions** and **Total**.
6. Since you received a shipment of some drugs during this period, type the following amounts in the Additions column, in the appropriate cells:
   - Dozehnaze: **200**
   - Mycolex: **350**
   - Zybox: **750**
7. To add a new drug, insert a row between rows 12 and 13.
   a. Type the label **Silease** in cell D13.
   b. In the Additions column for Silease, type **975**.
8. In cell G8, type a formula to calculate the total inventory on hand for the current period.
   ✓ *Take the previous count and add the additions that occurred during the period.*

9. Copy this formula to cells G9:G15.
10. Type these current inventory amounts in the appropriate cells in column H (Current Count):
    - Blador: **97**, Clumins: **203**, Clear All: **71**
    - Dozehnaze: **112**, Mycolex: **207**
    - Silease: **764**, Tempour: **57**, Zybox: **684**
11. In cell I8, type a formula that calculates the amount of Blador used during the period.
    ✓ *Take the Total for Blador minus the Current Count.*
    ✓ *Copy this formula to the range I9:I15*
12. Using the Cut and Paste buttons, move the contents of cells D7:I15 to the range beginning with cell D5.
13. Using drag and drop, move the contents of cells B3:D3 to the range F3:H3.
14. Widen columns, as necessary.
15. Spell check the worksheet.
16. Print the worksheet.
17. Close the file, saving all changes.

*Illustration A*

| | A | B | C | D | E | F | G | H | I |
|---|---|---|---|---|---|---|---|---|---|
| 1 | | | California Cardiology, Inc. | | | | | | |
| 2 | | | | | | | | | |
| 3 | | | | | | Pharmacy Inventory | | | |
| 4 | | | | | | | | | |
| 5 | | Date: | 12/1/2000 | Drug | Previous Count | Additions | Total | Current Count | Used |
| 6 | | | | Blador | 205 | | 205 | 97 | 108 |
| 7 | | | | Clumins | 312 | | 312 | 203 | 109 |
| 8 | | | | Clear All | 115 | | 115 | 71 | 44 |
| 9 | | | | Dozehnaze | 96 | 200 | 296 | 112 | 184 |
| 10 | | | | Mycolex | 74 | 350 | 424 | 207 | 217 |
| 11 | | | | Silease | | 975 | 975 | 764 | 211 |
| 12 | | | | Tempour | 187 | | 187 | 57 | 130 |
| 13 | | | | Zybox | 205 | 750 | 955 | 684 | 271 |
| 14 | | | | | | | | | |

# On Your Own

1. Open the file **OXL09**, created in the On Your Own section of Exercise 9, or open **10CDMANIA**.

2. Save the file as **OXL10**.

3. Insert two new rows above the Totals row, and enter sales data for two new stores.

4. Insert a column between March and April, and label the column **Qtr 1**.

5. In the Qtr 1 column, type formulas to total the first quarter sales (January through March) for each store.

6. Where the Totals row and the Qtr 1 column meet, type a formula that calculates the grand total for Qtr 1.

7. Using drag and drop, copy the store names (and the Store and Totals labels) to an area a few rows below the sales data—but in the same column.

   ✓ You're creating a duplicate sales area below the current area that will eventually store the sales amounts for the second quarter—April, May, and June.

8. Using Cut and Paste, move the April column totals to this new sales area, below the data for January.

9. Add labels for **May**, **June**, and **Qtr 2** in the columns to the right of the April column.

10. In the Qtr 2 column, type formulas to total the second quarter sales (May through June) for each store.

11. Spell check the workbook.

12. Print the worksheet.

13. Close the workbook, saving all changes.

# Exercise 11

Skills Covered:

◆ **Work with Worksheets**
◆ **Group Sheets** ◆ **Format Sheets**

## On the Job

Use workbook sheets to organize your reports. For example, instead of entering the data for an entire year on one worksheet, use multiple worksheets to represent each month's data. Excel gives you the freedom to add, delete, move and even rename your worksheets so you can keep a complex workbook organized. In addition, you can group multiple sheets and work on them simultaneously and quickly format an entire worksheet in one step.

You're the owner of an organic food chain called Golden Harvest, and you've asked Murray Hill Marketing to create a marketing campaign for you. They need to see your survey on people's buying habits, which you happen to have in Excel format. Before you print the survey for them, however, you want to add formatting and make a few adjustments.

## Terms

**Grouping** Worksheets that are selected as a unit; any action performed on this unit will affect all the worksheets in the group.

**Active sheet tab** The selected worksheet; the tab name of an active sheet is bold.

## Notes

### Work with Worksheets

- The default workbook window contains three sheets named Sheet1 through Sheet3.
- The sheet tab displays the name of the sheet.
- Right-click a sheet tab to display a shortcut menu that allows you to insert, delete, rename move, and copy worksheets. You can also change the color of a worksheet's tab.
- You do not need to delete unused sheets from a workbook since they do not take up much room in the file; however, if you plan on sharing the file, you may want to remove unused sheets to create a more professional look.
- Renaming sheets and coloring sheet tabs make it easier to keep track of the data on individual sheets.

*Sheet tab shortcut menu*

- Moving sheets allows you to place them in a logical order within the workbook.
- When you copy a worksheet, you copy all of its data and formatting. However, changes you later make to the copied sheet do not affect the original sheet.

**194**

- If you change the color of a sheet tab, that color appears when the tab is not selected. When a colored sheet tab is clicked, its color changes to white, with a small line of its original color at the bottom of the tab.

  ✓ *For example, an orange sheet tab changes to white with a thin orange line at the bottom when it is selected.*

## Group Sheets

- If you want to work on several worksheets simultaneously, select multiple worksheets and create a **grouping**.

- Grouped sheet tabs appear white when selected, and the name of the **active sheet tab** appears in bold.

- When you select a grouping, any editing, formatting, or new entries you make to the active sheet are simultaneously made to all the sheets in the group.

- ✓ *For example, you can select a group of sheets and format, move, copy, or delete them in one step. You can also add, delete, change, or format the same entries into the same cells on every selected worksheet.*

- ✓ *Remember to deselect the grouping when you no longer want to make changes to all the sheets in the group.*

## Format Sheets

- One way in which you can quickly give your worksheets a professional look is to format them using AutoFormat.

- Using AutoFormat saves you time, because you won't have to format the column labels, row labels, and data manually.

- After you select an AutoFormat, Excel applies that format throughout the worksheet.

- You can select only part of an AutoFormat's attributes to apply.

  ✓ *For example, you could apply just the number formats and fonts, but not the alignments, patterns, borders, widths, and heights.*

# Procedures

### Select One Sheet

1. If necessary, click tab scrolling buttons  to view hidden sheet tabs.
2. Click sheet tab to select it.

### Select All Sheets

1. Right-click any sheet tab.
2. Select **Select All Sheets** .............. , Enter

### Select Consecutive Sheets

1. If necessary, click tab scrolling buttons to view hidden sheet tabs.
2. Click first sheet tab in group.
3. If necessary, to view additional hidden sheet tabs click tab scrolling buttons.
4. Press **Shift** and click last sheet tab in group.

   ✓ *The word [Group] appears in the title bar.*

### Select Nonconsecutive Sheets

1. If necessary, click tab scrolling buttons to view hidden sheet tabs.
2. Click first sheet tab in group.
3. If necessary, to view additional hidden sheet tabs click tab scrolling buttons.
4. Press **Ctrl** and click each subsequent sheet tab to be included in group.

   ✓ *The word [Group] appears in the title and task bars.*

### Ungroup Sheets

1. Right-click any sheet tab in group.
2. Click **Ungroup Sheets**........ U

OR

- Click any sheet tab not in group.

### Delete Sheet(s)

1. Select sheet tab(s).
2. Right-click sheet tab.
3. Click **Delete**......................... D
4. Click **Delete** to confirm deletion of a sheet with data Enter

### Rename Sheet

1. Double-click sheet tab.
   OR
   a. Right-click sheet tab.
   b. Select **Rename**.............. R
2. Type new name.
3. Press **Enter**...................... Enter

### Insert Sheet(s)

1. Select number of sheet tabs as sheets to be inserted.
2. Right-click sheet tab.

   ✓ *The new sheets will be inserted before the first sheet in the group.*

3. Click **Insert** ......................... I
4. Select **General tab** of Insert dialog box.......... Ctrl + Tab
5. Select **Worksheet**............
6. Click **OK**........................... Enter

## Move Sheet(s) within Workbook

1. If necessary, click tab scrolling buttons to view hidden sheet tabs.
2. Click and drag selected sheet tab(s) to new sheet tab position.
   - ✓ Mouse pointer shape changes to 🔲. Black triangle indicates where sheet will be inserted.

## Copy Sheet

1. If necessary, click tab scrolling buttons to view hidden sheet tabs.
2. Select sheet tab.
3. Press and hold **Ctrl**, as you click and drag selected sheet tab to its final position.
   - ✓ Mouse pointer shape changes to 🔲 with a plus sign. Black triangle indicates where sheet will be inserted.

- ✓ To copy multiple sheets at once, select them, then choose *Edit, Move* or *Copy Sheet*. Select a location to place the copies from the Move or Copy dialog box, choose **Create a copy**, and then click **OK**.

## Change Tab Color

1. Select the sheet tab(s) you wish to make the same color.
2. Right-click sheet tab in group.
3. Click **Tab Color** .................. 🆃
4. Select a color .................... ⬚
5. Click **OK** ......................... Enter
   - ✓ You can remove the color on a tab by repeating these steps and choosing **No Color** in step 4.

## Use AutoFormat

1. Select the data range you want to format, or select multiple ranges if you like.
   - ✓ You can format the exact same range on multiple sheets by positioning the cursor within the data range, and selecting the tabs of the sheets you want to format.

2. Click **Format** ............... Alt + O
3. Click **AutoFormat** ............... A
4. Select the format you want to apply. .................... ⬚
5. To apply only selected parts of the format, click **Options** .... O
6. From the expanded dialog box, select only the formats you want to apply:
   a. **Number** ...................... N
   b. **Border** ......................... B
   c. **Font** ............................ F
   d. **Patterns** ...................... P
   e. **Alignment** .................... A
   f. **Width/Height** ............... W
7. Click **OK** .......................... Enter

# Exercise Directions

1. Start Excel if necessary.
2. Open 💿 **11ORGANIC**.
3. Save the file as **ORGANIC**.
4. Rename Sheet 1 **Frequency**. Rename Sheet 2 **Users**. Rename Sheet 3 **Buying Habits - Men**.
5. Make a copy of the Buying Habits – Men sheet, and place the copy in front of that sheet.
   a. Rename the copied sheet **Buying Habits – Women**.
   b. Change the percentages to match those shown in Illustration A.
   c. Change cell D9 to **Women**.
6. Move the Users worksheet in front of the Frequency sheet.
7. Insert a new worksheet in front of Users worksheet, and rename it **Basic Survey Info**.
8. Select the two Buying Habits worksheets to form a group.

9. Color the tabs of the worksheets in that group a light yellow.
10. Select the remaining worksheets, and color their tabs a light green.
11. Delete Sheet 4, since it contains duplicate data.
12. Group the two Buying Habits Worksheets.
13. Click cell C11 of the Buying Habits – Women worksheet, select the other Buying Habits worksheet, and apply the Colorful 2 AutoFormat.
14. Apply the Colorful 1 AutoFormat to the two Users and Frequency sheets.
    - ✓ Because the data on the Users and Frequency sheets is not laid out exactly the same, you must apply the AutoFormat to each sheet individually, by clicking within the data range and selecting the AutoFormat you want. You can't apply an AutoFormat to the Basic Survey Info sheet, since it does not contain any data.
15. Select all four sheets, and apply these formats to the following ranges:
    - ✓ If you do not have these exact same fonts, choose your own, using Illustration A as an example.
    a. D4:F4—Architect, 14, bold, tan fill

b. D6:D7—Architect, 10, bold, tan fill

c. E6—Light yellow fill

d. E7:I7—Light yellow fill

16. Select the two Buying Habits worksheets, and apply Architect, 10, bold, tan fill to cell D9.

17. Adjust column widths as needed to fully display data.

18. Spell check the workbook.

19. Print the entire workbook.

20. Close the file, saving all changes.

*Illustration A*

# On Your Own

1. Open a new workbook in Excel.

2. Save the file as **OXL11**.

3. Set up a worksheet for tracking weekly income.

   ✓ *For this exercise, assume that you receive income from a part-time job, along with a weekly allowance. Also, you've decided to sell some old CDs, so record the sales from that effort. In addition, your birthday falls during week 3 of this month, and you usually receive money gifts from several relatives.*

4. Delete Sheet 2 and Sheet 3.

5. On Sheet 1, enter a title for the worksheet in row 2.

6. Label columns B through H for the days of the week.

7. In the rows in column A, list your sources of income: **Job**, **Allowance**, **CD sales**, and **Gifts**.

8. Copy Sheet 1 three times, to create four worksheets.

9. Label the four sheets: **Week 1, Week 2, Week 3,** and **Week 4** respectively. Assign a unique color to each week's tab.

10. Enter data in all three worksheets. You may or may not have income for each day, or for each category (job, allowance, CD sales, or gifts).

11. Group the worksheets and enter formulas to calculate the total income for each category as well as for each day of the week.

    ✓ *Label the column and row where the results are displayed correctly.*

    ✓ *Select the data and totals, and apply the numeric format of your choice.*

12. Select the data range of one sheet, then group the worksheets and apply the AutoFormat of your choice—but do not apply the AutoFormat's Number format.

13. Spell check the workbook.

14. Print the entire workbook.

15. Close the file, saving all changes.

# Exercise 12

◆ **Critical Thinking**

You're the invoice clerk for California Cardiology, Inc., and one of the insurance companies you work with has asked for a detailed summary of their client's initial bills, payments made, and overdue amounts. Since you need to summarize several months' worth of data, you'll place each month's unpaid invoices on a separate worksheet. You'll add formulas, formatting, insert sheets, and make several other changes before you're finished.

## Exercise Directions

1. Start Excel, if necessary.

2. Open ⌨**OVERDUE** or 💿**12OVERDUE**.

3. Save the file as **OVERDUE**.

4. Apply the Classic 2 AutoFormat to the range B7:E10.

5. Add additional formatting:

   a. B8:B10—Right alignment.

   b. B12:B14 and A16:B16—Arial, 9 pt., violet fill, white text color, and adjust column widths as necessary.

   c. C8:C16—Currency format, 2 decimal places, and adjust column widths as necessary.

   d. B3:E3—Copperplate Gothic Bold, 14, pale blue fill.

   e. B5:E5—Arial, 11 pt., italic, light turquoise fill.

6. Make a copy of Sheet 1 and place that copy in front of Sheet 2.

   a. Rename Sheet 1 **April** and color its tab red.

   b. Rename Sheet 1 (2) **May** and color its tab blue.

   c. Delete Sheet 2 and Sheet 3.

   d. On the April sheet, change cell B5 to **Healthman HMO -- April Overdue Invoices**.

   e. On the May sheet, change cell B5 to **Healthman HMO – May Overdue Invoices**.

7. Select both worksheets.

   a. Insert two columns in front of column C.

   b. In cell C7, type **Original Amount**.

   c. In cell D7, type **Current Amount**.

   d. Change cell E7 to **% of Monthly Total**, and adjust the column width so all the text is visible.

   e. Using drag and drop, move the data in E8:E10 to D8:D10.

   f. Using Cut and Paste, move the data in E12:E16 to C12:C16.

   g. Select D12:D16, and remove the color fill.

8. With the sheets still selected, type a formula in cell E8 that computes the percentage of the total overdue amount (cell C14) the current amount due (cell D8) represents.

   ✓ In other words, how much of the total, $3,881.27, does the amount $2,147.48 represent? Is it 50%? 60%? Or something even higher?

   ✓ To calculate the percent, take the smaller number and divide by the bigger number.

   ✓ Since you want all the formulas to use the reference, C14, you'll need to make it an absolute cell address in the original formula.

9. Copy this formula to E9:E10, and apply Percent, 3 decimal place format.

10. Ungroup the worksheets, change to the April worksheet, and enter the following Original Amounts:

    a. J. Thomas Wilson: **$3,218.48**

    b. Carlos Riveria: **$375.97**

    c. Alice Thomson: **$4,893.21**

    d. Format the cells as currency with two decimals.

11. Change the information on the May worksheet to match Illustration A.

    ✓ Tell Excel to ignore the error that appears after you enter the invoice numbers as text.

12. Add a sheet after the May sheet, label it **Summary,** and color its tab yellow.

   a. Type the information shown in Illustration B.

   b. Copy the Current amount due and the Amount due if paid after 5/16 or 6/16 for April and May, and paste them in their appropriate spots on the Summary sheet as shown. Be sure to copy the values and number formats, and not the formulas.

   c. Apply the Classic 2 AutoFormat to the range B6:D8, and adjust the column widths as necessary.

   d. Apply Arial, 11 pt., italic, light turquoise fill to the range B4:E4.

   e. Apply Arial, 9 pt., right-align, violet fill, white text color to cell B10.

13. Adjust column widths to fit the data.

14. Spell check the workbook.

15. Preview each sheet, and print the workbook.

16. Close the file, saving all changes.

*Illustration A*

| | A | B | C | D | E | F | G |
|---|---|---|---|---|---|---|---|
| 1 | | | | | | | |
| 2 | | | | | | | |
| 3 | | **CALIFORNIA CARDIOLOGY, INC.** | | | | | |
| 4 | | | | | | | |
| 5 | | *Healthman HMO -- May Overdue Invoices* | | | | | |
| 6 | | | | | | | |
| 7 | | Patient | Original Amount | Current Amount | % of Monthly Total | Invoice Number | Date Due |
| 8 | | Henry Lee | $4,975.65 | $4,975.65 | 57.733% | 2189558 | 5/15/2001 |
| 9 | | Sendal Gundra | $2,497.86 | $2,497.86 | 28.983% | 219776 | 5/15/2001 |
| 10 | | Alice Thomson | $4,893.21 | $975.86 | 11.323% | 2049462 | 4/21/2001 |
| 11 | | | | | | | |
| 12 | | Overdue amount: | $8,449.37 | | | | |
| 13 | | Late charge: | $168.99 | | | | |
| 14 | | Current amount due: | $8,618.36 | | | | |
| 15 | | | | | | | |
| 16 | | Amount due if paid after 6/16: | $8,790.72 | | | | |

*Illustration B*

| | A | B | C | D | E |
|---|---|---|---|---|---|
| 1 | | | | | |
| 2 | | | | | |
| 3 | | | | | |
| 4 | | *Overdue Amounts for Healthman HMO - Summary* | | | |
| 5 | | | | | |
| 6 | | | Current | If Paid Late | |
| 7 | | April Overdue Amount | $3,881.27 | $3,958.90 | |
| 8 | | May Overdue Amount | $8,618.36 | $8,790.72 | |
| 9 | | | | | |
| 10 | | Grand Totals | $12,499.63 | $12,749.62 | |
| 11 | | | | | |
| 12 | | | | | |
| 13 | | | | | |
| 14 | | | | | |
| 15 | | | | | |
| 16 | | | | | |

April / May \ Summary /

# Exercise 13

## On the Job

Use an Excel function to help you write a formula to perform specific calculations in your worksheets. Excel's Paste Function feature provides a list of available functions with a wizard to assist you in "filling in the blanks" to complete a formula.

You work for Murray Hill Marketing, and you've just been assigned the account for Dan's Digital Camera Works, a new store that sells digital cameras exclusively. They are concerned about the competition, and they've asked you to create a report that lists the number of digital cameras sold and dollar sales by their four competitors for the last three years. You need to perform some analysis of this information, calculating averages, minimums, and maximums.

## Terms

**Function**  A predefined formula that depends on specific values to perform a specific calculation.

**Function name**  The name given to Excel's predefined formulas.

**Argument**  Part of a formula that contains the specific values necessary to perform the function.

**Nest**  To insert a function into another function.

**AutoCalculate**  A feature that temporarily performs the following calculations on a range of cells without making you write a formula: Average, Count, Count Nums, Max, Min, or Sum.

## Notes

### Use Functions

- Excel provides built-in formulas called **functions** to perform special calculations.

- A function contains these elements in the following order:

    - The equal symbol (=) starts the function.

    - The **function name** is entered in upper- or lowercase letters.

    - An open parenthesis separates the **arguments** from the function name.

    - The argument(s) identify the data required to perform the function.

- A closed parenthesis ends the argument.

    Example: =SUM(A1:A40)

    ✓ *This sum function adds the values listed in the argument, which in this case is a single range of cells A1 through A40.*

- Most functions allow multiple arguments, separated by commas.

    ✓ *For example, =SUM(A1:A40,C1:C40) adds the values in the ranges A1:A40 and C1:C40.*

- A function may be inserted into a formula.

    ✓ *For example, =B2/SUM(C3:C5)*

- When a function is used as an argument for other functions, it is **nested** within those functions.

## Common Functions

■ You'll find these functions to be the ones you use most often:

- =SUM( ) adds the values in a range of cells.
- =AVERAGE( ) returns the arithmetic mean of the values in a range of cells.
- =COUNT( ) counts the cells containing numbers in a range of cells (blank cells or text entries are ignored).
- =MAX( ) finds the highest value in a range of cells.
- =MIN( ) finds the lowest value in a range of cells.
- =ROUND( ) adjusts a value to a specific number of digits.

   ✓ *When a cell is formatted to a specified number of decimal places, only the display of that value is affected. The actual value in the cell is still used in all calculations. For example, if a cell contains the value 13.45687, and you decide to display only the last two decimal places, then the value 13.46 will display in the cell, but the value, 13.45687 will be used in all calculations.*

   ✓ *Let's say you have a long column of numbers such as this:*

      **Sales Projections**
      2147.8347
      2866.1633
      2593.0049
      **Total: 7607.0029**

   *You're not interested in the extra digits past a penny, so you simply change the formatting, and the numbers appear like this:*

      **Sales Projections**
      2147.83
      2866.16
      2593.00
      **Total: 7607.00**

   ✓ *So, if you plan on displaying a limited number of decimal places and not the whole number, you might want to use the ROUND function to adjust each value so that the displayed value is equal to the actual value used in calculations.*

   ✓ *For example, use the ROUND function to round the value 2147.8347 to 2147.8400, like this:*

      **Sales Projections**
      2147.8400
      2866.1600
      2593.0000
      **Total: 7607.0000**

   *If you then display only two decimal places, the total will display correctly:*

      **Sales Projections**
      2147.84
      2866.16
      2593.00
      **Total: 7607.00**

   ✓ *Of course, if you are interested in every digit of the calculated sales projections, then display them fully so that your totals will add up.*

- Use the drop-down arrow on AutoSum button Σ ▾ on the Standard toolbar to quickly insert a SUM, AVERAGE, COUNT, MIN, or MAX function.

## Insert a Function

■ You can enter a function by typing it, or you can use the Insert Function dialog box to help you locate a specific function and enter the correct arguments.

■ To insert a function instead of typing it, click the Insert Function button *fx* on the Formula bar; then type a brief description of the function you want help with (or type its name).

   ✓ *You can also display functions by category by choosing one from the Or select a category list.*

   ✓ *When you enter a formula using Insert Function, Excel automatically enters the equal sign in the formula.*

■ After selecting a function, you're prompted to enter the appropriate arguments into a second dialog box—Function Arguments.

- You can select cells instead of typing them by using the Collapse Dialog button located at the right of each text box.
- Required arguments are displayed in bold.
- As you enter the arguments, the value of that argument is displayed to the right of the text box.
- Excel calculates the current result and displays it at the bottom of the dialog box.

- If you need help understanding a particular function's arguments, click the Help on this function link.

*Insert Function dialog box*

*Function Arguments dialog box*

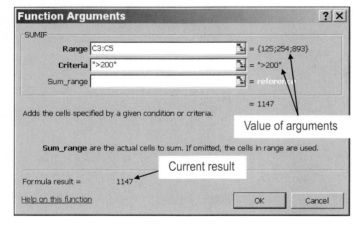

## AutoCalculate

- When you want to quickly calculate the Average, Count, Count Nums, Max, Min, or Sum for a range of cells on your worksheet, without actually entering a formula, use **AutoCalculate**.

- Using the mouse, drag across a range of cells to display the auto calculation (default is SUM) on the Status bar.

- To use a different function with AutoCalculate, right-click the AutoCalculate result on the Status bar and pick from the list of functions.

*AutoCalculate function list*

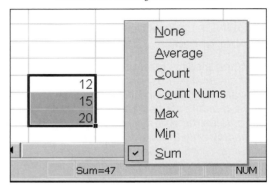

# Procedures

## Enter a Function Manually

1. Click cell where result should display ............................... 🔼🔽
2. Type **Equal** ......................... 🟦
3. Type function name.
4. Type **Left Parenthesis** ...... 🟦
5. Enter arguments, separated by commas.
   **You can enter:**
   - Numeric value
   - Cell reference
   - Range of cells
   - Range name
   - Function
6. Press **Right Parenthesis** ... 🟦
7. Press **Enter** ...................... Enter

## Insert a Function

1. Click cell where result should display ................... 🔼🔽
2. Click **Insert Function** button 🟦.
   OR
   a. Click **Insert** ............ Alt + I
   b. Click **Function** ............... F
3. Type the function name or a brief description in the **Search for a function** text box ....................... Alt + S
   OR
   Select category from **Or select a category** list ....... Alt + C, 🔼🔽
4. Select function from **Select a function** list ..... Alt + N, 🔼🔽
5. Click **OK** ........................... Enter
   ✓ *The Function Arguments dialog box appears.*
6. Click argument text box ....... Tab

7. Type data.
   You can enter:
   - Numeric value
   - Cell reference
   - Range of cells
   - Range name
   - Function
   ✓ *To enter a cell reference or range of cells from the worksheet, click the Collapse button located to the right of the argument text box, select the cell(s), and then click the Collapse button again to expand the dialog box.*
8. Repeat steps 6 and 7 to complete arguments.
9. Click **OK** ........................... Enter

## Enter a Common Function

1. Click cell where result should display ................... 🔼🔽
2. To enter SUM function, click **AutoSum** button Σ ▾.
   OR
   To enter AVERAGE, COUNT, MAX, or MIN function, click the arrow on **AutoSum** button Σ ▾ and select the function you want.
   ✓ *Excel guesses the range you want to use with the function you selected.*
3. If the selected range is not the one you want to use, select the range you want by dragging over it with the mouse.
4. Press **Enter** ...................... Enter
   ✓ *You can display the Insert Function dialog box to enter any function by selecting More Functions from the AutoSum list.*

## Edit a Function

1. Click result cell ................. 🔼🔽
2. Click in Formula bar.
3. Type correction.
   OR
   a. Click **Insert Function** button 𝑓ₓ on Formula bar to redisplay Formula Arguments dialog box.
   b. Click argument text box.
   c. Type correction.
4. Click **OK** ........................... Enter

## Enter a Function into a Formula

1. Click formula cell ............... 🔼🔽
   where answer will display.
2. Type **Equal** ..................... 🟦
3. Type the beginning part of the formula.
4. At the point in the formula where you wish to use a function, type the function name.
5. Type **Left Parenthesis** ........ 🟦
6. Type arguments(s).
7. Type **Right Parenthesis** ...... 🟦
8. Press **Enter** ...................... Enter

## Use AutoCalculate

1. Select cells ............... Shift + 🔼🔽
   you want to calculate.
2. View result of calculation on Status bar.
3. Right-click result.
4. Click desired function in list ..................... 🔼🔽, Enter

# Exercise Directions

1. Start Excel, if necessary.

2. Open 💿 **13COMPETE**.

3. Save the file as **COMPETE**.

4. In cell G6, use the AutoSum button to enter a formula that calculates the total digital cameras sold over the last three years by Mike's Camera World.

5. Copy this formula to cells G9, G12, and G15.

   ✓ Since you do not want to replace the formatting of the destination cells, you'll need to paste each cell one at a time, then select the Paste Option, Match Destination Formatting.

6. In cell G7, use the Insert Function button to enter a formula that calculates the total digital camera sales for Mike's Camera World.

7. Copy this formula to cells G10, G13, and G16. Do not overlay the formatting already in those cells.

8. In cell C20, use the AutoSum button to enter a formula that calculates the average number of units sold per year by all the competitors.

   ✓ You'll need to select each of the 12 cells that contain units sold data. (Do not select the four cells that contain total units sold.) You can calculate the average of a group of ranges by entering them as separate arguments, with a comma between each one. Just press **Ctrl** and click each range.

9. In cell C21, use the Insert Function button to enter a function that calculates the average sales of the competitors' combined sales.

   ✓ Again, select the 12 cells that contain the yearly sales data, not the total sales cells.

10. In cell C22, use the AutoSum button to enter a formula that calculates the minimum number of units sold during any one year by any competitor.

11. In cell C23, use the Insert Function button to enter a formula that calculates the maximum number of units sold during any one year by any competitor.

12. Widen any columns as necessary.

13. Use AutoCalculate to check your results.

   ✓ Remember that to select non-contiguous ranges, press Ctrl and drag over each range. The sum of the selected ranges appears in the Status bar. To view the results using other functions (such as AVERAGE), right-click the word **Sum** on the Status bar and select a different function.

14. Spell check the worksheet.

15. Print the worksheet.

16. Close the file, saving all changes.

*Illustration A*

| | A | B | C | D | E | F | G |
|---|---|---|---|---|---|---|---|
| 1 | | | | | | | |
| 2 | | **Murray Hill Marketing, LLC** | | | | | |
| 3 | | *Survey of the Competition* | | | | | |
| 4 | | | | | | | |
| 5 | | | | 1999 | 2000 | 2001 | Totals |
| 6 | | Mike's Camera World | Units Sold | 632 | 2741 | 4595 | 7968 |
| 7 | | | Sales | $ 287,000 | $1,507,550 | $2,986,750 | $4,781,300 |
| 8 | | | | | | | |
| 9 | | Enriz Photo | Units Sold | 331 | 521 | 978 | 1830 |
| 10 | | | Sales | $ 331,000 | $ 208,400 | $ 489,000 | $1,028,400 |
| 11 | | | | | | | |
| 12 | | Digital Den | Units Sold | 1247 | 3125 | 4388 | 8760 |
| 13 | | | Sales | $1,247,000 | $1,953,125 | $2,961,900 | $6,162,025 |
| 14 | | | | | | | |
| 15 | | Photos by Perez | Units Sold | 681 | 756 | 1033 | 2470 |
| 16 | | | Sales | $ 681,000 | $ 378,000 | $ 593,975 | $1,652,975 |
| 17 | | | | | | | |
| 18 | **Summary** | | | | | | |
| 19 | | | | | | | |
| 20 | | Average Units Sold each Year | 1752.33333 | | | | |
| 21 | | Average Sales each Year | $1,135,392 | | | | |
| 22 | | Minimum Units Sold by Any Competitor in One Yr. | 331 | | | | |
| 23 | | Maximum Units Sold by Any Competitor in One Yr. | 4595 | | | | |
| 24 | | | | | | | |

# On Your Own

1. Open the **OXL10** file you created in the On Your Own section of Exercise 10, or open ⊙**13CDMANIA**.

2. Save the file as **OXL13**.

3. Enter May and June sales data for each store.

4. Use the AutoSum button to enter formulas that calculate sales totals for May and June.

5. Apply Accounting Style, 2 decimal places, to the sales data and totals.

6. Widen any columns as needed.

7. Beginning in row 20, create a summary section that includes the following:

   a. In row 20, type the word **Summary**.

   b. In row 22, beginning in column B, enter the name of the months, January through June.

   c. In column A, beginning in row 23, type the labels **Average Sales**, **Maximum Sales by Any Store**, and **Minimum Sales by Any Store**.

   d. In row 23, enter formulas that calculate the average sales for each month—January through June.

   e. In row 24, enter formulas that display the sales total of the store that sold the most for that month.

   f. In row 25, enter formulas to display the total for the store that sold the least that month.

   g. In cell A27, type the label **Total number of times sales were over $25,000**.

   h. In cell B27, enter a formula that calculates the total number of times any store sold more than $25,000 in any given month.

      ✓ To calculate this, you'll need to use the COUNTIF function. Because COUNTIF only counts the valid cells in one range, you'll need to use two COUNTIF functions in one formula and add their results together.

      ✓ To use COUNTIF, select the range you want to analyze, then type the condition you want to compare against—which in this case, is >25000, which means "greater than 25000."

8. Use the AutoCalculate function to check the formula results.

9. Spell check the worksheet.

10. Apply formatting as you like, and print the worksheet.

11. Close the file, saving all changes.

# Exercise 14

## Skills Covered:

### ◆ Natural Language Formulas ◆ Comments

## On the Job

Write natural language formulas and add comments to your worksheet to help you read the formulas or remember why you included certain information in your worksheet.

You're the Detroit plant manager for Electron Consumer Industries, and you've been asked to prepare a report detailing the sales of the company's new computer chip for automobiles, the Super G 2001. You've got a lot of data to summarize, so you weren't looking forward to entering a lot of tedious formulas—until you discovered Excel's natural language formula option. Using real words like "Ford" and "GMC" with Excel's SUM and AVERAGE functions will make the task of entering proper totals easier. When you're through, you'll use the Comment feature to add some notes that will help your boss interpret the data.

## Terms

**Natural language formula** A formula that refers to column or row heading labels instead of a cell reference or range.

**Comment** A text note attached to a worksheet cell.

## Notes

### Natural Language Formulas

- Excel allows you to create **natural language formulas** that refer to column and row labels in place of the cell reference or range.

    ✓ *When "natural language" is used in a formula the column or row label must be spelled exactly as the column or row label appears.*

- For example, =SUM(Jan) totals the range of cells in the Jan column that are located either above or to the left of the formula.

*Column heading in a natural language formula*

|   | A | B | C |
|---|---|---|---|
| 1 | Jan | Feb | Mar |
| 2 | 1500 | 1700 | 1500 |
| 3 | 600 | 1300 | 1000 |
| 4 | 800 | 1200 | 900 |
| 5 | =SUM(Jan) | =SUM(Feb) | =SUM(Mar) |

- If you've used a label more than once in a worksheet, Excel may ask you to select the label to which you're referring in your natural language formula.

*Identify Label dialog box*

**Identify Label**   ? X

There is more than one cell with this label:

jan

Select the cell containing the label to use:

A1

OK    Cancel

- To use natural language formulas, you must first turn on that option on the Calculations tab of the Options dialog box, as explained in the Procedures.

## Comments

- To attach a text note to a cell (maximum of 255 characters), use the Insert Comment command.

- A red triangle appears in the upper-right corner of any cell with an attached **comment**.

- To display the comment, simply rest the mouse pointer on the comment indicator (the red triangle).

- Comments help explain data, formulas, and labels used in a complex worksheet. You can insert comments as reminders to yourself, but they are especially useful for explaining a worksheet shared with others.

*Comment displayed on worksheet*

|   | A | B | C |
|---|---|---|---|
| 1 | Jan | Feb | Mar |
| 2 | 1500 | 1700 | 1500 |
| 3 | 600 | 1300 | 1000 |
| 4 | 800 | 1000 | 900 |
| 5 | =SUM(Jan) | =SUM(Mar) | |
| 6 | | | |
| 7 | | | |
| 8 | | | |

**Jennifer Fulton:**
This cell uses a natural language formula.

- If you want, you can display all the comments on a worksheet with a single command.

# Procedures

**The following option must be checked for natural language formulas to work within a particular workbook:**

1. Click **Tools** ................. `Alt`+`T`
2. Click **Options** ..................... `O`
3. Click **Calculation** tab ... `Ctrl`+`Tab`
4. Select **Accept labels in formulas** option ................. `B`
5. **Click OK** ......................... `Enter`

### Create Natural Language Formula

1. Click formula cell ............... `⬍⬌` where answer will display.
2. Press equal symbol ............. `=`
3. Type name of function.
4. Type open parenthesis ........ `(`
5. Type argument using column or row labels instead of cell reference or range.
6. Type close parenthesis ....... `)`
7. Press **Enter** ..................... `Enter`

### Create Comment

1. Select cell to attach comment.
2. Click **Insert** ................ `Alt`+`I`
3. Click **Comment** .................. `M`
4. Type text.
   - ✓ Note that handles appear around the box to resize or move it.
5. Click outside box.
   - ✓ A red triangle now displays in the upper-right corner of the comment cell.

### Display Comment

- Move mouse pointer over cell that contains a comment.
  - ✓ Comment appears in a small yellow box beside the cell.
  - ✓ To display all comments in a worksheet, choose **View, Comments**. Select **View, Comments** again to get rid of them.

### Edit Comment

1. Right-click cell with comment.
2. Click **Edit Comment** ........... `E`
3. Make correction.
   - ✓ Drag a handle to increase or decrease the size of the box.
4. Click outside of box.

### Delete Comment

1. Right-click cell with comment.
2. Click **Delete Comment** ....... `M`

# Exercise Directions

1. Start Excel, if necessary.
2. Open ⊙ **14CHIPSALES**.
3. Save the file as **CHIPSALES**.
4. Turn on the natural language feature for this workbook.
5. In cell C16, use the SUM function to create a natural language formula that calculates the total sales for April.
6. Use the fill handle to copy this formula to cells D16:E16.
   - ✓ *Notice that Excel creates a series from your formula. For example, in cell D16, Excel creates the formula, =SUM(May) and does not simply copy the formula =SUM(April) from cell C16.*
7. In cell C17, use the AVERAGE function to create a natural language formula that calculates the average sales for April.
8. Copy this formula to cells D17:E17.
9. In cell F10, use the SUM function to create a natural language formula that calculates the total sales for the quarter to GMC.
10. Copy this formula to cell F11:F14.
11. Add a comment to cells E11 and E13 that indicates that these figures are not the final ones.
12. Using the mouse, view the comments one at a time.
13. Using the View, Comments command, display all the comments.
14. Delete the comment in cell E13.
15. Spell check the worksheet.
16. Print the worksheet.
17. Close the file, saving all changes.

*Illustration A*

| | A | B | C | D | E | F |
|---|---|---|---|---|---|---|
| 1 | | | | | | |
| 2 | | **Electron Consumer Industries** | | | | |
| 3 | | | | | | |
| 4 | SUPER G 2001 COMPUTER CHIP SALES | | | | | |
| 5 | PLANT # | 5147 | | | | |
| 6 | | | | | | |
| 7 | QUARTER 2, 2001 | | | | | |
| 8 | | | | | | |
| 9 | | | APRIL | MAY | JUNE | QTR 2 TOTAL |
| 10 | | GMC | 14,506,789 | 17,894,511 | 15,684,791 | 48,086,091 |
| 11 | | FORD | 7,452,138 | 11,689,728 | 10,978,455 | 30,120,321 |
| 12 | | DAIMLER-CHRYSLER | 28,314,548 | 25,418,964 | 19,154,974 | 72,888,486 |
| 13 | | TOYOTA | 9,748,111 | 6,418,795 | 7,854,972 | 24,021,878 |
| 14 | | HONDA | 6,487,551 | 5,784,612 | 6,484,572 | 18,756,735 |
| 15 | | | | | | |
| 16 | TOTAL UNITS SOLD | | 66,509,137 | 67,206,610 | 60,157,764 | |
| 17 | AVERAGE # OF UNITS SOLD | | 13,301,827 | 13,441,322 | 12,031,553 | |
| 18 | | | | | | |

# On Your Own

1. Open a new workbook in Excel.
2. Save the file as **OXL14**.
3. Create a worksheet to estimate your anticipated college or school expenses for next year.
4. Enter a worksheet title in row 1.
5. Label column B **September** for September's expenses.
6. Use the fill handle to create the column labels for October through May.
7. Enter row labels for each different type of expense.
   - ✓ *Examples might include books, school supplies (such as notebooks, pens, and paper), computer supplies, gas and car maintenance, parking, and extras (such as concert tickets and dinners out).*
8. Enter values for the expense items in each month.
   - ✓ *If some expenses are the same for every month, copy and paste the data, or use the fill handle.*

9. Label the row below the last expense item **Totals**, and then create a natural language formula to sum September's expenses.
10. Copy the formula to the other columns.
11. Format the worksheet data as currency.
12. Apply other formatting to improve the worksheet's appearance.
13. Adjust column widths as needed.
14. Add comments to several cells explaining your estimates.
15. Spell check the workbook.
16. Print the workbook.
17. Close the file, saving all changes.

*Illustration B*

| | A | B | C | D | E | F | G | H | I | J |
|---|---|---|---|---|---|---|---|---|---|---|
| 1 | Estimated College Expenses for 2002 | | | | | | | | | |
| 2 | | | | | | | | | | |
| 3 | | September | October | November | December | January | February | March | April | May |
| 4 | Books | $ 185.00 | | | | $ 235.00 | | | | |
| 5 | Supplies | $ 100.00 | $ 75.00 | $ 35.00 | $ 20.00 | $ 125.00 | $ 75.00 | $ 45.00 | $ 35.00 | $ 15.00 |
| 6 | Computer Stuff | $ 575.00 | $ 45.00 | | $ 275.00 | $ 50.00 | | | $ 75.00 | $ 55.00 |
| 7 | Gas | $ 35.00 | $ 25.00 | $ 25.00 | $ 45.00 | $ 35.00 | $ 25.00 | $ 30.00 | $ 25.00 | $ 55.00 |
| 8 | Repairs | | $ 225.00 | $ 75.00 | $ 50.00 | $ 125.00 | $ 55.00 | | | $ 35.00 |
| 9 | Parking | $ 225.00 | | | | $ 225.00 | | | | |
| 10 | Extras | $ 100.00 | $ 100.00 | $ 100.00 | $ 100.00 | $ 100.00 | $ 100.00 | $ 100.00 | $ 100.00 | $ 100.00 |
| 11 | Totals | $1,220.00 | $470.00 | $235.00 | $490.00 | $895.00 | $255.00 | $175.00 | $235.00 | $260.00 |
| 12 | | | | | | | | | | |

# Exercise 15

### ◆ Named Ranges

## On the Job

At times it may be easier to reference a cell or range of cells with a descriptive name. For example, a range name can make the formulas in your worksheet easier to understand, and the formatting and printing easier to accomplish.

You are the manager of a local Northwest Gear store, and you did such a great job creating a worksheet to track the sales for your new sleeveless cashmere sweaters that you've been asked to expand the worksheet to include two other new items. You've entered the additional data, and now you need to add grand total and percent of grand total formulas for each new item, and to create a summary. Since there are so many formulas to add, you've decided to use range names to keep the data straight.

## Terms

**Range name** An identification label assigned to a group of cells.

**Name box** The text box located to the left of the Formula bar.

## Notes

### Named Ranges

- A **range name** is a descriptive name assigned to two or more cells for identification.

- After naming a range, you can use the range name anyplace the range address might otherwise be entered—such as within a formula, defining the print range, selecting a range to format, and so on.

  ✓ As you learned in Exercise 14, you don't have to name ranges to use your row and column labels in formulas. See Exercise 14 for more information.

- Range names cannot be repeated within a workbook, even if they are located on different worksheets.

- Range names can be referenced across worksheets.

- A range name may use up to 255 characters, although short descriptive names are easier to read and remember.

- Some rules for naming ranges are:
  - Spaces are not allowed. Use the underscore character to simulate a space.
  - Do not use range names that could be interpreted as a cell address or a number, such as Q2 or Y2001.
  - A range name may include letters, numbers, underscores (_), backslashes (\), periods (.), and question marks (?).
  - You cannot begin a range name with a number.
  - Avoid using your column and row labels as range names, because they could confuse you when used with the natural language formula feature, should you turn that on.

✓ *For example, suppose you had a worksheet with column labels Jan, Feb, Mar and so on, and you created a range in the January column and named it Jan. Then suppose you forgot about that and turned on natural language formulas, typed the formula =SUM(Jan) at the end of the January column, and copied the formula to the Feb and Mar columns. If you hadn't created the range name Jan, then Excel would have created the formulas =SUM(Feb) and =SUM(Mar) as expected. But because you did, Excel treats the range name as an absolute reference and displays the formula =SUM(Jan) in both the February and March columns, resulting in errors.*

■ Use the Name, Define command or the **name box** to assign a name to a selected range.

*Name box*

Name box

■ If you have a lot of named ranges in a workbook, you might want to have Excel insert a list of all your named ranges with their corresponding cell references into the worksheet.

*Define Name dialog box*

# Procedures

## Name Range with Menu

1. Select range to name.
2. Click **Insert**.................. Alt+I
3. Click **Name**.......................... N
4. Click **Define** ........................ D

   ✓ *Note that the selected range appears in **Refers to** text box and the nearest column or row label appears in **Names in workbook** text box.*

5. Type name in **Names in workbook** text box...... Alt+W
6. Click **Add** button [ Add ] ...... Alt+A
7. Click **OK** ............................ Enter

## Name Range with Name Box

1. Select range on worksheet to name.
2. Click in name box.
3. Type name.
4. Press **Enter**...................... Enter

## Modify Named Range

1. Click **Insert**.................. Alt+I
2. Click **Name**.......................... N
3. Click **Define** ........................ D

   ✓ *Active cell reference appears in Refers to text box.*

   **To delete name:**

   a. Click name in list .................... Tab, ↕

b. Click **Delete** .......... Alt+D

**To change name:**

a. Click name in list .................... Tab, ↕
b. Double-click in **Names in workbook**.......... Alt+W
c. Type new name for range.
d. Click **Add** button [ Add ] .......... Alt+A
e. Click old name in list.................... Tab, ↕
f. Click **Delete** button [ Delete ] ............ Alt+D

### To change range defined by a name:

a. Click name in list ...................... `Tab`, `↑↓`

b. Drag through reference in **Refers to** text box... `Alt`+`R`

c. Use collapse button to select cells in worksheet.
   OR
   Type new cell reference.

4. Click **OK** ........................... `Enter`

### Select Cells in a Named Range

**Using name box:**

1. Click drop-down arrow in name box.
2. Click desired named range.

**Using Go To:**

1. Press **F5** ............................. `F5`
2. Click name in **Go to** text box ... `Alt`+`G`, `↕↔`
3. Click **OK** ........................... `Enter`

### Insert List of Named Ranges in Worksheet

1. Click in upper-left cell of range to receive list.
2. Click **Insert** ................. `Alt`+`I`
3. Click **Name** ......................... `N`
4. Click **Paste** ......................... `P`
5. Select range to paste.
6. Click **Paste List** button `Paste List` ....... `Alt`+`L`

   ✓ List includes range name with corresponding sheet name and cell references.

### Set Print Area for Named Range

✓ This option is useful when you want to print a specific area of the worksheet.

1. Click **File** ..................... `Alt`+`F`
2. Click **Page Setup** ............... `U`
3. Click **Sheet** tab........... `Ctrl`+`Tab`
4. Click **Print area** .......... `Alt`+`A` text box.
5. Type name of range.
6. Click **Print** button `Print...` ....... `Alt`+`P`

   ✓ Choose print options as needed.

7. Click **OK** ........................... `Enter`

### Print Named Range

1. Follow steps to select named range.
2. Click **File** ..................... `Alt`+`F`
3. Click **Print** ......................... `P`
4. Click **OK** ........................... `Enter`

# Exercise Directions

1. Start Excel, if necessary.
2. Open ⊚ **15NWGNEW**.
3. Save the file as **NWGNEW**.
4. On the Cashmere Tops worksheet, select the range B14:D19, and name it **Cash_Tops**.
5. Name cell B23 **GTCash_Tops**.
6. On the Surfer Shorts worksheet, select the range B14:D17, and name it **Surf_Shorts**.
7. Name cell B21 **GTSurf_Shorts**.
8. On the Fleece Tops worksheet, select the range B14:D17, and name it **Fleece_Tops**.
9. Name cell B21 **GTFleece_Tops**.
10. On the Cashmere Tops worksheet, use the Cash_Tops range name to create a formula in cell B23 (total sales). See Illustration A.
11. Use the GTCash_Tops range name to create the formula for cell B24 (October percentage of total sales). Apply 2 Decimal, Percent format.

    ✓ Take the monthly total for October and divide by the Grand Total to calculate the percentage of total sales for October.

12. Copy the formula in cell B24 to C24:D24.

    ✓ Notice that the range name acts as an absolute reference to cell B23—it's not adjusted as the formula is copied from cell to cell.

13. Repeat steps 10 and 11 to create similar formulas on the Surfer Shorts and Fleece Tops worksheets.

14. On the Summary worksheet, in cells B13:B15, use your range names to enter formulas that calculate the total units sold.

    ✓ In cell B13, for example, you could enter the formula =SUM(Cash_Tops) or =GTCash_Tops.

15. Adjust column widths as needed.
16. Spell check the workbook.
17. Print the workbook.
18. Close the workbook, saving all changes.

*Illustration A*

| 13 | | October | November | December |
|---|---|---|---|---|
| 14 | *Red* | 2415 | 2694 | 2421 |
| 15 | *Lt. Blue* | 3108 | 3278 | 4386 |
| 16 | *Brown* | 978 | 1105 | 1098 |
| 17 | *Burnt Umber* | 1027 | 1594 | 1655 |
| 18 | *Burgundy* | 2374 | 3497 | 4297 |
| 19 | *Cyan* | 2156 | 3387 | 4092 |
| 20 | | | | |
| 21 | *Monthly Totals* | =SUM(B14:B19) | =SUM(C14:C19) | =SUM(D14:D19) |
| 22 | | | | |
| 23 | *Grand Total* | =SUM(Cash_Tops) | | |
| 24 | *% of Grand Total* | =B21/GTCash_Tops | =C21/GTCash_Tops | =D21/GTCash_Tops |

*Illustration B*

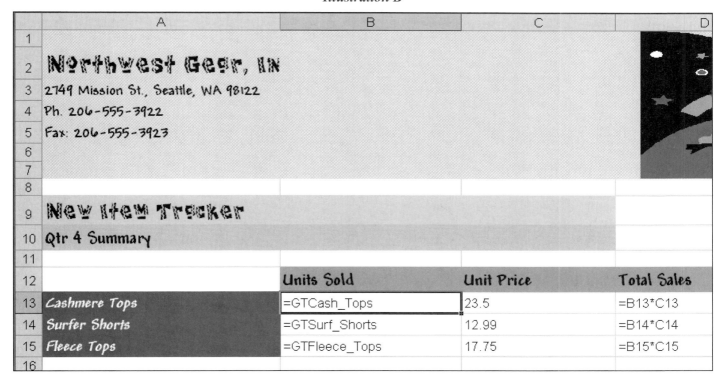

| | A | B | C | D |
|---|---|---|---|---|
| 1 | | | | |
| 2 | **Northwest Gear, In** | | | |
| 3 | 2749 Mission St., Seattle, WA 98122 | | | |
| 4 | Ph. 206-555-3922 | | | |
| 5 | Fax: 206-555-3923 | | | |
| 6 | | | | |
| 7 | | | | |
| 8 | | | | |
| 9 | **New Item Tracker** | | | |
| 10 | Qtr 4 Summary | | | |
| 11 | | | | |
| 12 | | Units Sold | Unit Price | Total Sales |
| 13 | *Cashmere Tops* | =GTCash_Tops | 23.5 | =B13*C13 |
| 14 | *Surfer Shorts* | =GTSurf_Shorts | 12.99 | =B14*C14 |
| 15 | *Fleece Tops* | =GTFleece_Tops | 17.75 | =B15*C15 |
| 16 | | | | |

# On Your Own

1. Open OXL13, created in the On Your Own section of Exercise 13, or open 15CDMANIA.

2. Save the file as **OXL15**.

3. Delete the data in the range B23:G27.

4. Name the range B4:B8 **JanTotal**.

5. Repeat step 4 for the Feb, Mar, Apr, May, and June data ranges.

   ✓ *For example, select the range C4:C8 and name it FebTotal.*

6. Using these new range names, reenter the formulas in cells B23:G25.

   ✓ *For example, in cell B23, enter =AVERAGE(JanTotal). In cell B24, enter MIN(JanTotal), and in cell B25, enter MAX(JanTotal).*

7. Name the range B4:E8 **Qtr1**. Name the range B13:E17 **Qtr2**.

8. Use these two range names to reenter the formula in cell B27, using the COUNTIF function.

9. Redefine the Qtr1 range to be A3:D8. Redefine the Qtr2 range to be A12:D17.

10. Print just the Qtr1 range, then print just the Qtr2 range.

11. Spell check the worksheet.

12. Print the worksheet.

13. Close the workbook, saving all changes.

# Exercise 16

## On the Job

IF functions allow you to test for values in your worksheet, and then perform specific actions based on the result. For example, with an IF function, you could calculate the bonuses for a group of salespeople on the premise that bonuses are only paid if a sale is over $1,000. With the SUMIF function, you could total up the sales in your Atlanta office, even if those sales figures are scattered through a long list of sales figures. And with the COUNTIF function, you could count the number of sales that resulted in a bonus being paid.

As the owner of Coastline Gourmet Importers, you're always concerned about your inventory, so you've decided to perform a little analysis on your product line to determine what items are your best sellers. You'll use this information to drop low-selling items from your inventory, and to add new ones.

## Terms

**Function** A pre-programmed Excel formula for a complex calculation.

**Condition** A statement in an IF function that if true yields one result and if false yields another result.

**Nesting** Inserting one function within another one. For example, you could nest the AVERAGE function within the IF function like this:
=IF(G2="","",AVERAGE(G2:G21))
In this example, the IF function prevents the AVERAGE from occurring if G2 is blank("").

**Argument** A variable entered into a function. An argument can be a number, text, formula, or a cell reference. A comma separates each argument in a function.

## Notes

### Understand IF Functions

■ With an IF **function**, you can tell Excel to perform one of two different calculations based on whether your data matches a certain **condition**.

✓ *For example, you can use an IF function to have Excel calculate a 10% bonus if total sales are over $500,000, and just a 3% bonus if they are not.*

■ The format for an IF statement is:
=IF(*condition,x,y*)

• The *condition* is a True/False statement.

• If the condition is true, the result is *x.*

• If the condition is false, the result is *y.*

■ To calculate the bonus described here, you would type =IF(B2>500000,B2*.10,B2*.03)

✓ This function says, "If total sales (cell B2) are greater than 500,000, then take total sales times 10% to calculate the bonus. Otherwise, take total sales times 3%."

✓ Notice that in the IF function, the value, $500,000, is entered without the dollar sign or the comma.

■ You can have words appear in a cell instead of the result of a calculation.

✓ For example, you might type **=IF(B2>500000,"We made it!","Good try.")** to display the words **We made it!** if total sales are over 500,000, or the words **Good try.** if they are not.

✓ Notice here that the words you want to use are surrounded by quotation marks " ".

■ IF statements may use the conditional operators below to state the condition:

| = | Equals | <> | Not equal to |
|---|--------|-----|--------------|
| > | Greater than | >= | Greater than or equal to |
| < | Less than | <= | Less than or equal to |
| & | Used for joining text | | |

■ For help in entering an IF function, Excel provides a screen tip that lists the IF function arguments in order.

■ You can also type =IF( and click the Insert Function button to display the Function Arguments dialog box which provides a text box for each argument, making it easier to enter them correctly.

*Function Arguments dialog box*

## Nested IF Functions

■ You can **nest** an IF function (or any other function) as one of the **arguments** in another function.

■ For example, the formula:

=IF(C3>92,"A",IF(C3>83,"B",IF(C3>73,"C",IF(C3>65,"D","F"))))

✓ If the average score is greater than 92, then the student gets an A, if the score is less than or equal to 92 but greater than 83, the student gets a B, if the score is less than or equal to 83 but greater than 73, the student gets a C, and so on.

## =SUMIF() Statements

■ A SUMIF statement is a logical function that uses a condition to add certain data.

■ If the condition is true, then data in a corresponding cell is added to the total; if it is false, then the corresponding data is skipped.

■ The format for a SUMIF statement is =SUMIF(*range, condition, sum_range*)
  • The *range* is the range of cells you want to test.
  • The *condition* is a True/False statement that defines which cells should be added to the total.
  • If the condition is true, the corresponding cell in *sum_range* is added to the total.
  • If the condition is false, the corresponding cell in *sum_range* is skipped (not added to the total).

  ✓ The condition is written using the same symbols (such as >,<>, etc.) as listed in the IF section. However, here, you must enclose the condition in quotation marks "".

■ For example, if you had a worksheet listing sales for several different products, you could total the sales for widgets only by using this formula: =SUMIF(D2:D55,"Widget",G2:G55)
  • Column D contains the name of the product being sold and column G contains the total amount for that sale.
  • If column D contains the word "Widget" then the amount for that sale (located in column G) is added to the running total.

  ✓ Because Widget is a text label, you must enclose it in quotation marks (" ").

■ You can leave the last argument off if you want to sum the same range that you're testing. For example: =SUMIF(G2:G10,"<=500")

  ✓ This formula calculates the total of all values in the range G2 to G10 that are less than or equal to 500.

## =COUNTIF() Statements

- A COUNTIF statement is a logical function that uses a condition to count the number of items in a range.

- If the result of the condition is true, then the item is added to a running count; if it is false, then the item is skipped.

- The format for a COUNTIF statement is =COUNTIF(*range, condition*).
  - The *range* is the range of cells you want to test.
  - The *condition* is a True/False statement that defines which cells should be counted.
    - ✓ The condition is written using the same symbols listed in the IF section. Again, enclose the condition in quotation marks " ".

- For example, if you count the number of individual Widget sales, you could use this formula: =COUNTIF(D2:D55,"=Widget")
  - Column D contains the name of the product being sold.
  - If column D contains the word "Widget" then that sale is added to the running total.
    - ✓ Because Widget is a text label, you must enclose it in quotation marks (" ").

- You can combine functions to create complex calculations: =SUMIF(D3:D13,"PASS",C3:C13) /COUNTIF(D3:D13,"PASS")
  - This computes the average score of all the students who passed the course.
  - Column D contains the words "Pass" or "Fail" based on the student's final score. The final score is located in column C.

# Procedures

### Enter IF Function

1. Click desired cell.
2. Press **Equal** ........................ ▣
3. Type **IF**.
   - ✓ You can click the Insert Functions button $fx$ at this point to display the Function Arguments dialog box, which may make entering the IF function easier, or you can simply type the rest of the function by following these steps.
4. Press **Left Parenthesis** ...... ▣
5. Type condition.
6. Press **Comma** ...................... ▣
7. Type argument if condition is true.
8. Press **Comma** ...................... ▣
9. Type argument if condition is false.
10. Press **Right** Parenthesis ..... ▣
11. Press **Enter** ...................... Enter

- ✓ IF statements may be used in combination with OR, AND, and NOT statements to evaluate complex conditions. For example, =IF(OR(B3>C3,B3<1000),D4*1 .05,D4*1.03), which says "If B3 is greater than C3 or less than 1000, take D4 times 105%, otherwise, take D4 times 103%"

### Enter SUMIF Function

1. Click desired cell.
2. Press **Equal** ........................ ▣
3. Type **SUMIF**.
4. Press **Left Parenthesis** ...... ▣
5. Type range to test.
   - ✓ You can select the range instead of typing it.
6. Press **Comma** ...................... ▣
7. Type condition in quotation marks.
8. Press **Comma** ...................... ▣
9. Type range to sum if condition is true.

- ✓ You can select the range instead of typing it.
- ✓ Skip steps 8-9 if the range you're testing is the same as the range you want to sum.
10. Press **Right Parenthesis** .... ▣
11. Press **Enter** ...................... Enter

### Enter COUNTIF Function

1. Click desired cell.
2. Press **Equal** ........................ ▣
3. Type **COUNTIF**.
4. Press **Left Parenthesis** ....... ▣
5. Type range to count.
   - ✓ You can select the range instead of typing it.
6. Press **Comma** ...................... ▣
7. Type condition to test.
8. Press **Right Parenthesis** .... ▣
9. Press **Enter** ...................... Enter

# Exercise Directions

1. Start Excel, if necessary.

2. Open ⊙ **16CGISALES**.

3. Save the file as **CGISALES**.

4. In cell E11, use the IF function to enter a formula that displays the words "Best Seller" if cell D11 is greater than $7,000, and nothing (blank) if it is not.

   ✓ *Enclose the text in quotation marks. Use two quotations together "" to represent blank. Do not include the $ or , in the value $7,000.*

5. Copy this formula to E12:E25.

6. In cell C30, use the COUNTIF function to count the number of best selling items (items in which the sales value in column D is greater than $7,000).

   ✓ *Be sure to enclose the condition in "".*

7. In cell C31, use the SUMIF function to calculate total sales for best sellers.

8. In cell C32, use the SUMIF and COUNTIF functions to calculate the average sales for the best sellers (sales over $7,000).

   ✓ *You could type just =C31/C30, but for the purposes of this exercise, use SUMIF and COUNTIF in one formula.*

9. In cells C34:C36, use SUMIF to calculate the total sales for each of the different types of ethnic food.

   ✓ *For example, in cell C34, you could type =SUMIF(C11:C25,"Chang Lo Lee Oriental Seafood",D11:D25).*

   ✓ *If you want, instead of typing "Chang Lo Lee Oriental Seafood," you can simply click any cell that contains that value, such as cell C13.*

10. Spell check the worksheet.

11. Print the worksheet.

12. Close the workbook, saving all changes.

*Illustration A*

| | A | B | C | D | E |
|---|---|---|---|---|---|
| 20 | | Sea Bass Sushi | Chang Lo Lee Oriental Seafood | $ 4,312.89 | |
| 21 | | Seared Scallops with Haricot Verts and Truffle Oil | Al Dente Italian Gourmet Foods | $ 14,947.21 | Best Seller |
| 22 | | Sesame Crab Claw | Chang Lo Lee Oriental Seafood | $ 5,894.81 | |
| 23 | | Shrimp Chipotle | Tejano Terone Mexican Gourmet Food | $ 11,594.31 | Best Seller |
| 24 | | Squid Paste | Chang Lo Lee Oriental Seafood | $ 2,175.84 | |
| 25 | | Zabaglione Tart with Marsala-Lemon Sauce | Al Dente Italian Gourmet Foods | $ 6,134.95 | |
| 26 | | | Total Sales for June | $ 113,850.43 | |
| 27 | | | | | |
| 28 | | | | | |
| 29 | Summary | | | | |
| 30 | | No. of Best Selling Items | 6 | | |
| 31 | | Total Sales for Best Sellers | $72,201.90 | | |
| 32 | | Average Sales for Best Sellers | $12,033.65 | | |
| 33 | | | | | |
| 34 | | Total Sales--Oriental | $38,291.49 | | |
| 35 | | Total Sales--Italian | $36,254.29 | | |
| 36 | | Total Sales--Mexican | $39,304.65 | | |
| 37 | | | | | |

# On Your Own

1. Open **OXL14**, the school expenses workbook you created in the On Your Own section of Excel Exercise 14, or open 💿 **16COLEXP**.

2. Save the workbook as **OXL16**.

3. Below the expense data, add a row labeled **Income**, and input monthly income figures.

   ✓ *Your income should be only slightly above your monthly expenses.*

4. Enter a formula that calculates your total income for the school year.

5. Enter a formula for calculating the net income (total income minus total expenses) for each month, and for the school year.

6. Use an IF function to determine if you will have enough money left in the budget at the end of the year to purchase a new color printer for your computer. The printer costs $279. If you have enough, the formula should display **Yes!**. If you do not have enough, the formula should display **Maybe next year**.

7. Spell check the workbook.

8. Print the workbook.

9. Close the workbook, saving all changes.

# Exercise 17

**Skills Covered:**

◆ **Chart Basics** ◆ **Select Chart Data** ◆ **Chart Elements**
◆ **Create Charts** ◆ **Change Chart Types** ◆ **Select a Chart**
◆ **Resize, Copy, Move, or Delete a Chart**

## On the Job

A chart presents Excel data in a graphical format—making the relationship between data items easier to understand. To present your data in the best format, you must select the proper chart type. For example, if you wanted to highlight your department's recent reduction in overtime, you might use a column or bar chart. Whereas, to compare your division's sales with other divisions, you might use a pie chart instead.

In the fourth quarter, sales for a new product, cashmere tops, exceeded expectations—at least, certain colors did. Now it's up to you to analyze the sales data and decide which color tops to carry in your store for the rest of the season. You've decided that Excel's chart feature will help you make sense of all that data. You'll create some charts to analyze the sales of some of your other products as well.

## Terms

**Chart** A graphic that allows you to compare and contrast data in a visual format.

**Embedded chart** A chart placed as an object within a worksheet.

**Chart sheet** A chart that occupies its own worksheet.

**Plot** To position data points on a graph.

**Data series** For most charts, a data series is the information in a worksheet column. If you select multiple columns of data for a chart, you'll create multiple data series.

**Legend** A key that identifies each of the data series in a chart.

**X-axis** The horizontal scale of a chart on which categories are plotted.

**Y-axis** The vertical scale of a chart on which the value of each category is plotted.

**Categories** For most charts, a category is information in a worksheet row. If you select multiple rows of data for a chart, you'll create multiple categories.

## Notes

### Chart Basics

- **Charts** provide a way of presenting and comparing data in a graphic format.
- You can create **embedded charts** or **chart sheets**.

- When you create an embedded chart, the chart exists as an object in the worksheet alongside the data.
  - ✓ *All illustrations in this exercise use embedded charts.*

**220**

- When you create a chart sheet, the chart exists on a separate sheet in the workbook.

- All charts are linked to the data they **plot**. When you change data in the plotted area of the worksheet, the chart changes automatically.

## Select Chart Data

- To create a chart, you first select the data to plot. Following are some guidelines for selecting your chart data:

  - The selection should not contain blank columns or rows.

    ✓ *Just press Ctrl and select each range separately, making sure not to select blank rows or columns that may separate the ranges.*

  - You can select multiple ranges to plot on a single chart.

  - You can hide columns or rows you do not wish to plot.

  - The selection should include the labels for the data when possible.

  - A blank cell in the upper-left corner of a selection tells Excel that the data below and to the right of the blank cell contains labels for the values to plot.

  - The selection determines the orientation of the data series (in columns or rows). However, you may change the orientation as desired.

*Adjacent and nonadjacent selections*

| | B | C | D | E |
|---|---|---|---|---|
| 3 | **Profit and Loss Statement** | | Adjacent | |
| 4 | **Spring Quarter, 1997** | | selection | |
| 5 | | | | |
| 6 | Income | January | February | March |
| 7 | Wholesale | $ 125,650 | $ 122,645 | $ 156,210 |
| 8 | Retail Sales | $ 135,120 | $ 125,645 | $ 145,887 |
| 9 | Special Sales | $ 10,255 | $ 21,541 | $ 15,647 |
| 10 | | | Non-adjacent | |
| 11 | Totals by Month | $ 271,025 | selection | 17,744 |
| 12 | | | | |
| 13 | Expenses | January | February | March |
| 14 | Disk Production | $ 15,642 | $ 14,687 | $ 18,741 |
| 15 | Packaging | $ 2,564 | $ 2,407 | $ 3,071 |
| 16 | Promotions | $ 4,525 | $ 4,248 | $ 5,420 |
| 17 | | | | |
| 18 | Totals by Month | $ 22,731 | $ 21,342 | $ 27,232 |
| 19 | | | | |

## Chart Elements

- The parts of a column chart are labeled in the illustration to the right.

- As you move your mouse over each part of a chart, the name of the object displays.

- Typically each chart includes the following parts:

  - **Data series**
    If you include data for more than one item (such as homes sold in the Oak Bend, River Knoll, and Glenview North communities), then you'll create a different **data series** for each item. Each series is represented on the chart by a different color bar, column, line, etc.

  - **Series labels**
    Labels identifying the charted values. These labels appear in the chart **legend**, which identifies each data series in the chart.

  - **Category labels**
    Labels identifying each data series shown on the horizontal or **x-axis**.

- For charts which use axes (all except pie charts):

  - The **y-axis** is the vertical scale, except on 3-D charts. The scale values are based on the values being charted.

  - The x-axis is the horizontal scale and typically represents the data series **categories**.

  - The x-axis title describes the x-axis (horizontal) data. (*Communities* in the illustration below.)

  - The y-axis title describes the y-axis (vertical) data. (*Homes Under Construction* in the illustration below.)

*Chart Elements*

## Create Charts

■ You create charts with the Chart Wizard, which uses tabbed dialog boxes to step you through the entire process.

■ As you make selections, the Chart Wizard shows you exactly how the chart will look.

✓ *Previewing your chart enables you to select the chart type and other elements best suited to your data.*

■ Each chart type contains chart subtypes, which are variations on the selected chart type.

■ Excel also offers several customized chart types for specialized data.

## Change Chart Types

■ After creating a chart, you can easily change its chart type to something else.

■ There are many chart types from which you can choose:

• **Column charts** compare individual or sets of values. The height of each bar is proportional to its corresponding value in the worksheet.

✓ *All of the chart types listed here are available in a 3-D format.*

• **Bar charts** are basically column charts turned on their sides. Like column charts, bar charts compare the values of various items.

• **Line charts** connect points of data and show changes over time effectively. Line charts are especially useful to plot trends.

• **Area charts** are like "filled in" line charts; you use them to track changes over time.

• **Pie charts** are circular graphs used to show the relationship of each value in a data range to the entire set of data. The size of each wedge represents the percentage each value contributes to the total.

✓ *Only one numerical data range may be used in a pie chart. For example, if you have sales data for 2000 and 2001 for tricycles, offroad bikes, and helmets, you can only chart one year. If you select all the data, it will be lumped into one big pie, with each element (2000 tricycles, 2001 offroad bikes, etc.) representing a slice.*

✓ *Pie charts may be formatted to indicate the percentage each piece of the pie represents of the whole.*

■ A chart can be copied and then edited to produce a different chart that uses the same worksheet data.

*Chart elements*

Bar chart — Column chart — Area chart — 3-D pie chart — Line chart

## Select a Chart

■ To resize, copy, or move a chart, you must first select it by clicking anywhere on the chart.

■ A selected chart displays sizing handles. In addition, the Chart toolbar usually appears.

## Resize, Copy, Move, or Delete a Chart

■ You can resize, copy, or move an embedded chart as needed.

■ You can't resize a chart on a chart sheet; however, you can copy or move it around on the sheet.

■ You can move a chart on a chart sheet to another sheet, creating an embedded object. You can reverse the process when needed to change an embedded chart into a chart sheet.

■ If you copy a chart, you can change the copied chart type to present data in a different way.

# Procedures

### Select Adjacent Data

1. Click on blank cell in upper left-hand corner of data range.
2. Drag downward and right, until you have selected entire data range, including label cells.

### Select Nonadjacent Data

1. Click and drag over cells in first range you want to select.
2. Press **Ctrl** and drag over another range of cells. ........ `Ctrl`
3. Repeat for additional ranges.

### Create Chart with Chart Wizard

1. Select data to chart.
2. Click **Chart Wizard** button `📊`.
   OR
   a. Click **Insert** ............ `Alt`+`I`
   b. Click **Chart** ...................... `H`
3. Follow steps to create standard or custom chart type.
4. Click the **Finish** button
    ................ `Alt`+`F`

### Select Embedded Chart

1. Click once on chart to select it.
2. To deselect chart, click anywhere in worksheet.

### Select Chart Sheet

1. Click chart sheet's tab.
2. To deselect chart sheet, click different worksheet tab.

### Change Chart's Type

1. Select chart or chart sheet.
2. Click **Chart** ................ `Alt`+`C`
3. Click **Chart Type** ................ `Y`
4. Select standard or custom chart type.

**To select standard chart type:**
a. Select chart type in **Chart type** list box .................. `Alt`+`C`
b. Select sub-type for selected chart in **Chart sub-type** list box .................. `Alt`+`T`
c. If desired, click and hold **Press and Hold to View Sample**

   to display preview ....... `Enter`

**To select custom chart type:**
a. Click **Custom Types** tab .............. `Ctrl`+`Tab`
b. Select **User defined** ......... `Alt`+`U`
   OR
   Select **Built-in** ........ `Alt`+`B`
c. Select desired custom chart in **Chart type** list .... `Alt`+`C`

5. To set current chart type as default, click **Set as default chart**
    ...... `Alt`+`E`

6. Click **OK** .......................... `Enter`

### Resize Embedded Chart

1. Select chart you want to resize.
2. Move mouse pointer to handle.
   ✓ *Mouse pointer becomes* ⬊ *when positioned correctly.*
   ✓ *To size object proportionally, press Shift and point to corner handle.*
3. Click handle and drag it outwards to make chart bigger, or inwards to make it smaller.
   ✓ *To align edges of chart to worksheet gridlines, press Alt key as you drag.*
4. Release mouse button and chart is resized.

### Move Chart

1. Select chart you want to move.
2. Click chart and drag it to its new location.
   ✓ *As you drag, outline of chart follows mouse pointer.*
3. Release mouse button and chart is moved.

### Switch from Embedded Chart to Chart Sheet or Vice-Versa

1. Right-click the chart.
2. Select **Location**. ........ `Alt`+`L`
3. Select **As new sheet** . `Alt`+`S`
   OR
   **As object in** .............. `Alt`+`O`
4. Click **OK** .......................... `Enter`

### Copy Chart

1. Select chart you want to copy.
2. Click **Copy** button `📋`.
3. Click elsewhere in worksheet.
4. Click **Paste** button `📋`.
   ✓ *You can change chart type of copied chart to view its data in a different way.*

### Delete Embedded Chart

1. Select chart you want to delete.
2. Press **Delete** ...................... `Del`

### Delete Chart Sheet

1. Click **Edit** .................... `Alt`+`E`
2. Click **Delete Sheet** .............. `L`
3. Click **OK** .......................... `Enter`
OR
1. Right-click sheet tab.
2. Select **Delete** ...................... `E`

# Exercise Directions

1. Start Excel, if necessary.
2. Open ⌨ **NWGNEW** or open 💿 **17NWGNEW**.
3. Save it as **NWGNEW**.
4. On the Cashmere Tops worksheet, select the range A13:D19.
5. Use the Chart Wizard to create your first chart. Make the following selections:
   a. Select the Clustered Column chart type.
   b. Display the data series in columns.
   c. Enter the chart title **4th Qtr Sales by Month**.
   d. Enter the Category Axis title **Cashmere Tops**.
   e. Enter the Value Axis title **Units Sold**.
   f. Display the legend at the bottom center of the chart.
   g. Save the chart as an embedded object on the Cashmere Tops worksheet.
6. Size and move the chart so that the chart appears in A26:H51.
   - ✓ *Some charts won't fully display their data no matter which you size you make them initially. Don't worry too much if this happens to you. You will format charts in the next exercise and learn how to achieve the effect you desire.*
7. To create a second chart that displays the data in a different format, copy the first chart to the worksheet range beginning at A53.
8. Change the chart type of the copied chart to Clustered bar with a 3-D visual effect. (See Illustration B. You'll learn how to fix the title in the next exercise.)
9. To create the third and last chart, change to the Surfer Shorts worksheet, and select the non-adjacent ranges B13:D13 and B19:D19.
10. Use the Chart Wizard to create the chart with the following selections:
    a. Select Exploded Pie with 3-D visual effect chart type.
    b. Display the series in rows.
    c. Add the chart title **4th Qtr Surfer Short Sales**.
    d. Don't show the legend.
    e. Select category name, value, and percentage data labels.
    f. Save the chart as a sheet titled **Surfer Short Chart**.
11. Spell check the workbook.
12. Print the workbook.
13. Close the workbook, saving all changes.

*Illustration A*

224

*Illustration B*

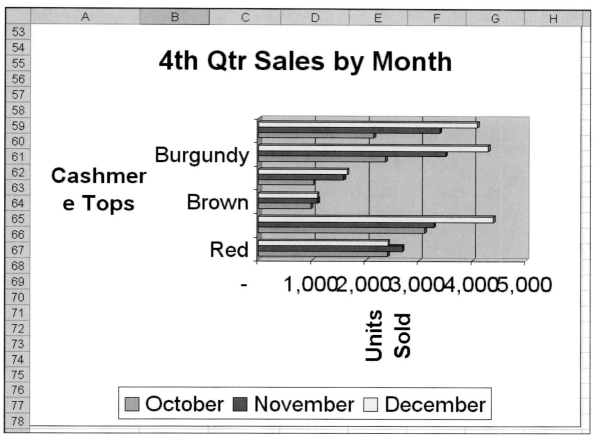

# On Your Own

1. Start Excel, if necessary.

2. Open **OXL15**, created in the On Your Own section of Exercise 15, or open **17CDMANIA**.

3. Save the workbook as **OXL17**.

4. Create two charts, stored on chart sheets, using the quarter 1 and quarter 2 totals, respectively.

   ✓ *Be sure to use two different chart types when creating the two charts.*

5. Add sheet titles, chart titles, legends, data labels, and other options as desired to each chart.

   ✓ *Some charts just won't look great until you format them, which you'll learn to do in the next exercise. So resize the charts as best you can to achieve a margin of respectability, then apply your formatting next exercise to create exactly the effect you want.*

6. Change the Quarter 1 chart to an embedded chart on Sheet 2. Resize and move the chart as needed to fully display its data.

7. Copy the Quarter 1 chart to another location on Sheet 2. Change the chart type of the copied chart.

8. Create a third chart that displays the average sales for January through June. Save the chart as an embedded object on Sheet 3.

9. Add sheet titles, chart titles, legends, data labels, and other options as desired. Resize and move the chart as needed.

10. Spell check the workbook.

11. Print the workbook.

12. Close the workbook, saving all changes.

# Exercise 18

**Skills Covered:**

◆ **Use Chart Toolbar** ◆ **Resize, Move, or Delete a Chart Object**
◆ **Change Chart Text** ◆ **Enhance Chart Background**
◆ **Format Category and Value Axes**

## On the Job

There are many ways in which you can enhance your chart: you can format the chart text, add color or pattern to the chart background, and format the value and category axes so that the numbers are easier to read.

Murray Hill Marketing has provided you with a pretty thorough analysis of your competition, but as the owner of Dan's Digital Camera Works, you're finding it hard to make sense of it all. So you've decided to take the data and chart it using Excel's charting feature. After the chart is created, you'll use your new Excel skills to apply formatting to the chart before printing it out.

## Terms

**Object** An item that is treated separately from the main document. In the case of a chart, each chart element is an object that can be manipulated independently.

**Chart area** The total area occupied by a chart.

**Plot area** The area defined by the x and y axes.

**Tick marks** Lines of measurement along the value and category axes.

## Notes

### Use Chart Toolbar

*Chart toolbar*

Chart Objects

Chart Type

Format Object Selected

By Row | Angle Clockwise

By Column | Angle Counterclockwise

Data Table
Legend

- Normally, when you select a chart or one of its parts, the Chart toolbar appears.
- If needed, you can access the Chart toolbar from the View menu.
- The Chart toolbar provides the following tools:

- Chart Objects allows you to select any part of a chart so you can delete or format it.
- Format Object presents format options for the selected chart object.
- Chart Type allows you to change the chart type associated with the selected chart.
- Legend hides or displays the chart legend.
- Data Table hides or displays data used in the chart.
- By Rows changes orientation of data series to rows.
- By Column changes orientation of data series to columns.
- Angle Clockwise angles selected text downward.
- Angle Counterclockwise angles selected text upward.

## Resize, Move, or Delete a Chart Object

■ Before you resize, move, or delete an **object**, you must select it first.

■ By resizing, moving, or deleting the parts of your chart, you may make it more attractive and easier to read.

■ If you resize an object that contains text, the font size of the text changes correspondingly.

■ When you delete an object from a chart, the remaining parts of the chart are enlarged to fill the gap.

■ You can change the value represented by a column or bar by resizing it.

## Change Chart Text

■ You can edit chart text or change its formatting. For example, you can change the size, font, and attributes of text.

## Enhance Chart Background

■ A chart actually has two backgrounds: the larger **chart area** and the smaller **plot area**, as shown in the figure to the right.

■ You can format the chart area, the plot area, or both.

■ To format either chart background, you can:
  • Add a border around the background area.
  • Apply a color to the background.
  • Apply a fill effect, such as gradient (a blend of two colors), texture (such as marble), pattern (such as diagonal stripes), or picture (a graphic file).
  • Add a shadow effect behind the border (chart area only).

• Round the corners (chart area only).

*Chart backgrounds*

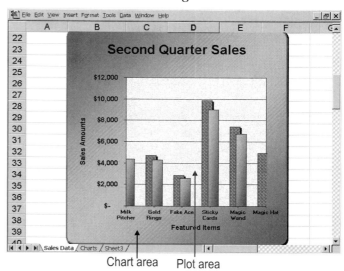

Chart area    Plot area

## Format Category and Value Axes

■ The category axis, or x-axis, represents the horizontal axis for most charts. Categories and data series are plotted along the category axis.

■ The value axis, or y-axis, represents the vertical axis for most charts. The values of various categories or data series are plotted along the value axis.

■ You can change the font, size, color, attributes, alignment, and placement of text or numbers along both the category and value axes.

■ You can also change the appearance of the **tick marks**.

■ In addition, you can adjust the scale used along the value axis.

# Procedures

### Select Chart Object

• Click the object you wish to select.

OR

• Select the object's name from the Chart Object list on the Chart toolbar.

### Resize Chart Object

1. Select object you want to resize.
2. Move mouse pointer over handle.

   ✓ *Mouse pointer becomes ⬦ when positioned correctly.*

   ✓ *To size object proportionally, press Shift and point to corner handle.*

3. Click handle and drag it outwards to make object bigger, or inwards to make it smaller.

4. Release mouse button and object is resized.

### Move Chart Object

1. Select object you want to move.
2. Click object and drag it to its new location.

   ✓ *As you drag, outline of object follows mouse pointer.*

3. Release mouse button and object is moved.

## Delete Chart Object

1. Select object you want to delete.
2. Press **Delete** ........................ Del

   ✓ *You can select the plot area, but your can't delete it.*

## Change Chart Text

1. Click chart object that contains text you wish to change.
2. Edit the text using normal text editing techniques.
3. Click anywhere outside of chart text when finished.

   ✓ *You can apply any formatting you want to the selected text.*

## Enhance Chart Background

1. Select either chart or plot area.
2. Click **Format Chart Area/Format Plot Area** button 📋.
3. On the Patterns tab under Border, select **Automatic** to apply normal border style.................. Alt + A

   OR

   a. Select **Custom**.
   b. Select border **Style**... Alt + S
   c. Select border **Color** .......... Alt + C
   d. Select border thickness, or **Weight** ............... Alt + W

   **To fill area with color:**

   • On the Patterns tab under Area, select **Automatic** to apply normal background color (usually white). ....... Alt + U

   OR

   • Select desired color from color palette............ Alt + O

   OR

   a. Click **Fill Effects**
      [Fill Effects...] .... Alt + I
   b. On Gradient tab, choose color option you want:

      • Select **One color** ......... Alt + O

      • Choose color you want to blend from **Color 1** drop-down list ... Alt + 1
      • Adjust transition from **Dark** to **Light**.... Alt + K

      OR

      • Select **Two colors**....... Alt + T
      • Choose two colors you want to blend from **Color 1** and **Color 2** drop-down list boxes .. Alt + 1 , Alt + 2

      OR

      • Select **Preset**.... Alt + R
      • Choose **Preset colors** option you want .. Alt + E

   c. Select one of the **Shading styles**.
   d. Select one of the **Variants** ........... Alt + A

   **To fill area with texture:**

   a. Click **Texture** tab.
   b. Select texture you want.

   **To fill area with pattern:**

   a. Click **Pattern** tab.
   b. Select **Foreground** color .. Alt + F
   c. Select **Background** color . Alt + B
   d. Click **Pattern** .......... Alt + T

   **To fill area with a picture:**

   a. Click **Picture** tab.
   b. Click **Select Picture** ....... Alt + L
   c. Select desired drive and folder from **Look in** drop-down list......... Alt + I
   d. Double-click graphic file.

4. Click **OK** .......................... Enter
5. Click **OK** .......................... Enter

## Format Category Axis

1. Select category axis.
2. Click **Format Axis** button 📋.
3. If desired, on Patterns tab, select setting:

   • Select **Automatic** to apply normal line style. .... Alt + A

   OR

   a. Select **Custom**.
   b. Select border **Style** .. Alt + S
   c. Select border **Color** .......... Alt + C
   d. Select border thickness, or **Weight**............... Alt + W

   OR

   Select **None** to remove the axis lines.

4. If desired, change **Major tick mark type** (change its location). ................. Alt + M
5. If desired, change **Minor tick mark type** (change its location). ................. Alt + R
6. If desired, change location of **Tick mark labels** ........ Alt + T
7. Click **Scale** tab.

   a. To change point at which y-axis intersects category axis, enter category number in **Value (Y) axis crosses at category number** text box. ................. Alt + C

   b. To change frequency of category labels, enter number in **Number of categories between tick-mark labels** text box. (Enter a 2 to display every other label, etc.)...... Alt + L

   c. To change frequency of tick marks along category axis, enter number in **Number of categories between tick marks** text box ....... Alt + K

   d. If you do not want first category to be placed right against y-axis, select **Value (Y) axis crosses between categories**.............. Alt + B

   e. If desired, select **Categories in reverse order**..... Alt + R

   f. To place y-axis on the right, select **Value (Y) axis crosses at maximum category**................ Alt + M

8. Click **Font** tab and make desired changes to font, size, and other attributes of data labels.

9. Click **Alignment** tab and angle label text:
   - Drag **Text** marker to set degree of rotation.

   OR

   a. Enter positive number in **Degrees** text box to angle text from lower left to upper right, or negative number to angle text from upper left to lower right .............. Alt+D

   b. Select amount of space you want between data labels and x-axis by adjusting **Offset** value ........... Alt+O

10. Click **OK** ........................... Enter

## Format Value Axis

1. Select value axis.

2. Click **Format Axis** button 🔲.

3. If desired, on Patterns tab, select setting:
   - Select **Automatic** to apply normal line style. .... Alt+A

   OR

   a. Select **Custom**.

   b. Select border **Style** .. Alt+S

   c. Select border **Color** ......... Alt+C

   d. Select border thickness, or **Weight**. .................. Alt+W

   OR

   Select **None** to remove the axis lines.

4. If desired, change **Major tick mark type** (location) ... Alt+M

5. If desired, change **Minor tick mark type** (location). .. Alt+R

6. If desired, change location of **Tick mark labels** ........ Alt+T

7. Click **Scale** tab.

   a. Set **Minimum** and **Maximum** values used on y-axis ........ Alt+N, Alt+X

   b. Adjust placement of major and minor tick marks along y-axis by changing values in **Major unit** and **Minor unit** text boxes .. Alt+A, Alt+I

   c. To change point at which x-axis intersects value axis, enter value in **Category (X) axis crosses at** text box................... Alt+C

   d. If desired, adjust **Display units** value ............. Alt+U

   e. To display values as powers of 10, select **Logarithmic scale** option............ Alt+L

   f. To display **Values in reverse order**, select that option.............. Alt+R

   g. To move category axis to top of plot area, select **Category (X) axis crosses at maximum value** .... Alt+M

8. Click **Font** tab and make desired changes to font, size, and other attributes of value labels.

9. Click **Number** tab and select format you wish for your value labels.

10. Click **Alignment** tab and angle label text:
    - Drag **Text** marker to set degree of rotation.

11. Click **OK** .......................... Enter

# Exercise Directions

1. Start Excel, if necessary.

2. Open 🖳COMPETE or 💿18COMPETE.

3. Save the file as **COMPETE**.

4. Press Ctrl and select the following cells: B6, B9, B12, B15, F6, F9, F12, and F15.

5. Click the Chart Wizard button 📊.

6. Follow the Chart Wizard steps and make the following selections:
   a. Select the Pie with 3-D visual effect chart type.
   b. Choose data series by columns.
   c. Add the title **Competitors' 2001 Sales**.
   d. Show percentage data value labels.
   e. Save the chart as an embedded object on Sheet 2.
   f. Resize the chart to fit in the range A1:H18.

7. Make the following improvements to the chart:
   a. Delete the Legend.

   b. Add category name and value data labels. Turn on the Show leader lines option as well.
      ✓ *Select the chart and use the Chart, Chart Options command to make this change.*

   c. Format the title in Architect, 24-point bold, green text.

   d. Format the Series 1 Data Labels with Arial, 8-point green, bold font.

   e. Select the plot area, and move it to the left, as shown in Illustration A. Resize the pie as shown.
      ✓ *To select the plot area, click right outside a slice. Then click on the plot area box and drag it to a new location.*

   f. Drag the data labels to reposition them as shown. This will make the leader lines (the lines pointing to the associated pie slice) appear as well.

   g. Apply Papyrus texture with a green rounded corner border of medium weight to the chart background.

8. Spell check the workbook.
9. Print the workbook.
10. Close the workbook, saving all changes.

*Illustration A*

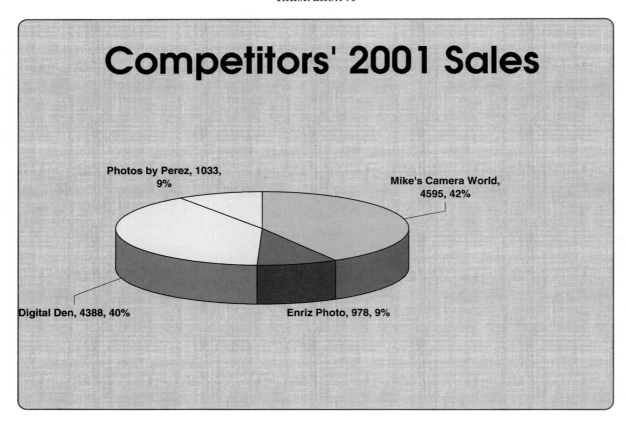

# On Your Own

1. Open **OXL17**, the workbook you created in the On Your Own section of Exercise 17, or open 🖸**18CDMANIA**.

2. Save the file as **CDMANIA**.

3. Rename Sheet 2 **Quarter 1 Sales Charts**.

4. Apply formatting to the two charts on the Quarter 1 Sales Charts sheet.

   ✓ *Be sure to make different selections for the two charts, so that they are unique in appearance.*

   a. Select a small font size for the labels and a larger font size for the title.

   b. Apply formatting to the chart background, and a different format to the plot area.

   c. Adjust the scale used on the y-axis.

      ✓ *For example, you could set the minimum to 50,000, and the major unit to 10,000.*

5. Rename Sheet 3 **Average Sales Chart**.

6. Apply formatting as desired to the chart on the Average Sales Chart sheet.

7. Spell check the workbook.

8. Print the workbook.

9. Close the workbook, saving all changes.

# Exercise 19

You're the director of sales at Regency General, Inc., a Web-based company specializing in Internet services such as company database management and purchasing. Your company sponsored a sales contest for June, and now that it's July, it's up to you to organize the sales information and award prizes. You'll use various functions to help you analyze the data, and then you'll create a chart that will enable you to compare the contest results by city.

## Exercise Directions

1. Start Excel, if necessary.

2. Open 📀 **19SALESCONT**.

3. Save the file as **SALESCONT**.

4. Assign the range name **GOAL** to the cell C8.

5. In cell F12, type a formula that computes the average sales amount per client.

   ✓ *Hint: Take the June Total and divide by the number of clients.*

6. Copy the formula to the range F13:F21.

7. In cell G12, type a formula that displays the word **Yes** if the person met the June sales goal, and nothing if he/she did not.

   ✓ *Use the IF function, and compare the value in cell D12 to the range name, GOAL, and if it is greater than or equal to GOAL, display "Yes." Otherwise, display blank "".*

8. Copy this formula to the range G13:G21.

9. In cell D23, type a formula that computes the total sales.

10. In cell D24, type a formula that computes the average sales for all the salespeople.

11. Using the SUMIF function, type a formula in cell D26 that computes the total sales for the people in the Chicago office. Copy the formula to D27 and D28.

12. Apply Accounting style, zero decimal places, to the range D26:D28.

13. If necessary, adjust column widths to fit the data.

14. Create a clustered bar chart using the range, C26:D28.

    a. Use the title **June Sales**.

    b. Display minor gridlines along the Y axis.

    c. Remove the legend.

    d. Place the chart on its own sheet, titled **June Sales**.

    e. Format each bar with a unique color—South Bend=pale blue, Ft. Wayne=tan, and Chicago=lavender.

    f. Apply the Water droplets texture to the chart background.

    g. Apply blue-gray fill to the plot area.

    h. Apply Arial, bold, 28-point text to the title.

    i. Apply Arial, bold, 12-point text to the Category Axis labels.

15. Create a second chart using the range C11:D21.

    a. Choose the clustered column with 3-D effect chart type.

    b. Use the title **Contest Results**.

    c. Use the Value Axis title **$25,000 Goal**.

    d. Remove the legend.

    e. Place the chart on its own sheet, entitled **Contest Results**.

    f. Apply Arial, bold, 18-point type to the title.

    g. Apply 90 degrees Orientation alignment to the Value Axis title.

    h. Apply 45 degrees Orientation alignment to the Category Axis labels.

    i. Apply the Canvas texture to the chart background.

16. Spell check the workbook.

17. Print the workbook.

18. Close the file, saving all changes.

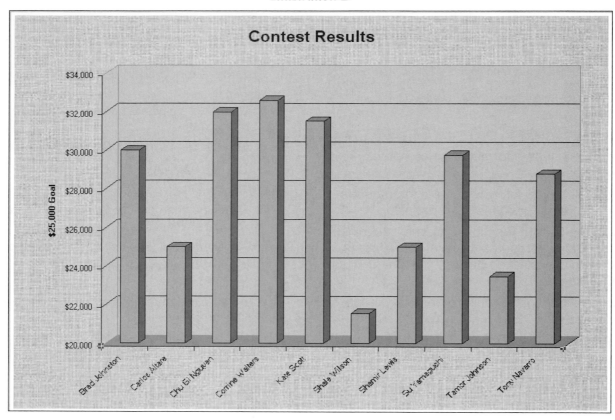

# Access 2002

## Lesson 1

**Getting Started with Access 2002**
**Exercises 1-6**

## Lesson 2

**Working with Tables and Datasheets**
**Exercises 7-10**

## Lesson 3

**Simplifying Data Entry with Lookups and Forms**
**Exercises 11-16**

# Directory of Data Files on CD

| Exercise # | File Name | Page # |
|:---:|:---|:---|
| 1 | AC01 | 244 |
| 2 | AC02 | 249 |
| 3 | AC03 | 254 |
| 4 | AC04 | 258 |
| 5 | AC05 | 264 |
| 6 | AC06 | 265 |
| 7 | AC07 | 270 |
| 8 | AC08 | 276 |
| 9 | AC09 | 280 |
| 10 | AC10 | 281 |
| 11 | AC11 | 285 |
| 12 | AC12 | 291 |
| 13 | AC13 | 296 |
| 14 | AC14 | 300 |
| 15 | AC15 | 305 |
| 16 | AC16 | 307 |

# Database Basics

Skills Covered:

◆ **What is Access?** ◆ **What is a Database?**
◆ **What is a Database Management System?**
◆ **How is an Access Database Organized?**
◆ **How are Access Tables Related?**

## Notes

### What is Access?

- Microsoft Access is the best-selling personal computer database management system. The notes below describe what a database management system is in more detail.

- You can share data created in Access with other Microsoft Office applications, especially Word and Excel.

### What is a Database?

- A **database** is an organized collection of information about a subject.

- Examples of databases include an address book, the telephone book, a CD tower full of music CDs, or a filing cabinet full of documents relating to clients.

- A name, address, and phone listing in an address book is an example of a common manual database. To update an address of a friend in Denver, you would search for the name, erase or cross out the existing address, and write in the new address.

*Examples of manual database records*

| | |
|---|---|
| Name: Jim Ferrara<br>Address: 84 Winthrop Rd.<br>City: Denver<br>State: CO    Zip: 80209<br>Telephone: 303-555-5576<br><br>Notes: Note new address and phone number. | Part Number:        001759<br><br>Part Description: Socket wrench<br>Cost:                     $3.50<br><br>List Price:            $14.99<br>Date Received:    2/23/99 |
| Address Book Entry | Inventory Card |

- While updating one or two address in a manual database may not take a lot of effort, searching for all friends in one city or sorting all clients who have done business with you in the last month would take considerable effort.

- An **Access database** is a computer-based equivalent of a manual database. Access makes it easy to organize and update information electronically.

### What is a Database Management System?

- A **database management system** such as Access includes both the database information and the tools to use the database. These tools allow you to input, edit, and verify your data.

- With Access, you can sort, find, analyze, and report on information in your database. For example, in a sales management database you could find all clients who bought a mountain bike in the last year and create mailing labels in order to send them an announcement of a new bike trails book.

### How is an Access Database Organized?

- Unlike other database software programs, Access maintains all its objects in one database file. This file uses the MDB extension.

#### The Database Window Organizes Objects

- When you open a database file, you see the **database window**, which displays seven buttons under the Objects button.

- Each button changes the database window to display a list of the database **objects** for each object type. (See next page for a description of each object type.) For example, click on the Forms button to see a list of all forms.

*Access database window*

Types of database objects

## Tables Store Information

- All Access database information is stored in tables. Each table contains information about a particular topic. For example, a sales inventory database may have separate tables for clients, products, and sales.

- Each row of an Access table is a **record**. A record is a set of details about a specific item. For example, a record for a client may contain the client's name, address, and phone number. A record about a product could include the part number, serial number, and price.

- Each column of an Access table is a **field**. Fields provide the categories for the details describing each record. In the client example above, there would be separate fields for name, address, and phone number.

- Each column is headed by a **field name**.

- The specific field data within a record is the **field contents**.

*Tables store information in rows and columns*

- Good database design may require you to break what you originally thought may be one field into multiple fields. For example, you would use separate fields for a client's first name, last name, address, city, state, and ZIP code.

- You can decide what to make into fields by thinking about how you will sort or look up the information. Many client lists, for example, sort by last name and then by first name.

## Database Objects Help You Search, Analyze, and Present Data

- Database objects are the elements that make up a database. Although each Access database has numerous objects, there are seven major object types that are visible as soon as you open a database.

  - **Table**
    You store database information in one or more tables. You view, edit, and input information in tables in Datasheet view, which has rows and columns, just like an Excel spreadsheet.

  - **Form**
    A form is a window for viewing the data in one or more tables. Forms make it easy to view, input, and edit data because forms typically show all the information for one record on a single page.

*Forms help you view, input, and edit data*

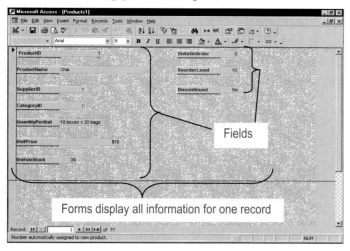

Fields

Forms display all information for one record

- **Query**

  A query allows you to see or work with a portion of a table by limiting the number of fields and by selecting specific records. For example, a bank may choose to see just the name, phone, and amount for all clients in Texas whose accounts are over $10,000.

*Design queries to sort and analyze data*

Table selected for query

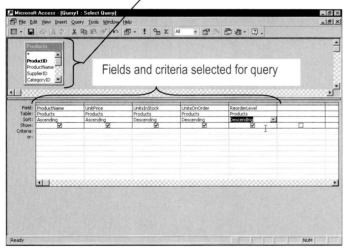

Fields and criteria selected for query

*Query results show a portion of table data*

Only selected fields appear in query result

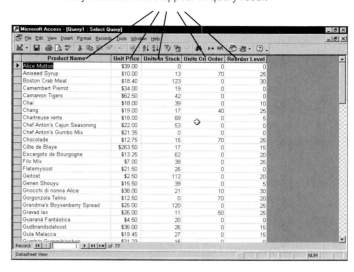

- **Report**

  A report is formatted information from a table or query that you can send to a printer. Reports can include a detailed list of records, calculated values and totals from the records, mailing labels, or a chart summarizing the data.

*Use reports to create printed summaries of data*

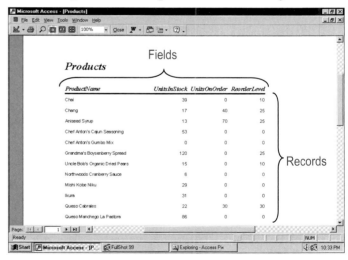

Fields

Records

- **Macro**
  Macros allow you to automate some processes within Access. Macros are beyond the scope of this book.
- **Module**
  Modules help automate Access tasks. Modules give you more flexibility for each automated process than macros do. Modules are also not included in this book.
- **Page**
  This new feature allows you to create Web-based forms that allow users to input and read data from your database via the Internet.

*Pages let users input and read data on the Web*

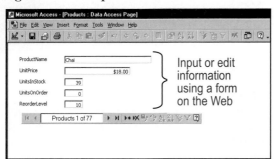

## How are Access Tables Related?

- Database tables that share common fields are **related**. Most Access databases have multiple tables that are related to each other, which means you can use Access to create a **relational database**.

- A relational database breaks the "big picture" into smaller, more manageable pieces. For example, if you were gathering information about a new product line, each type of information—product, suppliers, customers—would be stored in its own, related table rather than in one large, all-inclusive table.

- You relate one table to another through a common field. For example, the Products table will have a ProductID field that also appears in the Customers table.

- This capability to store data in smaller, related tables gives a relational database great efficiency, speed, and flexibility in locating and reporting information.

# Exercise 1

## Skills Covered:

◆ **Copy Data Files and Deselect the Read-only Attribute**
◆ **Start Access and Open a Database** ◆ **Navigate in a Database**
◆ **Sort Records**

## On the Job

Your first goal in working with a database is to start Access and open a database. You must then be able to identify and move around each of the various objects in the database. A quick sort of the data lets you find data quickly and perform a simple analysis of the information.

You've just been hired as the manager of Steel Dreams Motorcycle Emporium. One of your responsibilities is going to be maintaining and updating the store's databases. The owner of the shop wants you to explore the information stored in two of the database's tables and forms. You'll also perform a few simple sorts of the information to see how databases are used to analyze information.

## Terms

**Database file**  The file that contains all objects of your database.

**Database window**  The on-screen container that has a separate button for each object type (tables, queries, forms, reports, pages, and others).

**Switchboard**  An Access form with command buttons or other controls that lead to other switchboard forms, input forms, and reports.

**Datasheet view**  The view of a table that shows you the data in each record. Like a spreadsheet, the datasheet shows rows (records) and columns (fields).

**Sort**  To organize data alphabetically or in numerical order.

**Ascending**  To sort from the smallest to the largest (from A to Z and from 1 to 9).

**Descending**  To sort from the largest to the smallest (from Z to A and from 9 to 1).

## Notes

### Copy Data Files and Deselect the Read-only Attribute

- Access does not let you use the Save As command on a database as a whole.

- To use the data files for the Access exercises in this book, you must first copy the files from the CD to your hard drive. You can copy them all at once, or you can copy individual files as you need them.

- Files stored on a CD-ROM drive, when copied to another disk, have the read-only attribute turned on. You must turn it off in order to save your changes to the files.

- To turn off the read-only attribute for a file, you right-click it and choose Properties, and then deselect the Read-only check box in the Properties box that appears.

- You can remove the read-only attribute from many files at once by selecting multiple files before you right-click.

Deselect
Read-only
attribute

## Start Access and Open a Database

- As with other Office programs, you can start Access using the Start button, an icon on the desktop, or a button on the Office Shortcut bar.

- When you start the program, Access displays the New File Task Pane at the right, from which you can open an existing database or start a new one.

*Access's Task Pane provides shortcuts for opening and creating database files*

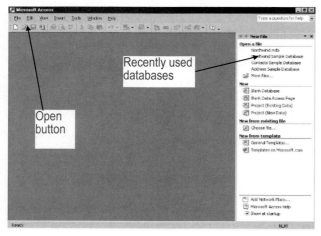

Recently used databases

Open button

- The last four databases you have opened appear in the *Open a file* section at the top of the Task Pane. You can quickly reopen one of them by clicking its name.

- If the database you want to open does not appear on that list, click More Files to use the Open dialog box to locate the file you want.

- You can also display the Open dialog box by clicking the Open button 📂 on the toolbar.

- If you need help with the Open dialog box, see Exercise 9 in Lesson 2 of the Word section in this book.

- After the **database file** opens, you see the **database window.**

*The database window is a central point from which you can open tables, queries, forms, and so on*

✓ *Notice that the title bar of the database window shown above reports that the database is in Access 2000 format. By default, all files created in Access 2002 are in Access 2000 format, for compatibility with the earlier Access version. You will learn more about file formats in upcoming exercises*

- Some databases, such as those created with the Database Wizard, display a **Switchboard** window when you open them. You can close the Switchboard window by clicking its Close button ⊠.

- After closing the Switchboard, you might need to maximize the minimized Database window. Double-click it to do so.

*Close the Switchboard window if it appears when you open a database, and restore the Database window*

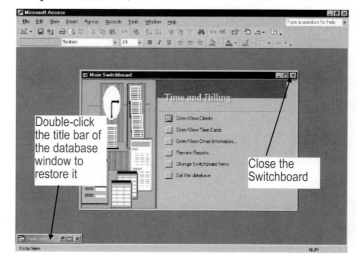

Double-click the title bar of the database window to restore it

Close the Switchboard

- You can start Access and open a database file at the same time by double-clicking the database file you want to open from Windows Explorer or My Computer.

- You can also use the Open Office Document command on the Start menu in Windows to select a database to open and start Access at the same time.

## Navigate in a Database

### Open Objects with the Database Window

- Use the database window to select the type of object you want to work with in Access. Click one of the Objects buttons in the Objects bar to view the available objects of that type, which are displayed in the right portion of the window.

*To open an object from the database window,*
*double-click it*

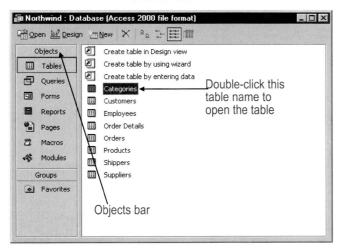

- Double-click an object to open it and begin work. For example, if you want to open a table called *Customers*, click the Tables button, and then double-click the icon for Customers. You can also click on the object icon and click the Open button.

### Move through a Datasheet

- When you open a table, data displays in a row and column format similar to a spreadsheet. Each column heading displays the caption or field name for the field, and each row contains all the information for a single record.

- This row and column display is called **Datasheet view**. This view enables you to see more than one record at a time on the screen.

*Datasheet view displays data in rows and columns*

- To move through the datasheet, you can use the navigation buttons at the bottom of the window.

- The navigation buttons also show the current record and the total number of records. You can type a record number in the specific record box and press Enter to move to that record.

*Datasheet navigation buttons*

- When you move into a field, you are in one of two modes: *field edit mode* or *navigation mode*. The insertion point displays in the field in edit mode; the entire field entry is highlighted when you are in navigation mode. To switch back and forth between the two modes, press F2.

- Press Tab to go from one column to the next column. In the last column, press Tab to go to the first column in the next record.

- You can use the arrow keys to move around the datasheet, and you can also use a number of shortcut keys to move to specific points in the datasheet.

### Move through a Form

- You can navigate through records on a form using the same navigation buttons that appear in Datasheet view of a table or form.

- If you are in navigation mode, you can also use the shortcut keys such as Ctrl+Home and Ctrl+End, to move to the first or last record on a form.

## Sort Records

- Sorting rearranges records in order by one or more fields. Most types of fields can be sorted.

- You can **sort** in **ascending** order (A to Z or 1 to 9) or **descending** order (Z to A or 9 to 1).

- Before sorting, you must first move the insertion point to the field you want to sort. For example, if you want to sort a table of clients by last name in ascending order, move to the Last Name field, then click the ⯭ button.

- Some reasons to sort might be to:
  - See groups of data (for example, all clients who live in New York or all of yesterday's sales).
  - See information organized from smallest or largest values.
  - Group all records that have blanks in a field.
  - Look for duplicate records.

- You can sort in Datasheet or Form view. It is easier to see the sort results in Datasheet view.

*You can sort a table by any field*

Sort buttons

Ascending sort has been done by this column

# Procedures

## Copy Data Files and Deselect the Read-only Attribute

1. Copy the Access data file(s) from your CD to a hard drive.
2. Open Windows Explorer, and locate the drive and folder where you stored the copies.
3. Click to select the file(s) you want to open.

   ✓ To select all the files in a folder at once, right-click and choose Select All.

4. Click **File** ..................... `Alt`+`F`
5. Click **Properties** ................. `R`
6. Deselect **Read-only** in the Attributes section... `Alt`+`R`
7. Click **OK** ....................... `Enter`

## Start Access

1. Click **Start** button `Start`.
2. Click **Programs**.
3. Click **Microsoft Access**.

## Open an Existing Database File when You Start Access

1. Click **Start** button `Start`.
2. Click **Open Office Document**.
3. Click the desired file.

   ✓ You can change to another folder, if needed, to locate file you wish to open.

   ✓ To change folders, select a new folder from Look in drop-down list.

4. Click **Open**.

## Open a Recently Used Database File

- Click the **file name** in the Open a file section of the New File Task Pane.

OR

1. Click **File** ............................. `F`
2. Click the **file name** at the bottom of the File menu.

## Open a Database File

1. Click **More files** on the Task Pane.

   OR

   Click the **Open** button 🖫 on the toolbar.

2. Click the file you want to open.
3. Click **Open** .......................... `O`

## Navigate in a Database

### Open objects with the database window:

1. Click an **Objects** button.
2. Double-click the object you want to open.

OR

1. Click on object icon to select it.
2. Click **Open** in datasheet window. ........ `Alt`+`O`

### Move through a datasheet:

- **Tab** into a field ................... `Tab`
- Press **Ctrl+End** to move to last field and last row ........ `Ctrl`+`End`
- Press **Ctrl+Home** to move to first field and first row .................. `Ctrl`+`Home`
- Press **End** to move to last field in row ............................... `End`
- Press **Home** to move to first field in row ...................... `Home`

### In Navigation mode, to move to:

- **Last field, last record of table** ..................... `Ctrl`+`End`
- **First field, first record of table** ....... `Ctrl`+`Home`

- **Last field, current record** .................. `End`
- **First field, current record** .............. `Home`
- **Last record, current field** ................ `Ctrl`+`↓`
- **First record, current field** ................ `Ctrl`+`↑`
- **Next field (or if in last field to first field of next record)** .... `Tab`
- **Previous field** ........... `Shift`+`Tab`

## Sort Records

1. Open datasheet or form.
2. Click in column to be sorted in Datasheet view or one field in Form view.
3. Click **Records** ............. `Alt`+`R`

   a. Click **Sort** ..................... `S`
   b. Select **Ascending** or **Descending** ..... `A` or `C`

   OR

   Click **Ascending** button `A↓` or

   **Descending** button `Z↓`.

## Close a Table

1. Click **File** ............................. `F`
2. Click **Close** .......................... `C`

   ✓ Text changes are saved automatically.

3. If you are prompted to save design changes, click **Yes** to save changes or **No** to cancel changes.

## Close Access

1. Click **File** ............................. `F`
2. Click **Exit** .............................. `X`

   OR

   Click the **Close** button `X` for the Access window.

# Exercise Directions

1. Start Access, if necessary.

2. Open 💿**AC01**.

   ✓ *You may have to copy the data files from your CD to the hard drive and deselect the read-only attribute.*

3. In the database window, click **Tables** on the Objects list.

4. Open the **tblClients** table.

5. Scroll vertically to review some of the client names.

6. Scroll horizontally to review the number of fields in the table.

7. Use the navigation buttons to find the record for **Anar Mitra**.

8. Move to the Last Name field and sort the client names in ascending order. After the sort, your table should look like the one shown in Illustration A.

   ✓ *Choose Records, Sort, Sort Ascending or click the Sort Ascending button.*

   ✓ *Now sort the table in ascending order by Client ID.*

9. Close the table without saving any changes.

10. Click the Forms button on the Database window.

11. Open the form **frmClients**.

12. Go to the record for **Jamal Joyner**.

13. Now go back to the first record. Scroll through the records and count how many of the clients have been to the store (have a check mark in the field). How many of the client prospects are classified as "Hot One"?

14. Sort the records in ascending order by City.

    ✓ *Move to the City field, then choose Records, Sort, Sort Ascending.*

15. Scroll through the records. Note that this sort groups the clients by city, starting with **Avon** and ending with **Westminster**.

16. Close the form.

17. Exit the database.

    ✓ *Close button* ☒ *or File, Exit.*

*Illustration A*

| | | Client ID | Last Name | First Name | Address | City | State | ZIP | Phone | Work |
|---|---|---|---|---|---|---|---|---|---|---|
| | + | 14 | Abrahamson | Jane | 324 Next Drive | Georgetown | CO | 80444 | (720) 555-2828 | |
| | + | 15 | Bair | Chip | 983 Dude Ranch | Idaho Springs | CO | 80452 | (720) 555-1222 | (303) 555-4143 |
| | + | 3 | Balto | Leanne | 818 Winter St. | Denver | CO | | (303) 555-2111 | (303) 555-2112 |
| | + | 17 | Betts | Elaine | 151 Kings Rd. | Denver | CO | 80238 | (303) 555-3983 | |
| | + | 22 | Bhimani | Korak | 425 Circle K. Rd | Denver | CO | 80838 | (303) 555-0929 | |
| | + | 25 | Braxton | Tyrone | 866 Silver Creek | Denver | CO | 80989 | (303) 555-8928 | |
| | + | 27 | Coffin | Jane | 3735 Brook Can | Avon | CO | 80178 | (720) 555-8917 | |
| | + | 23 | Gomez | Juan | 1344 Syracuse | Denver | CO | 80222 | (303) 555-4943 | |
| | + | 12 | Johnson | Michael | 108 Steele St. | Avon | CO | 80526 | (720) 555-1111 | (303) 555-1112 |
| ▶ | + | 9 | Joyner | Jamal | 1 Park Avenue | Denver | CO | 80234 | (303) 555-5192 | (303) 555-5193 |
| | + | 19 | Katsaropolu | Chris | 1800 Ridgewood | Georgetown | CO | 80483 | (720) 555-9100 | |
| | + | 24 | Lenardsen | Judy | 2010 Wall St. | Denver | CO | 80388 | (303) 555-1732 | |
| | + | 6 | Martinez | Jesus | 491 Cherokee S | Denver | CO | 80221 | (303) 555-3333 | (303) 555-9276 |
| | + | 11 | Martinez | Maria | 491 Cherokee S | Denver | CO | 80221 | (303) 555-3333 | (303) 555-9276 |
| | + | 20 | Mills | Ellen | 1110 Vine | Denver | CO | 80583 | (303) 555-1283 | |
| | + | 21 | Mitra | Anar | 778 Meadow Vie | Evergreen | CO | 80281 | (720) 555-8472 | |
| | + | 10 | Mitterand | Michele | PO Box 1556 | Blackhawk | CO | 80444 | (720) 555-8917 | (303) 555-8918 |
| | + | 16 | Moore | Minny | 888 Market St. | Denver | CO | 80201 | (303) 555-6633 | (303) 555-5193 |
| | + | 26 | Mozeliak | John | 110 N. Sadle Dr | Avon | CO | 80988 | (720) 555-1788 | |
| | + | 5 | Nehru | Al | 1551 James | Westminster | CO | 80030 | (720) 555-3010 | (303) 555-3011 |
| | + | 4 | O'Meara | Kathie | 154 Newton | Thornton | CO | | (720) 555-4987 | (303) 555-4988 |
| | + | 8 | Smythe | John | 15 Cosby Lane | Golden | CO | 80401 | (720) 555-9174 | (303) 555-9175 |

Record: ⏮ ◀ | 10 | ▶ ⏭ ▶* of 25

# On Your Own

1. Start Access and open the 💿**AC01** database.

2. Open the **tblClients** table.

3. Use keystroke shortcuts to go to the following locations in the table:
   - The current field of the last record.
   - The last field of the current record.
   - The previous field.
   - The first field of the first record.

4. Find the record for **Ellen Mills**. What is her address?

5. Sort the table in ascending order by ZIP. How many clients live in the **80444** ZIP Code?

6. Close the table without saving any changes.

# Exercise 2

**Skills Covered:**

◆ **Enter Records** ◆ **Edit Records** ◆ **Delete Records**
◆ **Print Datasheets and Forms** ◆ **Print Preview**

## On the Job

Your main task as a user of a database is to enter and edit data stored in the database. You must be able to enter new records, typically in a form or a datasheet. You will also edit records already stored in the database and correct entries as you enter them. Printing a table or form provides you with a hard copy of the database, which can be used, for example, by a manager for reviewing and on-paper editing.

As the manager of the Steel Dreams Motorcycle Emporium, you must keep the customer database up-to-date by entering records using both a form and a datasheet. You will make changes to existing records and correct information as you enter it. You will then print the updated database to create a hard copy of the information.

## Terms

**Enter** To type in data and press Tab to move to the next field.

**Preview** To produce a screen view of what a printed page will look like.

## Notes

### Enter Records

- To **enter** records in a datasheet or in a form, type the information you want in a field, and press Tab or Enter to go to the next field.

### Enter Records in a Datasheet

- To enter records in a datasheet, type the data below each field name as you would in an Excel worksheet.

- Type the information you want for the record, and press Tab or Enter to go to the next field.

- When you enter data in the last field for a record, press Tab or Enter to go to the first field of the next record. If you are at the last record of the table, this will automatically create a new record.

- Unlike other Office applications where you have to choose the Save command, Access automatically saves a record when you go to another record.

✓ *Each field has a drop-down list containing previous entries for that field; you can select from it instead of retyping an entry. You'll learn more about this feature in later exercises.*

### Enter Data Quickly Using Shortcut Keys

- Use shortcut key combinations shown in the Procedures on page 248 to enter data quickly.

### Copy Data

- Use the Copy and Paste commands to enter repetitive data. Select the data you want to copy, and then use the Copy command. Then move the insertion point to the location you want the data to appear. Use the Paste command to insert the copied data.

- There are three ways to issue the Copy and Paste commands. To copy, you can choose the Copy command from the Edit menu, press Ctrl+C, or click the Copy button .

- To paste, you can choose the Paste command from the Edit menu, press Ctrl+V, or click the Paste button .
- When you copy (or cut) twice in a row before you paste, the Clipboard appears in the Task Pane. This is a new feature in Access 2002.
- The Clipboard Task Pane enables you to store and paste multiple selections.
- If you want to paste a copied selection other than your most recently copied one, you can click it on the Task Pane before pasting.

*The Clipboard is available on the Task Pane*

## Move Data

- Moving data works the same way as copying it (see above, except you use the Cut command instead of the Copy command).
- To issue the Cut command, choose it from the Edit menu, press Ctrl+X, or click the Cut button .

## Copy an Entire Record

- To copy an entire record in Datasheet view, select the record by clicking its record selector button to the left of the record in the gray record selector bar. Copy it with the Copy command. Then select the destination location and use the Paste Append command (on the Edit menu). Existing information will be overwritten with the new information.
- The Paste Append command does not have a keyboard shortcut or toolbar button equivalent.

*Select a record, then copy it; then use
Paste Append to paste a copy of it elsewhere*

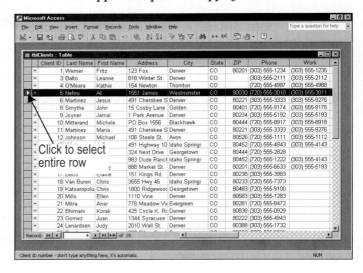

## Enter Records in a Form

- You enter records in Form view the same way you do in Datasheet view. Type in a field and press Tab or Enter to go to the next field.
- When you are on the last field of the form and you press Tab or Enter, Access automatically saves the current record and the insertion point moves to the first field of the next record.
- If you are displaying a current record and want to add a new record, choose the New Record command from the Insert menu or click the New Record button on the toolbar or navigation bar.

## Edit Records

- You may want to correct field information after you enter it. You can delete and add text in the same way you would in Word or Excel.
- Click to position the insertion point. Press Backspace to remove text before the insertion point or press Delete to remove text after the insertion point.
- You can also drag the mouse pointer to select text and then press Delete to remove the text.
- Select text and type new text to replace the selected text. You can double-click on a word to select a word, then type to replace it.
- If you move the mouse pointer to the beginning of a field, the pointer changes to a white plus sign. Click to select the entire content of that field.

- While you are making changes to a record, a pencil icon appears on the record selector button (to the left of the record). The pencil indicates that any changes are not currently saved.

- If you want to undo your changes, press Esc once to undo the change to the current field and press Esc again to undo all changes to the current record.

- Changes are automatically saved to the record when you go to another record or close the table or form.

## Delete Records

- You can delete the current record or one or more contiguous records.

- When you delete one or more records, Access will ask you to confirm the deletion. After you select *Yes*, you cannot reverse the deletion.

- Access shows the total number of records at the bottom of the window.

- If you have an AutoNumber field in the table, when you delete a record, Access will not reuse the numbers of the deleted records. AutoNumber fields are discussed in Exercise 5.

## Print Datasheets and Forms

- Print all the records of the current screen in Datasheet or Form view by clicking the Print button 🖨️.

- If you want to set print options, open the Print dialog box by choosing Print from the File menu.

*Print dialog box*

- The Name drop-down arrow in the Print dialog box allows you to choose a different printer.

- To print selected records, click the record selector to the left of one or more records in Datasheet or Form view. Then click File, Print and choose to print Selected Record(s) in the Print dialog box.

- If desired, type more than 1 in the Number of Copies box and then check Collate if you want to print the document in a complete set, or leave Collate unchecked if you want to print multiple copies of page 1, then page 2, and so on.

## Print Preview

- Click the Print Preview button 🔍 on the toolbar to see a screen **preview** of what your printing will look like.

- While in Print Preview, click the magnifying glass to see more details or to return to full-page view.

- The Navigation buttons at the bottom of the screen in Print Preview allow you to see the first, previous, specific, next, or last page.

*Print Preview shows what the data will look like when printed*

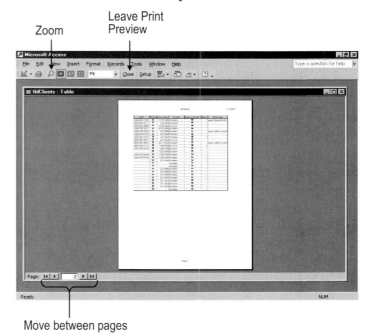

Zoom

Leave Print Preview

Move between pages

# Procedures

## Enter Records

### To enter records in a datasheet:

1. Click in the first blank cell in the first field (the first column and first row).
2. Type data for field.
3. To correct an error, press **Backspace** ....... `Backspace` and type again.
4. Press **Tab** to go to next field ........................... `Tab`
5. Repeat steps 2–4 for each field in record.
6. Click in first cell in the next row to begin new record.

### To enter data quickly using shortcut keys:

- Copy value from current field in previous record ........ `Ctrl`+`'`
- Enter current date ........ `Ctrl`+`;`
- Enter current time ........ `Ctrl`+`:`

### To copy data:

1. Select data to copy.
2. Click **Edit** ..................... `Alt`+`E`
3. Click **Copy** ........................... `C`
4. Move insertion point to where you want copied data to go.
5. Click **Edit** ..................... `Alt`+`E`
6. Click **Paste** ......................... `P`

### To copy entire record:

1. Click on record selector button to left of record.
2. Click **Edit** ..................... `Alt`+`E`
3. Click **Copy** ........................ `C`
4. Click **Edit** ..................... `Alt`+`E`
5. Click **Paste Append** ........... `N`

### To enter records in a form:

1. Type data in first field.
2. Press **Tab** .......................... `Tab`
3. Repeat steps 1 and 2 until complete.

## Edit a Field Entry

1. Click in the field you want to edit.
2. Position the insertion point:
   - Click where you want it.
   OR
   - Use arrow keys ........................... `↕↔`
3. Remove unwanted text using these keys:
   - **Backspace** .......... `Backspace` to delete to left.
   - **Delete** .......................... `Del` to delete to right.
4. Type replacement text.

## Replace a Field Entry

1. Select entire field.
2. Click at beginning of field, when mouse pointer shows black arrow.
3. Retype field content.

## Delete a Record

1. Select the record you want to delete.
2. Click **Delete Record** button .
   OR
   a. Click **Edit** ............... `Alt`+`E`
   b. **Click Delete Record** ..... `R`
   OR
   - Press **Ctrl** + minus sign ............. `Ctrl`+`-`
   OR
   - Press **Delete** ................. `Del`
3. Click **Yes** .......................... `Enter`

## Print Datasheets and Forms

1. Open datasheet or form to print.
2. If desired, click on record selector button on left of datasheet or form to select record(s) to print.
3. Click **File** ..................... `Alt`+`F`
4. Click **Print** .......................... `P`
5. Click **Print Range** option to select:
   - **All** .......................... `Alt`+`A`
   - **Pages** .................... `Alt`+`G`
   - **Selected Record(s)** . `Alt`+`R`
6. Select **Properties** ....... `Alt`+`P` to make any changes to printer setup.
7. Choose desired option tab and select options:
   - **Paper**
   - **Graphics**
   - **Fonts**
   - **Device Options**
   ✓ *The tabs may be different depending on your printer.*
8. Click **OK** .......................... `Enter`
9. Type number in **Number of Copies** text box ........... `Alt`+`C` if you want multiple copies.
10. Click **OK** .......................... `Enter`

## Print Preview

- Click **Print Preview** button.
OR
1. Click **File** ..................... `Alt`+`F`
2. Click **Print Preview** ............. `V`
3. Click magnifying glass to see more or less detail.
4. Click navigation buttons to see the first, previous, specific, next, or last page.

# Exercise Directions

1. Start Access, if necessary.

2. Open 💿 **AC02**.

   ✓ *You may have to copy the data files from your CD to the hard drive and deselect the read-only attribute.*

3. Open the **tblClients** table.

4. Move to the blank record after client 27, **Jane Coffin**.

5. Make sure the insertion point is in the Last Name field, then enter the three new records shown in Illustration A.

   ✓ *Press Tab or Enter to move from one field to the next.*

6. Change **Mark Wasser's** address to **89 Winthrop Rd**.

7. Add three more records shown in Illustration B. Use shortcut keys to enter the repeated information in the City, State, and ZIP fields.

8. Copy the entire record for **Gloria Sebastia** and paste it in the row for the next new record at the bottom of the table.

9. Change the First Name of the new record to **George**.

   ✓ *This new record is for Gloria's husband. All other record information is the same.*

10. Preview the datasheet and print one copy.

11. Close the table.

    ✓ *Close button* ⊠ *or File, Close.*

12. Open the **frmClients** form.

13. Insert a new record (Insert, New Record) and enter a new record with the following information:
    **Tracy Richards, 532 W. Albion Dr., Blackhawk, CO, 80356, (303) 555-7275**

14. Change the ZIP for **Tracy Richards** to **80444** and change the phone number to **(720) 555-2237**.

15. Delete the record for **Jane Coffin**.

16. Select the records for **George** and **Gloria Sebastia** as well as **Tracy Richards**.

17. Preview and print the selected records.

18. Close the table.

19. Exit the database.

*Illustration A*

| | | Client ID | Last Name | First Name | Address | City | State | ZIP | Phone | Work |
|---|---|---|---|---|---|---|---|---|---|---|
| | + | 23 | Gomez | Juan | 1344 Syracuse | Denver | CO | 80222 | (303) 555-4943 | |
| | + | 24 | Lenardsen | Judy | 2010 Wall St. | Denver | CO | 80388 | (303) 555-1732 | |
| | + | 25 | Braxton | Tyrone | 866 Silver Creek | Denver | CO | 80989 | (303) 555-8928 | |
| | + | 26 | Mozeliak | John | 110 N. Sadle Dr | Avon | CO | 80988 | (720) 555-1788 | |
| | + | 27 | Coffin | Jane | 3735 Brook Can | Avon | CO | 80178 | (720) 555-8917 | |
| ▶ | + | 28 | Gallup | Paul | 4215 Kessler A\ | Denver | CO | 80388 | (303) 555-9256 | (303) 555-3920 |
| | + | 29 | Wasser | Mark | 89 Guilford Ln. | Avon | CO | 80988 | (720) 555-3840 | |
| | + | 30 | Nguyen | Toby | 229 Kenlock Dr. | Evergreen | CO | 80281 | (720) 555-0035 | (303) 555-1182 |
| ✳ | | oNumber) | | | | | | | | |

| | | Client ID | Last Name | First Name | Address | City | State | ZIP | Phone | Work |
|---|---|---|---|---|---|---|---|---|---|---|
| | + | 23 | Gomez | Juan | 1344 Syracuse | Denver | CO | 80222 | (303) 555-4943 | |
| | + | 24 | Lenardsen | Judy | 2010 Wall St. | Denver | CO | 80388 | (303) 555-1732 | |
| | + | 25 | Braxton | Tyrone | 866 Silver Creek | Denver | CO | 80989 | (303) 555-8928 | |
| | + | 26 | Mozeliak | John | 110 N. Sadle Dr | Avon | CO | 80988 | (720) 555-1788 | |
| | + | 27 | Coffin | Jane | 3735 Brook Can | Avon | CO | 80178 | (720) 555-8917 | |
| | + | 28 | Gallup | Paul | 4215 Kessler A\ | Denver | CO | 80388 | (303) 555-9256 | (303) 555-3920 |
| | + | 29 | Wasser | Mark | 89 Winthrop Rd. | Avon | CO | 80988 | (720) 555-3840 | |
| | + | 30 | Nguyen | Toby | 229 Kenlock Dr. | Evergreen | CO | 80281 | (720) 555-0035 | (303) 555-1182 |
| ▶ | + | 31 | Phillips | Everett | 214 Ridge St. | Evergreen | CO | 80281 | (720) 555-9387 | |
| | + | 32 | Hastings | Laurie | 7789 Adams St. | Evergreen | CO | 80281 | (720) 555-8886 | (720) 555-3381 |
| | + | 33 | Sebastia | Gloria | 32 Florida Ct. | Evergreen | CO | 80281 | (720) 555-9402 | |
| ✱ | | oNumber) | | | | | | | | |

# On Your Own

1. Start Access and open the ⊚ **OAC02** database.

2. Open the **tblClients** table.

3. Enter records for 5 of your friends and family members into the table. Use their real addresses and phone numbers—or make up the address and phone information as you go.

4. Change the address information of the records you entered to fit with the Colorado city, state, ZIP, and phone number information already in the table. For example, use the cities of Denver, Thornton, Westminster, Golden, Blackhawk, etc., use CO for the state abbreviation, use phone numbers with either the 303 or 720 area code, and use some of the ZIP Codes already in the table.

5. Preview and print the table, then close it.

6. Open the **frmClients** form.

7. Scroll through the new records you added, then add 5 more records for your friends and family members. Make up Colorado city, state, ZIP, and phone number information similar to what you used in the **tblClients** table.

   ✓ *You can press Tab to move from field to field.*

8. Close the form, and open the **tblClients** table.

9. Select the new records you added.

10. Preview and print the selected records.

11. Close the form.

12. Close the database and exit Access.

# Exercise 3

## Skills Covered:

◆ **Plan a Database** ◆ **Create a New Database File**
◆ **Create a Table in Datasheet View**
◆ **Change Field Names in Datasheet View** ◆ **Save a Table Design**

## On the Job

As well as learning to work with existing databases, you must also learn to plan and create a new database of your own. In planning the database, you need to consider how the database will be used by asking: What information will it store? How will you use the database to analyze the information? After planning the database, you can easily create the new database file and the tables that store the data.

Now that you have become familiar with the Steel Dreams Motorcycle Emporium's current database, you've decided to create a new database and add a table to store information about the shop's client names, addresses, and phone numbers.

## Terms

**Primary key** The field that uniquely identifies each record in a table.

**Blank database** A database file that does not yet contain any objects (that is, tables, queries, reports, and so on).

**Template** A predefined group of settings for creating a new database, including what tables will be included, what fields will be used, and so on.

## Notes

### Plan a Database

- Before you create a database, you must decide which fields you want to include—and if you need a single table or more than one. Consider what information the database will store and how the information will be used.

- To begin, make a list of the fields you want to store in your database, such as last name, first name, address, phone, and so on.

- If you have a lot of categories in mind, break down the field list into specific categories such as Customers, Vendors, Inventory, and so on. Each category will form a separate table in your database.

- If you envision repeated information in a table, plan to split it into separate tables. For example, you might want to store employee contact information in a separate table and employee vacation usage data in another table so that you don't repeat information you already have in the contact table (address, phone, e-mail account, and so on).

- Think about the ways you will want to search or sort the data, and plan the fields to support them.

- For example, if you want to sort by last name, make sure you have separate fields for First Name and Last Name. The same goes for City, State, and ZIP Code. It would be hard, for example, to create mailing labels if client addresses are in one field.

- Each table should have a field in which each record will be unique, such as an ID Number field. This field will be the table's **primary key**.

- Plan the relationships between your tables. Make sure that tables to be related have a common field. For example, the Employee ID field in the Employee Contacts table might link to the Employee ID field in the Vacations table.

  ✓ *Relationships between tables are covered more thoroughly in Lesson 2, Exercise 9.*

- When you've finished identifying fields and tables, you are ready to create your new database file and create the tables within it.

## Create a New Database File

- The database file contains all Access objects, including tables, forms, queries, pages, and reports. Each database file is stored with an .mdb extension.

- You must create a database file, or open an existing one, before you can enter any data or create any objects (such as tables or queries).

- When you start Access, the New File Task Pane provides shortcuts for starting a new database or opening an existing one.

- You can reopen the task pane at any time by clicking the New button ⬜ on the toolbar.

*Start a new database from the Task Pane*

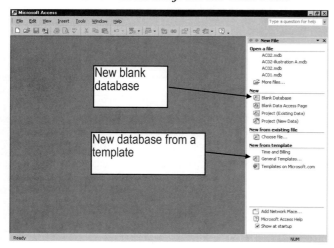

- To start a new database, you can choose to create a **blank database** or create a database based on a **template**.

  ✓ *You can also choose to start a new data access page for a Web page or a new project, but these are not covered in this course.*

✓ *A new feature in Access 2002 is the ability to create a new database by copying an existing one. Use the New from Existing File link in the Task Pane.*

### Create a New Blank Database

- To create a blank database, use the Blank Database link in the New File Task Pane.

- The File New Database dialog box appears, and you enter a file name and click Create.

*Enter a name for the database file you are creating*

## Create a Table in Datasheet View

- There are three ways to create a table: using Table Design view, using a wizard, and by entering data in a new datasheet.

- In this exercise, you will learn about the latter method. Other methods are covered in upcoming exercises.

- To create a new table with a datasheet, click the *Create table by entering data* shortcut from the database window. A new, blank datasheet appears with placeholder field names (Field1, Field2, etc.) in the column heads.

*A new table from Datasheet view*

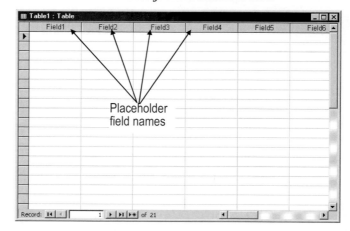

## Change Field Names in Datasheet View

- A new table in Datasheet view provides placeholder names for each field at the top of each column.

- To change a field name, double-click the existing name and then type a new one.

## Save a Table Design

- When you close a table after making design changes to it, Access asks whether you want to save your changes.

- This refers to the structural changes to the table, such as the field names, not to any data you have entered. Data is saved automatically.

- The first time you save changes to a table, Access prompts for a table name.

*Name the new table*

- If there is no primary key field defined for the table, Access asks whether you want to create one.

*Define the primary key*

- If you choose *Yes,* it creates a new field called *ID* in the table and sets it as the primary key.

- If you choose *No,* it saves your table without a primary key.

  ✓ *You cannot choose an existing field to be the primary key field from Datasheet view. In Exercise 5 you will learn about Table Design view.*

# Procedures

**Display the Task Pane**

1. Click **File** ..................... Alt + F
2. Click **New** ........................... N

**Create a New Blank Database**

**From Task Pane:**

1. Choose **Blank Database**.
2. Type file name.
3. Choose folder in **Save in** drop-down list.
   OR
   Click folder on the Places bar.
4. Click **Create** .................... Enter

**Create Table in Datasheet View**

**From database window:**

- Double-click **Create table by entering data**.
   OR
   a. Click **Insert** ........... Alt + I
   b. Click **Table** ................. T

   c. Choose **Datasheet View**.
   d. Click **OK** ...................... Enter

**Change Field Names in Datasheet View**

1. Double-click field name in column header.
2. Type new field name in column header.
3. Press **Enter** ..................... Enter
   OR
   Click in column to change.
4. Click **Format** .............. Alt + O
5. Click **Rename Column** ....... N
6. Type new field name in column header.
7. Press **Enter** ..................... Enter

**Save a Table Design**

1. Close the table ...................
   ✓ *If this is the first time you've saved the table, continue with the following.*
2. Click **Yes** ............................. Y
3. Type table name.
4. Click **OK** ......................... Enter
5. Click **No** .............................. N
   ✓ *To bypass creation of primary key.*
   OR
   Click **Yes** to create primary key ......................... Y

# Exercise Directions

1. Start Access and select Blank Database from the Task Pane.

2. Replace the default file name, *db1*, with **AC03** and press **Enter**.

3. Double-click on **Create table by entering data** in the database window.

4. In the Datasheet view for the new table, change the field names as shown in Illustration A.

   ✓ *As you can see, the field names for this table do not use spaces. Although you can use spaces in file names, spaces can sometimes result in database errors for certain advanced operations.*

   ✓ *Double-click on Field1 and type the new name.*

5. Add the records shown in Illustration A.

   ✓ *Press Tab after each entry to move to the next column.*

6. Save the table as **tblClients** and have Access create a primary key.

7. Close the table.

8. Exit the database.

*Illustration A*

| FirstName | LastName | Address | City | State | ZIP | Phone |
|-----------|----------|---------|------|-------|-----|-------|
| Fritz | Werner | 123 Fox | Denver | CO | 80201 | (303) 555-1234 |
| Jenny | Zimdahl | 234 Ivy | Aurora | CO | 80014 | (303) 555-2345 |
| Leanne | Balto | 83 Winter St. | Denver | CO | 80224 | (303) 555-2111 |
| Kathie | O'Meara | 154 Newton | Thornton | CO | 80221 | (303) 555-4987 |
| Al | Nehru | 1551 James | Westminster | CO | 80030 | (303) 555-3010 |
| Jesus | Martinez | 17 Tar Drive | Arvada | CO | 80030 | (303) 555-9275 |
| Pam | Wong | 3954 Maple | Evergreen | CO | 80219 | (303) 555-7283 |
| John | Smith | 15 Cosby Lane | Golden | CO | 80456 | (303) 555-9174 |
| Jamal | Joyner | 1 Park Avenue | Denver | CO | 80234 | (303) 555-5192 |
| Michele | Mitterand | PO Box 1556 | Blackhawk | CO | 80444 | (303) 555-8917 |

Table1 : Table

Record: 11 of 11

# On Your Own

1. Start Access and create a new database.

2. Save the database file as **OAC03**.

3. Create a table for storing a telephone list or roster. You can use friends, relatives, associates, club or organization members, or the members of a sports team.

4. Include fields for first name, last name, and telephone number.

5. Save the table with the name **Roster**.

6. Let Access create the Primary Key field.

7. Enter at least five records in the table.

8. Close your database and exit Access.

# Exercise 4

◆ **Create a Database with Database Wizards**
◆ **Start Database Wizards** ◆ **Use Database Wizards**
◆ **Use Switchboards**

## On the Job

Microsoft Access comes with several databases designed for typical purposes. You simply choose the desired wizard—which you can customize to more closely match your needs—and enter data. If you create a database using one of the database wizards, you can save a significant amount of time compared to designing a database from scratch. Access switchboards provide a convenient way to automate your database and make its features and data more *access*ible.

Before you spend a lot of time creating the database objects for Steel Dreams Cycle Emporium, you want to check out the templates that come with Access to see whether one of them might provide a suitable head start for your work. You will create a new database using the Database Wizard, to see whether it meets your needs.

## Terms

**Template** A predefined group of settings for creating a new database, including what tables will be included, what fields will be used, and so on.

**Database Wizard** A step-by-step process for creating a new database using a template.

**Switchboard** An Access form with command buttons or other controls that lead to other switchboard forms, input forms, and reports.

## Notes

### Create a Database with Database Wizards

■ Access offers ten different **templates** that help you create a database that may match what you need in a database.

✓ *You can also download additional templates from the Microsoft Web site if you have Internet access. Just click the* Templates on Microsoft.com *hyperlink on the New File Task Pane.*

■ In Access, **templates** are accessed through **Database Wizards**, so the terms *template* and *database wizard* are roughly synonymous in Access. This is not always the case in other Office programs, however.

■ These templates provide a basic set of tables, queries, forms, and reports, plus a Switchboard to help beginners navigate among them.

■ You cannot pick and choose among the tables and other objects that Access creates when you use a database wizard. However, you can delete any unwanted objects, or make changes to them, after the database wizard is finished creating the objects.

■ Using a template is helpful primarily if you want to create a database similar to one of the templates. If your database is fairly specific in purpose, whether simple or complex, it is probably easier to build from scratch.

## Start Database Wizards

- You can start a database wizard from within Access by clicking General Templates in the task pane to display the Templates dialog box.

- The Templates dialog box has two tabs: General and Databases. The General tab contains a template for a blank database, a data access page for the Web, and blank databases that are not designed around a specific purpose.

- Click the Databases tab to see icons for the database templates that Access offers. Then double-click the one you want, or click it and then click OK.

  ✓ *A preview pane exists in the Templates dialog box, but it only shows a simple graphic representation of the database. If you need more help choosing the right database template, open it up and examine its features.*

*Choose the template you want*

- After you choose a template, a File New Database dialog box appears, just like when you create a new blank database. Enter a name for the new database file in it and click Create. The database wizard then starts.

## Use Database Wizards

- The database wizard leads you through a series of dialog boxes that:
  - Show you the tables that appear in the new database and allow you to select optional fields for each table.

    ✓ *The basic list of fields for a particular table is fixed. The field names that appear in italics and that do not have a check mark next to them by default are optional. You can select any or all of these optional fields to include in the table.*

*Select optional table fields*

Optional fields

  - Provide choices for form and report formatting.

  - Enable you to enter a title for the database (different from the file name).

  - Enable you to specify a graphic to use as a logo on reports.

- The database wizard does not create any data; you will enter the data yourself, as you learned to do in Exercise 2.

- You can customize the tables and other database objects (queries, forms, and reports) after Access creates them for you.

## Use Switchboards

- Databases created with a database wizard automatically include a **switchboard** that allows you to navigate to forms and reports created for the database.

- The switchboard is actually a group of linked forms with buttons for opening certain forms, reports, or queries.

- The main switchboard form opens automatically each time you open that database.

- The database window starts minimized when the main switchboard appears; double-click it (in the bottom-left corner of the Access window) to restore it. You can minimize or close the main switchboard if desired to get it out of your way.

*A main switchboard*

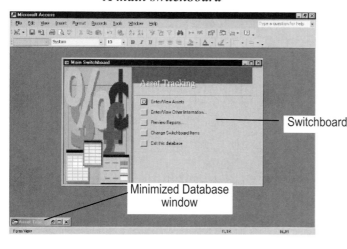

- You can change the content of a switchboard form, or choose a different form as the default, by clicking Change Switchboard Items on the main switchboard. Such editing is beyond the scope of this book, but you can try it on your own or with the assistance of an instructor.

### Modifying the Switchboard

- You can prevent the main switchboard from opening at startup by choosing Tools, Startup, and choosing None as the Display Form/Page entry.

# Procedures

### Create a Database with a Template

**From Task Pane:**

1. Choose **General Templates**.
2. Click the **Databases** tab.
3. Click the template.
4. Click **OK** ............................ Enter
5. Type file name.
6. Choose folder in **Save in** drop-down list.
   OR
   Click folder on left side of dialog box.
7. Click **Create** ..................... Enter
8. Click **Next** ........................ Enter
9. If desired, click on each table in database and click on check box in front of italicized entries to add optional fields.
10. Click **Next** ....................... Enter
11. Click style for screen displays.
12. Click **Next** ........................ Enter

13. Click style for printed reports.
14. Click **Next** ........................ Enter
15. Type a title for database.
    ✓ *This name appears on the title bar. It need not be the same as the file name.*
16. If you want a picture on every report, click **Yes, I'd like to include a picture** and click **Picture** button to choose picture.
17. Click **Next** ........................ Enter
18. Click **Finish** ...................... Enter
    ✓ *Some templates prompt you to enter your company's contact information after the database wizard runs; do so if prompted.*

### Use Switchboard

1. Click on button to open form, report, or another switchboard.
2. If another switchboard appears, click on **Return to Main Switchboard** to return.

### Close Switchboard

- Click **Close** ☒ on the Switchboard window.

### Restore Database Window

- Double-click the database window's **title bar.**
  ✓ *The database window's title bar is in the bottom-left corner of the Access window.*

### Prevent Switchboard from Opening Automatically

1. Click **Tools** ................. Alt + T
2. Click **Startup** ........................ U
3. Click down arrow next to **Display Form/Page** ▾.
4. Choose **(none).**
   ✓ *(none) is at the top of the list; scroll up to find it.*
5. Click **OK** ............................ Enter

# Exercise Directions

1. Start a new database using the Order Entry template.
   - ✓ *Click the General Templates link in the New File Task Pane, and choose Order Entry from the Databases tab.*

2. Name the database **AC04**. The database wizard starts.

3. In the Customer information table, add the E-mail Address and Notes fields (at the bottom of the Fields in customer information table list).

4. Pick your own styles for screen displays (forms) and reports.

5. Title the database **Orders** and choose Finish.

6. Access prompts you for company information. Click OK and enter the following information for the company:

   Company: **Steel Dreams Cycle Emporium**
   Address.: **P.O. Box 765**
   City: **Oyster Bay**
   State: **NY**
   ZIP: **11771**
   Sales Tax Rate: **8%**
   Default Terms: **Net 30**
   Phone Number: **(516) 555-2200**

7. Click the Close button ⊠ to exit the form.

8. On the switchboard, click Enter/View Other Information.

9. Click Enter/View Products, add the Products as follows.

   | Product Name | Unit Price |
   |---|---|
   | Leather saddlebag | 109.95 |
   | Vinyl seat cover | 24.95 |
   | Chrome polish | 9.50 |
   | Steel Dreams T-shirt | 10.95 |

   - ✓ *You do not enter the Product ID; Access enters this automatically.*

10. Click the Close button ⊠ to exit the form.

11. Close the switchboard and restore the database window.

12. Turn off the automatic display of the switchboard at startup.
    - ✓ *To do so, choose Tools, Startup and set Display Form/Page to None.*

13. Exit Access.

# On Your Own

1. Start Access and create a database using the Inventory Control Wizard.

2. Save the database as **OAC04**. You can use this database to store information about items sold as part of a fundraiser for a club or organization, for items sold in a retail store, or for items that you own, such as books or CDs.

3. Close the main switchboard and open the **Categories** table in Datasheet view.

4. Enter at least five product categories.

5. Open the **Products** table in Datasheet view.

6. Enter at least three products. Notice that the categories you created appear on a drop-down list in the Category ID field.

   - ✓ *You do not have to fill in all the fields in the Products table. Try to fill in the Product Name, Production Description, Category ID, and Unit Price, though.*

7. View the existing forms and tables and make modifications if you want.

8. Open the switchboard form. (Click on Forms in the Objects bar; click on switchboard to open it.)

9. Make some changes to the switchboard using the Switchboard Manager. To access it, click Change Switchboard Items on the Main Switchboard.

10. Close the database and exit Access.

# Exercise 5

Skills Covered:

◆ **Open a Database File** ◆ **Create a Table with the Table Wizard**
◆ **Start a New Table in Table Design View**
◆ **Work with Table Design View** ◆ **Select a Field for the Primary Key**
◆ **Open a Database Exclusively** ◆ **Set a Database Password**

## On the Job

You will probably want more than one table in your database. Good database design means having tables for different types of information as you learned in Exercise 3. Client information should be in one table (or tables) and employee information should be in another (or others) as you specialize tables for the different types of information. In this exercise, you will open the database file you created in Exercise 3 and add a few new tables to it. You will also learn how to set a password to protect your database from being modified by others.

You have decided to stick with creating your database from scratch rather than using the database wizard version from Exercise 4. You now need to create a new table to keep track of your employees, as well as a table to log customer inquiries and requests. You will also experiment with password-protecting the database.

## Terms

**Table Design view** A view in which you can add, edit, and delete fields from the table, change field types and descriptions, set a primary key, and more.

**Data type** The type of data that a particular field is designed to hold. Common types include *Text, Number, Date,* and *Memo.*

**Field description** An optional brief comment or explanation of a field. The field description appears in the status bar at the bottom of the window when its field is selected.

**Field properties** Characteristics of a field that determine how long an entry can be, how the entry will be formatted, whether there should be a default entry, and what can be entered (for example, numbers only or valid dates only).

## Notes

### Open a Database File

- To get to any tables or other objects within a database, you need to open the database first.

- Depending on when you last opened the database, you can choose from a list of recently used files on the New File Task Pane or at the bottom of the File menu.

- If you have not used the database recently, you may need to use the Open dialog box (File, Open) or the More Files link in the Task Pane.

259

## Create a Table with the Table Wizard

- The Table Wizard is a handy utility for creating new tables. You can choose fields from many different sample tables that Access provides.

- To create a table using the Table Wizard, you can double-click *Create table by using wizard* in the list of tables of the database window.

- Another way to start the Table Wizard is to display the list of tables in the Database window, click New 🔲 New , and then click Table Wizard in the New table dialog box that appears.

- The Table Wizard walks you step-by-step through all the decisions you must make.

*Two ways to start the Table Wizard*

Click here and then choose Table Wizard

Double-click here

### Choosing Table Fields

- The first decision to make is what fields to include. The Table Wizard lets you choose any field from any table in any of the database templates. There are over a hundred tables to choose from.

- The sample tables are broken into two categories: *Business* and *Personal*. Choose one of the two options to switch the sample table listing.

- When you select a sample table, a list of all its fields appears. You can select a field by clicking the ＞ button, or select all the fields in that table at once by clicking the ＞＞ button.

- You can choose fields from as many of the sample tables as you like before moving on.

*The Table Wizard helps you choose fields*

- You can rename a chosen field by clicking the Rename Field button. This keeps the field's properties but enables you to call it something else.

### Completing the Table Wizard

- The Table Wizard also prompts you for a table name, and lets you specify whether Access should create a primary key field.

- If you choose to create your own primary key field, the Table Wizard displays a list of the fields you have chosen, so you can specify which one should be the primary key.

  ✓ *You won't see this screen (below) if you let Access create a primary key field.*

*Select the primary key field*

- The Wizard also prompts you for a data type for your primary key field. You can make it an AutoNumber field, a Numeric field, or a Text field.

  ✓ *Data types are explained in the table on the next page.*

- The Table Wizard also asks about relationships to other tables in your database. The default is for the table to have no relationships.

  ✓ *You will learn about relationships in Exercise 9.*

## Start a New Table in Table Design View

■ You can also create a new table in **Table Design view**. The Table Design view method is more complex, but also more powerful and flexible.

■ To start a new table using Design view, you can double-click *Create Table in Design View* in the tables list of the Database window.

■ Another way is to click the New button ▦ New in the Database window, choose Design View from the New Table dialog box, and click OK.

## Work in Table Design View

■ Table Design view contains a list of the fields in the table, including name, **data type**, and **field description**.

■ When a field is selected, its **field properties** appear in the lower half of the Table Design view window. Field properties specify advanced options for the field, such as maximum entry length and default value.

 ✓ *Field properties will be covered in Exercise 7.*

*Table Design view*

Field Name    Data types                    Description

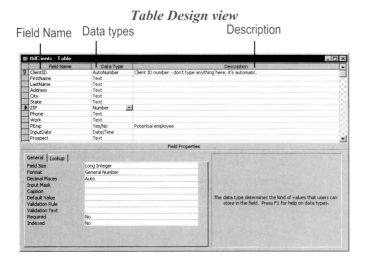

## Field Names

■ Type or edit a name in the Field Name column. Although you may use up to 64 characters, you should keep the name short.

 ✓ *As previously discussed, even though you can include underscores or spaces in the field name, you should avoid doing so. This will help avoid problems with formulas, programming, or converting your database to a different format.*

## Field Descriptions

■ The field description is optional. You can enter anything you want here, but most people use it to provide comments or hints about the intended use and/or limitations of the field.

■ The text you type in the description will appear on the status bar (bottom of the screen) when the user is in this field in Datasheet view or on a form.

## Data Types

■ The Data type column tells you what kind of information your field can store. Click the drop-down arrow in this cell to choose from the list of data types. You can also type the first letter of the data type to make this choice, if you prefer to use the keyboard:

| Data Type | Description |
|---|---|
| Text | Includes any characters up to a maximum of 255 characters (determined by field size). If the data includes a mix of numbers and any amount of letters, choose Text. Examples include name and address fields. <br><br> ✓ *The default data type is Text.* |
| Memo | Use this data type when Text is not large enough. Like Text, this data type can also have letters and numbers but can be much larger— up to 65,536 characters. Don't use Memo unless you need that extra length, however, because you can't perform certain actions (indexing, for example) on a memo field. |
| Number | Includes various forms of numerical data that can be used in calculations. |
| Date/Time | Date and time entries in formats showing date, time, or both. |
| Currency | Use for currency values with up to four digits after the decimal place. This data type is more accurate for large numbers than the Number data type, but generally takes up more space. |
| AutoNumber | Usually this is used to create an identification number for each record. The value for each record increases by one. |

| Data Type | Description |
|---|---|
| Yes/No | Only two possible values can be in this field. Options include Yes/No, True/False, or On/Off. The default style shows a check box with a ✔ for *Yes* or blank ☐ for *No*. |
| OLE Object | This data type allows you to place another file type into your record. Within the field, you can insert a picture (a company logo, for example), a Word document (employee resume), or an Excel spreadsheet (client summary chart). |
| Hyperlink | This allows you to insert a Web address such as *www.ddcpub.com*, which will launch when you click it in Datasheet view or on a form. You could also type a path and file name to a file on your hard drive (C:\docs\myres.doc) or a network drive. |
| Lookup Wizard | Creates a lookup column, which creates a list of values from which to choose when entering data. |

## Select a Field for the Primary Key

- As explained in Exercise 3, a table can have a primary key field that contains unique data for each record. The primary key field helps avoid duplicate records in a table.

- Each table can have only one primary key field.

- For the primary key field, choose a field that will be unique for each record. FirstName and LastName would not be good choices for the primary key because different records could have the same value.

- For an employee database, the primary key could be the Social Security Number, for example. You could also create an Employee ID field specifically to be the primary key field.

- When you create a table without choosing a primary key field, Access asks whether you want a primary key field to be created automatically. If you do so, the new field receives the name "ID."

- From Table Design view, you can choose an existing field to be your primary key by selecting it and then clicking the Primary Key button 🔑 on the toolbar.

## Open a Database Exclusively

- To set a database password, you have to open the database in exclusive mode (no one else can be in the database).

- Open Exclusive is most often used to ensure that only one user at a time is trying to change the design of database objects.

- In the Open dialog box, choose the down arrow on the Open button and select Open Exclusive.

*Use Open Exclusive rather than the normal Open operation when you want to set a password*

## Set Database Password

- When you set a password, you must type the password again to verify accuracy. The password does not show when you type; asterisks display instead. Note that passwords are case-sensitive.

*Enter the password to use, then reenter it to confirm*

### Remove Database Password

- You have to type the password again when you want to remove the password.

- If you forget your password, you will not be able to open the database.

# Procedures

## Open a Recently Used Database File

### From the New File Task Pane:
- Click the file name.

### From the menu bar:
1. Click **File** ..................... `Alt`+`F`
2. Click the file name.

## Open a Database File

1. Click **Open** button `📂`.
   OR
   a. Click **File** ................ `Alt`+`F`
   b. Click **Open** ..................... `O`
   OR
   - Click **More Files** on the Task Pane.
2. Select file to open.
3. Click **Open** ................. `Alt`+`O`

## Create a Table with Table Wizard

### From the Database window:
1. Click **Tables**.
2. Double-click **Create table by using wizard**.
3. Click **Business** ................... `S`
   OR
   Click **Personal** ............... `P`
4. Click a sample table.
5. Click a field you want.
6. Click > to add the field......... `>`
   - ✓ *Click >> to choose all fields from the sample table at once. Click < or << to remove fields from your list.*
7. Repeat steps 5–6 as needed.
8. Repeat steps 4–6 to choose more fields from another table.
9. (Optional) Rename a field:
   a. Click a **field** on the Fields in my new table list.
   b. Click **Rename Field** ....... `R`
   c. Type the new name.
   d. Click **OK** ...................... `Enter`

10. Click **Next** ............................ `N`
11. Type the table name.
12. Choose one:
    - Click **Yes**, set a primary key for me ............. `Alt`+`Y`
    - Click **No**, I'll set the primary key ........... `Alt`+`N`
13. Click **Next** ............................ `N`
    - ✓ *If you chose Yes in step 12, skip to step 18 now.*
14. Click the down arrow next to **What field will hold data that is unique for each record?**............. `Alt`+`W`
15. Click the primary key field you want.
16. Choose the data type for the primary key field:
    - **Consecutive numbers Microsoft Access assigns automatically to new records**................. `Alt`+`C`
    - **Numbers I enter when I add new records** .. `Alt`+`A`
    - **Numbers and/or letters I enter when I add new records**................. `Alt`+`L`
17. Click **Next** ............................ `N`
18. (Optional) Set relationships to other existing tables.
    - ✓ *Relationships are covered in Exercise 9. You can skip them for now.*
19. Click **Next** ............................ `N`
20. Click **Finish** ......................... `F`

## Create Table in Table Design View

### From the Database window:
1. Click **Tables**.
2. Double-click **Create table in Design view**.

## Create a Field in Table Design View

1. Click in the **Field Name column** of an empty row.

2. Type field name.
3. Press **Tab** ........................... `Tab`
4. Click the **down arrow** in the Data Type column ...... `▾`
5. Click the field type.
6. Press **Tab** ........................... `Tab`
7. (Optional) Type field description.

## Select a Field for the Primary Key

1. Click in the field to use.
2. Click **Primary Key** button `🔑` on toolbar.
   - ✓ *Click Primary Key button again to remove primary key.*
   - ✓ *Click in another field and click Primary Key button to change primary key.*

## Open a Database Exclusively

1. Click **File** ..................... `Alt`+`F`
2. Click **Open** ........................... `O`
3. Move to database file.
4. Click on **Open** drop-down arrow.
5. Click **Open Exclusive** ......... `V`

## Set Database Password

1. Open database exclusively.
2. Click **Tools**................. `Alt`+`T`
3. Click **Security** ..................... `T`
4. Click **Set Database Password** ........................... `D`
5. Type password.
6. Press **Tab** ........................... `Tab`
7. Type password again.
8. Click **OK** .......................... `Enter`

## Remove Database Password

1. Click **Tools**................. `Alt`+`T`
2. Click **Security** ..................... `T`
3. Click **Unset Database Password** ........................... `D`
4. Type password.
5. Click **OK** .......................... `Enter`

# Exercise Directions

1. Start Access, if necessary.

2. Open ⊘ **AC05**.

3. Start a new table using the Table Wizard.

4. Choose the **Employees** sample table, and transfer all of its fields to the Fields in My New Table list.

5. Remove the BillingRate, EmployeeID, and NationalEmplNumber fields from your Fields in My New Table list.

6. Rename the SocialSecurityNumber field to **SSN**.

7. Name the table **tblEmployees**.

8. Choose to set your own primary key field, and set it to the SSN field.

9. Specify that the primary key field should contain numbers that you will enter yourself.

   ✓ *Do not create any relationships at this point for the new table.*

10. Create a new table using Table Design view with the following information:

| Field Name | Data Type |
|------------|-----------|
| NeedID | AutoNumber |
| ClientID | Number |
| Needs | Memo |

11. Make the NeedID field the primary key.

12. Save the table as **tblNeeds**.

13. Close the **tblNeeds** table.

14. Close the database and reopen it with Open Exclusive.

15. Create a password for the database.

    ✓ *Start with Tools, Security.*

16. Close and reopen the file by typing the password.

17. Remove the password.

18. Close the database.

# On Your Own

1. Open ⊘ **OAC05**, which contains a simple database with the beginnings of a sports team roster.

2. Create a new table with the Table Wizard that will hold data about the equipment that the organization owns.

   ✓ *You might want to pull fields from several different sample tables.*

3. Create another new table, this time using Table Design view, to hold data about various categories of membership in the organization.

4. Password-protect the database, and then close it and reopen it.

5. Remove the password.

6. Close the database and exit Access.

# Exercise 6

You are in charge of tracking customer feedback for Wee-Soft, a company that produces educational software for children. The company includes a Feedback card with each product, which customers fill out and mail in. You need to create a database that records the feedback from those cards.

## Exercise Directions

1. Create a blank new Access database named **AC06**.

2. Create a new table using the fields in Part I of Illustration A.

   ✓ Do not use spaces in the field names.

   ✓ Separate the parent's first name and last name into separate fields: FirstName and LastName.

   ✓ Abbreviate long names; for example, abbreviate the How many children live in your home? field to NumChildren.

   ✓ Choose appropriate field types (Text or Number). The ZIP field should be set to Text rather than Number.

3. Insert a field at the top of the field list called **CustomerID**, set its type to Number, and make it the primary key.

4. Save the table design; name it **tblCustomers**.

5. Create another table using the fields shown in Part II of Illustration A.

   ✓ Use the Yes/No field type for the yes/no questions on the form.

   ✓ Abbreviate the question names; for example, you could use the following abbreviations:

| Field Name on Form | Field Name in Table |
|---|---|
| How old is the child who will use the product the most | ChildAge |
| Was the program easy to install? | InstallEasy |
| Did you encounter any installation errors or problems? | InstallProblems |
| Does your child enjoy using the program? | ChildEnjoy |

| Field Name on Form | Field Name in Table |
|---|---|
| Do you think that the program is helping your child learn? | ChildLearn |
| If you had it to do over, would you buy this program? | BuyAgain |
| Would you recommend this program to others? | Recommend |

   ✓ Use the Memo type for the Comments field.

6. Add a CustomerID field with the Number type at the top of the field list.

   ✓ You will use this field to join the two tables in a later exercise.

7. Add a FeedbackID field above the CustomerID field with the AutoNumber type, and make it the primary key.

   ✓ Since one customer might send in more than one feedback card on different products, the CustomerID field cannot be the primary key field in this table. The FeedbackID field serves that function instead.

8. Save the table design; name it **tblFeedback**.

9. Enter the data from the completed customer form shown in Illustration A into the tables.

10. Close the Access database.

# Wee-Soft
# Customer Feedback

**Part I: About You**

Parent Name: _Janice Rand_
Address: _108 Ponting Street_
City: _Macon_   State: _IL_   ZIP: _62544_
Telephone: (_217_) _555-2340_
How many children live in your home? _1_

**Part II: About the Product**

Product Purchased: _Learning Adventure_
Product Version: _2.0_
Date of Purchase: _3/15/01_
Place of Purchase: _Best Shopper_
How old is the child who will use the product the most? _8_
Was the program easy to install? ................................................... Yes ☑ No ☐
Did you encounter any installation errors or problems? ..................... Yes ☐ No ☑
Does your child enjoy using the program? ....................................... Yes ☑ No ☐
Do you think that the program is helping your child learn? ................ Yes ☑ No ☐
If you had it to do over, would you buy this program? ...................... Yes ☑ No ☐
Would you recommend this program to others? ............................... Yes ☑ No ☐

Comments:
I would like to see a version for younger children (ages 3-5).

# Exercise 7

◆ **Open a Table for Editing in Table Design View**
◆ **Rename a Field** ◆ **Add a Field** ◆ **Delete a Field**
◆ **Reorder Fields** ◆ **Change Field Properties**

## On the Job

After you design a table and begin to add data, you may discover that you don't have a place to put some of the information or that the data you have for a field doesn't fit. In this case, you will have to edit the design of the table. You may also want to set some field properties that help speed up data entry or help ensure that you enter the data correctly.

Now that you have begun working with the tables you created in Lesson 1, you realize that they could stand some improvement. You need to add more fields, rename some existing fields, and make changes to field type and field properties,

## Terms

**Field properties** Characteristics of a field that determine how long an entry can be, how the entry will be formatted, whether there should be a default entry, and what can be entered (for example, numbers only or valid dates only).

## Notes

### Open a Table for Editing in Table Design View

- To edit an existing table's design, select it from the list of tables in the Database window and then click Design 📝 Design.

- You can also right-click an existing table and choose Design View.

- While viewing an existing table in Datasheet view, you can also click the Design button 📝 ▾ on the toolbar to switch to Design view.

  ✓ *The Design button on the toolbar is also a drop-down list. You can switch among Design view, Datasheet view, PivotTable view, and PivotChart view.*

*Table Design view*

Field Name   Data types                          Description

Field properties for current field

- You can edit the name, data type, and field description just as you did when you created the table initially (see Exercise 5). Even if you created the table some other way, such as with the Table Wizard, you can still edit it in Table Design view.

- When a field is selected, its **field properties** appear in the Field Properties half of the Table Design window. Field properties specify advanced options for the field, such as maximum entry length and default value.

## Rename a Field

- To rename a field, move to the Field Name box and edit or replace the name there.

- Any forms, reports, or queries based on this table will need to be changed or recreated; the name change does not automatically transfer to related objects.

## Add a Field

- You can add new fields to your table in Design view. Move to a blank row and type the field name you want. Select a data type and enter a description for the field if you like.

- To insert a new field between two existing ones, or at the top of the list, select the field above which the new one should appear and click the Insert Rows button � on the toolbar (or choose Insert, Rows).

## Delete a Field

- If you make a mistake creating new fields, you can remove a field from Table Design view.

- Removing a field deletes all data that was entered in that field from the table.

- To delete a field, select it and press the Delete key, or click the Delete Rows button on the toolbar.

- You can also delete a row (that is, a field) by choosing Edit, Delete Rows from the menu bar.

## Reorder Fields

- The order in which fields appear in Table Design view does not directly affect objects based on the table, like queries and reports.

- However, when you build reports, queries, forms, and so on with a table, you work with a *field list,* and the order shown on that list is the order shown in Table Design view.

- To move a field on the list, select it by clicking the field selector (the gray square to the left of the field name) to select the entire row. Then drag it up or down on the list.

*Select a field and then drag it up or down*

| | Field Name | Data Type | |
|---|---|---|---|
| 🔑 | ClientID | AutoNumber | Cli |
| | FirstName | Text | |
| | LastName | Text | |
| ▶ | Address | Text | |
| | City | Text | |

tblClients : Table

## Change Field Properties

- In most cases you do not have to change the field properties at the bottom of the Table Design view window; you can accept the defaults.

- To see an explanation of each field property, click in the property and see the description on the right side of the screen or press F1 to see more detailed help.

### Set Field Size

- The field size for Text data types determines the maximum number of characters you can type.

- Choose a Field Size option on the drop-down list for Number data types to determine how large the number can be and if you can have decimal places. For numbers 0 to 255 with no decimal places, choose Byte. For the largest numbers without decimal places, choose Long Integer, and for the largest numbers with decimal places, choose Double.

*Field size options*

### Choose a Format

- Especially for number and date/time data types, choose an option on the Format drop-down list to choose how you want the values displayed. Each drop-down choice shows an example of what the value will look like.

*Format options for date/time data types*

| | |
|---|---|
| General Date | 6/19/94 5:34:23 PM |
| Long Date | Sunday, June 19, 1994 |
| Medium Date | 19-Jun-94 |
| Short Date | 6/19/94 |
| Long Time | 5:34:23 PM |
| Medium Time | 5:34 PM |
| Short Time | 17:34 |

■ You can also type codes in the Format box. (See Help for an explanation for codes). For example, type m/d/yyyy for a date type to display 1/1/2002.

### Enter a Caption

■ A caption is an alternative name for the field. For example, if you have a field called FNAME, you might assign a caption of First Name.

■ Captions appear on forms and reports instead of the field name, helping make those objects more understandable.

### Enter a Default Value

■ You can type a Default Value you want to appear in new records.

■ The Default Value is used for the most common value for records but the user can always type over any value in the field.

■ An example would be 0 for a sales field or CO for the state field in a table where addresses, for example, are typically located in Colorado.

### Use an Input Mask

■ The Input Mask is a field template to validate how each character is entered into the field.

■ For example, you can show parentheses for a telephone field or dashes for a social security number field. Some of the fields you worked with in the first few exercises used input masks for data like phone numbers and ZIP Codes.

### Use Data Validation

■ The Validation Rule property allows you to verify data as the user enters it into the table.

■ Examples include <Date() (less than today's date), Between 0 and 100, "CO", "TX", or Is Null (blank).

■ You can use the Expression Builder by clicking the Build button ... to the right of the field property box.

  ✓ *The Expression Builder is a dialog box from which you can choose various fields or objects and math operators. It is a very powerful tool, but not covered in any detail in this book; you might want to experiment with it on your own.*

■ The Validation Text appears in a dialog box when a Validation Rule is broken.

### Require an Entry

■ Required means that a user has to fill in this field before going to another record.

■ You might want to set a field to Required if that field is an essential part of the record, such as Invoice # or Customer ID.

### Index a Field

■ Indexed makes searches and sorts on this field go quicker.

■ Do not set all fields to Indexed; instead, set this value only for the field (or two) on which you think you will search or sort most often.

### Switch between Views

■ To switch to Datasheet view from Table Design view, click the View button 🔲 ▾ on the Standard toolbar. It is the left-most button on the toolbar.

■ When in Datasheet view, the button's face changes (📝 ▾), and clicking it switches you to Table Design view.

■ This button also has a drop-down list, so you can choose other views from it.

■ You can also choose a view from the View menu if you prefer.

# Procedures

## Open a Table for Editing

**In Database view:**

1. Click **Tables**.
2. Click the table to edit.
3. Click **Design** ............... `Alt`+`D`

## Rename a Field

1. Double-click the field's name.
2. Type a new name.

## Insert a Field

1. Select the field above which the new field should appear.
2. Click **Insert Rows** button `⊒←`.
   OR
   a. Click **Insert** ............. `Alt`+`I`
   b. Click **Rows** .................... `R`
3. Click in the **Name column** of the new row.
4. Type field name.
5. Press **Tab** .......................... `Tab`

6. Click the down arrow `▼` in the Data Type field.
7. Click the field type.
8. Press **Tab** .......................... `Tab`
9. (Optional) Type field description.

## Delete a Field

1. Select the field.
2. Click **Delete Rows** button `⊒→`.
   OR
   a. Click **Edit** ............... `Alt`+`E`
   b. Click **Delete Rows** ......... `R`

## Move a Field

1. Select the field.
2. Drag it up or down on the list.

## Change Field Data Type

1. Click in the field's Data Type column.
2. Click the down arrow `▼`.
3. Click the new field type.

## Set Field Properties

1. Select a field.
2. Click the property you want to change.
3. Type a value, or select from the drop-down list.
   ✓ *For example, to enter a caption, click in the caption field and enter the caption you wish to display.*
4. Repeat steps 2–3 as needed to set properties in other fields.

## Switch Between Views

1. Click **View** .................. `Alt`+`V`
2. Click **Datasheet View** ......... `S`
   OR
   Click **Design View** ............. `D`
   ✓ *You can also use the View button, the left-most button on the Standard toolbar, to switch views.*

# Exercise Directions

1. Start Access, if necessary.
2. Open ⊘**AC07**.
3. Open the **tblClients** table in Design view.
4. Change the ID field name to **ClientID** and include the description **Client ID number -- don't type anything here; it's automatic**.
5. Change the caption to **Client ID**.
6. Add an InputDate field with a Date/Time data type, Input Date caption, and Short Date format.
   ✓ *In Design view, move to a blank row and type the field name and then change the properties in the bottom of the window. For example, move to the Caption property and type **Input Date** and move to the Format property and choose Short Date on the drop-down list.*
7. Add a BeenToStore field with a Yes/No data type and **Been To Store?** as the caption.
8. Add a Cycles field with a Number data type, **Number of Cycles in Household** in the description, and Byte for the Field Size.
9. Add a WebPage field with a Hyperlink data type.
10. Add a Notes field with a Memo data type.

11. Create captions for all field names that contain more than one word. For example, type **First Name** as the caption for the FirstName field.
12. Save the table's design.
   ✓ *Click the Save button.*
13. Look at the table in Datasheet view.
   ✓ *Click first toolbar button.*
14. Return to Design view.
   ✓ *Click again on the first toolbar button.*
15. Insert a Suffix field (Text type) before the FirstName field.
16. Set the Suffix field's size to 5 characters.
17. Move the Suffix field below the LastName field.
18. Close the **tblClients** table, saving any changes, and open the **tblEmployees** table.
19. Delete the MiddleName field.
20. Close the **tblEmployees** table, saving your changes to it.
21. Close the database.

# On Your Own

1. Open the database **OAC05** that you worked with in the On Your Own section of Exercise 5, or open ⊙ **OAC07**.

2. In Design view, edit the **Roster** table to add two new fields. Make one of the fields a different data type. For example, you can add a Position field or a birthday field. If you add a birthday field, you can also add a Yes/No field to indicate whether or not you should send a card.

3. Enter captions for the FirstName, LastName, and SendACard fields that include spaces between the words.

4. Save the changes to the table.

5. Switch to Datasheet view. Scroll the window so you can see the new fields added to the table.

6. Close the table.

7. Close the database and exit Access.

# Exercise 8

## Skills Covered:

◆ **Switch among Open Objects** ◆ **Insert a Column** ◆ **Delete a Column**
◆ **Move a Column** ◆ **Hide and Unhide Columns** ◆ **Change Datasheet**
**Column Width** ◆ **Freeze Columns** ◆ **Remove Gridlines**

## On the Job

If you plan to work with your data in Datasheet view a lot, you might want to adjust the layout so you can see your data more clearly as you work. You can make changes that affect the underlying table, such as inserting and deleting columns (fields). You can also make cosmetic changes that affect only Datasheet view, such as hiding certain columns, freezing certain columns so they remain visible when you scroll, and adjusting the width of a column.

At the Steel Dreams Cycle Shop, customers can sign up for the shop's quarterly newsletter. You would like to add a field to your tblClients table to indicate whether each customer has signed up. You would also like to make some on-screen formatting changes to the tblClients table so you can enter and view records in it more easily.

## Terms

**Column header** The gray box containing the column (field) name.

**Hide** To remove an object, such as a column, from view on the screen without deleting it.

**Freeze** To fix the position of certain columns so that when you scroll to the right, those columns remain on-screen while other columns move.

**Gridlines** Lines that outline each row and column on-screen.

## Notes

### Switch among Open Objects

- The bottom of the Window menu shows you a list of all objects that are currently open. Click or type the number on the menu to move to the object.

- You can also see each object or document that is open on the Windows taskbar. Click on the document button on the taskbar to go to the object.

  ✓ *You can press F11 to go to the database window, no matter which window is currently displayed.*

*Switch between open windows within Access with the taskbar or Window menu*

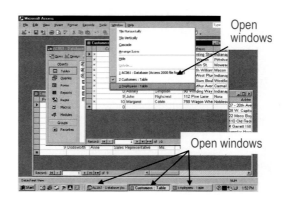

## Insert a Column

- When you add a column in Datasheet view you are adding a field to the underlying table.

- To insert a column, open the Insert menu and choose Column. The field name will be a placeholder name (Field#); you can change the name as you learned in Exercise 3.

- When you insert a column, it appears to the left of the column that was selected before you issued the insertion command.

*A new field inserted between two existing fields*

- If you want to add a description, change the data type, or change any properties, you must go to Design view.

- If you have already entered data into the table, you will need to go back and fill in the value for the new field for each record.

- Adding, deleting, and moving a column from a table does not change any forms, reports, or queries that you've created based on that table. You must modify these objects separately. For this reason, it is advantageous to finalize the lists of fields you plan to use in a table before you create forms, reports, or queries based upon it.

## Delete a Column

- Deleting a column on the datasheet removes the field from the underlying table, including any data that was stored in it.

  ✓ *To hide a field temporarily without deleting it, see Hide and Unhide Columns later in this exercise.*

- After deleting a field, you cannot get the data back that the field contained, so be careful when deleting fields.

## Move a Column

- After you select the column header, you can use the drag-and-drop method to move a column in Datasheet view.

- Click the **column header** to select it. The entire column becomes highlighted. Then drag the column name left or right to move the column.

- A black vertical line shows where the column is going. When you release the mouse button, the column drops into the new location.

*Move a column by dragging its header*

## Hide and Unhide Columns

- If you don't want to view or print certain columns in Datasheet view, you can **hide** them. Simply select the column(s) and choose the Hide Columns command from the Format menu. To redisplay the columns, choose the Unhide Columns command from the Format menu and check all the columns you want displayed.

## Change Datasheet Column Width

- If the field entry is too wide to see in Datasheet view, you can change the width to display more of the column.

- The column width does not affect the field size in table design; it is only for your convenience when viewing the datasheet.

- You can change column width for automatic fit to the widest entry by double-clicking the double-headed arrow mouse pointer between two column headers.

- Or, change the column width manually by dragging the right border of the column header to the desired width.

*Drag column dividers or double-click to autosize*

| Address | City |
|---------|------|
| 123 Fox | Denver |
| 818 Winter St. | Denver |
| 154 Newton | Thornton |
| 1551 James | Westminster |

Mouse pointer

- You can also change column width by choosing the Column width command from the Format menu and typing the width or clicking the Best Fit button.

## Freeze Columns

- If there are too many columns, you may not be able to see all fields at once in Datasheet view.

- If certain columns are important to view at all times, you can **freeze** them so that they remain on the screen as you scroll to the left or right.

- Before you can freeze a column, select it. To do so, move the mouse pointer over a column until the pointer becomes a down arrow. Then click and drag to the left or right to select multiple columns. Then open the Format menu and choose Freeze Columns.

- A divider line appears between the frozen columns and the unfrozen ones.

*Three columns have been frozen at the left*

Columns to the left of this line are frozen

- You can unfreeze columns by choosing the Unfreeze All Columns command from the Format menu.

## Remove Gridlines

- If you don't want the **gridlines** between rows and columns to appear on-screen and when you print the datasheet, you can choose to remove the gridlines.

- In the Datasheet Formatting dialog box, you can also change the color of the gridlines and background as well as the effect of shown gridlines.

*Datasheet Formatting dialog box*

274

# Procedures

### Switch among Open Objects

1. Click **Window**.............. `Alt`+`W`
2. Click number of desired object.
   OR
   Click desired object in Windows taskbar.
   OR
   Press **F11** to go to the database window................. `F11`

OR

- Press **Alt+Tab**............ `Alt`+`Tab`

### Insert a Column

1. Display Datasheet view.
2. Click in column to right of location for new column.
3. Click **Insert**.................. `Alt`+`I`
4. Click **Column** ....................... `C`

OR

1. Right-click column header.
2. Click **Insert Column** ........... `C`

### Delete a Column

1. Click on column header you want to delete.
2. Click **Edit**..................... `Alt`+`E`
3. Click **Delete Column** .......... `M`
4. Click **Yes** ............................. `Y`

OR

1. Right-click column header.
2. Click **Delete Column** .......... `M`
3. Click **Yes** ............................. `Y`

### Move a Column

1. Click on column header you want to move.
2. Click and drag the selected column to new position.

### Hide and Unhide Columns

**Hide Columns:**

1. Click in column you would like to hide.
2. Click **Format** ............... `Alt`+`O`
3. Click **Hide Columns** ........... `H`

**Unhide Columns:**

1. Click **Format** ............... `Alt`+`O`
2. Click **Unhide Columns** ...... `U`
3. Check column(s) to unhide.
4. Click **Close**....................... `Enter`

### Change Datasheet Column Width

**Menu:**

1. Click in field for column.
2. Click **Format** ............... `Alt`+`O`
3. Click **Column Width** .......... `C`
4. Click **Best Fit** ............. `Alt`+`B`
   OR
   Type column width.
5. Click **OK** .......................... `Enter`

**Mouse:**

- Double-click on right edge of field name cell.

OR

- Drag double-headed mouse pointer on right edge of field name cell.

### Freeze/Unfreeze Columns

1. Select one or more columns.
2. Click **Format** ............... `Alt`+`O`
3. Click **Freeze Columns** ........ `Z`
   OR
   - Click **Unfreeze All Columns** ................... `A`

### Remove Gridlines

**In Datasheet view:**

1. Click **Format** ............... `Alt`+`O`
2. Click **Datasheet** ................... `E`
3. Deselect Gridlines Shown for:
   - **Horizontal** ...................... `H`
   - **Vertical** .......................... `V`
4. Click **OK** .......................... `Enter`

# Exercise Directions

1. Start Access, if necessary.
2. Open ⊙ **AC08**.
3. Open the **tblClients** table.
4. Switch back to the database window without closing the datasheet.
5. Switch back to the datasheet again.
6. Delete the Suffix column.
7. Hide the ClientID column.
8. Increase or decrease the width of each column so that it is large enough to see all data within it but small enough that it does not waste space on-screen.
   - ✓ *Double-click the column heading borders.*
9. Freeze the first two columns.
10. Scroll all the way to the right, so the last field is visible on-screen (Notes).
11. Insert a new field to the left of the Notes field, and name it Newsletter.
    - ✓ *Select the Notes field, then choose Insert, Column. Then double-click the column header and type the new field name.*

12. Change the field type to Yes/No for the Newsletter field.
    - ✓ *Hint: you will need to go into Table Design view.*
13. Return to Datasheet view, and place a check mark in the Newsletter column for Leanne Balto.
14. Unfreeze all columns.
    - ✓ *Format, Unfreeze All Columns.*
15. Move the Newsletter field to the right of the Notes field.
16. Turn off the vertical gridline display. (Leave the horizontal gridlines showing.)
17. Unhide the ClientID column.
18. Close the datasheet, saving your changes to it.

# On Your Own

1. Open the database ⊙ **OAC08**.
2. Open the **Roster** table in Datasheet view, resize the columns as needed to create a pleasing display that shows all data in each column.
3. Place a checkmark in the Send a Card column for Leo, Shenille, Justin, and John.
   - ✓ *The best way to accomplish this is to freeze the first three columns. Then you can scroll to the right and see the Send a Card field on-screen at the same time as the First Name field. Unfreeze when you are finished.*
4. Make a printout that contains just the First Name, Last Name, and Position fields, and that does not contain any gridlines.
   - ✓ *To do so, hide all the fields except the ones you want, hide the gridlines for the table, and then print the datasheet. Don't forget to unhide the fields when you're finished.*

5. Insert a new field called OtherTeams, to the left of the Birthday field.
6. Use Design view to create a caption for the new field that includes a space between **Other** and **Teams**. Then go back to Datasheet view to see the change in the column header.
7. Close the table, saving your changes.
8. Close the database and exit Access.

# Exercise 9

Skills Covered:

◆ **Relate Tables** ◆ **Enforce Referential Integrity**
◆ **Print Relationships** ◆ **Close Relationships Window**
◆ **Show Related Records**

## On the Job

When you create relationships between tables, you associate a field in one table with an equivalent field in another. Then the two tables can be used in queries, forms, and reports together, even if there is not a one-to-one relationship between entries. For example, a Customers table can be linked to an Orders table by the customer ID number, so that you can pull up a customer's contact information on a form when entering a new order.

Since each entry in the tblNeeds table corresponds to a request made by one of the clients in your tblClients table, you have decided to create a relationship between those two tables so they can be used together in queries, forms, and reports.

## Terms

**Foreign key** A field in the child table that is related to the primary key in the parent table.

**Parent table** The main table of a relationship. When creating a relationship, this is the "one" side of the relationship and contains the primary key.

**Child table** The second table of a relationship. When creating a relationship, this is generally the "many" side of the relationship. One record from the parent table (such as clients) can be related to one or more records of the child table (such as sales).

**Referential Integrity** A property of a relationship between two tables. When Referential Integrity is on, the child table cannot contain a foreign key value that does not have a corresponding value in the primary key of the parent table.

**Orphan** A value in the foreign key that does not have a corresponding primary key in the parent table.

**Cascade Update** When the primary key field is updated in a relationship, the corresponding foreign key value(s) in the child table's related records automatically updates.

**Cascade Delete** When a record in a parent table is deleted, Access deletes all the related records from the child table where the value from the primary key matches the value in the foreign key.

**Subdatasheet** A child table related to the main (parent) table.

**Master field** The related field from the main (parent) table of the relationship.

**Child field** Related field from the child table of the relationship.

# Notes

## Relate Tables

- To create a relationship between two tables, the same field (or equivalents) must appear in both tables. It is desirable, but not required, to use the same field name in both tables.

- In most cases the field is unique in one table (usually the primary key) but not unique in the other. This results in a one-to-many relationship.

- The related field in the second table is called the **foreign key**. The foreign key field must have the same data type as the related primary key, unless the primary key is an AutoNumber type. In that case, the foreign key field must be a Number type.

- The table containing the primary key field being linked is in the **parent table**, and that field is the "one" side of the relationship, indicated by a "1" in the Relationships window.

- The table containing the foreign key field is the **child table**, and that field is the "many" side of the relationship, indicated by an infinity sign (∞) in the Relationships window.

- You set relationships in the Relationships window. In the Relationships window, primary key fields are indicated in bold.

- In the Relationships window, drag a primary key to the related foreign key to open the Edit Relationships dialog box. You can also double-click on the space between two tables in the Relationships window to open the Edit Relationships dialog box.

*Relationships window and Edit Relationships dialog box*

One side of relationship    Many side of relationship

Double-click line to open dialog box.

## Enforce Referential Integrity

- On the Edit Relationships dialog box, you can choose to Enforce **Referential Integrity** so that you won't have an **orphan** in the child table. For example, you won't be able to enter an order for a customer that does not exist.

- If you select Enforce Referential Integrity, you can choose two additional options: Cascade Update Related Fields and Cascade Delete Related Records.

- **Cascade Update** Related Fields means that when you change the value in the primary key of the parent table, the related foreign key field in all related records of the child table will automatically change as well. If you don't check this box, Access will give an error message when you try to change the primary key.

- **Cascade Delete** Related Records means that when you delete the record in the parent table, all related records in the child table will delete as well. If you don't check this box, Access will give an error message when you try to delete the record in the parent table.

- When referential integrity is enabled, the parent table shows a "1" next to the primary key and the child table most often shows an infinity symbol next to the foreign key.

- If the two related fields are primary keys, you'll see an "I" on both fields.

## Print Relationships

- To print the Relationships window contents, open the File menu and choose Print Relationships. Access creates a report that contains a replica of the window contents. Print it using the Print button on the toolbar or the File, Print command.

## Close Relationships Window

- After setting table relationships, click File, Close or click the window's Close button to close the Relationships window.

## Show Related Records

■ You can view the parent table and the child table in Datasheet view. After you create a relationship between tables, return to the Datasheet view of the parent table and click on the plus sign (+) on the left edge of a record to see the related rows from the child table.

✓ If you have more than one child table, you can change the **subdatasheet** attached to the datasheet. Choose Insert, Subdatasheet and in the dialog box choose the child table and if necessary, identify the **master fields** and **child fields**.

*Subdatasheet for current record*

*Insert Subdatasheet dialog box*

Subdatasheet

# Procedures

## Relate Tables

1. Click the **Relationships** button [icon] on the Standard toolbar.

   OR

   a. Click **Tools**............. Alt + T

   b. Click **Relationships**....... R

      ✓ *Relationships Window opens. The Show Table dialog box may open automatically. Use step 2 if it does not.*

2. Click the **Show Table** button [icon].

   OR

   a. Click **Relationships**........ Alt + R

   b. Click **Show Table**.......... T

3. Click table you want to include.

4. Click **Add** .................... Alt + A

5. Repeat steps 5–6 for all tables that are part of relationships.

6. Click **Close**................. Alt + C

7. Drag from primary key of one table to foreign key of another table.

✓ *Edit Relationships dialog box opens. See next procedure to enforce referential integrity.*

8. Click **Create** ..................... Enter

## Enforce Referential Integrity

1. If necessary, open Edit Relationships dialog box again and do steps a–c:

   a. Click **Enforce Referential Integrity**................ Alt + E

   b. Click **Cascade Update Related Fields**....... Alt + U

   c. Click **Cascade Delete Related Records** .. Alt + D

2. Click **OK** .......................... Enter

## Print Relationships

1. Click **File** .................... Alt + F

2. Click **Print Relationships** .. R

3. Click **Print** button [icon].

   OR

   a. Click **File** ............... Alt + F

   b. Click **Print**...................... P

   c. Click **OK**...................... Enter

✓ *After printing the relationships, a report remains on-screen.*

4. Click the **Close** button [X] to close the report.

5. Click **No** to not save changes .............................. N

## Close Relationships Window

● Click the **Close** button [X].

   OR

1. Click **File** .................... Alt + F

2. Click **Close** ........................ C

## Show Related Records

1. Click **Tables** object button on database window.

2. Click name of table.

3. Click **Open** ................. Alt + O

4. Click **+** before record to show subdatasheet for selected record.

5. Click **–** before record to hide subdatasheet.

## Set Subdatasheet

1. Open main table in Datasheet view.
2. Click **Insert** .................. `Alt`+`I`
3. Click **Subdatasheet** ............ `S`

4. Choose child table.
5. If necessary, choose an option from **Link Child Fields** drop-down list .............. `Alt`+`C`
6. Click **OK** ........................... `Enter`

# Exercise Directions

1. Start Access, if necessary.
2. Open 💿 **AC09**.
   - ✓ *Do not open any tables, queries, or forms. You cannot create a relationship to a table already in use.*
3. Relate the ClientID primary key from the **tblClients** table to the ClientID field of the **tblNeeds** table.
   - ✓ *Choose Tools, Relationships. Click Show Table button and add tables. Then drag between the fields.*
4. In the Edit Relationships dialog box, Enforce Referential Integrity between these two tables.
5. Set Cascade Update and Cascade Delete.
6. Print the Relationships window content, and then close the Relationships window. Close the report without saving it.

7. Open the **tblClients** table in Datasheet view.
8. Click on the + before Client ID to see the subdatasheet **tblNeeds** for Fritz Werner.
9. Click on the - before Client ID to close the **tblNeeds** subdatasheet for Fritz Werner.
10. Open the subdatasheet for Jenny Zimdahl.
11. Enter the following need for Jenny: **Wheel covers for 1968 Harley-Davidson**.
    - ✓ *Do not enter the NeedID; it is an AutoNumber field. Simply tab past it.*
12. Close the **tblClients** table, and open the **tblNeeds** table in Datasheet view. Verify that the new record you entered appears there.
13. Close the database and exit Access.

# On Your Own

1. Open 💿 **OAC09**.
2. Create a new field in the **Roster** table called CategoryID and set its type to Number.
3. Create a relationship between the **Roster** table and the **Categories** table based on the CategoryID field in each. Enforce Referential Integrity, and turn on Cascade Update Related Fields.
4. Set the category of each player in the Roster table to 1 (Active) except John Smith; set his to 5 (Inactive).
5. In the **Categories** table, try to delete record 5 (Inactive).
6. Go back to the Relationships window and turn off Enforce Referential Integrity for the relationship.

7. Go back to the **Categories** table and try again to delete record 5.
8. Return to the Relationships window and try to turn on Enforce Referential Integrity again.
9. Return to the **Roster** table and change John Smith's status to 4 (Retired).
10. Return to the Relationships window and turn on Enforce Referential Integrity.
11. Close the Access database, saving all changes, and exit Access.

# Exercise **10**

## ◆ Critical Thinking

Because of your experience with databases at Steel Dreams, you have volunteered to be the database coordinator for the Central Indiana Shetland Sheepdog Club. The club's secretary has started a database file, but now that you have taken over the project, you want to improve the database using the skills you have learned in the preceding exercises.

## Exercise Directions

1. Open the ⊙**AC10** database.

2. Open the **tblMembers** table.

3. Widen the Address column so that the complete addresses display.

4. Narrow the State and ZIP columns so that they are not wider than required to hold the data they contain.

5. In Datasheet view, move the JoinDate field between MemberID and FirstName.

6. In Table Design view, create captions for the fields in which the field names consist of two or more words, so that there are spaces in the captions between the words. For example, the caption for FirstName would be First Name.

7. Close the **tblMembers** table, saving your changes.

8. Open the **tblDogs** table.

   ✓ Notice that owner names in tblDogs have been entered with both the first and last names in a single field. You know from your work in this lesson that in order to create a relationship between the two tables, you must join the MemberID field from tblMembers to a field in tblDogs, but since MemberID is an AutoNumber field and Owner is a Text field, some work will be required.

9. Edit the entries in the Owner field so they show the owners' MemberID number rather than their names.

   ✓ You will need to open the tblMembers table for reference, and switch back and forth between the two tables using the Window menu or the taskbar.

10. Switch the **tblDogs** table to Table Design view and change the field type of the Owner field to Number.

11. Close all tables, saving your changes.

12. Open the Relationships window and create a relationship between the MemberID field in **tblMembers** and the Owners field in **tblDogs**. Choose all three Referential Integrity checkboxes.

    ✓ When you finish, the Relationships window should resemble Illustration A.

13. Close the Relationships window.

14. Open **tblMembers** in Datasheet view and hide the MemberID field.

15. View the list of Kenneth Kwan's dogs on the subdatasheet.

16. Using a subdatasheet, add the following information for Ralph Orton's dog:

    • Registered Name: **Orton's Spice of Life**
    • Call Name: **Skip**
    • Birthdate: **9/12/00**
    • Coloring: **Sable**

17. Close **tblMembers**, saving your changes.

18. Close the Access database.

*Illustration A*

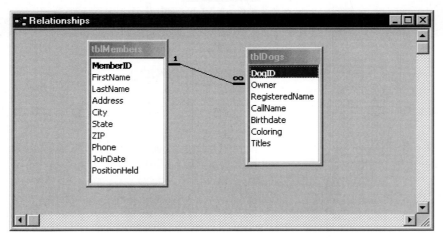

# Exercise 11

## Skills Covered:

◆ **Create a Lookup for a Field** ◆ **Create a Value List with the Lookup Wizard** ◆ **Lookup Field Values from another Table**

## On the Job

Some fields store data that can contains only a limited range of valid values, such as Marital Status or Gender. To simplify data entry and prevent entry errors, you can create a lookup for a field that presents the user entering records with a list of options from which to choose.

As you have started to fill in data in the Employees table in your Steel Dreams Cycle Shop database, you have noticed that some fields can contain only a few different entries. You would like to create lookups so that there are no typing mistakes in those fields that would prevent you from querying or generating reports based on those fields later.

## Terms

**Lookup Field** A list of values from which to choose when entering information into a field.

## Notes

### Create a Lookup for a Field

- If you have several values that can appear in a field, consider using a **lookup field**.

- A lookup field appears as a drop-down list during data entry, and you can choose from the list rather than typing an entry. This minimizes data entry errors and ensures consistent formatting (such as capitalization).

- When you enter data for a record, an arrow appears within the lookup field indicating that you can choose from a list of options.

*A lookup field during data entry*

- You can use the Lookup Wizard to create a lookup field with values you enter.

- You can also use the Lookup Wizard to create a lookup field that looks up values from another table.

- To create a lookup for a field, go to Table Design view and change the field's type to Lookup Wizard. The Lookup Wizard will automatically run.

### Create a Value List with the Lookup Wizard

- The Lookup Wizard provides a list in which you can type the values you want to appear on the list.

- This method works well when the values on the list will seldom or never change. If the values change frequently, use the table lookup method instead.

  ✓ *When creating your list, try to enter the values in a useful order. An alphabetical list of states, for example, is easier to use than one that doesn't have a recognizable order. A list of prospect levels might be ordered by the frequency with which they are used.*

## Lookup Field Values from Another Table

- If your list often varies, you can create a separate table for the list instead and then create a lookup field that looks into that table.

- Before creating the lookup, you must first create the additional table. Then run the Lookup Wizard and select the table to be used.

- The Lookup Wizard first helps you choose the lookup table or query.

*Select the table from which to look up values*

- It then prompts you to choose which fields from the table or query to include.

  ✓ *If the table you choose for the lookup has a primary key field, it's a good idea to choose it along with the field that you actually want to appear in the lookup list. You can then hide the primary key field. The users will choose from the "friendly" field, such as the text names, but the entry in the table will be the unique primary key value for that choice.*

*Select the fields to include*

- You next choose how wide to make each chosen field. By default the primary key field is hidden.

*Select the column widths for the lookup field(s)*

- On the last step of the wizard, you can change the field name. Keep the field name the same if you are changing an existing field and if you've already created a query, form, or report based on this table.

  ✓ *If you have text values in a field that you are converting to a lookup field, and the new lookup will contain the numeric ID numbers from the corresponding table rather than the values, creating the lookup will delete all the nonnumeric previous entries in that field, and you will need to reenter them. For this reason, it's best to set up any lookups you want to use before you do much data entry.*

# Procedures

### Create a Lookup List for a Field

1. Open the table in Table Design view.
2. Click in the **Data Type** column for the field.
3. Click the **down arrow** ▼.
4. Click **Lookup Wizard**.
5. Click **I will type in the values that I want**............... `Alt`+`T`
6. Click **Next**.................... `Alt`+`N`
7. Press **Tab**........................... `Tab`
8. Type a value for the list.
9. Press **Tab**........................... `Tab`
10. Repeat steps 8–9 as needed.
11. Click **Next**.................... `Alt`+`N`
12. Click **Finish**...................... `Enter`

### Use a Table as a Lookup

1. Create a **table** to be used as a lookup.
   OR
   Decide on an **existing table** to use as a lookup.
2. Open the **table** containing the field in which you want to use the lookup in Table Design view.
3. Click in the **Data Type** column for the field to receive the lookup.
4. Click the **down arrow** ▼.
5. Click **Lookup Wizard**.
6. Click **I want the look up column to lookup the values in a table or query** ..... `Alt`+`L`
7. Click **Next**.................... `Alt`+`N`

8. Click the table to use.
9. Click **Next**.................... `Alt`+`N`
10. Click a **field** to include.
11. Click `>` button................. `>`
12. Repeat **steps 10–11** as needed.
13. Click **Next**.................... `Alt`+`N`
14. Adjust column width if desired.
15. Click **Next**.................... `Alt`+`N`
16. Click **Finish**...................... `Enter`

### Use a Lookup Field in Data Entry

1. Click the **down arrow** ▼.
2. Click the **value** you want.

# Exercise Directions

1. Open ⊙ **AC11**.
2. Create a new table called **tblLocations** using Design view. Include these fields:

| LocationID | AutoNumber |
|------------|------------|
| Location | Text |

3. Make LocationID the primary key field. Then save the new table.
4. Switch to Datasheet view and enter the following locations:

| North |
|-------|
| Central |
| South |
| Warehouse |

5. Close **tblLocations**.
6. Open **tblEmployees** in Design view.
7. Change the data type for the OfficeLocation field to Lookup Wizard.
8. Create a lookup using the Lookup Wizard:
   - Choose to look up the values in the tblLocations table.

   - Choose to include both fields from that table.
   - Leave the column width and field name at the defaults.
9. Save **tblEmployees**, and switch it to Datasheet view.
10. Enter the following locations using the new drop-down list in the Office Location field:
    - Central: **Taiko, Raoul, and Shanda**
    - North: **Stanley and Peter**
    - Warehouse: **Richard**
11. Switch back to Design view and create a lookup for the DepartmentName field that uses the following internal list:

| Administration |
|----------------|
| Distribution |
| Sales |
| Maintenance |

12. Save the table, and then go to Datasheet view and change Taiko's department to **Administration** using the new drop-down list.
13. Save and close the table and the **AC11** database.

# On Your Own

1. Start Access and open ⊘ **OAC11**.

2. Remove the relationship between the Roster and **Categories** table.

3. In the **Roster** table, set up the CategoryID field to use the **Categories** table to look up values.

4. Save and close all tables, then go back to the Relationships window. Notice that the lookup recreated the relationship between the tables.

5. Edit the relationship to Enforce Referential Integrity.

6. Open the **Roster** table in Datasheet view, and notice that the CategoryID field now shows the text names of the categories rather than the numbers.

7. Enter the caption for the CategoryID field to **Category**.

8. Create a lookup for the Position field with these values:

| Catcher | Center field | First base |
|---|---|---|
| Second base | Third base | Right field |
| Left field | Center field | Left-center field |
| Shortstop | Any | |

9. Close the database and exit Access.

# Exercise 12

## Skills Covered:

◆ **Compare Datasheet and Form View** ◆ **Create an AutoForm**
◆ **Create a Form with the Form Wizard**
◆ **Create a Form from Scratch** ◆ **Enter Form Design View**
◆ **Work with Form Design View** ◆ **AutoFormat a Form**

## On the Job

If your table contains many fields, entering records in Datasheet view can become cumbersome. Many people find it easier to create a data entry form that displays all the fields on-screen at once, one record at a time.

As you add more information to the Steel Dreams Cycle Emporium database, you're finding that you're spending too much time scrolling through the records in Datasheet view. You've decided to create a form to help you navigate the information.

## Terms

**Form view**  The view that generally shows many fields for one record on one screen.

**Form Design view** The view in which you can edit the controls on a form.

**Form selector** A box at the upper left of Form Design view, where the two rulers intersect. Clicking this box selects the form as a whole.

**Control** An item such as a text box, label, or line on a form or report.

**AutoFormat** A feature that applies a formatting template to a form, including background and fonts.

## Notes

### Compare Datasheet and Form View

- In Datasheet view, each row is a record and each column is a field.

- If there are many fields, you must scroll to the left/right to move among them.

*Datasheet view*

- **Form view**, on the other hand, displays one record at a time, and shows all the fields at once (in most cases).

*Form view*

- Think of a form as a window to the table. When you add data to a form, it automatically fills in the underlying table(s).

## Create an AutoForm

- There are several ways to create a new form. The easiest is to use AutoForm, which creates a simple form containing all the fields in a particular table or query.

- An AutoForm is very basic and might not be formatted exactly the way you want. However, you can edit it in **Form Design view** after you create it.

- You have a choice of several types of AutoForms. The most common type is Columnar, which arranges the field names in columns. The form shown on the preceding page is a columnar AutoForm.

- Other types resemble datasheets, or enable you to drag-and-drop fields into a PivotTable or PivotChart.

- To create an AutoForm, display the Forms tab on the database window, click the New button, and choose the type of AutoForm you want and the table or query on which the form should be based.

## Create a Form with the Form Wizard

- The Form Wizard offers a good compromise between the simplicity of an AutoForm and the time needed to create a form from scratch.

- It asks questions in a series of dialog boxes, walking you step-by-step through the process of selecting tables/queries, fields, and formatting.

- To start a form with the Form Wizard, display the Forms tab in the database window and double-click *Create form by using wizard.*

*The Form Wizard*

## Create a Form from Scratch

- You can also create a new form from scratch in Form Design view. This creates a blank form, onto which you can place fields and other controls.

- To start a form in Design view, double-click Create form in design view from the Forms tab of the database window.

Form selector          *A blank form*

- If you start a new form using the above method, no table or query is associated with it. You can edit the form properties to attach one by right-clicking the **form selector** (the box in the top left corner, where the rulers intersect) and choosing Properties, and then choosing a table or query from the Record Source list on the Data tab.

*Edit a form's properties to change the table or query on which it is based*

- The attached table/query will become important in Exercise 13, when you learn how to add fields to a form from the Field List.

■ If you would prefer to specify a table or query when creating a new form, use the New button in the database window. The New Form dialog box enables you to choose a table or query before creating the form.

*Using the New Form dialog box enables you to select a table or query for your new blank form*

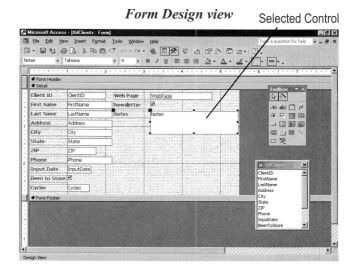

*Form Design view*     Selected Control

## Enter Form Design View

■ If you start a form using AutoForm or the Form Wizard, you might want to edit the form in Design view.

■ You can switch between Form view and Form Design view by making a choice on the View menu or by clicking the View button [icon] ▾ on the toolbar.

■ You can open a saved form in Design view by selecting it in the database window and clicking the Design button.

## Work with Form Design View

■ Each item on a form (or report) is called a **control**. Controls include text boxes where you type in the information for a field, labels to describe the field and the form, lines, and many other items.

■ While you are in Form Design view, click on a control to select it. Selection boxes surround the control.

■ You will learn more about controls and Form Design view in upcoming exercises.

## AutoFormat a Form

■ When you create a form with the Form Wizard, it asks you to choose a design to apply. The design includes a background, font choices, and color choices.

■ You can choose a different design at any time, or apply a design to a form that was not created with the Form Wizard at all.

■ To choose a different format, choose Format, **AutoFormat** or click the AutoFormat button [icon] on the toolbar.

■ Then select a format from the AutoFormat dialog box that appears.

*Select an AutoFormat*

# Procedures

## Create a Columnar AutoForm

1. Open table in Datasheet view.
2. Click **AutoForm** button .

## Create Any Type of AutoForm

**From the database window:**

1. Click **Forms**.
2. Click **New** ..................... `Alt`+`N`
3. Click **AutoForm: Columnar**.
   OR
   Click **AutoForm: Tabular**
   OR
   Click **AutoForm: Datasheet**
   OR
   Click **AutoForm: PivotTable**
   OR
   Click **AutoForm: PivotChart**
4. Click **down arrow** next to Choose the table or query where the object's data comes from.
5. Click the **table** or **query** to use.
6. Click **OK** .......................... `Enter`

## Create a Form with the Form Wizard

**From the database window:**

1. Click **Forms**.
2. Double-click **Create form by using wizard**.
3. Click **down arrow** next to Tables/Queries.
4. Click **table** or **query**.
5. Click **Available Fields** to include.
6. Click **right arrow button** `>`.
7. Repeat steps 5–6 as needed.
8. Return to step 4 to select fields from other tables/queries if needed.
9. Click **Next** .................... `Alt`+`N`
10. Click a layout:
    - **Columnar** ............... `Alt`+`C`
    - **Tabular** .................. `Alt`+`T`
    - **Datasheet** .............. `Alt`+`D`
    - **Justified** ................. `Alt`+`J`

- **PivotTable** ............. `Alt`+`I`
- **PivotChart** ............. `Alt`+`V`
  - ✓ *Columnar is the most common type, and the one that produces a traditional type of form.*
11. Click **Next** .................... `Alt`+`N`
12. Click a format style.
13. Click **Next** .................... `Alt`+`N`
14. Type a title.
15. Click **Finish** ..................... `Enter`

## Create a New Form from Scratch

**From the database window:**

1. Click **Forms**.
2. Double-click **Create form in Design view**.
   - ✓ *The above steps do not attach a table or query to the form.*

OR

**From the database window:**

1. Click **Forms**.
2. Click **New** .................... `Alt`+`N`
3. Click **Design View**.
4. Click **down arrow** `▼`.
5. Click the **table** or **query** name.
6. Click **OK**.

## Attach a Table or Query to a Form

- ✓ *You can also use the following procedure to change which table or query is attached.*

1. In Design view, right-click **form selector**.
   - ✓ *The form selector is the box at the top left, at the intersection of the vertical and horizontal rulers.*
2. Click **Properties** .......... `Alt`+`P`
3. Click the **Data** tab.
4. Click **down arrow** `▼` next to Record Source.
5. Click **table** or **query** to use.

## Switch from Form View to Form Design View

1. Click **View** .................. `Alt`+`V`
2. Click **Design View** ............. `D`
   OR
   Click **Design View** button `▦ ▼`.

## Switch from Form Design View to Form View

1. Click **View** .................. `Alt`+`V`
2. Click **Form View** ................ `F`
   OR
   Click **Form View** button `▦ ▼`.

## AutoFormat a Form

**From Form Design view:**

1. Click **Format** .............. `Alt`+`O`
2. Click **AutoFormat** .............. `F`
3. Click the desired format.
4. Click **OK** .......................... `Enter`

# Exercise Directions

1. Start Access, if necessary.
2. Open ⊚ **AC12**.
3. Create a columnar AutoForm based on the **tblNeeds** table.
4. Save the new form as **frmNeeds** and close it.
5. Create a form based on the **tblClients** table using the Form Wizard. Use the following settings:
   - Use all the fields.
   - Use a Columnar layout.
   - Choose the Industrial design.
   - Name the form **frmClients**.
6. Change the form's AutoFormat to the Expedition style.
7. Close the form, saving your changes.
8. Start a new, blank form without specifying a table.
9. Attach the **tblEmployees** table to the form using the form's Properties box.
10. Save the form as **frmEmployees** and close it.
11. Close the form and database.

# On Your Own

1. In Access open the ⊚ **OAC12** database.
2. Create a form for the **Roster** table using the Form Wizard. Include all fields.
3. Save the form with the name **Roster**.
4. Display the form in Design view.
5. Apply an AutoFormat to it.
6. Switch to Form view, and enter a new record into the table using the form.
7. Close the form, saving your changes.
   - ✓ When you enter Form view through Form Design view, the design changes you have made to the form are not immediately saved. They are not saved until you close the form, whether from Form view or Form Design. That's why you're prompted to save your changes when you close the Form view in step 7.
8. Create a new form for the Equipment table using AutoForm:Tabular. Name it **Equipment**.
9. Close the database and exit Access.
   - ✓ In these On Your Own exercises, you are creating some forms and tables with the same names. Although this is not such a great idea from a database design perspective because of the potential for confusion, many people do create databases that way in real life. These exercises give you the opportunity to try it out and see whether you find it confusing or convenient.

# Exercise 13

## Skills Covered:

◆ **Add a New Field to a Form**  ◆  **Select Controls on a Form**
◆ **Delete a Control from a Form**  ◆  **Move Controls**  ◆  **Reset Tab Order**
◆ **Change Control Formatting**  ◆  **Resize Fields and Other Controls**
◆ **Align Controls**  ◆  **Form Backgrounds**

## On the Job

Regardless of how you created your form, you might like to make some changes to it. The AutoForm and Form Wizard methods create nice basic forms, but sometimes field labels are truncated or there is not enough space between fields. In addition, you might want to add more fields to the form that you originally omitted, or change the text formatting.

You have decided to add another field to your tblClients table, and you want it to appear on the frmClients form as well. You would also like to apply some additional formatting on the form to make it more attractive.

## Terms

**Field List**  A floating box in Form Design view containing the names of all the fields in the associated table or query.

**Control**  A field, label, option group, box, or other object on a form.

**Selection handles**  Black squares around the border of a control that indicate it is selected.

**Tab order**  The order in which the insertion point moves from field to field on a form.

## Notes

### Add a New Field to a Form

■ To add a new field, drag it from the **Field List**. If the Field List does not appear, click the Field List button on the toolbar.

*Adding fields to the form*

✓ *Don't worry if you don't get the positioning exactly right; you can move the field and/or its associated label at any time.*

292

## Select Controls on a Form

■ To select a field or other **control**, click on it. **Selection handles** appear around it.

■ When you select a field, its associated text label is also selected, so that moving the field also moves the label. It works in reverse, too: clicking a text label also selects the associated field.

*A selected field and label*

Associated label has a single large selection handle

Selected field has a full set of selection handles

■ To select multiple controls, click on the first control, hold the Shift key down, and click on additional controls. You can also "lasso" controls by dragging a box around them.

## Delete a Control from a Form

■ To delete a field or other control, select it and press the Delete key.

■ When selecting a field for deletion, click on the field itself, not its associated text label. If you select the label before pressing Delete, only the label will be deleted, and the field itself will remain.

## Move Controls

■ To move a field, select it, and then position the mouse pointer anywhere over it *except* over a selection handle, so the pointer becomes an open hand. Then drag to a new location.

*Drag a field and its label as a pair with the open-handed mouse pointer*

Mouse pointer

■ The field and its associated label move as a pair when you drag with the open-hand mouse pointer.

■ If you want to move the field or the label separately from one another, click on the one you want to move and then drag it by the large selection handle in the top-left corner. The mouse pointer appears as a pointing finger in this case.

*Drag a field or label separately by dragging by the selection handle in the upper-left corner*

Mouse pointer

## Reset Tab Order

■ If you add or move controls, you may want to reset the order in which each field appears when you or another database form user presses Tab to navigate in the form.

■ You might also want to set an alternate **tab order** so that users don't have to tab past a seldom-used field such as Suffix or Middle Initial during data entry.

■ Choose the Tab Order command from the View menu.

■ In the Tab Order dialog box, drag the fields into the order you want them.

■ Click the Auto Order button to set the order from left to right and top to bottom based on the fields' current positions on the form.

*Set tab order*

## Change Control Formatting

■ While a control on a form is selected, you can click on the Formatting toolbar to do any of the following:

● Change the item's font type or font size.

● Change whether the text is bold, italic, or underlined.

● Choose left-aligned, centered, or right-aligned.

● Choose the color of the background, text, and border.

● Choose the style and width of the line or of the border surrounding the box.

- All of the above formatting features work just as they do in other Office programs that you might already be familiar with.

- When you select multiple objects, you can use the Formatting toolbar to change more than one at a time.

- If you make an error while formatting, choose the Undo command immediately after a change.

- To copy all enhancements, select a control with the enhancements you want to copy, click the Format Painter button  and then click the object to change.

- If you want to change multiple objects with Format Painter, double-click the Format Painter button and click on each control you want to change. Click the Format Painter button again to turn it off.

## Resize Fields and Other Controls

- To resize a control, drag any selection handle except the one in the upper-left corner.

- To resize several controls at once, select them all and then resize one; the others will resize, too.

- If you need to resize a text box so that text is not truncated, double-click a selection handle to automatically expand or contract the size so that the text exactly fits.

- To make a group of controls the same size, select them all, choose Format, Size, and then select To Widest, To Narrowest, To Tallest, or To Shortest.

## Align Controls

- One of the challenges in creating a form from scratch is to get all the fields precisely aligned with one another.

- To align several fields, place the first one where you want it, and then choose Format, Align. You can choose alignment options such as Left, Center, Top, or To Grid.
  - ✓ *The dots on the background in Form Design view form the grid referred to in the To Grid option.*

## Form Backgrounds

- You can change the color of any part of a form by clicking on the background in Design view, and then clicking the drop-down arrow of the Fill/Back Color button on the Formatting toolbar and choosing a color from the palette.

*Make a choice from the Fill/Back Color palette*

- You can add a logo or other graphic as a background for the form. You do this through the Property sheet of the form.

- Double-click on any object to open its Property sheet. For the form, use the Form selector above the vertical ruler and to the left of the horizontal ruler.

*Property sheet*

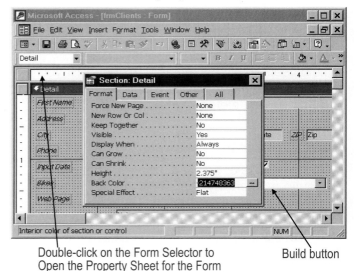

Double-click on the Form Selector to Open the Property Sheet for the Form

Build button

- The Build button appears on the toolbar and as an ellipses (...) button at the end of some properties when you select them, such as the Picture property. This button opens a dialog box that allows you to make a choice from a list.

- If you want the picture repeated throughout the form, change Picture Tiling to Yes.

# Procedures

✓ *All the following procedures take place in Form Design view.*

## Display the Field List

1. Click **View** .................. Alt+V
2. Click **Field List**.................... L

   OR

   Click the **Field List**

   button 🗐 .

## Add a Field

- Drag field from field list to form.

## Select a Field or Other Control

- Click on a **control** to select it.

OR

1. Click on first control.
2. Hold down **Shift** and click on additional controls to select them.

OR

1. Position **mouse pointer** outside first control.
2. Drag a box around all controls to select.

## Delete a Field or Other Control

1. Select **control** to delete.

   ✓ *If deleting both a field and its label, click on the field itself, rather than the label.*

   ✓ *If deleting only a field label, select the label.*

2. Press **Delete key** ............... Del

## Move a Field or Other Control

**Move a field and label as a pair, or move other type of control:**

1. Click on **field** you want to move.
2. When the mouse pointer is a hand 🖑, drag control and attached label and drop in new location.

## Move a field or label separately:

1. Click on **field** or **label** you want to move.
2. Point **mouse pointer** to upper-left selection handle.
3. When mouse pointer is a pointing hand 👆, drag and drop to new location.

## Reset Tab Order

1. Click **View** .................. Alt+V
2. Click **Tab Order** ................. B
3. Click **Auto Order** ............... A

   OR

   Drag fields into order you want.

4. Click **OK** .......................... Enter

## Change Control Formatting

1. Select **control** you want to format.
2. Click desired button from Formatting toolbar.

OR

1. Click **Format** ............... Alt+O
2. Click desired change from Format menu.

## Resize Controls

1. Click on **control** you want to size.
2. Point to **selection handle** so mouse pointer becomes an arrow ↘ ↔ ↕ .
3. Drag to resize.

OR

1. Change first item to proper size.
2. Select first item and other items to size.
3. Click **Format** ............... Alt+O
4. Click **Size** ........................... S
5. Click **To Widest** ................. W

## Align Controls

1. Move first item to proper location.
2. Select first item and other items to align.
3. Click **Format** .............. Alt+O
4. Click **Align** .......................... A
5. Click desired alignment option.

## Change Form Background Color

1. Click the **form background**.
2. Click down arrow on **Fill/Back Color** button 🎨 ▾.
3. Click the desired **color**.

## Use a Background Image

1. Click the **Form Selector**.
2. Click **View** .................. Alt+V
3. Click **Properties** ................. P
4. Click **Format** tab.
5. Scroll down to **Picture** field and select it.
6. Click **Build** button … next to Picture field.
7. Choose a file that contains the picture you want.
8. Click **Open** ...................... Enter
9. Click the **Close** button ✕.

## Remove a Background Image

1. Click the **Form Selector**.
2. Click **View** .................. Alt+V
3. Click **Properties** ................. P
4. Click **Format** tab.
5. Delete the entry in the **Picture** field.
6. Click the **Close** button ✕.

# Exercise Directions

1. Start Access, if necessary.
2. Open ⊘ **AC13**.
3. Open the **tblClients** table in Table Design view, and add a new field directly above the Notes field called **WhenBuy**.
4. Set the field type to Text and set its caption to **Anticipated Purchase**.
5. Close the table, saving changes.
6. Open the **frmClients** form in Form Design view, and add the new field to a blank spot on the form.
7. Move the field to the right (separately from its label) so that the label and field do not overlap.
8. Remove the colon from the end of the Anticipated Purchase label.
9. Rearrange the form fields so that the new field is directly above the Notes field.

10. Resize the Web page, Anticipated Purchase, and Notes fields, and right align the text boxes, as in Illustration A.
11. Use the Align feature to make sure that those three fields are precisely aligned at their right edges.
12. Reset the tab order so that the WhenBuy field falls between Newsletter and Notes.
13. Select all the field labels and italicize them (as a group).
14. Change the font color of the field labels to dark green.
15. Set the background color for the Detail area of the form to pale yellow.
16. Remove the background image from the form so that the yellow background shows.
17. Preview the form in Form view; then return to Form Design view and save your changes.
18. Close the form and database.

*Illustration A*

# On Your Own

1. Open ⊘ **OAC13**.
2. Create a new blank form with the **Equipment** table associated with it.
3. Manually add and arrange the fields from the Field List.
   - ✓ *You can enlarge the form size by dragging its bottom-right corner of the grid area outward.*
4. Format the fields in whatever way you think is attractive. This can include:

- Aligning fields with one another
- Changing font, text size, and color
- Rearranging fields
- Increasing or decreasing field or label size
- Changing the background color or adding a background picture

5. Check the tab order, and reset it if needed.
6. Save the new form as **Equipment2**.
7. Close the database and exit Access.

# Exercise 14

## Skills Covered:

◆ **Use Form View Toolbox** ◆ **Add Labels** ◆ **Add Lookups to Forms**
◆ **Add an Option Group** ◆ **Add a List Box or Combo Box**

## On the Job

You might want to dress up your basic form with some extra text labels, or place special controls on the form that make data entry easier for the user. Some of these extras include option groups, list boxes, and combo boxes. They're similar in function to the lookups you created in Exercise 11, but work only within the form on which they are created.

As store employees use the frmClients form you have created, you notice that they are making some data entry errors. You think that perhaps creating option groups or combo boxes for some fields will help improve data entry accuracy. You would also like to add a note to clarify the purpose of the Notes field.

## Terms

**Toolbox**  A floating toolbar in Form Design view that provides buttons for adding various types of controls to the form.

**Option group**  A set of buttons or check boxes on a form that present a finite set of acceptable values from a lookup.

**List box**  A box on a form that lists a finite set of acceptable values for a field from a lookup.

**Combo box**  Like a list box, except the user can also enter new values of none if the existing values in the lookup are appropriate.

**Label**  A frame containing descriptive text on a form. A label is different from a text box in that a text box can be bound to a field in a table, while a label exists only on the form.

**Text box**  A box on a form that contains text and that can be bound to a field in a table. Fields on a form appear as text boxes, for example.

## Notes

### Use Form View Toolbox

- The **Toolbox** appears in Form Design view. It can be used to add items (controls) to a form.

- If the toolbox does not appear, click the Toolbox button on the toolbar.

*Display the Toolbox if it does not already appear*

Toolbox button

- The toolbox contains a Wizard button near the top. It is an on/off switch; by default it is on.

*The Toolbox*

Wizard button

- When the Wizard feature is on, a wizard walks you through the process of creating certain types of controls (such as **option groups** and **list/combo boxes**).

- When the Wizard button feature is off, all types of controls can be manually placed on the form without using a wizard.

- Using the wizards makes learning about the different kinds of controls easier.

## Add Labels

- A **label** is a descriptive bit of text that you add to a form that is not associated with a field in a table. The label exists only on the form.

- To add a label, click the Label button *Aa* on the Toolbox and then drag on the form to create the label's frame. Then type your text.

*Create a new label from the Toolbox*

Label button

- The button to the right of the Label button is the **Text Box** button *Aa*. You can use it to create unbound text boxes that will later be associated (manually) with fields. Beginners will not do this very often.

## Add Lookups to Forms

- Access offers various types of lookups you can add on a form. These are like the lookups you can set for fields in Table Design view (see Exercise 11), except you create them from the form.

- You do not need to create lookups on the form for fields that have already been set up with the Lookup Wizard in Table Design view; these appear with lookups by default when placed on a form.

- The default setting for a field with a lookup is Combo Box when placed on a form, but you can change that setting. To do so, go to the Lookup tab for that field's properties in Table Design view and set the Display Control setting to Text, List Box, or Combo Box.

## Add an Option Group

- An option group is a group of mutually exclusive buttons representing various lookup choices. You can make them appear as square buttons, as round dots, or as check boxes.

*An option group*

- The Option Group Wizard makes it easy to create an option group on a form. Click the Option Group button in the Toolbox and then click or drag on the form where you want it to appear.

*Create an option group from the Toolbox*

Option Group button

- Then step through the wizard to complete the option group.

*The Option Group Wizard at work*

- A limitation of an option group is that you cannot specify that it take its values from a table or query; you must manually type in the values to appear in the group.

- If you need the values to come from a table or query, use a list box or combo box instead.

## Add a List Box or Combo Box

- List boxes and combo boxes work the same way, except a combo box enables users to enter additional values, while a list box restricts them to the choices you provide.

- Both a list box and a combo box can either take their values from a list you provide or from a table or query, just like a lookup (from Exercise 11).

    ✓ *Make sure you have completed Exercise 11 before working on this exercise, so you will understand the concepts behind lookups.*

- A combo box, by default, appears as a single-line text box with an associated drop-down list. Users can type in the text box normally, or select from the list.

- If there are more entries for a list box than will fit in the allotted space on the form, Access automatically adds a scroll bar to the list box.

*A combo box (left) and a list box (right)*

- To create a list box or combo box, click the corresponding button on the Toolbox and then follow the Wizard's prompts. Just like with the Lookup Wizard, you can specify a table or query, or you can type the values you want.

*Create a list box or combo box*

### Adding Other Types of Controls

- The Toolbox has other buttons as well, for other kinds of controls you can place on a form.

- To find out what type of control a button inserts, point to it and review the ScreenTip that appears.

- Some of the more common additional controls include Image, Page Break, Tab Control, Line, and Rectangle. These can be used to dress up the form or to organize a complex form into manageable sections.

# Procedures

### Display the Toolbox

**From Form Design view:**

- Click on **Toolbox** button 🔨.

OR

1. Click **View** .................. Alt+V
2. Click **Toolbox** ...................... X

### Add a Label

1. Click **Label** button *Aa*.
2. Drag diagonally on form.
3. Enter text.
4. Resize box as necessary.

### Create an Option Group

1. With the Control Wizard on, click **Option Group** button.
2. Click on form.
3. Type **label names**, pressing Tab after each.
4. Click **Next** .................... Alt+N

5. Do one of the following:
    a. Click **down arrow** ▼.
    b. Click choice of **default label**.
    OR
    - Click **No, I don't want a default**.
6. Click **Next** .................. Alt+N
7. Accept the default values.
    OR
    Enter values to correspond to each label.
8. Click **Next** .................. Alt+N
9. Click **down arrow** ▼.
10. Click the **field** to store the value in.
11. Click **Next** .................. Alt+N
12. Click the **button type** to use.
13. Click the **button style** to use.
14. Click **Next** .................. Alt+N
15. Type a caption.
16. Click **Finish** ...................... Enter

### Create a List Box or Combo Box using Values from a Table or Query

1. Click **List Box** button.
    OR
    Click **Combo Box** button.
2. Click **Next** ................... Alt+N
3. Click the table to use.
    OR
    a. Click **Queries** ......... Alt+Q
    b. Click the query to use.
4. Click **Next** ................... Alt+N
5. Click the field from which to take data.
6. Click > >.
    ✓ *Usually you will want only one field. However, in some cases you might want two or more, such as First Name and Last Name.*
7. Click **Next** ................... Alt+N

8. Drag edge of sample list to adjust width.
9. Click **Next**.....................Alt + N
10. Click **down arrow** ▾.
11. Click field to store value in.
12. Click **Next**.....................Alt + N
13. Type a label for the list or combo box.
14. Click **Finish**.....................Enter

## Create a List Box or Combo Box by Typing Values

1. Click **List Box** button ▦.
   OR
   Click **Combo Box** button ▦.
2. Click **I will type in the values that I want** .................Alt + T
3. Click **Next**.....................Alt + N
4. Type the number of columns you want.
   ✓ *One column is sufficient in most cases.*

5. Press **Tab**.........................Tab
6. Type a list entry.
7. Repeat steps 5-6 as needed.
8. Drag edge of list to adjust width.
9. Click **Next**.....................Alt + N
10. Click **down arrow** ▾.
11. Click field to store value in.
12. Click **Next**.....................Alt + N
13. Type a label for the list or combo box.
14. Click **Finish**.....................Enter

# Exercise Directions

1. Start Access, if necessary.
2. Open ✏AC14.
3. Open **frmClients** in Form Design view.
4. Move the Notes field down, and add a label above it with the following text:

   **Enter any information gathered during conversation with customer, such as spouse name, hobbies, or favorite brands.**

5. Format the text in the new label as 8-point italic.
6. Switch to Form view to check your work. It should resemble Illustration A. Then switch back to Form Design view.
7. Delete the City field from the form, and create a combo box in its place called **City** that takes its values from the following list:

   **Denver**
   **Indianapolis**
   **Noblesville**
   **Beech Grove**
   **Lafayette**

8. Set the combo box to store its value in the City field, and name the combo box **City**.
9. Delete the State field from the form, and create a list box called **State** in its place that takes its values from the **tblStates** table and stores its value in the State field.
10. Use Format Painter to copy the label formatting from existing fields and field labels to the new ones.
11. Resize/reposition fields as needed. You might want to move some fields into the second column to make room for the new State list box, as in Illustration B.
12. Close the database.

*Illustration A*

*Illustration B*

# On Your Own

1. In Access, open the database ✐**OAC14**.

2. Display the **Equipment** table in a datasheet. Which fields do you think would benefit from a combo box, list box, or option group?

3. Create a new table based on one of the fields you identified in step 2, and include values in that table for all the current field entries.

   ✓ *For example, if you decided to create a combo box for Item Type, your new table would include Ball, Bat, Miscellaneous, and Safety.*

4. Open the **Equipment2** form in Form Design and create a combo box based on the table you just created that replaces the existing field on the form.

5. Create other combo boxes, list boxes, or option groups for any other fields that you identified in step 2.

   ✓ *For example, you might change the Insured field to Yes and No option buttons in an option group.*

6. Close the database and exit Access.

# Exercise 15

◆ **Work with Headers and Footers** ◆ **Display Header and Footer Areas**
◆ **Add Page Numbers or Date and Time** ◆ **Page Setup**

## On the Job

Form headers and footers help users to identify a form's purpose and to give the form a professional, attractive appearance both on-screen and in printouts. If you think you might want to print your records in Form format at some point, the Page Setup features in Access will be helpful in setting margins and page orientation.

You would like to add a title to the form you have been working on, and you think the form header might be a good place to add it. You would also like to print a copy of your client list using the form and would like to adjust the margins and page layout before you print.

## Terms

**Page header** Same as form header except it applies to individual printed pages instead of to the form as a whole.

**Form header** An area at the top of the form, above the Detail area, in which you can enter titles, explanatory text, graphics, or anything else that applies to the form as a whole.

**Page footer** Same as form footer except it applies to individual printed pages.

**Form footer** Same as form header, except it appears below the Detail area.

**Margin** The space on all sides of a page where no printing appears.

**Orientation** The direction the printing appears on the page, either across the width of the page (portrait) or the length of the page (landscape).

## Notes

### Work with Headers and Footers

■ Headers and footers on a form provide a place to enter objects that relate to the entire form or entire page, rather than to an individual record.

■ On-screen, headers and footers appear at the top and bottom of a form (or page, on a multipage form), providing information. For example, you might enter a form title in the Form Header area.

■ When you print in Form view, the headers and footers appear on the printout.

■ There are two kinds of headers: page header and form header.

■ Whatever you enter in the **page header** appears in each page of a multipage form or printout. You might place a page numbering code here, for example, to print a page number at the top of each page.

■ Whatever you enter on the **form header** appears only once, at the top of the on-screen form or at the beginning of the printout.

■ The **form footer** displays in Form view and on the last page of a printout. The form's footer is a good place for controls that you always want to see if the detail section requires scrolling.

■ Footers work the same way; you can have a **page footer** and a **form footer** that appear on the bottom of each page and at the bottom of the last page, respectively.

## Display Header and Footer Areas

■ By default, only the Detail area appears in Form Design view. To display form headers/footers or page headers/footers, choose them from the View menu.

■ You can drag the bars for each section up or down to increase or decrease the section's size.

■ Refer to the vertical and horizontal rulers on-screen to help gauge the size of the header or footer when printed. However, the actual size that appears on-screen will depend on the monitor size and resolution.

*Form with all headers and footers displayed*

■ The page header and footer prints at the top and bottom of the page but does not display in Form view.

■ After displaying the header or footer area, use the Toolbox tools to place objects into it, such as text labels.

## Add Page Numbers or Date and Time

■ You can also add controls that will show page numbers and the date in the header or footer section of a form.

■ To do so, click on the section in which you want the item, and then use the Page Numbers or Date and Time command on the Insert menu.

■ These commands place codes in text frames on the form.

■ Page Numbers codes can be inserted only in a page header or footer, and do not display anything on-screen.

■ Date and Time codes can be inserted only in a form header or footer, and *do* display in the on-screen form.

## Page Setup

■ Page Setup enables you to change the way your datasheet or form appears on the page. You can set Page Setup settings from either Form Design or Datasheet views.

✓ *Page Setup settings are saved with a form, but not with a datasheet. The settings go back to the defaults when you close a table after changing page setup. If you want to save settings with a datasheet, create a datasheet-style form.*

■ The Page Setup dialog box contains tabs for Margins and Page for both Datasheet and Form view, and an additional tab, Columns, in Form view.

■ To open the Page Setup dialog box, choose File, Page Setup.

### Margins Tab

■ Use the **Margins** tab of the Page Setup dialog box to change the margins.

✓ *Before you print, use File, Print Preview to check what the page settings will look like.*

■ The Print Data Only option specifies that the field names not be printed, only the data within the fields will be printed.

*Set print margins*

### Page Tab

■ Use the Page tab of the Page Setup dialog box to change the print **orientation** to landscape or portrait.

*Set page orientation and size*

- You can also specify a paper size and source, and choose to use a specific printer for the print job. This can be useful if you have multiple printers with different capabilities.

**Columns Tab**

- Here you can set the spacing between rows and the number and width of columns in which to print.

*Set number and width of columns*

✓ *The width of the detail section plus the left and right margins must be equal to or less than the width of the page for the form to print correctly. If you get two pages for each form when you expect one, try reducing the margins or decreasing the form width in Form Design view.*

# Procedures

### Display or Hide Headers or Footers

**From Form Design view:**

1. Click **View** ................... Alt + V
2. Click desired option to select or delete:
   - **Page Header/Footer** ..... A
   - **Form Header/Footer** ..... H

### Insert Page Numbering

**From Form Design view:**

1. Click **Insert** ................. Alt + I
2. Click **Page Numbers** .......... U
3. Select page number format:
   - **Page N** ................... Alt + N
   - **Page N of M** .......... Alt + M
4. Select location:
   - **Top of Page** ........... Alt + T
   - **Bottom of Page** ..... Alt + B

5. Select **Alignment**:
   - **Left**
   - **Center**
   - **Right**
   - **Inside**
   - **Outside**
6. Click **OK** ........................... Enter
   ✓ *Control is inserted on document.*
7. If desired, drag control to different location.

### Insert Date and Time

**From Form Design view:**

1. Click **Insert** ................. Alt + I
2. Click **Date and Time** .......... T
3. Select options.
4. Click **OK** ........................... Enter
5. If desired, drag control to different location.

### Page Setup

**Change page orientation:**

1. Click **File** .................... Alt + F
2. Click **Page Setup** ............... U
3. On **Page** tab, select orientation:
   - **Portrait** .................. Alt + R
   - **Landscape** ............ Alt + L
4. Click **OK** .......................... Enter

**Change margins:**

1. Click **File** .................... Alt + F
2. Click **Page Setup** ............... U
3. On **Margins** tab, enter margins:
   - **Top** ...................... Alt + T
   - **Bottom** ................. Alt + B
   - **Left** ..................... Alt + F
   - **Right** .................... Alt + G
4. Type margin in inches.
5. Click **OK** ......................... Enter

**Change columns settings:**

1. Click **F**ile ..................... Alt + F
2. Click **Page Setup** ............... U
3. On **Columns** tab, enter settings for:
   Grid Settings:
   - **Number of Columns** ............... Alt + C
   - **Ro**w **Spacing** ........ Alt + W

**Column Size:**

- **W**idth ..................... Alt + I
- **H**eight ................... Alt + E

**Column Layout:**

- **D**own, then **Across** .......... Alt + O
- **Across,** the**n Down** ............ Alt + N

4. Click **OK** .......................... Enter

# Exercise Directions

1. Start Access, if necessary.
2. Open 💿 **AC15**.
3. Open **frmClients** in Design view.
4. Enlarge the Form Header area to about 3/4" in height.
5. Change the form header's background color to match that of the Detail area.
6. Create a **Clients** label in the center of the form header area (using the Label tool in the Toolbox), and format it as Arial 28-point bold. See Illustration A.
7. Display the page header/footer, and place a page number code in the footer. Make the page number right-aligned.
8. Save your work.
9. Use Print Preview to see how the printout will look; then return to Form Design view for the form.
   ✓ Click the Print Preview button on the toolbar. When you are finished, click the Design View button to return.

10. Insert a date code only (no time) in this format: dd/mm/yy in the form header.
11. Move the date code to the form footer.
    ✓ By default the form footer has no area; drag the Form Footer bar downward to create some space for it.
12. Change the form footer's background color to match that of the Detail area.
13. Change the page margins to .5" on all sides.
14. Change the page layout to Landscape.
15. Change the number of columns to 2.
16. Preview your printout in Print Preview.
    ✓ Access reports a problem. Why?
17. Change the paper size to Legal.
18. Preview the printout again.
19. Close the database, saving all changes.

*Illustration A*

# On Your Own

1. In Access, open ⊙OAC15.

2. Add a title to the **Equipment2** table in the Form Header area. Use any font, size, and color you like.

3. Place page numbering in the page footer area. Then turn off the page footer with the View menu. What happens?

4. Experiment with various settings to find settings that allow you to print on the fewest number of pages possible. Use different sizes of paper, different orientations, and different numbers of columns. You can adjust the form size too if that will help.

5. When you find the right combination of settings, print your work.

6. Close the database and exit Access.

# Exercise 16

◆ **Critical Thinking**

As you learn more about Access, you have new ideas for improving the database for the Central Indiana Shetland Sheepdog Club that you worked on in Exercise 10. Now that you know about lookups and forms, you would like to use some of those elements to enhance the club's database.

## Exercise Directions

1. Open the ⊘**AC16** database.
2. Create a new form using AutoForm:Columnar based on the **tblDogs** table.
3. Save the form as **frmDogs** and close it.
4. Create a new form using the Form Wizard based on the **tblMembers** table.
   - Use all the fields.
   - Use a columnar layout.
   - Choose the Expedition style.
   - Name the new form **frmMembers**.
5. In Form Design view, add the title **Membership List** to the form header area. Center the label and format it as 18-point.
6. Switch to Form view to review the changes. Use Window, Size to Fit Form if necessary to view the entire form.
7. Close the form, saving your changes.
8. Create a new table called **tblPositions** with a single field called **Positions**. Make that field the primary key.
9. Create these entries in the new table:
   - **President**
   - **Vice-President**
   - **Secretary**
   - **Treasurer**
10. Use the newly created table as a lookup for the PositionHeld field in the **tblMembers** table (in Table Design view). Then close **tblMembers**, saving changes.
11. Return to **frmMembers** in Design view, and delete the PositionHeld field.

12. Re-add it to the form from the Field List, so that the new lookup takes effect there.
13. Format and reposition the added field and its label to match the other fields on the form.
14. Save and close the **frmMembers** form, and open the **frmDogs** form in Form Design view.
15. Add the title **Dogs** to the form header and format it attractively.
16. Add a page number code to the page footer.
17. Replace the Owner field with a list box that takes its values from the FirstName and LastName fields from the **tblMembers** table.
18. Rearrange the other fields on the form, and make the form larger overall, if necessary, to accommodate the larger size of the new list box. Illustration A shows an example, previewed in Form view.
19. Replace the Coloring field with a Coloring list box that uses the following values, and stores its value in the Coloring field in **tblDogs**:
    - **Bi-black**
    - **Bi-blue**
    - **Blue merle**
    - **Sable**
    - **Sable merle**
    - **Tri-color**
20. Resize the new list box so that it takes up only a single line.
21. Switch to Form view to inspect your work; then save the form and close it.
22. Save your work and exit Access.

# PowerPoint 2002

## Lesson 1

**Getting Started with PowerPoint 2002**
**Exercises 1-7**

## Lesson 2

**Editing and Formatting a Presentation**
**Exercises 8-16**

## Lesson 3

**Setting up a Slide Show**
**Exercises 17-24**

# Directory of Data Files on CD

| Exercise # | File Name | Page # |
|---|---|---|
| 1 | N/A | N/A |
| 2 | 02Gourmet | 322 |
| 3 | 03Gourmet | 326 |
| 4 | 04Gourmet | 330 |
| 5 | 05Gourmet | 334 |
| 6 | 06IMPORTOUTLINE 06WORKSH.xls | 338 |
| 7 | N/A | N/A |
| 8 | 08West | 347 |
| 9 | 09West | 351 |
| 10 | 10WestPrinting | 357 |
| 11 | 11WestPrinting | 364 |
| 12 | N/A | N/A |
| 13 | 13Marvel | 371 |
| 14 | 14Marvel | 377 |
| 15 | 15Marvel | 382 |
| 16 | N/A | N/A |
| 17 | 17Marvel | 392 |
| 18 | 18Marvel 18Marvel2 | 396 |
| 19 | 19Marvel | 400 |
| 20 | 20Marvel2 | 404 |
| 21 | 21Marvel2 21Marvel | 407 |
| 22 | 22Marvel2 | 410 |
| 23 | 23Marvel2, Internet Simulation | 414 |
| 24 | 24DitexInc | 415 |

# Exercise 1

◆ **About PowerPoint** ◆ **Start PowerPoint**
◆ **The Blank Presentation Option** ◆ **Apply a Slide Layout**
◆ **The PowerPoint Screen** ◆ **Use Shortcut Menus**
◆ **Use Slide Design Templates** ◆ **Use Placeholders**
◆ **Add Slides to a Presentation** ◆ **Save a Presentation**
◆ **Save File as a Web Page** ◆ **Close a Presentation/Exit PowerPoint**

## On the Job

Use a presentation to supplement a speech or lecture. You can show an audience the main topics you will discuss as you illustrate items with charts or tables. For example, you might present a talk to prospective customers about services your company performs or products you sell.

You are in charge of creating a slide presentation for Coastline Gourmet Importers. Coastline Gourmet Importers is importing a new line of Indian spices and wants you to create a presentation advertising some of their newest products. As a bonus, you will save the presentation for the Web because you know the company uses the Internet to sell many products.

## Terms

**Presentation** A set of slides or handouts that contain information you want to convey to an audience.

**Clip art** Predrawn artwork that you can insert into your files.

**Design template** A preformatted slide design that contains colors and graphics to make your presentation consistent and attractive.

**Slide layout** Pre-determined sets of placeholders for various types of slide content.

**Placeholder** Designated areas in PowerPoint layouts that can be used to easily insert text, graphics, or multimedia objects.

**HTML** Hypertext Markup Language is the file format used for files accessed on the World Wide Web.

## Notes

### About PowerPoint

■ PowerPoint is a presentation graphics program that lets you create slide shows that can be shown with a projector, a computer screen, or as a Web page.

■ A **presentation** can include handouts, outlines, and speaker notes.

■ PowerPoint slides may contain text and various objects, such as charts and **clip art**.

■ You can import data from other Office programs to a PowerPoint slide.

## Start PowerPoint

- When you start PowerPoint, the screen appears with a slide, ready for you to work.

### *The PowerPoint Screen*

- PowerPoint offers a variety of designs and **design templates** on which to base a new presentation. There is also a blank template so you can create your own design.

## The Blank Presentation Option

- A blank presentation doesn't have any graphics or backgrounds applied to it, but it does contain a single slide with the Title Slide layout applied. You can change the layout, create additional slides, apply colors, background patterns, and other formatting. You can then insert text, charts, drawings, clip art, and various multimedia effects to build your presentation content.

- The different kinds of slide layouts offer placeholders for entering content and text formats.

- After you create the presentation, you can add design elements, such as backgrounds, font styles, and color, if you want.

- If you do not have time to create your own design—or if you're new to creating presentations—you can use one of PowerPoint's predesigned design templates to enhance the appearance of your slides quickly and consistently.

### *Task Pane*

Click to start a blank presentation

Click to use a design template

## Apply a Slide Layout

- When you start a new presentation or add a slide to a presentation, it will appear with a default **slide layout**. You can use that layout, or select a new layout from the Slide Layout Task Pane.

- The Slide Layout Task Pane supplies 27 different slide layouts you can use to build your own unique presentation.

- Slide layout arranges the standard objects of a presentation—titles, charts, and clip art, for example—on the slide to make it attractive.

- The placeholders and options for slide layouts help you create the text and content for each slide of a presentation.

### *Slide Layout Task Pane*

## The PowerPoint Screen

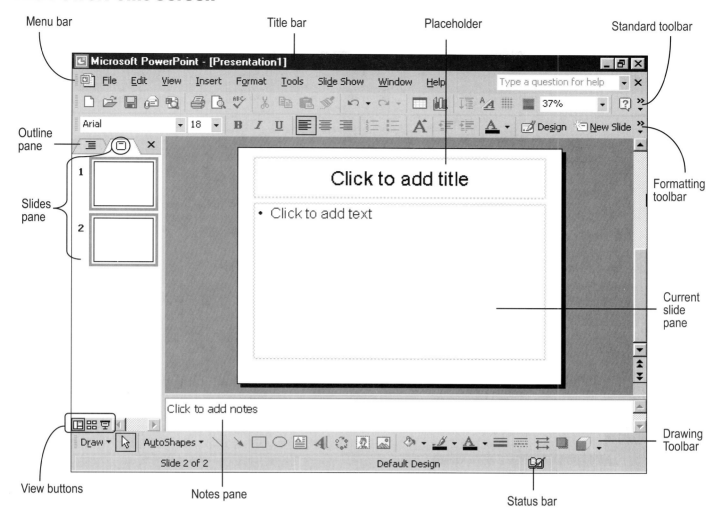

Menu bar    Title bar    Placeholder    Standard toolbar

Outline pane

Slides pane

View buttons    Notes pane    Status bar

Formatting toolbar

Current slide pane

Drawing Toolbar

- PowerPoint supplies the default title "Presentation" and a number in the title bar of each presentation you create. This title can be changed when you save the presentation with a new and descriptive name.

- A menu bar displays below the title bar.

- The Standard toolbar contains some buttons you'll see in other applications, such as Open, Save, and Print, as well as buttons unique to PowerPoint.

- The Formatting toolbar, which also contains some familiar buttons, lets you change font styles and sizes, among other things.

- The Formatting toolbar also includes buttons for common tasks, such as adding a design or a new slide by activating the Task Pane.

- The Drawing toolbar contains line, color, shape, and other drawing tools to use in your presentation.

- View buttons can be used to quickly switch among the three views: Normal (where you enter content on slides or in an outline format), Slide Sorter (the view used to rearrange and organize slides), and Slide Show (the presentation mode).

- The status bar displays information about the presentation, such as the slide number and template name.

- Normal view contains four panes: Slides, Current slide, Notes panes, and Outline, which you can access by clicking its tab. You can use these panes to enter information, arrange objects on the slide, and navigate between different slides.

## Use Shortcut Menus

- Right-clicking elements in PowerPoint—such as **placeholders**, slides, text, and graphics—displays a shortcut menu that lets you quickly perform tasks and procedures.

## Use Slide Design Templates

- The Template option lets you create slides with a planned layout. There are two types of templates—design templates and content templates.

- Design templates contain various colorful backgrounds, graphics, and text colors to apply to a presentation.

- Content templates contain sets of slides with design elements and content suggestions for specific presentations, such as a company handbook or financial overview.

## Use Placeholders

- PowerPoint displays placeholders to define the arrangement and location of text and other objects you can add to a slide.

- There are three types of text placeholders: title, subtitle, and text (bulleted lists of content). Each of these contains preset formatting for text font and size.

- When you type into a placeholder, PowerPoint selects the box, displays sizing handles for sizing, and a cursor for typing.

*Placeholders*

Placeholders

Handles

Selected placeholder

- Graphic placeholders provide a place for charts, clip art, tables, and other objects you can add to the presentation.

- If you are new to creating presentations, placeholders can help you create a professional-looking slide set.

## Add Slides to a Presentation

- PowerPoint inserts a new slide immediately after the slide currently displayed or selected.

- When you add a second slide to your presentation, the Title and Text slide layout is automatically applied. You can replace it with another layout from the Slide Layout Task Pane.

*Title and Text Slide Layout*

- The bulleted list layout supplies a title placeholder plus a text placeholder with five bullet levels, each with a different bullet shape to identify it.

## Save a Presentation

- If you want to have a file available for future use, you must save it on a removable disk or on an internal fixed drive.

- Save a PowerPoint presentation using the same procedures you use to save a Word document or Excel spreadsheet.

- PowerPoint automatically adds a .ppt extension to a saved presentation and changes the presentation's name in the title bar when you give the slide a new name.

- As in Word, you can also add summary information—title, author, keywords, and so on—about the presentation and view statistics.

## Save File as a Web Page

- You can save a presentation in **HTML** (Hypertext Markup Language) format for publishing on the World Wide Web.

- When you save a presentation in HTML, you can open it in a browser, such as Internet Explorer.

## Close a Presentation/Exit PowerPoint

■ PowerPoint prompts you to save a presentation that has not been saved or has been modified before letting you close the presentation or exit the program.

■ Follow the same procedures for closing a presentation file and exiting PowerPoint as in Word and Excel applications.

■ Close a document when you are finished working on it.

# Procedures

### Start PowerPoint

1. Click **Start** [🏁 Start] .... [Ctrl]+[Esc]
2. Click **Programs**.
3. Click **Microsoft PowerPoint 2002**.

### Open a New Presentation

1. Start PowerPoint.
2. In the Task Pane, click **Blank Presentation**
   [📄 Blank Presentation].

   ✓ If the New Presentation Task Pane isn't displayed, click View, Task Pane.
3. In the Task Pane, click the Slide Layout you want to use.

### Use Template Option

1. Start PowerPoint.
2. In the New Presentation Task Pane, click **From Design Template**
   [📄 From Design Template].
3. Click the design template you want to use.

### Use Right-clicks

1. Point to a PowerPoint item.
2. Right-click the mouse.
3. Click a command.

### Use Placeholders

1. Click once in text placeholder.
2. Enter text.
OR
1. Click on content placeholder.
2. Insert specific type of content, such as clip art.

### Insert New Slide (*Ctrl+M*)

1. Click **Insert**................ [Alt]+[I]
2. Click **New Slide** ............ [N]
   OR
   Click **New Slide** button [⬚].
3. From Slide Layout Task Pane, select layout.

### Add Summary Information about Presentation

1. Click **File** .................. [Alt]+[F]
2. Click **Properties**.......... [I]
3. Add desired information.
4. Click **OK** .................... [Enter]

### Save Presentation (*Ctrl+S*)

1. Click **File** ................ [Alt]+[F]
2. Click **Save** ............... [S]
   OR
   Click **Save** button [💾].
3. Click **Save in** drop-down arrow ...... [Alt]+[I]
4. Select **drive** and **folder**.
5. Double-click **File name** text box.............. [Alt]+[N]
6. Type **file name**.
7. Click **Save** .............. [Alt]+[S]

### Save as Web Page

1. Click **File** ............... [Alt]+[F]
2. Click **Save as Web Page**.... [G]
3. In **File name** text box, type file name.......... [Alt]+[N]
4. Click **Save** .............. [S]

### Close Presentation

1. Click **File** ............... [Alt]+[F]
2. Click **Close** ............. [C]

### Exit PowerPoint

1. Click **File** ............... [Alt]+[F]
2. Click **Exit**............... [X]

# Exercise Directions

1. Start PowerPoint, if necessary.
2. Create a new blank presentation.
3. Save the file as **01Gourmet**.
4. Accept the default Title Slide layout for the first slide.
5. Type the title and subtitle as shown in Illustration A.
6. Insert a new slide and accept the Title and Text layout for the second slide.
7. Type the title and bulleted list as shown in Illustration B.

8. Fill in the summary information for the file as follows:

   | | |
   |---|---|
   | Title: | **Coastline Gourmet Importers** |
   | Subject: | **Indian Spices** |
   | Author: | **Your name** |
   | Manager: | **Your supervisor or teacher's name** |
   | Company: | **Communications Solutions, Inc.** |
   | Category: | **Promotion** |
   | Keywords: | **Spices, Indian** |

9. Save the file, but don't close it.
10. Save the presentation as a Web page using the same name.
11. Close the file and exit PowerPoint, saving all changes.

*Illustration A*

# Coastline Gourmet Importers

## Indian Spices

*Illustration B*

# New Indian Spices

- Arrowroot-a starch used for sweetmeats
- Asafoetida-a sour spice with a strong aroma
- Carom seeds-a digestive seasoning spice
- Mace-a sedative and carminative spice
- Nigella-a seed used in pickles
- Fenugreek-a strong flavor, rich in iron

## On Your Own

1. Start PowerPoint and use a design template to create a presentation about yourself.

2. Select the default title slide layout and type a title for the presentation. For example, you might type My Life, or All About Me. Enter your name as the subtitle.

3. Insert a second slide using the Bulleted list layout.

4. Type a title on the second slide, and then type at least three items describing what the presentation will be about. For example, the first item might be "The Early Years," the second item might be "A Budding Athlete," and so on.

5. Insert a third slide using the Title, Text, and Clip Art layout.

6. Type a title on the third slide based on the first bulleted item that you entered on the second slide.

7. Type at least three bulleted items related to the topic.

8. Insert a fourth slide using the Title, Clip Art, and Text layout.

9. Type a title on the fourth slide based on the second bulleted item that you entered on the second slide.

10. Type at least three bulleted items related to the topic.

11. Save the presentation with the name **OPP01**.

12. Close the presentation and exit PowerPoint.

# Exercise 2

**Skills Covered:**

◆ **Open an Existing Presentation** ◆ **Slide Views**
◆ **Move from Slide to Slide** ◆ **Spell Check** ◆ **Print a Presentation**
◆ **Change a Slide's Layout or Design Template**

## On the Job

Check the spelling and otherwise refine the design of your presentation to make the best impression possible. For example, you may show a presentation to a prospective client who might purchase your product. A well-designed presentation can be the turning point in a sale.

You want to make some changes to the slide presentation for Coastline Gourmet Importers to make sure that your client will like it. Any presentation you plan to show a client should be spell checked. Also, you should review the design and organization of the presentation to make sure it is suitable for the client's tastes and requirements. Often, printing the presentation to hard copy gives you a better idea of how it will look to the customer.

## Terms

**Views** PowerPoint offers several different ways you can view the presentation as you work on it: Normal view, which includes the Slide, Note, and Outline panes, Slide Sorter, and Slide Show views. Each view has its own advantages and features.

**Automatic spell checking** A feature that checks spelling as you enter text. A wavy red line in the text indicates a possible spelling error.

## Notes

Standard toolbar

### Open an Existing Presentation

- PowerPoint opens with a blank presentation, consisting of a title slide, ready to work on.
- Open an existing presentation to modify, add or delete material, print, or run the presentation as a slide show.

### Slide Views

- In PowerPoint, you can create and view a presentation in three different **views** plus two tabs that display panes within Normal view.

318

Outline pane

*Normal view*

Slides pane          Notes pane          Slide pane

- Normal view (default) provides two panes, or views, of the slide and its contents—Slide pane and Notes. It also includes two tabs—Slides and Outline.
  - The Slide pane displays the contents as it will look on the slide.
  - The Notes pane lets you add text for personal reference.
  - The Slides tab lets you organize slides and easily see a thumbnail of each slide.
  - The Outline tab lets you view the slides content in outline format.
- Slides pane in Normal view displays the slides in the presentation so that you can quickly switch to the slide you want to view.
- The Outline pane in Normal view displays the outline of the presentation (slightly reducing the size of the Slide pane as it does so).

*Outline pane*

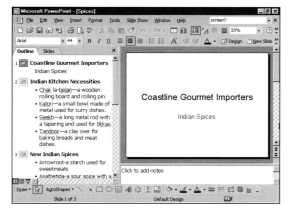

- Slide Sorter view displays the entire presentation in large thumbnails so you can easily identify slides as well as add, delete, and rearrange slides. This view is also suitable for easily adding and previewing animations, transitions, and sound effects to an entire presentation.
- Slide Show view displays one slide at a time, displaying a slide as it would be displayed in a slide show. This view is used to run an on-screen slide show.

## Move from Slide to Slide

- Most presentations include multiple slides.
- You will need to move from slide to slide to enter text and modify the presentation.
- PowerPoint offers a variety of ways to select and display slides.

*Move from slide to slide on scroll bar*

Next slide ⟶                    ⟵ Previous slide

## Spell Check

- PowerPoint provides two methods of spell checking in your presentations: automatic and manual.
- **Automatic spell checking** works while you're typing.
- Automatic spell checking displays a wavy red line under words PowerPoint doesn't recognize.
- PowerPoint activates the automatic spell checker by default.
  - ✓ *You can use manual spell checking at any time.*
- The use of the spell checker is similar to that in other Microsoft Office applications.
- A professional presentation must have no spelling errors.

## Print a Presentation

- Printing PowerPoint slides is similar to printing pages in other Office programs, with a few exceptions.
- A presentation can be printed as speaker's notes, handouts, slides, or as an outline. You choose the settings in the Print dialog box.

*Print dialog box*

## Print Options

| Option | Description |
|---|---|
| Properties | Click to change printer conditions, such as paper size, orientation, and graphics. |
| Print to file | Creates a printer file (.PRN) that can be printed on another computer that doesn't have the PowerPoint program. |
| Print range | Defines whether to print all slides, the current slide only, or a range of slides in the presentation. |
| Copies | Defines the number of copies to print. |
| Collate | Prints the slides in their order in the presentation. |
| Print what | Select to print slides, handouts, notes, or an outline. |
| Handouts | Select the number of slides to print per page. |
| Order | Select horizontal or vertical order of the slides on the handout page. |
| Grayscale | Select to print colors in shades of gray. |
| Pure black and white | Select this option to print slides in only black and white. |
| Scale to fit paper | Changes the size of the slide to fit the selected paper size. |
| Frame slides | Adds a frame border around the slides when printed. |
| Include animations | Check the option to include animations in the printed slides. |
| Print hidden slides | Prints any hidden slides in the presentation. |

- You specify page setup before you print the contents of the presentation. Select Page Setup from the File menu.
- Page setup lets you define the page size and orientation.
- Sometimes printing a slide set helps you to see any flaws to the design and to proofread content.

*Page Setup dialog box*

## Change a Slide's Layout or Design Template

- You may need to change a slide's layout or a presentation's template as you work.
- Change a slide's layout to add additional text or elements, like a graph or chart.
- Change the template to modify background, text color, or design elements.

*Slide Design Task Pane*

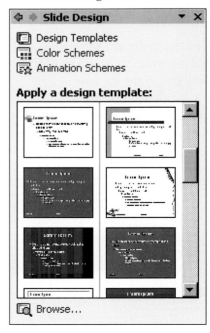

- Try to choose a template design that suits the subject matter.

■ You can view a color presentation in black and white or grayscale while you are working on it.

■ When viewing a presentation in grayscale or black and white, PowerPoint automatically displays a Grayscale View toolbar.

*Black and White view*

# Procedures

### Open Existing Presentation

1. Start PowerPoint.
2. Click **File** ..................... Alt + F
3. Click **Open** ......................... O
4. Click on file to open.
5. Click **Open** button.................. O

OR

1. Click the **Open** button 📂 on the Standard toolbar.
2. Browse to locate and open the file.

OR

• Click to open a file on the New Presentation Task Pane.

### Slide Views

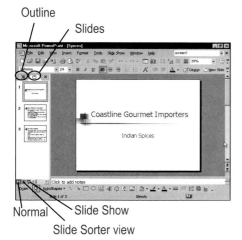

• To change views, click appropriate button on View bar or click appropriate tab.

OR

1. Click **View** ................... Alt + V
2. Click one of the following:

   **Normal**.............................. N
   **Slide Sorter**........................ D
   **Slide Show**.............. W or F5

### Move from Slide to Slide

1. Press **Page Down** to display next slide.
2. Press **Page Up** to display previous slide.

OR

1. Click **Next Slide** button ▼ on vertical slide scroll bar.
2. Click **Previous Slide** button ▲ on vertical slide scroll bar.

OR

• Click on a slide on the Slides or Outline pane.

OR

• Double-click on a slide in Slide Sorter view.

### Disable or Activate Automatic Spell Checker

1. Click **Tools**.................. Alt + T
2. Click **Options** ...................... O
3. Click **Spelling and Style** tab..................... Ctrl + Tab
4. To disable, select **Hide all spelling errors** check box.. S

   OR

   To activate, check **Check spelling as you type**.......... P
5. Click **OK** ........................... Enter

### Manually Spell Check Presentation (*F7*)

1. Click **Tools**.................. Alt + T
2. Click **Spelling and Grammar** ........................... S

   OR

   Click **Spelling and Grammar** button ✓.

### Change Page Setup

1. Click **File** .................... Alt + F
2. Click **Page Setup**................ U
3. Indicate page specifications.
4. Click **OK** ......................... Enter

### Change Slide Layouts

1. Click **Format** .............. Alt + O
2. Click **Slide Layout**.............. L
3. Click layout you want to apply.
4. Click the **Close** button ✕.

### Change Design Templates

1. Click **Format** .............. Alt + O
2. Click **Slide Design**.............. D
3. Select template design from Slide Design pane.

   ✓ Clicking the arrow on the design preview gives the option of applying the design to all slides or selected slides.
4. Click the **Close** button ✕.

### View Slide in Black and White

1. Click **View** .................. Alt + V
2. Click **Color/Grayscale**........ C
3. Click **Pure Black and White**... U
4. To change view back to color, repeat steps 1 and 2 and then click **Color**.

### Print Presentation (*Ctrl+P*)

1. Click **File** .................... Alt + F
2. Click **Print** ........................... P
3. Choose desired print options.
4. Click **OK** ........................... Enter

OR

• Click **Print** button 🖶.

   ✓ Your presentation will print based on the default or last options you selected in the Print dialog box.

# Exercise Directions

1. Start PowerPoint, if necessary.
2. Open ⌨01Gourmet or 💿02Gourmet.
3. Save the file as **02Gourmet**.
4. Move to slide 1 and insert a new slide using the Title Slide layout.
5. Enter the text as shown in Illustration A.
6. Switch to Outline pane. In the Notes pane, enter the following text:
   **Add recipes for some spices in sidebars**.
7. Switch to Slide pane.
8. Move to slide 3 and insert another slide using the Title and 2-Column Text layout.
9. Enter the text shown in Illustration B.
10. Change to Slide Sorter view.
11. Check the presentation for spelling errors.
    - ✓ *Note the spelling checker will find errors in some of the Indian words. Check the spelling yourself for these and then simply ignore the words in question.*
12. Apply the design template Edge.
13. Print a handout with three slides per page.
14. Close the file and exit PowerPoint, saving all changes.

*Illustration A*

# Indian Cookery

## Exotic Spices, Ingredients, and Kitchen Accessories

*Illustration B*

# Indian Essentials

- Beans
  - Lentils
  - Chick Peas
  - Black Beans
- Baked flat breads
  - Naan
  - Chapati
  - Wafers
  - Roti

- Preserves
  - Apple
  - Carrot
- Pickles
  - Chili Pickles
  - Lemon Pickles
- Desserts
  - Sweetmeats
  - Puddings
  - Toffee

# On Your Own

1. Open the **OPP01** presentation you created in the On Your Own section of Exercise 1, or open ⊙ **02MYLIFE**.
2. Save the file as **OPP02**.
3. Check the spelling in the presentation.
4. Scroll through the second, third, and fourth slides.
5. Change to Slide Sorter view.
6. Display the Outline pane.
7. Change to Normal view.
8. Display the slide in black in white.
9. Display the title slide.
10. Change back to color.
11. Change the design template.
12. Display slide four.
13. Change the slide layout to Title, Text, and Clip Art.
14. Print the entire presentation.
15. Save the presentation, close it, and exit PowerPoint.

# Exercise 3

## Skills Covered:

### ◆ Work with Content Layouts ◆ Use Undo

## On the Job

Add objects to your slides to make them more interesting to the audience. You might, for example, add clip art to a slide presentation to break up the text or emphasize certain points.

The client has supplied your company with information for use in a chart and other slides. They also asked that you add clip art to the presentation to make it more interesting for their prospective clients. In this exercise, you will enhance your presentation with clip art and **WordArt**.

## Terms

**WordArt** A feature used to transform text into a picture object.

**Object** An item other than text, such as a table, chart, clip art, WordArt, or worksheet.

**Embed** Inserting an object created in another application into your PowerPoint presentation. Embedded objects are easy to edit and update.

## Notes

### Work with Content Layouts

- The Slide Layout Task Pane supplies placeholders for **objects**, such as clip art and charts, in addition to placeholders for text.

- In PowerPoint, the Slide Layout Task Pane provides previews of various layouts that use text placeholders, or a combination of text and content placeholders.

- A content placeholder helps you add objects by displaying an icon box in the placeholder.

- You can also insert objects manually into new and preexisting slides using menus and toolbar buttons.

- **Embed** a content object, such as an Excel worksheet, so you can edit it easily within PowerPoint.

- Objects add interest to a presentation.

*Icon box for adding an object*

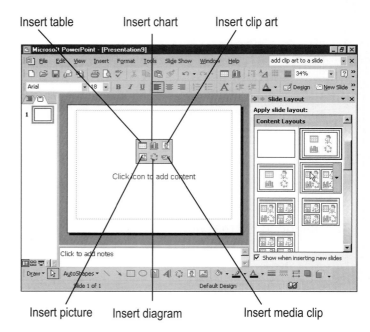

Insert table    Insert chart    Insert clip art

Insert picture    Insert diagram    Insert media clip

*Add clip art to a presentation*

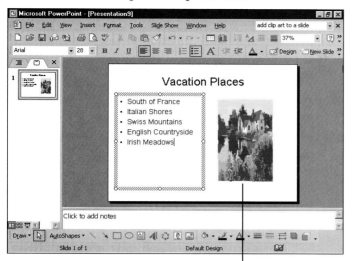

Clip art

## Use Undo

- PowerPoint contains an Undo feature, as in other Microsoft applications, that reverses the most recent action.
- With Undo, you can often reverse one or multiple actions you have performed in PowerPoint.
- You can redo actions after you undo, if you change your mind.

# Procedures

### Insert Object into Placeholder

1. Add new slide layout that contains a content placeholder.
2. Click the appropriate object icon.
3. In the resulting dialog box, choose the appropriate options.
4. Click **OK** ............................ Enter

### Insert Clip Art

1. Add new slide layout that contains a content placeholder.
2. Click **Insert Clip** Art icon 🖼.
3. In Select Picture dialog box, click desired art.
   OR
   a. Type a keyword in the Search text box.
   b. Click Search.
4. Select desired clip art.
5. Click **OK**.

### Insert WordArt

1. Click **Insert** ................... Alt + I
2. Click **Picture** ...................... P
3. Click **WordArt** .................... W
   ✓ You can add WordArt to a new or existing slide.
4. Click the WordArt style you'd like to apply.
5. Click **OK**.
6. Type text.
7. Click **OK** ........................... Enter
8. Select options from WordArt toolbar.

### Insert Object using No Placeholder

1. Open a new or existing slide.
2. Click **Insert** ................. Alt + I
3. Click one of the following:
   - **Picture** .......................... P
   - **Diagram** ........................ G
   - **Text box** ....................... X
   - **Movies and Sounds** ..... V

- **Chart** .............................. H
- **Table** .............................. B
- **Object** ............................ O

4. Choose from the submenu or dialog box that appears depending on the object you selected.

### Insert a Text Box

✓ Drawing toolbar must be displayed.

1. Click **Text Box** button 📧 on the Drawing toolbar.
2. Click and drag the text tool on the slide.
3. Type the text.

### Undo (*Ctrl+Z*)

1. Click **Edit** ..................... Alt + E
2. Click **Undo** ........................ U

### Undo Multiple Actions

1. Click **Undo** button's down arrow ▾.
2. Click the recent actions you want to undo.

*Insert WordArt Object toolbar*

Edit Text    Format Placeholder    WordArt Same Letter...    WordArt Alignment

Insert WordArt    Edit Text...    WordArt gallery    WordArt Shape    WordArt Vertical text    WordArt Character Spacing

# Exercise Directions

1. Start PowerPoint, if necessary.
2. Open 📷02Gourmet or 💿03Gourmet.
3. Save the file as **03Gourmet**.
4. Move to slide 4 and insert a new slide.
5. Select Title, Content, and Text slide layout.
6. Enter the text as shown in Illustration A.
7. Insert a relevant clip art in the content placeholder. Select a clip and then double-click it to insert into the document.
8. Insert a new slide at the end of the presentation.
9. Double-click the Title Only slide layout.
10. Type the title shown in Illustration B.
11. Insert a text box and type the text as shown in Illustration B.
    - ✓ *See procedures for inserting text boxes.*
12. Insert a relevant clip art. Resize or move the art as necessary.
    - ✓ *To resize the clip art click on the clip to select it and then drag one of the sizing handles. To move a clip, click on the clip to select it. Holding down the mouse button, drag the clip to a new location.*
13. Insert a new slide after slide 5 using any Slide Layout.
14. Undo the new slide insert.
15. Move to the end of the presentation and insert a new slide.
16. Select the Title Only slide layout.
17. Enter the title text as shown in Illustration C.
18. Click Insert, Picture, and WordArt.
19. Choose a WordArt style and click OK.
20. For the WordArt, type **Sizzling Spices**.
21. From WordArt's toolbar, choose any design or text formatting you want and close the WordArt by clicking OK. You can resize or reformat the WordArt.
22. Spell check the presentation.
23. Print the slides as handouts, with four slides to the page.
24. Close the file and exit PowerPoint, saving all changes.

*Illustration A*

Make Your Own or Buy Our GHEE

- Melt 5 pounds of butter in a saucepan. Bring to boil, stirring constantly.
- Simmer butter for 30 minutes then remove from heat.
- Skim the top layer. Let cool 2 hours.
- Transfer to jar.

*Illustration B*

## Presentation

Unless a dish looks nice, it doesn't matter how many exotic spices and wonderful flavors you add. Make sure the presentation of the dinner is attractive. Use fresh flowers, play some soft music, and arrange the napkins and dishes in an attractive manner.

*Illustration C*

Just what you need:

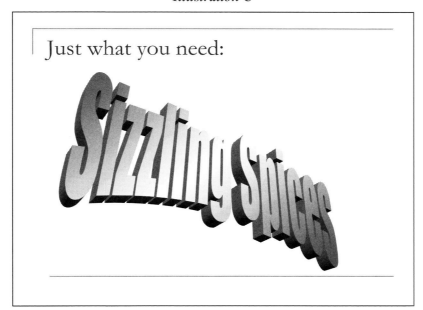

# On Your Own

1. Open the **OPP02** presentation you created in Exercise 2, or open ☺**03MYLIFE**.

2. Save the file as **OPP03**.

3. Insert a clip art picture on to slide 3. Try to select a picture that is somehow related to the text on the slide.

4. Insert a clip art object on slide 4.

5. Undo the insertion.

6. Insert a different clip art object on slide 4.

7. Print the presentation as handouts with two slides on a page.

8. Save the presentation, close it, and exit PowerPoint.

# Exercise 4

## ◆ Move, Copy, Duplicate, and Delete Slides
## ◆ Slide Sorter View

## On the Job

As you work on a presentation, you can move slides around, copy slides, and even delete slides you don't want in the presentation to make it more compact or descriptive. You might also, for example, create a presentation for one group of people in your company and then customize the presentation for another group by copying and changing some slides.

After reviewing your presentation, you decided to change the presentation's organization and make some additional changes before showing it to the client. In this exercise, you will duplicate slides and add new slides to your presentation.

## Terms

**Duplicate**  To create a copy of a slide that includes all text, content objects, and formatting of the original. A duplicate slide is inserted after the original slide in the presentation.

**Slide Sorter view**  A method of viewing multiple slides in the presentation at one time so you can easily move them.

## Notes

### Move, Copy, Duplicate, and Delete Slides

- A presentation contains multiple slides, any of which you can move, copy, **duplicate**, or delete.

- To move a slide, click the slide in the Slides tab or Outline tab in Normal view or in Slide Sorter view and drag it to the new position.

- You can also move and copy slides from one presentation to another.

- Duplicating creates a copy of a slide so you can make use of custom formatting and other features of the original slide to create a new slide.

- If you move, copy, duplicate, or delete a slide, you can use the Undo command to reverse the action.

- Save a presentation before you edit a slide so you can revert to the previous version if you make a mistake or lose data.

*Move slides*

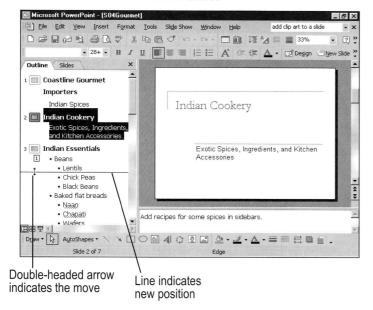

Double-headed arrow
indicates the move

Line indicates
new position

## Slide Sorter View

- **Slide Sorter view** enables you to organize your presentation as a whole.
- Slide Sorter view displays slides as miniatures so you can arrange them as you work or as the final step to completing the presentation.
- You cannot edit slide content in Slide Sorter view.
- To edit slide content, double-click a slide to display it in Normal view.

*Slide Sorter view*

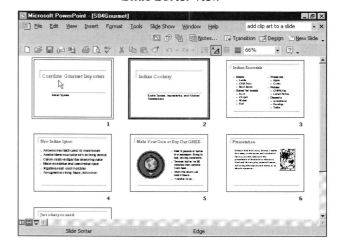

# Procedures

## Copy Slide (*Ctrl+C*) and Paste Slide (*Ctrl+V*)

1. In the Slides or Outline pane of Normal view or in Slide Sorter view, select slide to copy.

2. Click **Copy** button 🗐.
   OR
   a. Click **Edit**............... Alt + E
   b. Click **Copy** ..................... C
   
   ✓ *If you want to copy slide from one presentation to another, display the other presentation.*

3. In the Slides or Outline pane of Normal view or in Slide Sorter view, select slide after which the copied slide will be pasted.

4. Click **Paste** button 🗐.
   OR
   a. Click **Edit**............... Alt + E
   b. Click **Paste**..................... P

## Duplicate Slide

1. In the Slides or Outline pane of Normal view or in Slide Sorter view, select slide.

2. Click **Insert**.................. Alt + I

3. Click **Duplicate Slide**.......... D

## Delete Slide

1. In the Slides or Outline pane of Normal view or in Slide Sorter view, select slide.

2. Press **Delete** key............... Del
   OR
   a. Click **Edit** .............. Alt + E
   b. Click **Delete Slide**.......... D
   OR
1. Right-click slide in the Slides or Outline pane of Normal view or in Slide Sorter view.

2. Click **Delete Slide**.............. D

## Move Slide

1. In the Slides or Outline pane of Normal view or in Slide Sorter view, select the slide thumbnail.

2. Drag the slide thumbnail button to new position.

3. Release mouse button.

## Change to Slide Sorter View

- Click **Slide Sorter View** button ⊞.
  OR
1. Click **View** .................. Alt + V
2. Click **Slide Sorter**................ D

# Exercise Directions

1. Open ⌨️**03Gourmet** or 💿**04Gourmet**.

2. Save the file as **04Gourmet**.

3. Select slide 2 and copy it.

4. Paste the slide so it becomes slide 3.

5. Change the contents of slide 3 as shown in Illustration A.

6. If necessary, switch to the Slides pane in Normal view.

7. Duplicate slide 5.

8. Switch to Slide Sorter view.

9. Delete slide 5.

10. Move slide 4 to the second slide position.

11. Edit slide 8 to change the title to **The Key to Indian Cooking**.

12. Add a new slide after slide 8 and choose the Title, Text, and Content slide layout.

13. Add the text as shown in Illustration B.

14. Insert appropriate clip art.

15. Spell check the presentation.

16. Print handouts with 6 slides per page.

17. Close the file and exit PowerPoint, saving all changes.

*Illustration A*

Indian Cookery

Recipes are included with every purchase!

*Illustration B*

# Indian Ingredients

- Almonds
- Aniseed
- Artichokes
- Bay leaves
- Lamb
- Buttermilk
- Cabbage
- Lemons
- Mangos

# On Your Own

1. Open the **OPP03** presentation you created in Exercise 3, or open ☁ **04MYLIFE**.

2. Save the file as **OPP04**.

3. Insert a new slide after slide 2 using the Title and 2-Column Text layout.

4. Give the slide a title related to the third topic on slide 2.

5. Type at least two items in each column.

6. Change to Slide Sorter view.

7. Move the new two-column slide to the end of the presentation.

8. Make of copy of the fourth slide and paste it at the end of the presentation.

9. Undo the paste.

10. Save the presentation.

11. Close the presentation and exit PowerPoint.

# Exercise 5

## On the Job

Use the Outline pane in Normal view to help you organize a presentation. For example, you can add new slides and move slides around in the Outline pane so you can better organize the slides you already have.

You will continue working on the sample slide presentations for your client, Coastline Gourmet Importers. In this exercise, you will check each slide for organization, spelling, and other details in the Outline pane, so that you can easily rearrange text and make modifications to the presentation.

## Terms

**Outline pane**  Selecting the Outline pane in Normal view lets you see the outline of a slide presentation in text form on the Outline pane, as well as with slide thumbnails on the Slide pane.

**Collapse**  Hiding all except main, or selected, headings in an outline.

**Expand**  Showing all levels of an outline.

**Outline**  A technique of arranging topics and their subordinates to organize a presentation.

## Notes

### Outline Pane

- The **Outline pane** displays a presentation so that you can see an overview and organize content more easily.

- You can create a presentation in Normal view with the Outline pane displayed.

- Use the Outline pane to check the text content of a presentation for consistency and an overall flow of information.

- You can print a customized Outline view by **collapsing** or **expanding** certain headings or showing all formatting, for example.

- The Outlining toolbar makes it easy to rearrange content throughout the entire presentation.

- The Outlining toolbar also helps you view the **outline** in different ways, for easier organization.

*Outline pane*

Outline pane      Slide pane      Notes pane

## Outlining toolbar

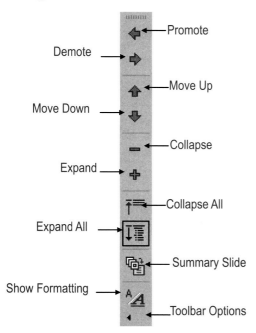

Promote

Demote

Move Up

Move Down

Collapse

Expand

Collapse All

Expand All

Summary Slide

Show Formatting

Toolbar Options

- Promote/Demote buttons change the heading levels and apply styles, such as bulleted text to selected text.

- Move Up/Move Down buttons let you move text up or down on the outline.
- Expand button displays the title, subtitle, and all bullet levels of the text in the selected slides.
- Collapse button hides the text levels in the selected slides and displays only the title text.
- Expand All button displays all levels of text for all slides in the presentation.
- Collapse All button displays only the title text for all slides in the presentation.
- Summary Slide button creates a new slide consisting of the titles of selected slides in Outline view.
- Show Formatting button displays text formatted as it will look on the slide.

## Summary Slide

- Create a Summary Slide made up of the titles of each slide in your presentation.
- A Summary Slide can be used as an agenda or overview.

# Procedures

### Display Outlining Toolbar
1. Click **View** ................... `Alt`+`V`
2. Click **Toolbars** .................... `T`
3. Click **Outlining**.

### Move Text in Outline View
1. Select the text to move.
2. Click **Move Up** `↑` or **Move Down** `↓` buttons.
3. Click **Demote** `→` or **Promote** `←` buttons to change the outline level of the text.

OR
1. Select the text to move.
2. Drag the text to new location.
3. Release mouse button.

### Select Slides in Outline View
1. Click the slide's number or Slide icon ⁵ `▨`.
2. To select additional slides, press Shift and then click Slide button for each slide.

### Display Titles in Outline View
- Click the **Collapse All** button `↑≡`.

### Insert Summary Slide
1. Select all slides in presentation ................`Ctrl`+`A`
2. Click **Summary Slide** button `▤` on the Slide Sorter toolbar.

### Print an Outline (*Ctrl+P*)
✓ *Collapse or expand slide titles and text as you want them to appear on printout.*
1. Click **File** .................... `Alt`+`F`
2. Click **Print** .......................... `P`
3. Click Outline View in **Print what** drop-down list............. `Alt`+`W`
4. Click **Outline View**.
5. Click **OK** ......................... `Enter`

# Exercise Directions

1. Open ⌨04Gourmet or 💿05Gourmet.
2. Save the file as **05Gourmet**.
3. If necessary, click the Outline pane.
4. Move slide 4 to the third slide position.
5. Move slide 2 so it appears after slide 4.
   - ✓ *Hint: Collapse the slides before you move slide 2.*
6. Move the following bullets on slide 9:
   - Lamb to the first bullet position on the slide.
   - Cabbage to the second bullet position.
   - Buttermilk to the third bullet position on the slide. See Illustration A.
7. Collapse all.
8. Select all slides and add a summary slide at the beginning of the presentation.
9. On the summary slide, as shown in Illustration B:
   - Delete one of the Indian Cookery bullets.
   - Move the Presentation bullet to the second position on the Summary Slide.
10. Expand the outline.
11. Spell check the presentation.
12. Print the outline.
13. Close the file and exit PowerPoint, saving all changes.

*Illustration A*

Indian Ingredients

- Lamb
- Cabbage
- Buttermilk
- Almonds
- Aniseed
- Artichokes
- Bay leaves
- Lemons
- Mangos

*Illustration B*

## Summary Slide

- Coastline Gourmet Importers
- Presentation
- Indian Cookery
- Indian Essentials
- New Indian Spices
- Make Your Own or Buy Our GHEE
- The Key to Indian Cooking
- Indian Ingredients

# On Your Own

1. Create a new, blank presentation.

2. Save the new presentation as **OPP05**.

3. In the Outline pane, enter text for at least four slides. Make the presentation about an organization or club to which you belong, about the place where you work, about a class you are taking, or about school in general.

4. Change to Slide Sorter view.

5. Create a Summary slide from the headings on the slides in the presentation.

6. Move the Summary slide to the end of the presentation.

7. Change back to Normal view and the Outline pane.

8. Use the Outlining toolbar to rearrange slides and promote/demote text.

9. Print the collapsed outline and then print the expanded outline.

10. Apply a design template to the presentation

11. Check the spelling.

12. Save the presentation.

13. Close the presentation and exit PowerPoint.

# Exercise 6

## Skills Covered:
### ◆ Import/Export an Outline
### ◆ Link an Excel Worksheet

## On the Job

Use data created in other programs for slide material to save time. You might have written a paper that when collapsed in Word creates the perfect outline for a presentation. Or, you created an Excel worksheet that you can link to a presentation that gives your audience the most up-to-date material.

Your client, Regency General, Inc., has supplied you with files that they want you to use in the presentation you're creating for them. Using the client's files from Word and Excel means the data is accurate and up-to-date and the organization is already arranged as the client wants. You'll also add some design elements to spice up the presentation.

## Terms

**Import** To bring a copy of text or data created in another program into PowerPoint.

**File formats** Each program saves a file as a specific type, or format. Many programs can convert file types so they can be used by several different programs.

**Export** To send a copy of text or data from one program, such as PowerPoint, to another program.

**Link** To connect two files so that when an original file is updated, the linked file reflects the changes.

**Source** The file from which you are copying or moving information.

**Destination** The file to which you are copying or moving information.

## Notes

### Import/Export an Outline

- You can use text created in other programs, such as Word, in your PowerPoint presentation.

- You might want to **import** text so that you don't have to retype the text or because you prefer organizing the presentation in Word.

- Import a DOC, RTF, TXT, or HTM format, as well as other formats from Excel, WordPerfect, and other programs.

  - ✓ *You may need to install a file converter to load certain types of files.*

- PowerPoint recognizes many **file formats**. When you open a file created in another format, PowerPoint automatically converts it to a PowerPoint outline.

  - ✓ *Some files you open may not be suitable for a PowerPoint outline. When you choose the Outline Files type when importing an outline, PowerPoint lists only those formats that do work as outlines.*

- Word formats an outline exported from PowerPoint with headings and bullets that are indented.

■ You might **export** an outline to Word so that you can use the text in another document, such as a report or letter.

*Import an Excel worksheet*

Excel worksheet

## Link an Excel Worksheet

■ You can **link** an Excel worksheet to a PowerPoint presentation to keep your information up-to-date and accurate.

■ A linked object is one that's created in a **source** file and inserted into a **destination** file.

■ A linked object does not become a part of the destination file.

■ The link connects the files so that when the source is modified, the destination automatically updates the information.

■ You can link to any program that supports linked and embedded objects.

■ PowerPoint lets you create a new object to link or select an existing file to link to your PowerPoint presentation.

■ An inserted worksheet may display empty cells, but you can crop unnecessary cells and resize the worksheet to better fit the slide.

■ When you click in an inserted Excel worksheet, the Excel toolbar appears for you to use.

# Procedures

### Import Outline from Word
*(Ctrl+O)*

1. Click **File** ..................... Alt + F
2. Click **Open** ........................... O
3. In **Files of type**, click **All Outlines**.
4. In **Look in** list, select the folder where the Word file is stored.
5. Select file to import.
6. Click **Open** .......................... O

### Export Outline to Word

1. Click **File** ..................... Alt + F
2. Click **Send To**...................... D
3. Click **Microsoft Word** ......... W
4. Click **Outline only**.............. O
5. Click **OK** ........................... Enter

### Insert New Excel Worksheet
*(Ctrl+M)*

1. Click **Insert**.................. Alt + I
2. Click **Object** ....................... O
3. Click **OK** ......................... Enter
4. In Insert Object dialog box, select **Create new**....... Alt + N
5. In **Object type** list box, select **Microsoft Excel Worksheet**.
6. Click **OK** .......................... Enter
7. Enter data in worksheet.
8. Click outside of worksheet to return to presentation and display data.

### Insert Existing Object File

1. Click **Insert**.................. Alt + I
2. Click **Object** ....................... O
3. Click **OK** .......................... Enter
4. In Insert Object dialog box, click **Create from file** ... Alt + F

5. Click **Browse** ....................... B
6. Select file.
7. Click **OK** ........................... Enter
8. Select **Link** check box ......... L
9. Click **OK** ........................... Enter

### Crop Excel Worksheet

1. Double-click worksheet.
2. Click any of the eight handles on border of object.
3. Drag double-headed arrow to resize object box.

### Size Worksheet

1. Select worksheet by clicking it once.
2. Drag corner handle to resize.

### Move Worksheet

1. Click worksheet to display four-headed arrow.
2. Drag object box to new position.

# Exercise Directions

1. Start PowerPoint, if necessary.
2. Open  **06IMPORTOUTLINE.doc** as an outline in PowerPoint.
   - ✓ You will need to select All Outlines from the Files of type drop-down list in the Open dialog box.
3. Save the file as **06InternetServices**.
4. Apply an appropriate design template to the presentation.
5. Go to slide 1 and add the bulleted text shown in Illustration A.
6. Go to slide 2 and insert a clip art. Resize and move the clip art to fit the slide content.
7. Insert a new slide after slide 3. Choose the Title Only text layout slide.
8. Add the title: **Communications**.

9. Insert a new Microsoft Excel Worksheet and add the data as shown in Illustration B.
   - ✓ Set the view to 100% to make working in the worksheet easier. The toolbar changes, which allows you to format the table as needed.
10. Crop and resize the worksheet so it looks similar to the one in Illustration B.
11. Move slide 4 to the slide 3 position.
12. Add a new slide to the end of the presentation. Use the Title Only text layout.
13. Add the title: **Services**.
14. Insert an existing worksheet and link it. Use the worksheet **06WORKSH.xls**.
15. Crop, size, and move the worksheet if necessary, as shown in Illustration C.
16. Modify the chart in Excel and then go to PowerPoint to view the modified chart.
17. Spell check the presentation.
18. Print the presentation as slides.
19. Close the file and exit PowerPoint, saving all changes.

*Illustration A*

## Regency General, Inc.

- Single Web pages to custom integration
- Business-2-Business Internet Services
- Small businesses to large enterprises
- Government and educational institutions
- Leased-line access

*Illustration B*

# Communications

|  | Consulting | Sales | Return Business |
|---|---|---|---|
| Intranet | 25% | 20% | 20% |
| Extranet | 15% | 15% | 15% |
| Telecommunications | 35% | 30% | 35% |
| Internet | 25% | 35% | 30% |

*Illustration C*

# Services

|  | September | October | November |
|---|---|---|---|
| Consulting | 15% | 25% | 20% |
| Website Design | 25% | 20% | 20% |
| Business Solutions | 5% | 5% | 0% |
| eCommerce | 30% | 20% | 30% |
| Web Project Management | 0% | 5% | 5% |
| Internet Marketing | 10% | 10% | 5% |
| Search Engine Optimization | 5% | 10% | 5% |
| Website Management | 10% | 10% | 15% |

# On Your Own

1.  Start PowerPoint and create a presentation outline from the ⊙**OPP06OUT.doc** Word document file.

2.  Save the presentation as **OPP06**.

3.  Use the outline to create a presentation telling people why they should donate money to a particular charity. You can select any charity you want. Personalize the outline text by replacing the sample text in the outline.

4.  Apply a design template to the presentation.

5.  Change slide layouts as necessary to set up the slides for titles and bulleted lists. Include space for clip art and an Excel worksheet.

6.  Insert clip art where necessary.

7.  Save the presentation.

8.  Start Excel and create a new workbook, or open ⊙**OPP06XL.xls**.

9.  Save the worksheet as **OPP06-2**.

10. Enter or edit the data to set up a worksheet to insert in your presentation. For example, list the income and expenses for the charity, or how much money comes from fundraising.

11. Save the worksheet, close it, and close Excel.

12. Insert the **OPP06-2.xls** worksheet on a slide in the **OPP06** presentation.

13. If necessary, move, crop, or resize the worksheet on the slide so it looks good.

14. Print the slides.

15. Save the presentation and exit PowerPoint.

# Exercise 7

◆ **Critical Thinking**

When presenting an advertising campaign to a client, you want to offer two or three different designs so that the client can compare layouts and then make a choice. In this exercise, you will create another sample presentation for your client Coastline Gourmet Importers.

## Exercise Directions

1. Start PowerPoint, if necessary.
2. Create a new presentation using the Watermark design template.
3. Save the file as **07Gourmet**.
4. Use the Title Slide design as your first slide.
5. In the Outline pane of Normal view, enter the text as shown in Illustration A.
6. Move to slide 1. Add a clip art or WordArt to one corner of the slide that serves as a logo for Coastline Gourmet Importers. You might use a food or herb clip art.
7. Resize and move as necessary. The logo should be small.
8. Create three more slides adding text to each slide and clip art, if you want.
9. Switch to Slide Sorter view.
10. Move slide 2 after slide 4.
11. Switch back to Normal view.
12. Edit slide 6 by inserting an Excel spreadsheet using the following data:

|  | 1st Qtr | 2nd Qtr | 3rd Qtr | 4th Qtr |
|---|---|---|---|---|
| Spices | 125 | 175 | 200 | 250 |
| Ingredients | 75 | 125 | 150 | 125 |
| Accessories | 75 | 100 | 125 | 75 |

13. Resize the worksheet so it fits on the slide and is easy to read.
14. If necessary, switch to the Outline pane in Normal view.
15. Collapse all and print the outline.
16. Select all slides and create a summary slide.
17. Move the summary slide to the end of the presentation and insert a logo on to that slide.
18. Spell check the presentation.
19. Expand all and print the outline.
20. Switch to Normal view and print handouts with 3 slides per page in pure black and white.
21. Save the file.
22. Close the file and exit PowerPoint, saving all changes.

*Illustration A*

1 ■ **Coastline Gourmet Importers**

Indian Spices and Cookery

2 ■ **Indian Spice Line**

- Cookery
- Tools and Equipment
- Ingredients
- Spices
- Recipes

3 ■ **Indian Spices**

- Arrowroot
- Asafoetida
- Carom seeds
- Mace
- Nigela
- Fenugreek

4 ■ **Indian Ingredients**

- Beans
- Flat breads
- Preserves
- Pickles
- Desserts
- Rice
- Ghee

5 ■ **Indian Recipes**

- Check out our cookbooks and printed recipes for Indian foods.

6 ■ **Sales Statistics**

- Spices
- Ingredients
- Accessories

7 ■ **Contact Information**

- Coastline Gourmet Importers
- 7334 Sunshine Pkwy.
- 12th Floor
- Miami, FL  33132
- Voice: 305-555-7300
- Fax: 304-555-7301
- E-mail: mail@ddcpub.com/coastlinegourmet

1

# Exercise 8

Skills Covered:

◆ **Select Text** ◆ **Align Text** ◆ **Change the Appearance of Text**
◆ **Change Case** ◆ **Change Slide Color Scheme**
◆ **Change Slide Background**

## On the Job

You can change the appearance of text to make it fit the space on the slide better or to add emphasis and interest. Change color schemes or text styles to give a presentation more interest or excitement. For example, a presentation about a sale would use bright colors and informal font styles, whereas a presentation about a financial institution would use more simple colors and formal fonts.

You work for Regency General, Inc. as a Web site designer. West Printing Company, a company that prints books and other publications, wants you to help them with a Web site to which they can refer prospective customers. One of West Printing Company's employees created a PowerPoint presentation. West's owner wants you to improve upon the design of the presentation.

## Terms

**Justified** Text is spaced so that both left and right edges of text are even.

**Format** To change the text appearance by applying a new font face, size, alignment, color, or style.

**Color scheme** A set of compatible colors in a slide used for background, type, lines, and objects.

## Notes

### Select Text

■ You select text so that you can modify it in some way, like making it larger or bold.

■ You can use the mouse pointer either as an I-beam or arrow to select text in PowerPoint. Drag the I-beam across the text you want to select. Point the arrow at a line of text to select one or more lines.

■ You can select and edit text in Normal view.

### Align Text

■ Align text to the left, center, or right in a placeholder to add interest and to enhance the design.

■ You can also use **justified** text alignment, although too much justified text can be difficult to read.

■ You can align any one paragraph of text in a text placeholder without changing the other paragraphs of text. In a title placeholder, however, aligning one paragraph realigns all of the paragraphs.

■ Align text in the slide pane in Normal view to see the effects on the slide.

### Change the Appearance of Text

■ You can **format** the appearance of text to emphasize it or to make your presentation more interesting and unique.

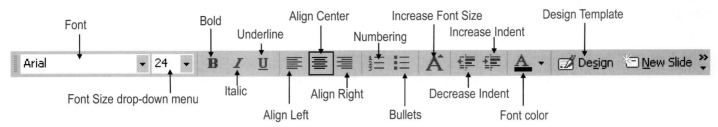

*Formatting toolbar*

- Text appearance attributes include font face, size, color, style, and special effects.

- You can change text attributes using techniques similar to those that you used in Word and Excel.

- As in Word, when changing the appearance of a single word, you do not need to select the word first. You can simply click in the word and apply a new text attribute.

- Use the Formatting toolbar to change one text attribute at a time.

  ✓ *If you cannot see all of the above buttons, drag the Formatting toolbar below the Standard toolbar to display all of its tools.*

- Use the Font dialog box to change multiple attributes at one time.

*Font dialog box*

- You can modify text appearance in Normal view.

  ✓ *Formatting doesn't change the appearance of the outline in the Outline pane even though you can format the text of the slide by selecting and formatting outline text.*

- When changing a font face, you can change a selection on one slide or you can replace one font with another throughout the entire presentation.

- Be aware that too many text attributes can make a presentation appear "busy" instead of adding to its power to communicate.

## Change Case

- You can change the case of existing text to make it consistent or to correct a typing error.

- As in Word, you can change the case of text to one of the following:

  - Sentence case: Initial capital letter and lowercase for the rest of the text in the sentence.

  - lowercase: All selected text is lowercase.

  - UPPERCASE: All selected text is uppercase.

  - Title Case: Each word is capitalized.

  - tOGGLE cASE: Reverses the case of the selected text.

## Change Slide Color Scheme

- PowerPoint's design templates each come with a set of predesigned **color schemes** from which you can choose.

- Each color scheme consists of eight colors that are applied to the slide background, text, lines, shadows, title text, fills, and accents.

- Click Design on the Formatting toolbar to access the Slide Design Task Pane. Click Color Schemes to view the different color schemes.

*Color Schemes in Task Pane*

- You can apply a different color scheme to an entire presentation or to just one slide. You might, for example, change the colors on one slide to emphasize that portion of the presentation.

- You can customize a color scheme by changing the colors of individual items, such as the background, title text, or shadows.

*Edit Color Scheme Custom tab*

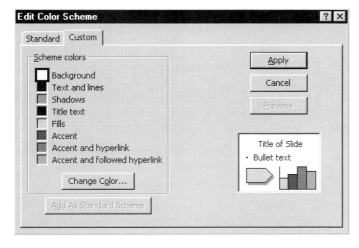

- Avoid using too many different colors, which can make a presentation hard to read.

## Change Slide Background

- You can change the color of a slide background, enhance it with a color gradient or pattern, or replace it with a texture effect or picture.

- Change background colors in the Background Color dialog box.

*Background Color dialog box*

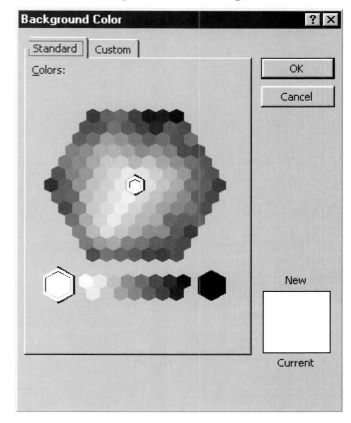

- Although you can combine a background color with a pattern or color gradient, you cannot combine a picture or texture with any other effect.

- You can change the background for a single slide, selected slides, or all slides in a presentation.

# Procedures

## Select Text

- Double-click to select word.
- Triple-click to select paragraph.
- Point mouse arrow ⟍ at text in Outline pane and click to select it.
  - ✓ *When you select an upper-level title all sub-titles and bullets beneath it are selected as well.*
- Click the I-beam at the beginning of the text and drag the mouse to the end of the text to select it.
- Click the text placeholder border to select the text box.

## Align Text *(Ctrl+L, Ctrl+E, Ctrl+R)*

1. Select text or click mouse anywhere in paragraph you want to align.
2. Click **Left Align** ▤, **Center** ▤, or **Right Align** ▤ button.

OR

1. Click **Format** ............... `Alt`+`O`
2. Click **Alignment** ................... `A`
3. Click appropriate alignment:
   - **Align Left** ....................... `L`
   - **Center** ........................... `C`
   - **Align Right** .................... `R`
   - **Justify** ........................... `J`

## Change Appearance of Text

1. Select text or click mouse within text to be changed.
2. Click appropriate button on Formatting toolbar.

OR

1. Click **Format** ............... `Alt`+`O`
2. Click one of the following:
   - **Font** ............................... `F`
   - **Bullets and Numbering** ................... `B`
   - **Line Spacing** ................. `S`
   - **Replace Fonts** .............. `R`
3. Make desired changes.
4. Click **OK** ......................... `Enter`

## Change Case

1. Select text.
2. Click **Format** .............. `Alt`+`O`
3. Click **Change Case** ............ `E`
4. Click one of the following:
   - **Sentence case** ............. `S`
   - **lowercase** ...................... `L`
   - **UPPERCASE** ................... `U`
   - **Title Case** ..................... `T`
   - **tOGGLE cASE** .............. `G`
5. Click **OK** ........................ `Enter`

## Change Slide's Color Scheme

1. Click **Format** .............. `Alt`+`O`
2. Click **Slide Design** ............... `D`
3. Click **Color Schemes** in the Task Pane.
4. Click one of the color scheme drop-down arrows to display the pop-up menu.
5. Click one of the following:
   - **Apply to All Slides** to apply the scheme to all slides.
   - **Apply to Selected Slides** to apply scheme to selected slides.
   - **Show Large Previews** to view the color schemes in a larger preview.

## Change Color within Color Scheme

1. Click **Format** ............... `Alt`+`O`
2. Click **Slide Design** .............. `D`
3. Click **Edit Color Schemes** in the Task Pane.
4. Click the **Custom** tab ................. `Ctrl`+`Tab`
5. In the **Scheme colors** list, select an element ........ `Alt`+`S`
6. Click **Change Color** button `Change Color...` .......... `O`

## Change Slide Background... *(continued)*

7. Click **Standard** tab ...... `Ctrl`+`Tab` for standard colors.
   OR
   Click **Custom** tab ........ `Ctrl`+`Tab` to add custom color.
8. Click **OK** .......................... `Enter`
9. Click one of the following:
   - **Preview** `Preview` ............. `Alt`+`P` to view scheme on slide.
   - **Apply** `Apply` ............. `Alt`+`A` to apply scheme to selected slides.

## Change Slide Background

1. Click **Format** .............. `Alt`+`O`
2. Click **Background** ............. `K`
3. Click color drop-down box and choose one of the following:
   - **Automatic** to choose assigned scheme color.
   - **Color box** to choose color within scheme.
   - **More colors** to choose custom color ................. `M`
   - **Fill effects** to choose gradient, texture, or pattern ...................... `F`
4. Select **Omit background graphics from master** check box to remove any lines, boxes, or other graphics but retain color on all slides .......................... `Alt`+`G`
5. Click one of the following:
   - **Preview** `Preview` ............. `Alt`+`P` to view scheme on slide.
   - **Apply** `Apply` ............. `Alt`+`A` to apply scheme to selected slides.
   - **Apply to All** `Apply to All` .............. `Alt`+`T` to apply scheme to all slides.

# Exercise Directions

1. Start PowerPoint, if necessary.
2. Open 📀 **08West**.
3. Save the file as **08West**.
4. In slide 1, select the title **West Printing Company** and enlarge its font size to 72 points.
5. Select the subtitle text that begins **Printing Services**… and change it to Times New Roman, italic, 42 points.
6. In slide 2, change the title to **Full-Service Printing** and left align it. Change the title to uppercase.
7. In slide 3, left align the title. Change the title to uppercase.
8. Change the remaining slide titles in the presentation to uppercase and left aligned.
9. In slide 4, select the title **Typesetting**… and change that text to Algerian, centered, and enlarge the text size to 66 points.
10. In slide 5, change the bulleted list to a numbered list.
11. Replace all occurrences of the Arial font with Times New Roman.
12. In slide 7, select row 1 of the table and change the font to Arial, 18-point bold.
13. Select column 1 of the table and change the text to Arial, 18-point bold. Select the rest of the table and right-align the text.
14. Select the text **Prices are per page** and change it to Arial, 14 point. See the example in Illustration A.
15. Change the design template to the Network template.
16. Change the slide color scheme to the first color scheme. Change the background color in the scheme to a dark blue and look at each slide.
17. Change the color scheme to another scheme and change the background color in that scheme to a lighter color. Apply the change to all of the slides in the presentation.
18. Spell check the presentation.
19. Print the slides.
20. Close the file and exit PowerPoint, saving all changes.

*Illustration A*

## Sample Prices

|  | One-Color | Two-Color | Three-Color | Four-Color |
|---|---|---|---|---|
| **2-page** | $1.09 | $1.60 | $2.05 | $2.55 |
| **4-page** | $2.09 | $2.60 | $3.05 | $4.55 |
| **8-page** | $3.09 | $3.60 | $4.05 | $6.55 |
| **16-page** | $4.09 | $4.60 | $5.05 | $7.55 |
| **24-page** | $5.09 | $5.60 | $6.05 | $8.55 |

Prices are per page

# On Your Own

1. Open **OPP06**, the presentation you used in the On Your Own section of Exercise 6, or open ⊚ **08DONATE**.

2. Save the file as **OPP08**.

3. Change the case of the titles on all of the slides.

4. Change the font of the subtitle on the Title slide.

5. Change the color scheme for all slides.

6. Change the background for the first slide and the last slide.

7. Save the changes, close the presentation, and exit PowerPoint.

# Exercise 9

**Skills Covered:**

◆ **Copy Text Formatting** ◆ **Move and Copy Text**
◆ **Increase/Decrease Paragraph Spacing**
◆ **Move, Size, Copy, and Delete Placeholders and Other Objects**

## On the Job

Modify text formatting and size placeholders to make more room on a slide for text or objects. For instance, you might need to add an extra bullet to the list, add a chart to a slide, or move text from one slide to another.

Your client asked that you revise the presentation to make it a bit less crowded and change some of the formatting. In this exercise, you'll enhance and edit the presentation for West Printing Company.

## Terms

**Format Painter** A tool that lets you copy text formatting from one selection and apply it to any other text in the presentation.

**Paragraph spacing** The amount of space between two blocks of text, such as two bullets.

**Placeholder border** A screened area around the edge of a placeholder, used to move a placeholder. You can also click on a placeholder to select the text or apply font changes.

**Sizing handles** Any of eight small black boxes located on a placeholder's border, used to resize the placeholder.

## Notes

### Copy Text Formatting

- Just as in Word, you can quickly copy and apply text formatting in PowerPoint by using the **Format Painter**.

- You can copy text and object formatting and apply it to one or multiple text blocks or objects.

### Move and Copy Text

- As you review a slide or presentation, you may rearrange the text to make it easier to follow.

- Just as in Word, you can move text in PowerPoint using drag-and-drop or cut-and-paste methods.

- Use the drag-and-drop method to move text to a nearby location. When you move text, a vertical line moves with the mouse to help you position the text.

- Use the cut-and-paste method to move text between two locations that are set far apart.

- You can use the drag-and-drop feature to move text on a slide or between slides in a presentation from the Outline pane. You can move text within a slide in the Slide pane.

- You can cut and paste text to a new location on the same slide, a different slide, or a different presentation using either the Slides or the Outline pane.

- You can also copy and paste text between slides and between presentations.

## Increase/Decrease Paragraph Spacing

- Adjust **paragraph spacing** between bullets or other paragraphs to make it easier to read or to fill the space better.

- You can adjust the space between paragraphs gradually by using the Increase ‖≣ and Decrease ‖≣ Paragraph Spacing buttons.

- To set paragraph spacing to a specific amount, use the Line Spacing dialog box.

*Line Spacing dialog box*

## Move, Size, Copy, and Delete Placeholders and Other Objects

- You can move or size any text or object placeholder or any other object, such as a clip art image.

- You can also delete or copy any placeholder or other object.

- To move, size, copy, or delete an object, you need to select it first so that its **placeholder border** and **sizing handles** appear.

*Placeholder border and handles*

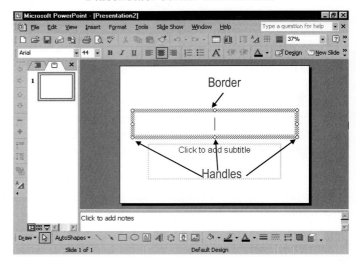

- Then drag the border or sizing handles to complete the task.

- When you click on a placeholder and drag it, the border changes from cross-hatching to dots.

# Procedures

### Copy Text Formatting to One Item

1. Select text containing format you want to copy.
2. Click **Format Painter** button  on the Standard toolbar.
3. Select text that you want to change.

### Copy Text Formatting to Multiple Items

1. Select text containing format you want to copy.
2. Double-click **Format Painter** button 🖌 on the Standard toolbar·
3. Select text that you want to change.
4. When you're done formatting, press **Esc** or click the **Format Painter** button 🖌 to deactivate Format Painter.

### Drag-and-Drop Text

1. Position mouse to left of text so pointer changes to four-headed arrow ✛.
2. Click once to highlight a bullet item and its subitems.
3. Drag mouse pointer to its new position.
4. Release mouse button.
   - ✓ *When moving text, make sure horizontal line representing text is in appropriate position before you release mouse button.*

## Cut or Copy and Paste Text

1. Select text to be moved or copied.
2. Click **Cut** button ✂ to move text.
   OR
   Click **Copy** button 📋 to copy text.
3. Position mouse where you want to insert text.
4. Click **Paste** button 📋.

## Add Increase/Decrease Paragraph Spacing Buttons to Toolbar

1. Display Formatting toolbar. ✎
2. Click **More Buttons** button ▾.
3. Click **Add or Remove Buttons**..................[A]
4. Click the **Increase Paragraph Spacing** and **Decrease Paragraph Spacing** buttons.
5. Click outside of menu to close it.

## Increase/Decrease Paragraph Spacing

1. Select paragraphs you want to adjust.
2. Click **Increase** or **Decrease Paragraph Spacing** button until space is as you want it.

## Move Placeholder or Other Object

1. Click in placeholder or graphic to select it.
2. Position mouse on border so pointer changes to four-headed arrow ✛.
3. Drag object to new position.

## Size Placeholder or Other Object

1. Click in placeholder or graphic to select it.
2. Position mouse on sizing handle so pointer changes to two-headed arrow ↘.
3. Drag handle until placeholder is desired size.

## Copy Placeholder (Ctrl+C, Ctrl+V)

1. Click in object placeholder to select it.
   OR
   Select text placeholder and click placeholder border.
2. Click **Edit**....................[Alt]+[E]
3. Click **Copy**...........................[C]
4. Move to slide, presentation, or position in which you want the copied material to appear.
5. Click **Edit**....................[Alt]+[E]
6. Click **Paste**..........................[P]

## Delete Placeholder

1. Click in object placeholder to select it.
   OR
   Select text placeholder and click placeholder border.
2. Press **Delete** key...............[Del]
   ✓ *The placeholder "Click to add" returns when you delete the placeholder's contents.*

# Exercise Directions

1. Start PowerPoint, if necessary.
2. Open 📇**08West** or 💿**09West**.
3. Save the file as **09West**.
4. In Normal view, go to slide 2. Change the text in the title **FULL-SERVICE PRINTING** to Times New Roman, 44 point.
5. Copy that formatting to all titles in the remaining slides of the presentation, except for the title on slide 4, **TYPESETTING**.
6. In slide 3, delete the third and fourth bullets: **Work with your word processing document** and **Multiple layouts for every document**.
7. Resize the placeholder to close up empty space left by the deleted bullets and add an appropriate clip art image.
8. Move and size the clip art to fit in the lower-right corner, as shown in Illustration A.

9. In slide 4, change the first bullet to read: **We provide over 200 typefaces for your printing needs**. Move the first bullet to the end of the bulleted list.
10. Change the text format of all of the bullets on slide 4 to Times New Roman, 28 point. Resize the placeholder so the text appears more to the left side of the slide. Add a clip art to the right corner of the slide, as shown in Illustration B.
    ✓ *Resizing a placeholder can result in changing the font size.*
11. Change the slide layout in slide 6 to Title and 2-Column Text and move the **Four-color work** bullet to the second bulleted list. Move the headings, resize the placeholders and adjust positions, as shown in Illustration C.
12. In slide 7, move the text box (**Prices are per page**) down about ½". Move the table down about ½" as well.
    ✓ *Moving text boxes and tables is the same as moving a placeholder.*

13. Change the title **Sample Prices** to uppercase to match the other titles in the presentation, as shown in Illustration D.

14. Spell check the presentation.

15. Print the slides in Slide view.

16. Close the file and exit PowerPoint, saving all changes.

*Illustration A*

# LAYOUT AND DESIGN

- Graphic artists available
- Free consultation
- Logo design

*Illustration B*

# TYPESETTING

- We use multiple desktop publishing programs to suit your needs
- We can scan your documents or work from scratch
- Bring in a disk with the material typed for a typesetting discount
- We provide over 200 typefaces for your printing needs

*Illustration C*

# ONE-, TWO-, AND FOUR-COLOR

- We can print your documents in one-color if you prefer black, red, or blue ink
- Two-color jobs include red and blue, green and yellow, or any other combinations

- Four-color work with Pantone colors gives your publications that professional look

*Illustration D*

# SAMPLE PRICES

|  | One-Color | Two-Color | Three-Color | Four-Color |
|---|---|---|---|---|
| 2-page | $1.09 | $1.60 | $2.05 | $2.55 |
| 4-page | $2.09 | $2.60 | $3.05 | $4.55 |
| 8-page | $3.09 | $3.60 | $4.05 | $6.55 |
| 16-page | $4.09 | $4.60 | $5.05 | $7.55 |
| 24-page | $5.09 | $5.60 | $6.05 | $8.55 |

Prices are per page

## On Your Own

1. Open **OPP08**, the presentation you used in Exercise 8, or open **09DONATE**.

2. Save the file as **OPP09**.

3. Copy the formatting from the subtitle on the Title slide to the bulleted text on all other slides.

4. Move the bulleted items on slide 5 to rearrange them.

5. Increase the paragraph spacing on all slides to improve the appearance of bulleted items.

6. Decrease the size of a clip art object on a slide and position it so it looks good.

7. Save the presentation, close it, and exit PowerPoint.

# Exercise 10

## Skills Covered:

◆ **Use Slide and Title Masters** ◆ **Slide Master View**
◆ **Insert Slide Numbers, Date and Time, and Footer Text**
◆ **Format Bullets**

## On the Job

Use a slide or title master to make each slide in the presentation consistent with the others. You might, for example, want to add the same art or logo to each slide and to change the format of the bullets so they all match throughout the presentation.

You have created a second presentation to show your client West Printing Company because you know it is always best to give a client at least two ideas from which to choose. You still need to go over the second presentation to make it more interesting and professional.

## Terms

**Slide master** A template slide that contains colors, text, placeholders, and other items that appear on all slides in a certain design. If you make a change to the slide master, all slides in the set change, too.

**Title master** A template slide that contains text or design elements for the title slide only.

**Footer** An area at the bottom of a slide in which you can enter a date, slide number, or other information. A footer appears on all slides in the presentation.

## Notes

### Use Slide and Title Master

- Each design template has its own **slide master**.

- A slide master contains text characteristics, background and other colors, and placeholders.

- If you want to make a change to all the slides in a presentation (except for the title slide), change the slide master. You might, for example, want to add a logo or slogan to each slide.

- Changes that affect all slides might include adding a picture, adjusting a placeholder, or changing fonts.

- To add text or objects to a slide master, insert a text box or an object box.

- If you want to use different default elements for the title slides in a presentation, use the **title master**.

- A title master contains characteristics and elements for only the title slide.

## Slide Master View

■ You edit the slide master in Slide Master view.

*Slide Master view*

Title master   Slide master

■ Changes you make in Slide Master view apply to all slides within the presentation, except title slides.

■ You can make changes to the title or master slide at any time during the creation of a presentation.

■ Formatting changes that you make to individual slides after you finalize the slide master will override slide master settings.

■ You can also customize individual slides to omit slide master background graphics.

## Insert Slide Numbers, Date and Time, and Footer Text

■ Include a slide number in the **footer** of a slide to identify the slide's position in the presentation.

■ Add the date and time to a slide footer so you can tell when it was created or updated.

*Slide footer with date and time*

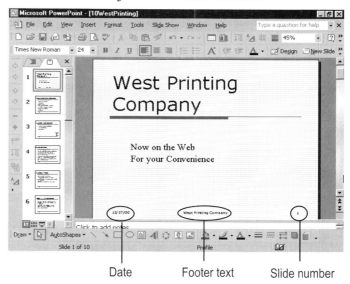

Date        Footer text        Slide number

■ You can use a slide footer to identify a presentation's topic, author, client, or other information.

*Header and Footer dialog box*

■ You can include numbers, dates, times, and other footer text on one slide or every slide in a presentation.

■ Placeholders for slide numbers, the date and time, and footer text appear on the slide and title masters.

■ If you want to change the location of an element in the footer, you must do so on the slide master.

## Format Bullets

- You can change the color, size, and/or character of any bullet.

*Bullets and Numbering dialog box*

Click here to change bullet size

Click here to change color

Click here to choose a different character

- Change the characteristics of a bullet on one slide to make the item stand out.
- Change the characteristics of bullets in a slide master so the bullets change throughout the presentation.
- Bullets that you format on individual slides after you finalize the slide master will override the slide master settings.
- As in Word or Excel, you can turn a bullet off if you prefer text without bullets.
- Too many bullet types in a slide put emphasis on design instead of on the content, so use discretion.

# Procedures

### View Slide Master

1. Click **View** .................... `Alt`+`V`
2. Click **Master** ..................... `M`
3. Click **Slide Master** .............. `S`

   OR

   Press Shift and click the **Slide Master View** button `⊞`.

   ✓ *The Normal View button changes to the Slide Master View button when Shift is pressed.*

4. In the Slide pane, click on either the slide master or title master to make changes.

### Create Text Boxes

   ✓ *The Drawing toolbar must be displayed.*

1. Click **Text Box** button `▣`.
2. Click or drag text box mouse pointer `⊥` on slide.
3. Enter text.

### View Footers

1. Click **View** .................. `Alt`+`V`
2. Click **Header and Footer** .... `H`

### Enter Date and Time

1. Click **View** .................. `Alt`+`V`
2. Click **Header and Footer** .... `H`
3. Select **Date and time** check box ........................... `D`
4. Click one of the following:
   - **Update automatically** ........ `Alt`+`U`
     Select date/time format.
   - **Fixed** ..................... `Alt`+`X`
     Enter date and/or time.
5. Click one of the following:
   - **Apply** button `Apply` to apply change to one slide ................ `Alt`+`A`

- **Apply to All** button
  `Apply to All` to apply change to all slides... `Alt`+`Y`

### Enter Slide Number

1. Click **View** .................. `Alt`+`V`
2. Click **Header and Footer** .... `H`
3. Select **Slide number** check box ................... `Alt`+`N`
4. Click one of the following:
   - **Apply** button `Apply` to apply change to one slide ................ `Alt`+`A`
   - **Apply to All** button
     `Apply to All` to apply change to all slides... `Alt`+`Y`

**Enter Footer Text**

1. Click **View** .................. `Alt`+`V`
2. Click **Header and Footer**.... `H`
3. Click **Footer** check box ....... `F`
4. Enter text in **Footer** text box.
5. Click one of the following:

   - **Apply** button `Apply` to apply change to one slide ................ `Alt`+`A`

   - **Apply to All** button `Apply to All` to apply change to all slides... `Alt`+`Y`

**Format Bullets**

1. Select bulleted text.
2. Click **Format** .............. `Alt`+`O`
3. Click **Bullets and Numbering** ................. `B`
4. Click **Bulleted** tab ....... `Ctrl`+`Tab`

5. Click bullet example or choose your own **Picture** to use art or **Customize** to change the bullet character.
6. Click **Color** ................ `Alt`+`C` to change bullet color. (You may need to repeat steps 1-4 if the dialog box closed.)
7. Click **OK** .......................... `Enter`

# Exercise Directions

1. Start PowerPoint, if necessary.
2. Open the file ⊙ **10WestPrinting**.
3. Save the file as **10WestPrinting**.
4. Go to title Slide Master view and display the title master. Reduce the width of the title placeholder by about 1" on the right so you can fit a logo in the upper-right corner of the slide.
5. Follow the steps to create a logo for West Printing Company using an appropriate clip art image with a text box over it, as shown in Illustration A.

   a. Insert appropriate clip art.

   b. Resize and move the clip art to the upper-right corner as shown in the illustration.

   c. Insert a text box and enter the text **WPC**.

   d. You may want to change the color or typeface of the text so it stands out (Format, Font, Color or Font).

6. Follow these directions to copy the logo (hold the Shift key as you select the clip art and the logo text) and paste it to the bulleted list slide master.

   a. Copy the logo in Slide Master view.

   b. Click the slide master in the Slides pane.

   c. Paste the logo in the upper-right corner.

7. Resize the title text placeholder so that the text does not interfere with the logo.

   ✓ *If text interferes with the logo, you can resize the placeholder of the bulleted text to make room for the logo.*

8. Display the title master. Change the color scheme on the title master. Add a striped background (Format, Background).
9. Switch back to Normal view.
10. Go to the end of the slide presentation and add a slide. Choose the Title Slide layout. Enter the text as shown in Illustration B.
11. Add a new slide using the Title and 2-Column Text slide layout. Add text as shown in Illustration C.
12. Move to slide 1. Insert an automatically updating date and a descriptive footer, as shown in Illustration D.
13. Move to slide 3 and change the color of the bullets.
14. Resize the placeholder to close up the empty space on the bottom.
15. Add a clip art to the bottom of the slide, as shown in Illustration E.
16. Increase the paragraph spacing between the bullets in slide 5.
17. On slide 5, change the bullets into a different character, size, and color to make them stand out more than the others in the presentation. Illustration F offers one example.
18. Spell check the presentation.
19. Save the file.
20. Print handouts of the slide presentation with 4 slides per page.
21. Close the file and exit PowerPoint, saving all changes.

*Illustration A*

# West Printing Company

Now on the Web
For your Convenience

**WPC**

*Illustration B*

## Customer Service

Personal service on the Web
New Teleconferencing!

**WPC**

*Illustration C*

## Teleconferencing

- Talker display
- Participant list
- Online orders
- Online call control
- Shared presentations
- Conference calling
- Low costs
- Flat rates

**WPC**

*Illustration D*

# West Printing Company

Now on the Web
For your Convenience

**WPC**

4/10/01     West Printing Company

*Illustration E*

## LAYOUT AND DESIGN

- Graphic artists available
- Free consultation
- Logo design

**WPC**

4/10/01     West Printing Company

*Illustration F*

## CAMERA WORK

- Expert camera operators
- Professional paste-up artists
- Metal plates are checked thoroughly for accuracy
- Bluelines provided for every job

**WPC**

4/10/01     West Printing Company

# On Your Own

1. Open **OPP09**, the presentation you used in Exercise 9, or open ☉ **10DONATE**.

2. Save the file as **OPP10**.

3. Add the date, time, and slide number in the footer of all slides except the title slide.

4. Change the slide master to include the name of the organization in the upper-right corner of all slides.

5. Select a different marker for the bullets on the slide master.

6. On one slide in the presentation, use a different bullet marker in a different color.

7. Save the presentation, close it, and exit PowerPoint.

# Exercise 11

## Skills Covered:

◆ **Use Rulers and Guides** ◆ **Floating Toolbars**
◆ **Draw Graphic Objects** ◆ **AutoShapes**
◆ **Group and Ungroup Objects** ◆ **Layer Objects**

## On the Job

Use PowerPoint's many drawing tools to help enhance a presentation. You might use rulers and guides to line up text or drawing objects, for example. You might draw logos, illustrations, or other objects to add to your slides.

The owner of West Printing Company is thinking about putting the presentation that you are designing on the Web. In this exercise, you will add design elements to the second presentation you created for West. You'll also add some buttons that make the presentation more suitable to the Web.

## Terms

**Guides** Nonprinting vertical and horizontal lines you can use to align objects on a slide.

**Floating toolbar** Any toolbar that you can move with the mouse around on the screen for easier access and viewing.

**Dock** To affix a floating toolbar to the edge of the PowerPoint screen.

**AutoShapes** A set of tools that makes drawing common geometric shapes fast and easy.

**Group** To join multiple objects into a single object so that they are easier to move and manipulate.

## Notes

### Use Rulers and Guides

*Rulers in Normal view*

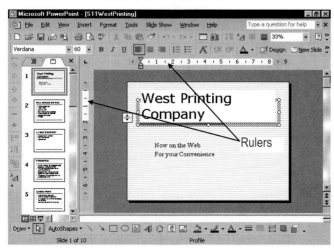

- PowerPoint provides a vertical and horizontal ruler that you can show or hide at any time.
- Use the rulers to adjust indents or add tabs to text.
- You can also use rulers to align objects on the slide.
- The ruler's origins (0 measurement on the ruler) change depending on whether you're using text or an object.
- The origin appears on the edge of the ruler when you're working with text and in the center point of the ruler when you're working with an object.
- As you move the mouse pointer, an indicator moves on each ruler showing your horizontal and vertical locations.

■ **Guides** are alignment tools that help you line up objects and text.

*Guides in Normal view*

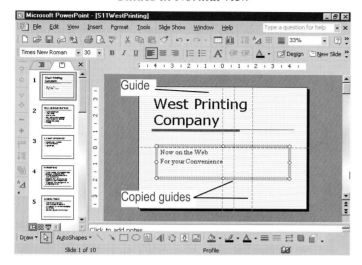

■ PowerPoint supplies one vertical and one horizontal guide that you can move and copy.

■ Use rulers and guides to make your work look more exact and professional.

## Floating Toolbars

■ A **floating toolbar** is one that is not attached to the edge of the program window. Certain toolbars float by default, such as the WordArt and Tables and Borders toolbars. The Standard and Formatting toolbars do not float by default, but they can be dragged from their position and float anywhere in the program window.

■ A move handle on a floating menu's submenu enables you to create a floating toolbar from the submenu.

■ You can resize a floating toolbar and move it anywhere on the screen.

*Floating toolbars*

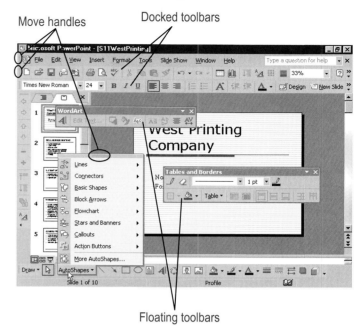

■ Use a floating toolbar to see all available buttons on it or to move it closer to a section on which you're working.

■ You can **dock** a floating toolbar on the left, top, or bottom of the program window. The Standard and Formatting toolbars are typically docked by default.

# Draw Graphic Objects

*Drawing toolbar*

- Use the Drawing toolbar to create objects such as lines, rectangles, and ovals.

- Drawings are objects that you can move, size, copy, and delete, just like any other object in PowerPoint.

- You can only draw in the Slide pane, on a slide master, or on a slide in Notes Page view, but whatever you draw on a notes page will not be reflected on slides in any other view.

- Using the Drawing toolbar, you can also fill the shapes and draw lines with colors. You can change line styles and colors, arrow styles, and fill colors.

- The Drawing toolbar displays with all views except Slide Sorter.

## AutoShapes

- Use AutoShapes to draw arrows, stars, circles, and other shapes into a slide quickly and easily.

- AutoShapes are objects, so they can be copied, resized, and moved just like placeholders and other objects.

- You can use the tools on the Drawing toolbar to enhance and modify AutoShapes.

  - Use Lines to create curves, arrows, and freeform lines.

  - Use Connectors to connect objects on a slide.

  - Basic Shapes include circles, rectangles, triangles, parentheses, brackets, and so on.

  - Block Arrows are decorative arrows of all kinds.

  - Use Flowchart to create organizational chart shapes.

  - Stars and Banners include ribbon and star shapes.

  - Use Callouts to create special text boxes that can be used to create labels in slides. There are several styles, including cartoon bubbles.

- Use Action buttons to create navigation buttons such as Next, Back, and Help. You use Action Buttons to give users control over the presentation.

## Group and Ungroup Objects

- You can **group** the objects within a drawing to make them into one composition that will keep the position of each object. Grouped objects are also easier to copy or move.

- When you group objects, you only need to click once to select the entire group of objects.

- You can ungroup objects when you want to edit or delete an individual object in the group.

*Ungrouped and grouped objects*

## Layer Objects

- You can layer objects one on top of another to create depth or add perspective in a drawing.

- After drawing an object, you can move it to the front or to the back of a layered stack.

- You can also move objects forward or backward in a layer one object at a time.

# Procedures

## Display Rulers and Guides

1. Click **View** .................. Alt + V
2. Click **Ruler** .......................... R
3. Click **View** .................. Alt + V
4. Click **Grid and Guides** ....... I
5. Click **Display drawing guides on screen** ........................... I
6. Click **OK**.

## Copy Guide

- Hold **Ctrl** key and drag existing guide.

## Delete Guide

- Drag guide off screen.

## Floating Toolbars

**To create floating toolbar:**

1. Drag toolbar's handle away from program window's edge.
   - ✓ *Some toolbars float by default but can be docked.*
   
   OR
   
   Drag move handle away from submenu to create floating toolbar.
2. Move floating toolbar by dragging its title bar.
3. Size floating toolbar by

   dragging its border ⬍ .

**To dock floating toolbar:**

- Move toolbar to edge of program window.

## Draw Graphic Objects

1. Click **Line** 乀 , **Arrow** 乁 , **Oval** ◯ , or **Rectangle** ☐ tool on Drawing toolbar.
2. Position crosshair ┼ on slide and drag to create object.
3. Click **Select** tool ☐ .
4. Select object by clicking it.
5. Click one of the following buttons on Drawing toolbar to apply to selected object:
   - **Fill Color** 🖌 ▾ to display colors and fill effects
   - **Line Color** 🖌 ▾ to display colors and fill effects
   - **Line Style** ≡ to display various line widths
   - **Dash Style** ▦ to display available dash types
   - **Arrow Style** ⇄ to display various arrow shapes
   - ✓ *Press Shift key as you draw rectangle or oval to create a straight line, a perfect square, or circle.*

## Draw AutoShapes

1. Click **AutoShapes** menu ..... Alt + U on Drawing toolbar.
2. Click one of the following:
   - **Lines** ............................. L
   - **Connectors** ................... N
   - **Basic Shapes** ............... B
   - **Block Arrows** ................ A
   - **Flowchart** ...................... F
   - **Stars and Banners** ........ S
   - **Callouts** ......................... C
   - **Action Buttons** .............. I
   - **More AutoShapes** ......... M
3. Select shape you want from submenu.
4. Click or drag mouse on slide to create shape.

## Group Objects

1. Click first object.
2. Hold down **Shift** key while clicking other objects to be grouped.
3. Click **Draw** .................. Alt + R
4. Click **Group** ......................... G

## Ungroup Objects

1. Select object.
2. Click **Draw** .................. Alt + R
3. Click **Ungroup** ..................... U

## Layer Objects

1. Select object.
2. Click **Draw** .................. Alt + R
3. Click **Order** ......................... R
4. Click one of the following:
   - **Bring to Front** ............... T
   - **Send to Back** ................ K
   - **Bring Forward** .............. F
   - **Send Backward** ............. B

# Exercise Directions

1. Start PowerPoint, if necessary.

2. Open 🖅10WestPrinting or 💿11WestPrinting.

3. Save the file as **11WestPrinting**.

4. Display the Slide Master view and click on the title master. Add two horizontal lines near the bottom of the slide, above the footer area, similar to those in Illustration A.

   ✓ *Press and hold the Shift key while drawing the line to make it absolutely straight. Release the mouse button before you release the Shift key.*

5. Apply colors to the lines that match the slide color scheme by selecting the line and clicking the Line Color button.

6. Create a West Printing Company logo in the title master. You can use AutoShapes, lines, WordArt, and other drawing tools. Apply a color fill to part of the logo, such as gray or yellow. An example appears in Illustration B.

7. Change to Normal view.

8. Switch to slide 7. Draw three AutoShape stars as in Illustration C, and apply a different fill color to each. Make sure the colors match the slide's color scheme.

9. Overlap the stars as shown in Illustration C. Move the last star you drew to the back and the first star to the front. Group the stars and position them as shown in Illustration C.

10. Add a text box below the stars with the text shown in Illustration C. Format the text to Times New Roman, 24 points, bold, and italic.

11. Display the rulers.

12. Move to slide 3. Remove the bullets from the bulleted text.

13. Widen the placeholder so it reaches the right side of the slide and, using the ruler, set tabs so that the second line of text is 1" and the third line another 1".

    ✓ *Note: You may have to adjust the indent markers.*

    ✓ *Refer to the Word section for information about setting tabs.*

    ✓ *You can set tabs easily using the horizontal ruler.*

14. Resize the placeholder.

15. Add a clip art to the bottom of the slide. Resize the clip art if necessary.

16. Go to slide 10. Insert any Action button from AutoShapes. In the Action Settings dialog box, select the First Slide hyperlink. Select any sound option you want. Position the button as shown in Illustration D.

17. Run the presentation to make sure the effects work.

    ✓ *To run the presentation, Click View, Slide Show.*

18. Spell check the presentation.

19. Print the presentation.

20. Save the file, but don't close it.

21. Save the file as a Web page using **11WestPrinting-2.htm** as the file name.

22. Close the file and exit PowerPoint, saving all changes.

*Illustration A*

# West Printing Company

Now on the Web
For your Convenience

*Illustration B*

# West Printing Company

Now on the Web
For your Convenience

*Illustration C*

## FOUR-COLOR PRINTING

❑ Four-color work with Pantone colors gives your publications that professional look

*All-Star Printing!*

*Illustration D*

## MAILINGS

❑ We can include mailing information on the printed piece
❑ Mailing labels printed
❑ We can sort your mailings
❑ We can even take them to the post office for you

# On Your Own

1. Open **OPP10**, the presentation you used in Exercise 10, or open ⊙ **11DONATE**.

2. Save the file as **OPP11**.

3. Display the slide rulers.

4. Insert an AutoShape on the title slide. For example, insert a lightning bolt, a star, or any other object.

5. Use the drawing tools to draw a simple picture on a different slide. For example, draw a bunch of balloons, or a flower.

6. Group the drawn objects and move them to a different location on the slide.

7. Save the presentation, close it, and exit PowerPoint.

# Exercise 12

◆ **Customize a Template**

◆ **Save and Apply a Custom Template**

## On the Job

Customize a template to create your own unique presentations. Your custom template, for example, might contain the same color scheme and graphic images that you use in your other company materials, such as a newsletter, letterhead, and brochure.

You work for Murray Hill Marketing, LLC. Marvel Enterprises is a client of your company. Marvel Enterprises produces cleaning products for home and businesses. The owner of Marvel Enterprises wants you to create a custom template in PowerPoint that you can use for several presentations as part of a special public relations campaign for the company.

## Terms

**Template** A foundation on which to build a presentation; a template may contain colors, graphics, fonts, and type styles.

## Notes

### Customize a Template

- You can customize a **template** to suit your presentation topic better. Or, you can create a template from a presentation you have already created. Any text, graphics, or other contents of the existing presentation will be saved with the template.

- Customize a template to change color schemes, background graphics, font formatting, and so on.

- Use the slide master to add modifications to all slides in a template.

- After you create the look you want, save the template so you can base other presentations on it.

### Save and Apply a Custom Template

- You can save any presentation as a custom template.

- After you save a custom template, you can use it as a basis for other presentations.

- Modifying a content template can make creating custom presentations quick and easy.

# Procedures

**Create Custom Template**

1. Open existing presentation.
   OR
   Open new blank design template or content template presentation.
2. Modify slide master, fonts, contents, color schemes, and other design elements.
3. Click **File** ..................... `Alt`+`F`
4. Click **Save As** ..................... `A`
5. Click **Save as type**...... `Alt`+`T`
6. Select **Design Template**.
7. Save template in default folder: Windows/Application Data/Microsoft/Templates.
8. Name the template.
9. Click **Save** ................... `Alt`+`S`

**Add Custom Template to AutoContent Wizard** *(Ctrl+N)*

1. Click **File** ..................... `Alt`+`F`
2. Click **New** ............................ `N`
3. In the Task Pane, click **From AutoContent Wizard**.
4. Click **Next**.................... `Alt`+`N`
5. Click **General** button... `Alt`+`G`
   - ✓ You cannot add content template to All category.
6. Click **Add** ................... `Alt`+`D`
7. Select your custom template.
8. Click **OK** .......................... `Enter`
9. Click **Finish**................ `Alt`+`F`

**Apply Custom Template**

1. Click **File** ..................... `Alt`+`F`
2. Click **New**............................ `N`
3. In the Task Pane, click **General Templates**.
4. Click the **General** tab.
5. Select the custom template on which to base new presentation.
6. Click **OK**........................... `Enter`

# Exercise Directions

1. Start PowerPoint, if necessary.
2. Add a slide color scheme. You can customize the colors, if you want. Apply the color scheme to all slides.
3. Go to the Slide Master view. Replace all Arial or Times New Roman fonts with Goudy Old Style or any other serif font.
4. On the slide master, add some graphic lines, shapes, clip art, and/or other design effects to make the slide interesting. See Illustration A for an example.
5. Create a logo for Marvel Enterprises. You can use clip art images or create a drawing. Place the logo on the slide master.
6. Save the file as a template: **Marvel.pot**.

7. Close the file.
8. Start a new presentation using the custom template.
9. Save the file as **12Marvel.ppt**.
10. Enter text in the title slide as shown in Illustration B.
11. Add a bulleted list slide and enter the text as shown in Illustration C.
    - ✓ You may have to resize the placeholder.
12. Spell check the presentation.
13. Print the presentation.
14. Close the file and exit PowerPoint, saving all changes.

*Illustration A*

*Illustration B*

*Illustration C*

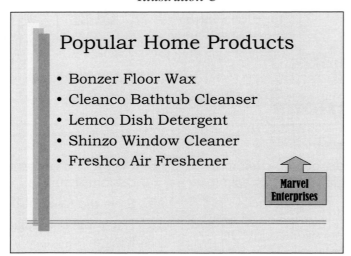

# On Your Own

1. Create a new presentation based on a blank template.

2. On the master slide apply colors, select fonts, select bullets, and insert graphics as desired to customize the template.

3. Save the presentation as a template with the name **OPP12.pot**.

4. Create a new presentation based on the **OPP12.pot** template.

5. Save the presentation as **OPP12-2.ppt**.

6. Create a presentation about a friend, family member, or pet. Include at least three slides.

7. Save the presentation, close it, and exit PowerPoint.

# Exercise 13

## On the Job

Add an organization chart to your presentation to illustrate the structure of your organization. For example, show the relationship between store managers and their staff or between the vice presidents of the company and their assistants and managers.

Recently there have been changes in employee status at Marvel Enterprises—several people were promoted and others left the company. The owners of Marvel have asked you to create an organization chart showing the current company structure.

## Terms

**Organization chart** An illustration of the top-down structure (the *hierarchy*) of positions within an organization, usually starting with the chief executive.

## Notes

### Insert Organization Chart Slide

- An **organization chart** can illustrate a company's or organization's structure.

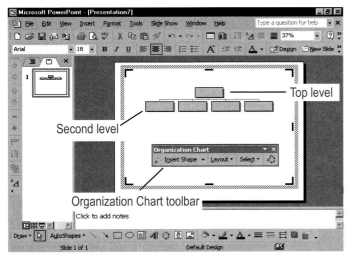

*Organization chart*

- It can also show the structure of a department, project, exercise, process, procedure, or family tree.

- You can create an organization chart using any layout that includes a content placeholder and clicking the Insert Diagram or Organization Chart icon or insert one without a placeholder using the Insert menu.

- You can choose to insert any diagram type, including the Organization Chart, a Pyramid Diagram, Target Diagram, or others.

- When you insert an organization chart, five boxes appear. You can add, delete, and type in the boxes as desired.

- PowerPoint includes an Organization Chart toolbar that has menus for adding boxes, changing the layout of the chart, and selecting parts of the chart.

- An organization chart can be moved, copied, and deleted like any other object.

# Procedures

## Create Organization Chart

1. Apply a layout that contains a content placeholder.
2. Click the Insert Diagram or Organization Chart icon.
3. Click the Organization Chart diagram style.
4. Click **OK**.
5. Click in any box and begin typing to enter text.
6. Press **Enter** to add another line of text in box.
7. Click mouse on box to which you want to attach new box.
8. To add box, click **Insert Shape** ..........................`Alt`+`N` and then press up or down.
   - **S**ubordinate ................. `S`
   - **C**oworker ....................... `C`
   - **A**ssistant ....................... `A`
9. Repeat steps 8 and 9 until chart is complete.

## Select Box

- Click the border of a box.

## Type in a Box

- Click within the box and enter text.

## Select Multiple Boxes

1. From Organization Chart toolbar, click **Sele**c**t** ..... `Alt`+`C`
2. Choose one of the following:
   - All **A**ssistants ................ `A`
   - **B**ranch .......................... `B`
   - **L**evel ............................. `L`
   - All **C**onnecting Lines ... `C`

   OR
   - Hold down **Shift** key and click on multiple boxes.

## Delete Box

1. Select box.
2. Press **Delete** key ............... `Del`

## Format Fonts

1. From Organization chart, select text.
2. Click **F**ormat ............... `Alt`+`O`
3. Click **F**ont .................... `F`
   - ✓ *Format fonts the same as you would any font in PowerPoint.*
4. Click **OK** ........................... `Enter`

## Change Chart Layout

1. From Organization Chart toolbar, click **L**ayout .... `Alt`+`L`
2. Click one of the following:
   - **S**tandard ...................... `S`
   - **B**oth Hanging ............... `B`
   - **L**eft Hanging ................ `L`
   - **R**ight Hanging .............. `R`
   - **F**it Organization Chart to Contents ........ `F`
   - **E**xpand Organization Chart ...... `E`
   - S**c**ale Organization Chart ...... `C`
   - **A**utoLayout ................... `A`

## Change Alignment

1. From Organization chart, select text.
2. Click **F**ormat ............... `Alt`+`O`
3. Click **A**lignment ................. `A`
4. Click one of the following:
   - Align **L**eft ...................... `L`
   - Align **R**ight ................... `R`
   - **C**enter ......................... `C`
   - **J**ustify ........................... `J`

## Change Box Color

1. From Organization chart, double-click box.
2. Click **Colors and Lines** tab.
3. Click **C**olor ..................... `C`
4. Select color.
5. Click **OK** ........................... `Enter`

   OR

1. Select the box to be formatted.
2. Click the drop-down arrow of the **Fill** button  on the Tables and Borders or the Draw toolbar.
3. Select a color from the display.

- **M**ore Fill Colors ............ `M`
  - ✓ *This option displays a color palette from which you can select a suitable color.*

- **F**ill Effects ..................... `F`
  - ✓ *This option displays a dialog box from which you can choose:*
    - **Gradient**
    - **Texture**
    - **Pattern**
    - **Picture**
  - ✓ *The row of colors under Automatic lets you apply a color that is consistent with the color scheme of the design template you are using for the presentation.*
  - ✓ *Other colors may appear if you have selected fill colors on other slides.*

## Change Box Border

1. From Organization chart, double-click box.
2. Click **Colors and Lines** tab.
3. Click one of the following:
   - Line C**o**lor ..................... `O`
   - **S**tyle .............................. `S`
   - **W**eight .......................... `W`
   - **D**ashed ......................... `D`
4. Click **OK** ........................... `Enter`

## Edit Organization Chart

- Click chart.

# Exercise Directions

1. Start PowerPoint, if necessary.
2. Open 🖾**12Marvel** or 💿**13Marvel**.
3. Save the file as **13Marvel**.
4. Add a slide after slide 2 and choose a Content slide layout that includes a title.
5. Add the title **Sales Staff**.
6. Add an organization chart.
7. Use the toolbar buttons to add a co-worker, subordinates, and assistants as shown in Illustration A and enter the text in each box as shown.
   - ✓ Hint: Colin Smith is a subordinate of Mary Frank.
8. Scale the chart to better fit the slide. Move the chart as necessary to fit the chart on the slide.
9. Select the boxes and change the color to any color that matches the color scheme.
   - ✓ Hint: You should make all assistants one color, all associates another color, and so on, to differentiate between levels.
10. Click outside of the chart to deselect the organization chart.
11. Add another slide, using a Content slide layout that includes a title.
12. Enter the title on the slide **Human Resources**.
13. Add an organization chart. Enter text and boxes as shown in Illustration B.
    - ✓ Hint: Use the both hanging layout.
14. Change the color of the boxes to similar colors you used on the previous chart.
15. Scale and move the chart to center it on the slide.
16. Spell check the presentation.
17. Print the presentation.
18. Close the file and exit PowerPoint, saving all changes.

*Illustration A*

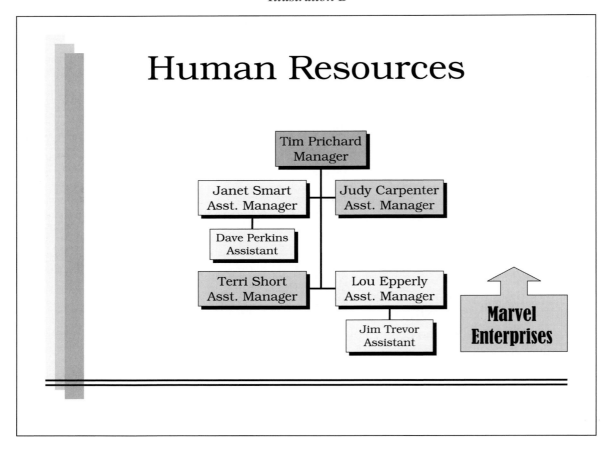

# On Your Own

1. Open **OPP04**, the presentation you created about yourself, or open ⊛**13MYLIFE**.

2. Save the file as **OPP13**.

3. Insert a new slide using the Organization Chart slide layout.

4. Create a family tree organization chart on the new slide.

5. Format the chart any way you want.

6. Place the slide in the order in which it belongs in the presentation. It should make sense in the flow of the presentation.

7. Format the slides using fonts, colors, and drawing objects, if you want.

8. Save the presentation, close it, and exit PowerPoint.

# Exercise 14

## On the Job

Add charts or tables to a presentation to illustrate data in an easy-to-read format. Sales figures represented in a chart, for example, are easier to understand than if they're simply listed or just read aloud to the audience.

The owner of Marvel Enterprises has given you some data that you can add to the presentation in the form of charts, tables, and worksheets. In this exercise, you will continue work on the Marvel Enterprises project using the custom template you created.

## Terms

**Chart**  A graphic illustration of numbers, percentages, or other data.

**Datasheet**  A worksheet for the graph and charting program. A datasheet contains columns and rows in which you can enter text.

**Data label**  Text that identifies your data.

**Table**  A structure for organizing data in rows and columns.

## Notes

### Create a Chart

- You can add a **chart** to your presentation to illustrate data in an easy-to-understand format or to compare and contrast sets of data.

- You can create a new chart and data in PowerPoint using Microsoft Graph, a charting program that comes with PowerPoint.

Format Chart Area — Import file — View Datasheet — Data Table — Chart Type

MS Graph menu

Chart toolbar

Chart area

Datasheet

- As you learned in Exercise 6, you can also insert an existing chart as an object from Excel to use in a slide.

*Import Data Options dialog box*

- You can insert a chart into a content slide layout or add it without a placeholder using the Insert Chart button on the Standard toolbar.

- When you insert a new chart, a Chart toolbar is added to the Standard toolbar and several charting tools appear on the Formatting toolbar.

- A sample chart and a **datasheet** window containing sample data also appear. You can type in replacement data or import data from an existing Excel file.

*Datasheet window*

| | | A | B | C | D |
|---|---|---|---|---|---|
| | | 1st Qtr | 2nd Qtr | 3rd Qtr | 4th Qtr |
| 1 | East | 20.4 | 27.4 | 90 | 20.4 |
| 2 | West | 30.6 | 38.6 | 34.6 | 31.6 |
| 3 | North | 45.9 | 46.9 | 45 | 43.9 |
| 4 | | | | | |

S14Marvel - Datasheet

- The default chart type is 3-D Column. You can, however, choose from several chart formats, including bar, line, pie, area, scatter, doughnut, radar, surface, bubble, and stock.

- You can move, copy, size, and delete a chart just like any other slide object.

- You can show or hide gridlines, or measurement guides, within a chart to help you read the chart information.
- You can include a title, **data labels**, and a legend with your chart. A legend identifies the data in a chart by listing each type of data with a color key to its corresponding chart element.

## Create a Table

- Use a **table** to organize information into rows and columns.
- You can create a new table using the placeholder in a Title and Table layout, or insert a table without a placeholder by using the Insert Table button on the Standard toolbar.

- When you insert a table, you may need to adjust row or column width or resize and move the table.
- When you insert a new table or click an existing table, the Tables and Borders toolbar appears with tools you can use to edit the table.
- The Tables and Borders toolbar appears on the right side of the screen. You can move the toolbar to show more buttons.
- After creating a table, you can format the text, resize the cells, insert and delete columns and rows, and change borders on the table.
- You can format the font, color, and size of table text just as you would regular slide text.

*Insert Table dialog box*

*Tables and Borders toolbar*

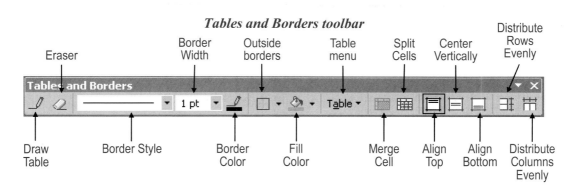

# Procedures

## Create New Chart

1. Click **Insert Chart** button .
   OR
   a. Click **I**nsert ............ `Alt`+`I`
   b. Click **N**ew Slide ............. `N`
   c. Select any layout with a chart object included.
   d. Double-click chart placeholder.
2. Enter data for chart in datasheet.
3. Click outside chart and datasheet to close datasheet and update chart on slide.
4. Return to chart for edits by double-clicking chart.

## Import Chart from Excel

1. Click **Insert Chart** button.
   OR
   a. Click **I**nsert ............ `Alt`+`I`
   b. Click **C**hart ..................... `H`
   c. Double-click chart placeholder on Chart slide.
2. Click **Import File** button.
3. In the **Look in** drop-down list, locate the folder where the Excel chart is stored.
4. Select Excel file to insert.
5. Click **O**pen ................. `Alt`+`O`
6. Select sheet you want to use from list.
7. Click **OK** ......................... `Enter`
8. Click outside chart and datasheet to close datasheet and update chart.
9. Return to datasheet for edits by double-clicking chart.

## View Datasheet

- Double-click chart.

## Close Datasheet

1. Click datasheet.
2. Click the **Close** button `X`.

## Change Chart Type

1. Double-click chart to display the datasheet.
2. Click down arrow on **Chart Type** button.
3. Select chart type from drop-down palette.

OR
1. Click **C**hart .................. `Alt`+`C`
2. Click Chart T**y**pe ................. `Y`
3. Select chart type.
4. Click **OK** ........................... `Enter`

## Show/Hide Gridlines and Show/Hide Legend

1. Double-click chart.
2. Click **Category Axis Gridlines** button.
   OR
   Click **Value Axis Gridlines** button.
   OR
   Click **Legend** button.

## Insert Table

1. Click **Insert Table** button and drag down and to the right to select number of cells to include in table.
   OR
   a. Click **I**nsert ............. `Alt`+`I`
   b. Click **N**ew Slide ............. `N`
   c. Select any layout with a table object included.
   d. Double-click table placeholder in the slide.
   e. Enter **Number of columns** .. `Alt`+`C`, *number*
   f. Enter **Number of rows** .... `Alt`+`R`, *number*
   g. Click **OK** ...................... `Enter`
2. Click in a cell to enter text.
3. Press **Tab** key to move insertion point from cell to cell.
4. Click outside of table to return to slide.
5. Return to table for edits by clicking table.

## Format Table

1. Click **Table and Borders** button if necessary to display Tables and Borders toolbar.
   OR
   Right-click the Standard toolbar and click Table and Borders.
2. Use Table and Borders toolbar to format table.
3. To format a border:
   a. Click from following buttons and make selection:
   - **Border Style**: choose solid, dashed, or dotted lines for table border.
   - **Border Width** `1 pt`: choose thickness of border line.
   - **Border Color**: choose color for borders.
   - **Outside Borders**: use Borders button to apply formatting to selected

borders: outside, inside, all, or individual.

b. Click the border to apply formatting, or draw lines to add new cells in the selected border settings.

4. Select cell(s) and then click from the following buttons.

- **Fill Color** [icon] : fill table with color. Select a color or fill effect.

- **Merge Cells** [icon] : joins two or more cells.

- **Split Cell** [icon] : divides cell in half.

- **Align Top** [icon] : aligns table text to top of cell.

- **Center Vertically** [icon] : aligns table text to vertical center of cell.

- **Align Bottom** [icon] : aligns table text to bottom of cell.

**Change Column Width/Row Height of Table**

1. Position mouse over border line.
2. Mouse pointer changes to double-headed arrow [icon] .
3. Click and drag border to move it.

# Exercise Directions

1. Start PowerPoint, if necessary.
2. Open [icon] **13Marvel** or [icon] **14Marvel**.
3. Save the file as **14Marvel**.
4. Add a new slide at the end of the presentation using the Title and Chart layout. Enter the slide title **Cleaning Agents**.
5. Insert a chart and delete the data from the datasheet. Enter the data as shown in Illustration A.
6. Close the datasheet and adjust the chart position or resize the chart so you can view all of the data.
7. Change the chart type to a 3-D Bar Chart.
8. Add value axis gridlines if they are not showing.
9. Add a new slide at the end of the presentation using the Title only slide layout. Enter the slide title **Best Sales**.
10. Insert a chart using the Chart button and import Sheet 1 of the file [icon] **14Marvel.xls** to the datasheet.
11. Close the datasheet and adjust the chart on the slide as shown in Illustration B.

    ✓ *Hint: You can resize the chart separately from the chart area placeholder. You can also move the legend.*

12. Add a new slide at the end of the presentation using the Title and Table slide layout. Add the slide title **Sales Analysis**.
13. Insert a 5 x 5 table and enter the text as shown in Illustration C. Do not press Enter after typing the chart information.
14. Format the text in the first row and the first column of the table as Arial Narrow, 18 points, and centered. Format the rest of the table text to 18 points and centered.
15. Resize the table to fit on the slide without overlapping other elements and adjust the row and column widths to fit the text.

    ✓ *To resize the table, click on the table to select it and drag the sizing handles.*

16. Spell check the presentation.
17. Print the slides as handouts with four per page.
18. Close the file and exit PowerPoint, saving all changes.

*Illustration C*

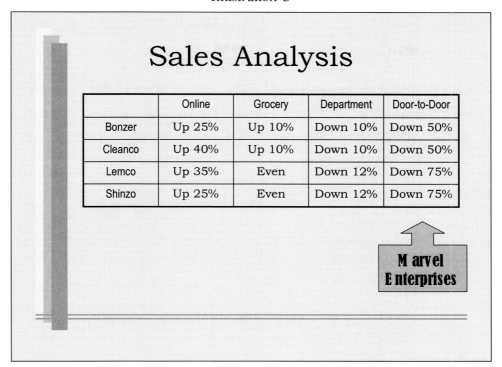

# On Your Own

1. Open **OPP11**, the charity presentation you last worked with in Exercise 11, or open 💿 **14DONATE**.

2. Save the file as **OPP14**.

3. Insert a chart slide illustrating where income for the organization came from last year. For example, it might come from donations, fundraising, grants, membership dues, and so on.

4. Insert another chart slide and import the Breakdown of Expenses pie chart from the 💿 **14CHART.xls** Excel workbook file.

5. Format the chart so it is easy to read and looks good on the slide.

6. Insert another slide showing a table listing the officers of the organization.

7. Save the presentation, close the presentation, and exit PowerPoint.

# Exercise 15

## On the Job

Share information between two applications to save yourself work and to provide consistency between documents. You might, for example, create a presentation in PowerPoint that contains information you can use in a report you're preparing in Word. Rather than type the information over again, export the text to Word.

The owner of Marvel Enterprises wants to create a report in Word for the partners of her company. Since she's not familiar with PowerPoint, you are going to help by creating several sample documents using various data and slides from the PowerPoint presentation. After she picks the one she wants, you can then explain to her how to complete her report.

## Terms

**Embed**  To insert a copy of an object from one application into another so that object in the second program is not affected by changes to the original object. Compare *Link*.

**Object**  Any text, table, picture, slide, spreadsheet, or data treated as a unit for formatting, copying, or moving.

**Link**  To insert a copy of an object from one application to another so that the copied object is automatically updated when it is changed in the original file.

**Export**  To send a copy of an object from one application to another application. The object may be embedded in the other application or it may be linked to the original.

## Notes

### Embed a PowerPoint Slide in a Word Document

- You can use simple copy and paste to **embed** a slide in a Word document to illustrate a report or enhance the document.

- The slide appears in Word in full color, with graphics and text.

- You can size and move the slide after it's copied to the Word document.

- Embedded **objects** are similar to **linked** objects except that the embedded object does not change when the original file changes.

### Export PowerPoint Slides and Notes to a Word Document

- You can send PowerPoint slides and notes to a Word document to enhance a report or other document.

- When you use the Send To command to export slides, miniatures of your slides appear in the Word document. You also can print blank lines with the slides for notes or comments.

- You can choose to link to the PowerPoint source document. Then, when you make a change to the presentation, the linked document in Word updates automatically.

## Export PowerPoint Text to a Word Document

- You can **export** PowerPoint text to a Word document to save yourself from retyping the text.
- You can choose to export only the text to the document, not graphics.

# Procedures

## Embed PowerPoint Slide in Word

1. Open presentation in PowerPoint.
2. Go to Slide Sorter view.
3. Select slide to copy.
4. Click **Copy** button 📋 .... Ctrl + C
5. Switch to Word document and position cursor.
6. Click **Paste** button 📋 .. Ctrl + V

   OR

   a. Click Paste **S**pecial ........ S
   b. Click **Paste link** ............. L
   c. Click **OK** ...................... Enter

## Export PowerPoint Slides and Notes to Word

1. Open presentation in PowerPoint.
2. Click **File** ..................... Alt + F
3. Click **Send To** ..................... D
4. Click **Microsoft Word** ......... W
5. Select one of the following options for Page layout in Microsoft Word.
   - ✓ The images beside each option indicate the Page layout.

- **Notes next to slides**..... N
  - ✓ The presentation is inserted into a new Word document in a three-column table. The slide number appears in the left column, the slide in the center column, and any notes in the right column.
- **Blank lines next to slides** ........................ A
  - ✓ The presentation is inserted into a new Word document in a three-column table. The right column contains blank lines for notes or comments.
- **Notes below slides** ...... B
  - ✓ The presentation is inserted into a new Word document with one slide per Word page. The slide is preceded by its number in the upper left and any notes are displayed below the slide image.
- **Blank lines below slides** ................. K
  - ✓ The presentation is inserted into a new Word document with one slide per Word page with blank lines under each slide for notes or comments.
- **Outline only** .................. O
  - ✓ Only the text of the presentation is inserted into a new Word document.

6. For all options except Outline only, select either:
   - **Paste** .................... Alt + P
   - **Paste link** ............. Alt + I
7. Click **OK** .......................... Enter
8. Save the Word document.

## Export PowerPoint Outline to Word

1. Open presentation in PowerPoint.
2. Click **File** ..................... Alt + F
3. Click **Save As** ...................... A
4. Click **Save as type** ..... Alt + T
5. Select **Outline/RTF (*.rtf)**.
6. Click **Save** ................... Alt + S
7. Switch to Word.
8. Click **File** ..................... Alt + F
9. Click **Open** ......................... O
10. Click **Files of type** ...... Alt + T
11. Select **Rich Text Format (*.rtf)**.
12. Select the file.
13. Click **Open** ................. Alt + O

OR

1. Open presentation in PowerPoint.
2. Click **File** ..................... Alt + F
3. Click **Send To** ..................... D
4. Click **Microsoft Word**.......... W
5. Select **Outline only** ............. O

# Exercise Directions

1. Start PowerPoint, if necessary.

2. Open ⌨14Marvel or 💿15Marvel.

3. Save it as **15Marvel**.

4. In Slide Sorter view, copy slide 5 and paste it into a new Word document. Press Enter in the Word document to leave space at the top of the page. Enter the text you see in Illustration A to show how the slide and text look together in a document.

5. Select the slide and center it.

   ✓ *Hint: you can use View, Print Layout in Word or check the results in Print Preview if you're not sure of the position of the slide.*

6. Save the document in Word as **15Marvel.doc**. Print the document and close it.

7. In PowerPoint, using the same presentation, export the file to a new Word document using the Send To command. Show the slides next to notes, as shown in Illustrations B, C, and D.

8. Save the document as **15Marvel2.doc**. Print the document and close it.

9. In PowerPoint, using the same presentation, save the file as an Outline/RTF file named **15Marvel3.rtf**. Switch to Word and open that file into a new Word document.

   ✓ *Note: Only the text saves in Outline/RTF format. The tables, charts, and organization charts do not save to the Word document.*

10. Save the file as **15Marvel3.doc**. Print the document and close it. Exit Word.

11. Close the file and exit PowerPoint, saving all changes.

*Illustration A*

*Illustration B*

*Illustration C*

*Illustration D*

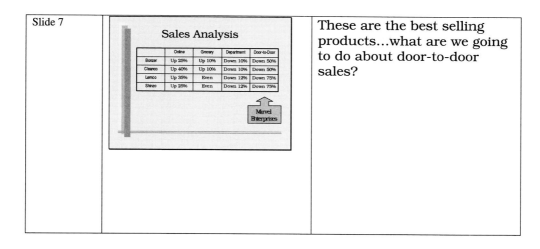

Slide 7

Sales Analysis

These are the best selling products...what are we going to do about door-to-door sales?

## On Your Own

1. Open **OPP14**, the presentation you were working with in Exercise 14, or open ⊙ **15DONATE**.

2. Save the file as **OPP15**.

3. Start Word, create a new document, and type a letter to the president of your organization explaining the presentation you have created, or open the document ⊙ **15LETTER**.

4. Save the Word document as **OPP15-2.doc**.

5. Select the Income chart in the **OPP15** presentation, and paste it at the end of the **OPP15-2.doc** document.

6. Export the entire presentation to a new Word document, including blank lines for notes.

7. Save the document as **OPP15-3.doc**.

8. Save all open Word documents, close them, and exit Word.

9. Save the PowerPoint presentation, close it, and exit PowerPoint.

# Exercise 16

Although the owner of Marvel Enterprises is pleased with your work so far, she would like another presentation design to choose from. She's also given you some additional information to use for this presentation. In this exercise, you will create one more presentation for Marvel Enterprises.

## Exercise Directions

1. Start PowerPoint, if necessary.

2. Create a new blank presentation.

3. Save the file as **16Marvel**.

4. Using the slide master, create a new presentation background for Marvel Enterprises. Apply a color scheme, clip art, AutoShapes, or other design elements to make it attractive. Make sure that you insert at least one clip art graphic and that you apply a custom color scheme or background colors.

   ✓ Hint: The background for the illustration is changed in the Background dialog box accessed by choosing Format, Background; instead of picking a color, try Fill Effects in the Background fill drop-down list.

5. Create a logo for Marvel Enterprises and place it on the slide master. Combine a clip art image or an AutoShape with a text box to create the logo to fit in the corner of the slide as shown in Illustration A.

6. Change all Arial fonts on the slide master to Times New Roman or any other serif font. Return to Normal view.

7. On the title slide, enter the text as shown in Illustration A. Select the title text and enlarge it to 48 points and left align the title text.

8. Show the rulers and use tabs to indent the subtitle text as shown.

9. Add a slide based on the Title and Table slide layout. Enter the text as shown in Illustration B.

10. Resize the cells to fit the text as shown in Illustration B. Center the text in the heading row both horizontally and vertically. Resize the table on the slide if necessary.

11. Add a Bulleted List slide and enter the text as shown in Illustration C.

12. Change the bullet characters to any desired shape. Increase the paragraph spacing in the bullet text.

    ✓ Hint: Use Wingdings characters for the larger bullets.

13. Add a fourth slide and use the Title Only slide layout. Add the title **Product Sales**.

14. Insert a bar chart using the following data:

|          | Qtr 1 | Qtr 2 | Qtr 3 | Qtr 4 |
|----------|-------|-------|-------|-------|
| **Bonzer**  | 2349  | 2400  | 2300  | 2250  |
| **Cleanco** | 3030  | 3230  | 3123  | 3144  |
| **Lemco**   | 1800  | 1989  | 1956  | 2000  |

15. Adjust the position of the chart on the slide to fit the space without overlapping other slide items.

16. Change the chart type, as shown in Illustration D.

17. Send the PowerPoint presentation to Word with blank lines below the slides for notes to be added.

18. Spell check the presentation.

19. Save the file as **16Marvel.doc** and print it.

20. Close the file and exit PowerPoint.

*Illustration A*

# Marvel Enterprises

Products for your future…

Products for your life…

Products for you…

*Illustration B*

# Alternate Product Uses

|  | Original | New | Improved | Best Yet |
|---|---|---|---|---|
| **Bonzer** | Floor wax | Car wax | Window polisher | Siding cleaner |
| **Cleanco** | Tub cleanser | Tile cleanser | Floor cleanser | Window cleaner |
| **Lemco** | Dish detergent | Car cleaner | Dog wash | Bath soap |
| **Shinzo** | Window cleaner | Tile cleaner | Floor cleaner | Car cleaner |

*Illustration C*

# Product Benefits

➢ All of our products are environmentally safe.

➢ Our products are concentrated, so you can add water to extend their usefulness.

➢ All of our products have multiple uses.

➢ You can order our products from a catalog, from our Web page, or from your local grocery store.

*Illustration D*

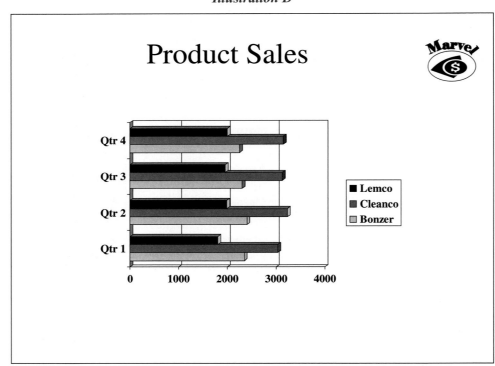

# Exercise 17

## Skills Covered:

◆ **Check Slides for Style and Consistency** ◆ **Show a Presentation**
◆ **Add Transitions** ◆ **Add Sound** ◆ **Advance Slide** ◆ **Hide Slides**

## On the Job

When you show your presentation, you can add certain elements to make it more interesting. You might want to show a presentation automatically, in which case you can use timings to give the audience the right amount of time to read each slide. Transitions and sound can be set to play as each slide changes into the next.

The owner of Marvel Enterprises informed you that she will present the slide show to a large audience. She wants automatic timings, although she also wants the capability to advance the slides manually. Additionally, she wants transitions and sounds. In this exercise, you will prepare the custom presentation you created for viewing.

## Terms

**Kiosk** A computerized machine that displays continuously running presentations, usually found in visitors' centers, trade shows, or conventions.

**Transitions** The visual effect used when one slide moves off of the screen and another moves onto the screen.

**Sound clip** Recorded audio clips that you can play automatically as a slide changes from one to the next or by clicking a sound button on the slide.

**Advance Slide timing** A setting that controls the amount of time a slide displays on the screen.

## Notes

### Check Slides for Style and Consistency

■ You can set PowerPoint to check your slides as you create them for style and consistency, such as the number of font types and the minimum font sizes.

■ PowerPoint displays a light bulb to warn you of errors. Click the light bulb to read suggestions.

■ You can change the style items that PowerPoint checks or turn the Check style feature off.

### Show a Presentation

■ You can show a presentation on your computer screen, project it on a larger screen, or show it using a **kiosk**.

■ You can present a slide show automatically or manually when you click the mouse.

■ You can also run a show continuously.

■ Each slide displayed in the slide show fills the entire computer screen.

■ PowerPoint displays a black screen with the words *End of slide show* at the end of the presentation.

### Add Transitions

■ PowerPoint provides **transitions** that you can use to make the slide show more interesting.

■ You can apply transitions in any view. However, Slide Sorter view is the easiest because it provides several transition tools on its toolbar and you can apply transitions to several slides at once.

- Apply an animation effect to one slide by selecting the effect. Apply to all slides by clicking the Apply to All Slides button on the Slide Transition Task Pane.

*Slide Sorter toolbar*

Hide slide · Summary Slide · Slide Transition · Rehearse Timings · Speaker Notes

- To access all of the transition options at once, open the Slide Transition Task Pane.

*Slide Transition Task Pane*

- You can preview transitions before you apply them and you can control the speed of each transition from the Slide Transition Task Pane.

- Slides with transitions are marked by a Slide Transition icon in Slide Sorter view. You can click the icon to preview the transition.

*Slide with transition*

Slide Transition icon

- If you use too many different transitions, the viewer may find it distracting.

## Add Sound

- Use a **sound clip** in your presentations to add interest and emphasis.

- You can add any sound file to a slide. Sound files often have a .wav or .mid extension. You can insert a sound from Microsoft's Clip Gallery or from any file on your computer. You can even record your own sounds.

- Sound files play when you move from one slide to another, or when you click the sound button on the slide.

- You can also play CD tracks or recorded narration in a slide show. See Exercise 19 for information.

## Advance Slide

- If you do not want to advance slides manually, by mouse clicks in a presentation, you can have PowerPoint advance each slide automatically.

- **Advance Slide timing** defines the amount of time a slide is on the screen before PowerPoint automatically advances to the next slide.

- You can set Advance Slide timing in the Slide Transition Task Pane for individual slides or for all slides in a presentation. Set advance slide timing in seconds or minutes and seconds.

- Even if you set advance timings for your slides, you can also choose to advance the slide manually.

- PowerPoint provides a play feature you can use to set and check advance slide timings.

- The advance slide timing for each slide is indicated in Slide Sorter view by a number below each slide.

*Slide with advance slide timing*

☆ **03:00**　　　　　　6

## Hide Slides

■ You can hide slides in your presentation so they do not show when you run the slide show. For example, you might hide some slides to shorten the presentation, or hide slides that don't apply to a specific audience.

■ Hidden slides remain in the file and can be displayed again at any time.

■ PowerPoint places an indicator under a hidden slide in Slide Sorter view.

*Hidden slide*

☆ **00:10**　　　　　　**3**

Hidden slide indicator

# Procedures

## Set Options for Style and Consistency

1. Click **Tools** .................. Alt + T
2. Click **Options** ...................... O
3. Click **Spelling and Style** tab ..................... Ctrl + Tab
4. Click **Check style** .............. C
5. Click **Style Options** button Style Options... .... Alt + T
6. Make necessary changes in Style Options dialog box.
7. Click **OK** ........................... Enter
8. Click **OK** again ................ Enter

## Start Slide Show *(F5)*

1. Click **Slide Show** button 🖳.
   OR
   a. Click **Slide Show** .......... D
   b. Click **View Show** .......... V
2. Press Page Down to advance to next slide. Press Page Up to go to previous slide.
   OR
   Click mouse to advance slide show.
3. Click the page to end the show.
   OR

Click **Esc** to end slide show ......................... Esc
OR
Right-click and select **End Show** .......................... S

## Add Transitions

1. Display slide to add transition effect in Normal view.
   OR
   Select one or multiple slides to affect in Slide Sorter.
2. Click **Slide Show** ........ Alt + D
3. Click **Slide Transition** ........ T
4. Select a transition in the **Apply to selected slides** list.
5. Click modify transition speed:
   • **Slow**
   • **Medium**
   • **Fast**
6. Click Apply to All Slides if you want the transition to apply to more than the selected slide.

## Add Transition Effect from Slide Sorter Toolbar

1. Switch to Slide Sorter view.
2. Select slide or slides to affect.
3. Select options from Slide Transition Task Pane.

## Add Sound

1. Select slide or slides to affect.
2. Click **Slide Show** ........ Alt + D
3. Click **Slide Transition** ......... T
4. Select a sound in the **Modify Transition** Sound drop-down list.
5. Click **Loop until next sound** for continuous sound.
6. Click Apply to All Slides if you want the sound to apply to more than the selected slide.

## Insert Sound Objects

1. Display slide in Normal view.
2. Click **Insert** ................. Alt + I
3. Click **Movies and Sound** .... V
4. Click one of the following:
   • **Sound from Media Gallery** ............... S
   • **Sound from file** ............ N
5. Select sound.
6. Click **OK** ........................... Enter
7. Choose **Yes** to play sound automatically or **No** to play sound when you click **Sound** button 🔊.

## Add Advance Slide Timings

1. Switch to Slide Sorter view.

**391**

2. Select a slide to apply timing to or select multiple slides by pressing the **Shift** key as you click the slides.
3. Click **Sli_de Show** ........ **Alt**+**D**
4. Click **Slide _Transition** ........ **T**
5. In **Advance slide**, click **Automatically after.**
6. Enter time in spin box.
7. Click **On mouse click** to add manual advance as option.
8. Click [Apply to All Slides] if you want the timing to apply to all slides.

### Check Timings

1. In Slide Sorter view, click **Rehearse Timings** button ⌨️.
2. Walk through the presentation, reading slide contents and any comments you intend to make in the presentation.
3. Advance from slide to slide as you intend to during an actual presentation.
4. When you're done, press **Esc** .......................... **Esc**
5. PowerPoint asks if you wish to save these timings. Select **Yes** to save them.

### Hide Slide

1. Switch to Slide Sorter view.
2. Select slide to hide.
3. Click **Hide Slide** button 🔲.
4. Click **Hide Slide** button 🔲 a second time to redisplay hidden slide.

### Remove Slide Transition.

1. Click the slide.
2. Display the Slide Transition Task Pane.
3. Click **No Transition** in the **Apply to selected slides** list.

# Exercise Directions

1. Start PowerPoint, if necessary.
2. Open 💾**15Marvel** or 💿**17Marvel**.
3. Save the file as **17Marvel**.
4. Check the presentation for any spelling errors or style inconsistencies.
5. Show the presentation as a slide show.
6. Switch to Slide Sorter view.
7. Apply the Random Transition effect to all slides using a slow speed. Show the presentation.
8. Apply one or two transitions to the entire slide show.
9. Rehearse the show to set transition timings. As you rehearse, read each slide. Allow enough time for the speaker to discuss the topics.

10. After rehearsal, in slide 2, set the timing to 2 minutes. On slides 5, 6, and 7, set the timing to 3 minutes.
11. Hide slides 3 and 4.
12. Run the presentation.
13. Add transition sounds to the slides. You can add one sound to all slides or use different sounds for multiple slides.
   ✓ *Your computer may not be equipped to play sound.*
14. Spell check the slide presentation.
15. Print the presentation.
16. Show the slide presentation.
17. Close the file and exit PowerPoint, saving all changes.

# On Your Own

1. Open **OPP15**, the presentation for the charity that you last used in Exercise 15, or open 💿**17DONATE**.
2. Save the file as **OPP17**.
3. Run the slide show.
4. Set the slide show to run automatically with an interval of 5 seconds.

5. Add a dissolve transition effect to all slides at a medium speed.
6. Add the sound of applause to the title slide and the final slide.
7. Run the slide show again.
8. Save the presentation, close it, and close PowerPoint.

# Exercise 18

## Skills Covered:

### ◆ Animate Text and Objects ◆ Preset Animation
### ◆ Custom Animation

## On the Job

Animate text and objects to add interest and emphasis to certain slides and items in the presentation. Animate a bulleted list of topics that build in importance, for example, with timed pauses to catch the audience's attention.

The owner of Marvel Enterprises liked your presentation but she wants more movement and some sound added for emphasis. The owner also asks that you prepare a second presentation with sound and movement, so she has a choice. In this exercise, you will add animation to the custom presentation you created.

## Terms

**Animate** To apply movement to text or an object. For example, text might fly onto the screen from the left or drop in from above.

**Preset animation** Several types of movements included in PowerPoint that you can apply quickly and easily.

## Notes

### Animate Text and Objects

- You can **animate** text on slides to add interest to your presentation or to emphasize special points.

- You can make animated text appear one letter or one paragraph at a time, for example. Or, you can animate text to fly in or bounce in, for example.

- You can use PowerPoint's **preset animations** or design your own custom animations.

- You can preview animations and adjust timing before you show the presentation.

- Apply an animation effect to one slide by selecting the effect. Apply to all slides by clicking the Apply to All Slides button in the Animation Schemes Task Pane.

*Slide Design - Animation Schemes Task Pane*

- Use the Animation Schemes Task Pane to apply preset animation effects quickly and preview those effects.

## Preset Animation

- PowerPoint supplies Subtle, Moderate, and Exciting animation schemes you can apply to your slides.

- Use preset animations on bulleted lists, titles, subtitles, and other text.

- You can apply preset animations from Normal or Slide Sorter view using the Animation Schemes Task Pane.

- You can click AutoPreview to preview an animation when you select it from the Animation Scheme list box.

## Custom Animation

- Use the Custom Animation Task Pane to set animation effects, direction, property and speed for text in a slide.

- You can apply custom animations to tables, charts, and organization charts. You can also apply custom animations to lines, shapes, clip art, and AutoShapes.

*Custom Animation Task Pane*

- You can choose the order in which objects and text appear on a slide.

*Custom animation order*

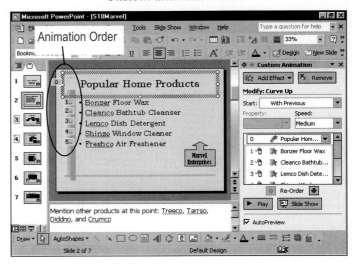

- You can also apply various properties to the animations. For example, you can choose the amount of spin or the direction of a checkerboard effect.

- You can set the speed of the animation.

- You can set details for each effect applied to bullet text, for example.

*Set details for single animations*

- You can set effect details, such as direction or size. Most effects also include sound enhancements.

*Set effect details*

■ You can set timing details, such as speed, delay, or repeat, for each effect.

*Set timing details*

■ You can set details for text animation, such as text grouping and order of the effect.

*Set text animation details*

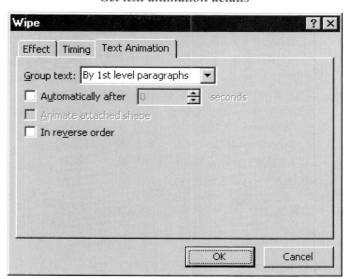

# Procedures

**Display Animations Effects Task Pane**

1. Click **Slide Show** ................. D
2. Click **Animation Schemes**. C

**Preset Animation**

1. In Normal or Slide Sorter view, display slide.
2. Click in text or object to be animated.

3. Click desired animation effect in Animation Schemes Task Pane.

OR

Click **Apply to All Slides**.

**Preview Animations**

● Click **Animation Preview** button ☆.

OR

1. Open Animation Schemes Task Pane.

2. Click **Play**.

**Custom Animation**

1. In Normal view, display slide.
2. Click the item to be animated.
3. Click **Slide Show** ........ Alt + D
4. Click **Custom Animation** .... M
5. Click **Add Effect** button

☆ Add Effect ▼ .

6. Choose appropriate command:
   - **Entrance** ........................ E
   - **Emphasis** ...................... M
   - **Exit** ................................ X
   - **Motion Paths** ................. P
7. Choose effect you want to apply.
8. Click **Start** drop-down arrow. Choose appropriate option:
   - **On Click**
   - **With Previous**
   - **After Previous**
9. Click the property drop-down arrow and choose appropriate option.

10. Click **Speed**. Choose appropriate option:
    - **Very Slow**
    - **Slow**
    - **Medium**
    - **Fast**
    - **Very Fast**
11. Click **Close** button X to close the Task Pane.

### Set Effect Details

1. Open the Custom Animation Task Pane.
2. Click the effect in the Effects list.
3. Click the drop-down arrow.
4. Click **Effect Options** ........... E

5. Click the appropriate tab:
   - **Effect**
   - **Timing**
   - **Text Animation**
6. Set the details.
7. Click **OK** .......................... Enter

### Turn Animation Off

1. Select text or object from which to remove animation.
2. Open Animation Schemes Task Pane.
3. Click No Animation in the Apply to selected slides list box.

# Exercise Directions

1. Start PowerPoint, if necessary.
2. Open 🖳**17Marvel** or 💿**18Marvel**.
3. Save the file as **18Marvel**.
4. Switch to Slide Sorter view.
5. Remove all transition effects from all slides; keep the timings.
6. Switch to Normal view.
7. In the first slide, select the title text and apply the preset animation Big Title (an Exciting animation).
8. Remove Hide Slide from slides 3 and 4.
9. Select slide 3 and apply the Faded zoom animation.
10. Select slide 4 and apply Faded Zoom.
11. Switch to slide 2.
12. Apply the following custom animation:
    - Display the title first, using any entrance effect.
    - Display the bulleted text with applause and by word.
13. Switch to slide 6 and apply any custom Emphasis effect to the chart. Repeat the effect 3 times.
    - ✓ Hint: Use the Timing tab to set the details of the effect.

14. Switch to slide 7 and apply any custom exit effect to the table.
15. Switch to Slide Sorter view.
16. Play the effects on each slide and make any adjustments you think necessary.
    - ✓ Illustration A shows that you do not see transitions and animations in this view.
17. Spell check the presentation.
18. Print the presentation.
19. Close the file, saving all changes.
20. Open 🖳**16Marvel** or 💿**18Marvel2**.
21. Save the file as **18Marvel2**.
22. Apply transitions, preset animations, timings, and custom animations to the show any way you'd like.
23. Preview the slide show and make any adjustments.
24. Close the file and exit PowerPoint, saving all changes.

*Illustration A*

# On Your Own

1. Open **OPP17**, the presentation you used in the On Your Own section of Exercise 17, or open ⊚ **18DONATE**.

2. Save the file as **OPP18**.

3. Display the Animation Schemes Task Pane.

4. Apply an animation scheme to the AutoShape on the title slide. (If you do not have an AutoShape on the title slide, use one on a different slide or create one.)

5. Animate the slide text for all slides with bullet lists.

6. Use Custom Animation to animate one of the charts in the presentation.

7. Run the presentation.

8. Save the presentation, close it, and exit PowerPoint.

# Exercise 19

## Skills Covered:

◆ **Annotations** ◆ **Pause and Resume Show**
◆ **Add Music** ◆ **Add a Movie**

## On the Job

Use annotations during a slide show to highlight certain information or items. For example, you can underline points to emphasize or check off topics as you discuss them. For a really dynamic presentation, you can add music or movie clips. Adding a limited amount of multimedia to a presentation can make it more interesting and entertaining.

The owner of Marvel Enterprises is pleased with the content of the presentation, but she wants you to add some pizzazz to it. She is planning on showing the presentation to a new group of investors and wants to really impress them.

## Terms

**Annotation feature** A method of writing or marking on the slide during a presentation.

## Notes

### Annotations

- You can add annotations such as writing or drawing to a slide during a slide show.
- When you use the **annotation feature**, the mouse becomes a pen.
- You may want to annotate a chart or data in a table, for instance, as you present a slide show.
- Annotations do not change the slide; they only appear during the presentation.
- PowerPoint suspends automatic timings while you use the annotations feature.
- You can choose different colors to use for the pen.

### Pause and Resume Show

- You can pause a slide show when you want to discuss elements in the show. When you are ready, you can resume the show.

### Add Music

- You can add music clips to your presentation to make it more interesting or to emphasize a slide.
- Your computer must have speakers and a sound card to play music during the presentation.
- You might want music to play in the background as the viewer reads the slide or as you talk.
- Insert a music clip as a slide object in Normal view.
- A music clip is indicated by a sound button .
- You can choose to have the music play when you advance to the slide containing the clip or when you click its icon.
- You can insert a music file, CD track, or music from Microsoft's Clip Gallery.
- Microsoft's Windows\Media folder often includes sounds, music, and other clips for you to use with a presentation. You can also find additional sound files on the Internet.

## Add a Movie

- You can insert movie clips or videos into a presentation.
- Insert a movie clip in Normal view.

- You can choose to have the video begin when you advance to the slide containing the object or to play when you click the movie icon.
- Movies are often files ending with an .avi, .mpe, or .mpg extension.

# Procedures

### Add Annotations

1. Show the presentation.
2. Click the shortcut menu 🖊️ 📐 that appears in the lower-left corner of the screen.
3. Click **P**ointer Options ........ O
4. Click **P**en ........................... P
   OR
   Press **Ctrl+P** .............. Ctrl + P

### Erase Annotations

- Press **E** on keyboard ........... E
OR
1. Right-click the slide or click the Annotation icon.
2. Click **S**creen ...................... S
3. Click **E**rase Pen ................. E

### Change Pen Color

1. Click the shortcut menu 🖊️ 📐 that appears in the lower-left corner of the screen.
2. Click **P**ointer Options ........ O
3. Click Pen **C**olor .................. C
4. Click one of the following:
   - **Black**............................ B
   - **White** ........................... W
   - **Red** .............................. R
   - **Green**........................... G
   - **B**lue .............................. L
   - **C**yan ............................. C
   - **M**agenta........................ M
   - **Y**ellow........................... Y
   - **Gr**ey ............................. E
   - **Re**set ........................... S

### Pause Show

1. Right-click the screen.
2. Click **S**creen ...................... C
3. Click **P**ause ...................... S

### Resume Show

1. Right-click the screen.
2. Click **S**creen ...................... C
3. Click **R**esume .................... S

### Turn Off Annotation Feature

1. During slide show, right-click any slide.
2. Click **P**ointer Options ........ O
3. Click **A**utomatic ................. U
OR
- Press **Esc**.......................... Esc

### Add Sound

Insert sounds and movies in Normal view.
1. Select slide with which to associate music.
2. Click **I**nsert ................. Alt + I
3. Click **Mo**vies and Sounds... V
4. Click one of the following:
   - **S**ound from Gallery...... S
   - **Sou**nd from File........... N
   - Play **C**D Audio Track.... C
5. Select a sound and click **OK**............................. Enter
6. Click **Yes** to play music automatically when slide advances.
   OR
   Click **No** to have music play when you click Sound button.

### Add Movie

1. Open slide presentation.
2. Select slide with which to associate video clip.
3. Click **I**nsert ................. Alt + I
4. Click **Mo**vies and Sounds....V
5. Click one of the following:
   - **Movie from Media Gallery**................M
   - **Movie from File** ............F
6. Choose file to add.
7. Click **OK**.......................... Enter
8. Click **Yes** to have movie play automatically in the slide show or **No** to have it played when you click it.

# Exercise Directions

1. Start PowerPoint, if necessary.
2. Open ⌨18Marvel or 💿19Marvel.
3. Save the file as **19Marvel**.
4. Run the slide show. On the second slide, activate the annotation feature and circle **Bonzer Floor Wax** with the pen. Change the color of the pen and draw an arrow to point to **Shinzo Window Cleaner**. Erase the annotations.
5. On slide 5, draw a star beside the first quarter in the chart.
6. On slide 6, circle **Mary's** name in the legend. Erase the annotations.
7. Move to slide 7 and pause the show.
8. Resume the show and end it.
9. In Slide view, insert a Title Only slide at the end of the presentation.
10. Insert the title **Marvel Enterprises Rocks**.
11. Insert a sound or movie clip. Have the sound or movie play automatically in the slide show.
12. Size the sound or movie clip as you would size any type of object.
13. Show the presentation.
14. Close the file and exit PowerPoint, saving all changes.

# On Your Own

1. Open **OPP18**, the presentation you used in the On Your Own section of Exercise 18, or open 💿**19DONATE**.
2. Save the file as **OPP19**.
3. Add a music clip or a video clip to one or more of the slides.
4. Run the slide show. Stop the show to annotate one of the slides. For example, circle important text.
5. Run the presentation.
6. Save the presentation, close it, and exit PowerPoint.

# Exercise 20

## Skills Covered:

◆ **Create Notes Pages and Handouts**
◆ **Notes Master and Handout Master** ◆ **Pack and Go**
◆ **Meeting Minder** ◆ **Incorporate Meeting Feedback**

## On the Job

PowerPoint provides ways for you to maximize your presentations. You can distribute handouts with a presentation, for example. Or, you can also pack up your presentation to display it on another computer. You can even show a presentation to different people on different computers during an online meeting.

The owner of Marvel Enterprises wants you to create notes pages and handouts of a presentation for her audience. She also needs the presentation saved to a disk so she can show it on a computer that doesn't have PowerPoint. Finally, the owner has asked you to show her how to take notes during an online presentation so she can create a report of the notes after the presentation.

## Terms

**Notes** Comments added to the presentation that can be for the speaker's eyes only.

**Handouts** Printed copies of the presentation for the audience to refer to during and after the slide show.

**Pack and Go** A feature that lets you save the presentation to a floppy disk and then show it on a computer that doesn't have PowerPoint loaded.

## Notes

### Create Notes Pages and Handouts

- **Notes** help you remember key points about each slide in the presentation.

- You can enter speaker's notes for a slide in the Notes pane in Normal view, or in a placeholder below the slide in Notes Page view.

- You can then print your presentation in Notes Page format for reference while giving a presentation or to hand out to the audience.

- You can also print and hand out notes pages with a blank notes' area, so that audience members can take their own notes in the empty placeholders.

- You can give the audience **handouts** of the presentation for future reference.

- Printed handouts do not show notes.

### Notes Master and Handout Master

- You can add text, pictures, and other information to a notes or handout master.

*Notes Master view*

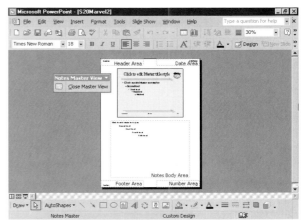

401

## *Handout Master view*

- Anything added to a master appears in all notes or handouts you print.

- Either master can list your company logo, the date, and your phone number, for instance.

- You can enter a header or footer, page numbers, and dates in a master as well.

## Pack and Go

- Use the **Pack and Go** Wizard when you want to run a slide show on another computer.

- If the computer you plan to run the packed show on doesn't have PowerPoint, you can include the Viewer in the Pack and Go file.

- The Viewer is a program that lets you run a PowerPoint slide show without the use of PowerPoint.

- The Pack and Go Wizard guides you through saving the presentation and Viewer.

- You can unpack the slide show on any PC.

### *Pack and Go Wizard*

## Meeting Minder

- You can use the Meeting Minder to take notes during a slide show.

### *Meeting Minder dialog box*

- During an online meeting, anyone can take notes in the Meeting Minder and everyone can view those notes while online.

- After the slide show, you can view the notes and comments in the Meeting Minder.

## Incorporate Meeting Feedback

- During a slide show, you can enter action items in the Meeting Minder as a way of involving online participants. Action items direct the participants to complete tasks related to the meeting.

- An action item may be a task you want someone to complete, such as performing research on a meeting topic and reporting back to the group.

### *Meeting Minder dialog box: Action Items tab*

- After the show, you can e-mail the interested parties by exporting the action item.

- PowerPoint also creates a slide at the end of the presentation on which you can store the action items so you can discuss them with your audience.

- You can also send meeting minutes and action items to Word to use in a report or other document.

# Procedures

### Create Notes Pages

- Enter notes in Notes pane in Normal view.

OR

1. Click **View** ................ `Alt`+`V`
2. Click **Notes Page** ............... `P`
3. Click in notes placeholder and enter notes.

### Print Notes Pages *(Ctrl+P)*

1. Click **File** ................ `Alt`+`F`
2. Click **Print** ........................... `P`
3. Click **Notes Pages** in **Print what** drop-down list.
4. Click **OK** ........................... `Enter`

### Create Handouts *(Ctrl+P)*

1. Click **File** ................ `Alt`+`F`
2. Click **Print** ........................... `P`
3. In the **Print what** drop-down list, click **Handouts**.
4. In **Slides per page** drop-down list, choose 2, 3, 4, 6, or 9 ............... `Alt`+`R`
5. Choose slide order:
   - **Horizontal** .............. `Alt`+`Z`
   - **Vertical** .................. `Alt`+`V`
6. Click **OK** ........................... `Enter`

### Edit Notes or Handout Master

1. Click **View** ................ `Alt`+`V`
2. Click **Master** ........................ `M`
3. Click **Notes master** ............ `N`

   OR

   Click **Handout master** ....... `D`
4. Enter any text or graphic you want to display on all notes or handouts.
5. Click **Close Master View** button `Close Master View`.

### Pack and Go

1. Open presentation.
2. Click **File** ..................... `Alt`+`F`
3. Click **Pack and Go** .............. `K`
4. Follow directions in Pack and Go Wizard.
5. Unpack show and run it to check for errors.

   OR

   Click the **Close** button `X` in the Master toolbar.

### Unpack Presentation

1. Insert floppy disk in computer.
2. Open Windows Explorer and locate the pack and go file.
3. Double-click **Pngsetup** on floppy disk.
4. Enter hard drive destination in which to unpack presentation.
   - ✓ Note: Use an empty folder on the hard drive. Pack and Go overwrites everything in the folder.
5. Click **Yes** to run unpacked show.

   OR

   Click **No** to wait to run show.

### Show Presentation

1. Open destination folder in Explorer.
2. Right-click presentation.
3. Click **Show**.

### Take Notes during Slide Show

1. Right-click slide in Slide Show view.
2. Click **Meeting Minder** ......... `T`
3. Enter notes or comments.
4. Click **OK** ........................ `Enter`

### Read or Enter Notes after Presentation

1. Click **Tools** ................. `Alt`+`T`
2. Click **Meeting Minder** ........ `T`

### Create Action Items in Meeting Minder

1. During slide show, right-click slide.

   OR

   After show,
   click **Tools** ................... `Alt`+`T`
2. Click **Meeting Minder** ........ `T`
3. Click **Action Items** tab.
4. Enter appropriate text.
5. Click **Add** .................... `Alt`+`A`
6. Click **Export** ............... `Alt`+`E`
7. Click **Post action items to Microsoft Outlook** ............. `P`

   OR

   Click **Send meeting minutes and action items to Microsoft Word** ................................... `S`
8. Click **Export Now** ............... `E`

# Exercise Directions

1. Start PowerPoint, if necessary.

2. Open ⌨ **18Marvel2** or 💿 **20Marvel2**.

3. Save the file as **20Marvel2**.

4. Switch to Normal view and select the first slide. Add the following notes in the Notes pane:

   **Mention research and development of future products**.

5. View notes pages. Print the notes page for slide one.

6. Print as handouts with 4 per page.

7. Go to the Notes Master view and add a header and date. Use your name as the header and the month and year as the date as shown in Illustration A. Print all slides as notes pages.

8. Go to the slides master and copy the logo plus logo text.

9. Switch to the handout master and copy the logo and text to the top middle of the page. Add the following footer **Marvel Enterprises**, as shown in Illustration B.

10. Print the handout for the slide show.

11. Run the presentation. During the presentation, open the Meeting Minder and enter the following notes in the meeting minutes:

    **Suggestions:**

    **Personal care products such as foot pumice, foot powders, foot creams and lotions**.

    **Dog care products? Shampoo and dips?**

12. In Normal view, open the Meeting Minder and add the following to the Action Items tab:

    **Research Dog Products**

    **Timothy**

    **6-01**

    and

    **Research Foot Care Products**

    **Debbie**

    **6-01**

    ✓ *Hint: Type the first action item, click the Add button. Type the second action item, click the Add button.*

13. Export the action items and meeting minutes to Word and print the Word document.

14. Save the document as **20Marvel2.rtf**.

15. Close the Word document and the file. Return to PowerPoint.

16. Save the file.

17. Pack the presentation to a floppy disk.

    ✓ *Hint: Embed the fonts. Include the Viewer only if you plan to show the presentation on a computer that does not have PowerPoint installed.*

18. Close PowerPoint.

19. Unpack the presentation and run it to make sure it works.

*Illustration A*

*Illustration B*

# On Your Own

1. Open **OPP19**, the presentation you used in Exercise 19, or open 💿 **20DONATE**.

2. Save the file as **OPP20**.

3. Type notes for at least three slides.

4. Open the handouts master.

5. Add your name, the date, and the page number to the notes master and the handouts master.

6. Insert a clip art image on the handouts master.

7. Set formatting options as desired.

8. Insert a different clip art image on the notes master.

9. Set formatting options as desired.

10. Create notes and handouts for the presentation and print them.

11. Save the presentation, close it, and exit PowerPoint.

# Exercise 21

## Skills Covered:

### ◆ Set Up a Presentation ◆ Set Up Show Dialog Box Options

## On the Job

Set up a slide show so you can use it in different situations. For example, if you run a slide show on a kiosk, you will want the show to run continuously so no one has to monitor it. At the same time, you don't want anyone to alter the show or add to it while it's running. You can control this by setting up the show.

The owner of Marvel Enterprises wants you to set up two presentations—one she can use on a kiosk and a second she can use at a computer at a trade show.

## Terms

**Custom Show** A show in which you specify the slides and the order in which the slides appear during presentation.

**Narration** A voice recording that describes or enhances the message in each slide.

## Notes

### Set Up a Presentation

- You can set up PowerPoint to show a presentation on a computer, either accompanied by a speaker, or running on its own continuously in a kiosk or trade show booth.

*Set Up Show dialog box*

### Set Up Show Dialog Box Options

| Option | Description |
|---|---|
| Presented by a speaker | Shows the presentation full screen. |
| Browsed by an individual | Shows the presentation in a window on the screen with menus and commands an individual can use to control and change slide show. |
| Browsed at a kiosk | Shows the presentation full screen; automatically sets the show to loop continuously; viewer can advance slides and use action buttons/hyperlinks but cannot change slide show. |
| Loop continuously until 'Esc' | Runs a presentation over and over continuously. |
| Show without narration | Displays the slide show with no voice. |
| Show without animation | Displays the show with no animation. |
| Pen Color | Enables you to choose a pen color for annotation. |

| Option | Description |
|--------|-------------|
| Show scrollbar | Shows scrollbar on-screen with presentation; available only when Browsed by an individual is selected. |
| Slides | Choose All or enter numbers of specific slides to show. |
| **Custom show** | Choose specific slides or presentations. |
| Advance slides | Choose Manually or Using timings if present. |
| Multiple monitors | Default is primary monitor; choose if second monitor is attached. |

- You may want to show the presentation at a trade show or convention or at your place of business.
- You can choose to set up a presentation so that the viewer can manipulate the screen or set it up so the viewer cannot manipulate or change the slide show.
- You can run a presentation in a continuous loop.
- PowerPoint lets you run a presentation with or without **narration** and animation.
- If you run a slide show that is unattended you should include timings and voice narration.

# Procedures

**Set Up and Run Presentation**

1. Open presentation.
2. Click **Slide Show** ........ Alt + D
3. Click **Set Up Show** ............. S
4. Choose one of the following show types:
   - **Presented by a speaker** ......................... P
   - **Browsed by an individual** ................ B
   - **Browsed at a kiosk** ...... K
5. Choose other options.
6. Click **OK** ........................... Enter

**Set Up Custom Slide Show**

1. Click **Slide Show** ............... D
2. Click **Custom Shows** ......... W
3. Click **New** ............................. N
4. Click slide to add to presentation.
5. Click **Add** ............................. A
6. Click **OK** ......................... Enter
7. Name the show.
8. Click **Close** ........................ C

# Exercise Directions

1. Start PowerPoint, if necessary.
2. Open ⌨20Marvel2 or 💿 21Marvel2.
3. Save the file as **21Marvel2**.
4. Set the slide show up to be browsed by an individual, with all slides and using timings.
5. Loop the show continuously.
6. View the show.
7. Change the setup so it doesn't show the animation.
8. View the show.
9. Close the file, saving all changes.
10. Open ⌨19Marvel or 💿 21Marvel.
11. Save the file as **21Marvel**.
12. Set the show up to run on a kiosk. Change timings in the show so it runs more quickly on the kiosk.
13. View the show.
14. Close the file and exit PowerPoint, saving all changes.

# On Your Own

1. Open **OPP20**, the presentation you used in Exercise 20, or open 💿 **21DONATE**.
2. Save the file as **OPP21**.
3. Set up the slide show to be presented by a speaker and to loop continuously.
4. Run the slide show. (Press Esc to stop it.)
5. Save the file as **OPP21-2**.
6. Set up the slide show to be browsed at a kiosk without animation.
7. Run the slide show.
8. Save the presentation, close it, and exit PowerPoint.

# Exercise 22

◆ **Save a Presentation as a Web Site** ◆ **Publish a Presentation**
◆ **Make Your Web Presentation More Efficient**

## On the Job

Publish a presentation to the Web so that a larger audience can view it. You might, for example, already have a Web site established for customers to view your products or services. Add a presentation to the site to interest more customers and provide an additional resource.

The owner of Marvel Enterprises wants to use one of the presentations you created as a Web site. You will need to check the presentation for consistency and add a few things to it before you save it as a Web page and publish it.

## Terms

**Web site**  A collection of Web pages; a site usually contains information with a common focus.

**HTML**  (Hypertext Markup Language) A formatting language used on the Internet.

**Browser**  A program, such as Internet Explorer, used to view Web pages and sites.

**Web page**  One document on the Web, usually containing information related to one topic.

**Publish**  To set options to make the presentation more suitable for viewing on the Web.

## Notes

### Save a Presentation as a Web Site

■ Save a presentation as a **Web site** so you can publish it to the World Wide Web.

■ PowerPoint lets you save a presentation in **HTML** format so you can open it in a Web **browser**, such as Internet Explorer.

■ When you save as a **Web page**, PowerPoint stores all HTML files in a folder named for the saved file. PowerPoint also saves the original file so you can open the presentation any time you want.

■ You can save a PowerPoint slide as a Web page or save multiple PowerPoint slides as a Web site.

### Publish a Presentation

■ You **publish** a presentation to prepare it for the Web.

*Publish as Web Page dialog box*

■ Publishing lets you choose options for how people will view the pages.

■ Organize files and locations in the Web site for efficiency.

*Web Options dialog box*

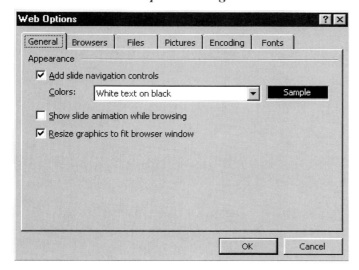

*Files tab of the Web Options dialog box*

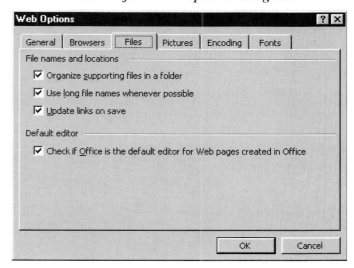

■ Choose browser support when you publish a presentation. Browser support determines which browsers can view the Web page.

*Browsers tab of the Web Options dialog box*

■ Change colors and resize graphics when you publish to the Web so the text and objects look their best on the page.

## Make Your Web Presentation More Efficient

■ An efficient Web site makes it easy for people to display topics quickly. If your site is easy to navigate, people will spend more time looking at your site.

■ Add Action buttons for easier navigation.

■ Use small graphics and pictures to cut downloading time.

■ Use one major heading on each page to let viewers know where they are.

■ Don't squeeze too much text on one slide or one page.

■ Use lists or tables when possible, because they are easier and faster to read than paragraphs of text.

■ Use the GIF image format for cartoons, line drawings, or pictures with few colors.

■ Use JPEG format for scanned photographs or images with several colors.

■ Use PNG format for buttons, bullets, and small images.

# Procedures

## Preview Presentation in Web Page View

1. Open a presentation.
2. Click **File**..................... `Alt`+`F`
3. Click **Web Page Preview**.... `B`
4. Close browser to return to PowerPoint.

## Save Presentation as Web Page

1. Open or create presentation.
2. Click **File**..................... `Alt`+`F`
3. Click **Save as Web Page**.... `G`
4. Click **Save in** and select a folder in which to save the Web page .............. `Alt`+`I`
5. Accept or change suggested **File name**..................... `Alt`+`N`

   ✓ *See your system's administrator for information on saving your Web page to a Web server.*

6. Click **Change Title** button

   Change Title... ............. `Alt`+`C`

   to display the Set Page Title dialog box and change the page title:

   a. Type the **Page title** ............... `Alt`+`P`
   b. Click **OK**..................... `Enter`

7. Click **Save** button 💾 ................... `Alt`+`S`

## Publish Web Page

1. Open or create presentation.
2. Click **File** .................... `Alt`+`F`
3. Click **Save as Web Page**.... `G`
4. Click **Save in** and select a folder in which to publish the Web page.............. `Alt`+`I`
5. Accept or change suggested **File name**................... `Alt`+`N`

6. Click **Publish** button

    ............. `Alt`+`P`

7. Click desired options.
8. Click **Web Options** button  .. `Alt`+`W`
9. Click desired options.
10. Click **Browsers** tab..... `Ctrl`+`Tab`
11. Click desired options.
12. Click **Files** tab ............. `Ctrl`+`Tab`
13. Click desired options.
14. Click **Pictures** tab ....... `Ctrl`+`Tab`
15. Click desired options.
16. Click **OK**......................... `Enter`
17. Click **Publish** button

    Publish ............... `Alt`+`P`

# Exercise Directions

1. Start PowerPoint, if necessary.
2. Open 💾**21Marvel2** or 💿**22Marvel2**.
3. Save the file as **22Marvel2**.
4. Switch to Normal view and add the following Action buttons to the presentation (AutoShapes, Action Buttons). You can place the buttons anywhere on the slide, as shown in Illustration A.

   Slide 1: add the End button
   Slide 5: add the Home button
   ✓ *See Exercise 11 for review of Action Buttons.*

   ✓ *Hint: Leave the hyperlinks as they are by clicking OK in the Action Settings dialog box.*

5. Save the presentation.
6. Save the presentation as a Web page and publish the complete presentation. Do not display speaker notes. Set browser support for Microsoft Internet Explorer 4 or later.
7. Change the following Web option when you publish the presentation:

   Show slide animation while browsing.

8. View the Web pages using your browser.
9. Close Internet Explorer.
10. Close the file and exit PowerPoint, saving all changes.

    ✓ *Some formatting may change when you save in HTML.*

*Illustration A*

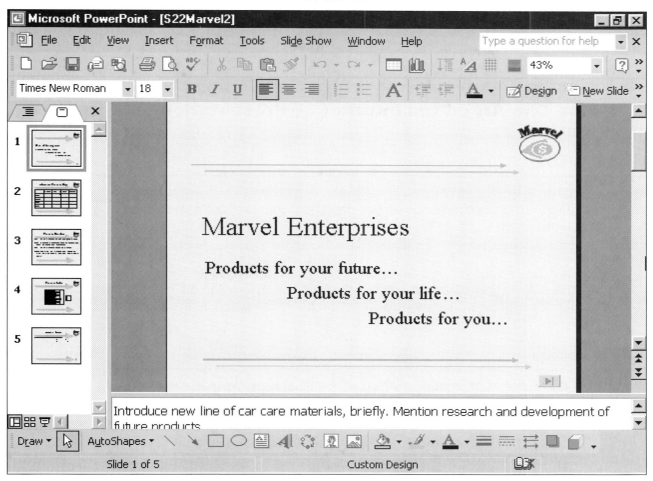

## On Your Own

1. Open **OPP21**, the presentation you used in Exercise 21, or open 💿**22DONATE**.

2. Save the file as **OPP22**.

3. Save the presentation as a Web page, changing the name to **OPP22-2**.

4. View the presentation in your Web browser.

5. Close the browser.

6. Save the presentation, close it, and exit PowerPoint.

# Exercise 23

## Skills Covered:

◆ **Export to Overhead Transparencies** ◆ **Export to 35mm Slides**
◆ **Find Clip Art on the Internet** ◆ **Presentation Conferencing**

## On the Job

Export a presentation to another format, such as slides or overheads, so you can show it on a projection system. For instance, export to overheads so you can show your presentation to a larger audience than you could on a computer screen.

Marvel Enterprises has asked you to prepare a presentation to send to an imaging company for slides and transparencies. Also, they've asked you to assist them in holding an online meeting with the owner of Marvel Enterprises and co-workers to review the presentation and discuss possible modifications.

## Terms

**Transparencies** Clear sheets of plastic on which you print a slide so it can be shown on an overhead projector, which displays the slide on a large screen.

**Imaging company** A company that specializes in printing 35mm slides, transparencies, and other computerized images to various media.

**Real time** An event that is taking place live, as opposed to in delayed time.

**Whiteboard** A tool, similar to a blackboard, on which you can enter text.

## Notes

### Export to Overhead Transparencies

■ PowerPoint lets you save a presentation so you can create **transparencies** to show on an overhead projector.

*Export to Overhead in Page Setup dialog box*

■ For best results, let a professional **imaging company** print the transparencies for you.

■ Check with the imaging company for the correct file format, although the PPT file format generally works well.

### Export to 35mm Slides

■ You can save a presentation in a format appropriate for creating 35mm slides.

■ You should send your presentation to a professional imaging company to have the slides made.

■ Avoid a blue and red color scheme because it can be hard to read or visually distracting.

## Find Clip Art on the Internet

- In addition to the clip art that is included with Office XP, you can also buy clip art collections from other resources or download clip art from the Internet.

## Presentation Conferencing

- You can share your presentation with others online via NetMeeting, Microsoft's **real** (actual) **time** conferencing program.

- Your computer must be networked or attached to the Internet to use NetMeeting.

- You can start a spontaneous meeting as long as co-workers are running NetMeeting and are online. You can schedule the meeting beforehand using e-mail or the telephone.

- During a meeting, you can show and edit a presentation.

- The person who initiates and controls an online meeting is called the host. The host can show the presentation to others without allowing them to edit the presentation.

- The host controls the online meeting by clicking the appropriate button on the Online Meeting toolbar, which appears when you connect with NetMeeting.

- The host can also allow co-workers to edit the presentation, if desired, by turning on the collaboration feature.

- Only one person can control/edit the presentation at a time. The initials of that person are displayed next to the mouse pointer.

- While others edit the presentation, the host cannot use the cursor.

- Only the host of an online meeting needs to have the file and application installed.

- The host can start the Chat feature to allow participants to discuss the presentation with co-workers.

- The host can start the **whiteboard** feature to allow participants to make notes and record comments.

- Several people can simultaneously send messages or files in Chat or add notes to the whiteboard if the collaboration feature is turned off.

- The first time you use the online conferencing feature, you must enter some basic information.

# Procedures

### Export to Overhead

1. Open presentation.
2. Click **File** ..................... `Alt`+`F`
3. Click **Page Setup** ............... `U`
4. Click **Slides sized for** ..................... `Alt`+`S`
5. Click **Overhead**.
6. Click **OK** ........................... `Enter`
7. Save presentation.

### Export to 35mm Slides

1. Open presentation.
2. Click **File** ..................... `Alt`+`F`
3. Click **Page Setup** ............... `U`
4. Click **Slides sized for** ..................... `Alt`+`S`

5. Click **35mm slides**.
   - ✓ *Image size changes to 11.25 x 7.5. Leave it at this size.*
6. Click **OK** ........................... `Enter`
7. Save presentation.

### Start Online Meeting

1. Click **Tools** .................. `Alt`+`T`
2. Click **Online Collaboration** ..................... `N`
3. Click **Meet now** .................. `M`
   - ✓ *If you've never used NetMeeting, the NetMeeting dialog box appears.*
   - a. Enter your personal and server information for NetMeeting.
     - ✓ *For help with this information, see documentation on NetMeeting.*

   b. Click **OK** ..................... `Enter`
   OR
   - ✓ *If you have used NetMeeting or after you enter your information in NetMeeting dialog box, continue with:*
4. Click **Type name or select from list** ......... `Alt`+`T`
5. Enter names of desired participants or select them from list.
6. Click **Call**.
7. Computer dials number.
8. When the receiving computer answers and displays NetMeeting, you can begin the meeting.

# Exercise Directions

✓ *Use the Internet simulation provided on the CD that accompanies this book to complete this exercise.*

1. Start PowerPoint, if necessary.

2. Open 📠**22Marvel2** or 💿 **23Marvel2**.

3. Save the file as **23Marvel2**.

4. Display the Web toolbar.

5. On the Address line, type the following and press Enter:
   **D:/Internet/Ppt/Ex23/barrysclipart.htm**
   ✓ *If you've copied the Internet simulation on to your hard drive or your CD-ROM drive is not D:, substitute the correct letter for D.*

6. To find appropriate clip art for your online presentation follow these steps:
   a. Type **business** in the Find box and click **Go**.
   b. Scroll the page to locate a clip art.
   c. Right-click the second clip art in the second row and click Save Picture As.
   d. In the Save As dialog box, choose the folder in which to save the clip art and click Save.

7. Close the Internet simulation by clicking the Close button ☒.

8. View slide 1 of the presentation.

9. Insert the picture from a file (Insert, Picture, From File).

10. Size and position the clip art above the slide's title.

11. Change the page setup of the presentation to overhead transparencies.

12. Print the presentation as slides.

13. Change the page setup to 35mm slides.

14. Print the presentation as slides and compare the size and shape of the slides to the first set you printed.

15. Schedule an online meeting with others in your network.
    ✓ *If your computer is not networked or NetMeeting is not installed to your computer, you may skip this part of the exercise.*

16. Start the online meeting and run your presentation.
    ✓ *You run a presentation the same way, whether you're online or not.*

17. End the meeting by clicking the End Meeting button on the Online Meeting toolbar.

18. Close the file and exit PowerPoint, saving all changes.

# On Your Own

1. Open **OPPT 22**, the presentation you used in Exercise 22, or open 💿 **23DONATE**.

2. Save the file as **OPPT23**.

3. Change the page setup of the presentation to overhead transparencies.

4. Print the presentation as slides.

5. Change the page setup to 35mm slides.

6. Print the presentation as slides and compare the size and shape of the slides to the first set you printed.

7. If you're attached to a network, hold an online meeting and run the presentation during the meeting.

8. Save the presentation, close it, and exit PowerPoint.

# Exercise 24

## ◆ Critical Thinking

When you show a presentation, you want to make sure the audience gets the most out of the information you present. By setting transitions, adding sound, and otherwise setting up a presentation, you can present the slide show in the best possible way for your audience to understand and enjoy.

## Exercise Directions

1. Start PowerPoint, if necessary.
2. Open 💿 **24DitexInc**.
3. Save the file as **24DitexInc**.
4. Apply transitions, sounds, and timing to all slides. View the presentation.
5. Hide slide 3.
6. Animate the bullets on slide 2 with preset animations.
7. Animate the text and objects on slides 3 and 4 with custom animations. You can choose to use sounds, if desired. View the presentation.
8. Save the timings.
9. Add a slide at the end of the presentation using the Title Only layout. Add the title **Thank You!**
10. Add a music or video clip to the last slide. The clip should play automatically when the slide is displayed.
11. On the notes master, add the following header:
    **DitexInc**
    **Sue Bender, owner**
12. In Notes Page view, add notes to slide 3 as shown in Illustration A.
13. Add notes to slide 5 as shown in Illustration B.
14. Print the notes pages as handouts, 4 per page.
15. Pack the presentation onto a disk and view it on another computer.

16. Show the presentation from your own computer. During the presentation, open the Meeting Minder and enter these notes:
    **Get price quote for 3 types of Input data: Catalog, Brochures, Annual Reports**.
17. In the Action Items, add the following:
    | | | |
    |---|---|---|
    | **Annual report** | **Dave** | **3/01** |
    | **Catalog design** | **Tom** | **4/01** |
    | **Catalog final** | **Willa** | **4/01** |
18. Export the information from Meeting Minder to Word.
19. Save the Word file as **24DitexInc.rtf** and print it.
20. Close the file and exit Word. Click OK to close the Meeting Minder.
21. Finish showing the presentation and then set up the slide show to run on a kiosk. View the slide show.
22. Save the presentation as a Web page (**24DitexInc.htm**). Publish the presentation using all slides, no speaker notes, and open it to a Web browser.
23. Run the presentation and then close the browser.
24. Close the file and exit PowerPoint, saving all changes.

*Illustration A*

DitexInc
Sue Bender, owner

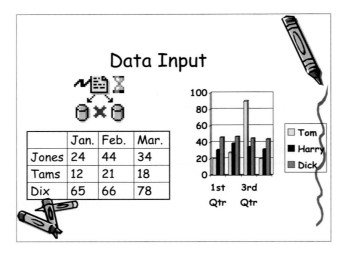

Our prices include data input, plus double-proofing. Every fact, word, and figure is double-checked by special proof-readers so you are guaranteed correct data. We guarantee our services with your money back if you find one single mistake.

Backups are also stored on tape for up to 6 months, longer if you want to pay for that option.

*Illustration B*

DitexInc
Sue Bender, owner

Please contact us if you have any questions or comments. For a free estimate of your input data, call us today. You can also email us or stop by the office.

# Index

## 3

35mm Slides .................................................413
    export to .................................................412

## A

Absolute cell reference .................................186
Accounting format ...............................181, 183
Active cell ......................................150, 151
    change .................................................153
    change using Go To .................................153
    change using mouse .................................153
    change using Name Box .............................153
Active sheet tab .................................194
Adjacent Components
    select .................................................126
Advance slide timing .................................389
Align entry .................................................170
Align horizontally .................................................23
Align vertically .................................................23
Alignment
    change .................................................370
    horizontal .................................................23
    in table cell .................................................130
    label .................................................169
    of table on page .................................131, 132
    vertical .................................................23
    within table cells .................................132
Animate .................................................393
Animation
    custom .................................................394
    preset .................................................393, 395
    preview .................................................395
    turn off .................................................396
Animations Effects toolbar
    display .................................................395
Annotation
    add to presentation .................................399
    erase .................................................399
    turn on/off .................................................399
Annotations .................................................398
Antonyms .................................................15
Argument .................................................200, 215
Ask a Question box .................................................5
Attachment .................................................99
    to e-mail message .................................100
AutoCalculate .................................................200, 202
    use .................................................203
AutoComplete .................................162, 163, 164
AutoCorrect .................................20, 21, 162, 164
    create replacement .................................165
    use .................................................22
AutoFill .................................................186
AutoFormat
    apply .................................................126
    use .................................................196
Automatic format checking
    turn on .................................................89
Automatic spell checking .................................318, 319
AutoShapes .................................360, 362,363

## B

Background .................................................110
    apply .................................................112
    change .................................................346
    Web page .................................................111
Blank presentation .................................................312
Blank workbook .................................................156
Bookmark .................................................115
Border .................................................124
Borders
    cell .................................................141
Box
    border, change .................................................370
    color, change .................................................370
    delete .................................................370
    select .................................................370
    select multiple .................................................370
    type in .................................................370
Browse by Object button .................................................5
Browser .................................................408
Bullet .................................................77
Bulleted lists .................................................77
Bullets
    format .................................................356
    format in PowerPoint .................................357
Business letter
    format .................................................28

## C

Caps Lock .................................................20
Caps Lock key .................................................21
Carbon copy .................................................99
Case .................................................26
    change .................................................27, 344, 346
Categories .................................................220
    in charts .................................................221
Category labels .................................................221
Cell .................................................124, 150
    clear contents .................................................157
    split .................................................137
Cell editing
    enable .................................................159
Cell reference .................................................150
Cells .................................................124, 150
    merge and split .................................................136
Change case .................................................344
Chart .................................................220, 373
    basics .................................................220
    change text .................................................227, 228
    change type .................................................222
    copy .................................................222, 223
    create .................................................222, 373
    create in PowerPoint .................................376
    delete .................................................222, 223
    delete object .................................................228
    elements .................................................221
    enhance background .................................227, 228
    format category axis .................................227
    format value axis .................................227, 229

import from Excel .................................................. 376
move ...................................................... 222, 223
move object ........................................................ 227
resize .................................................... 222, 223
resize object ....................................................... 227
select ............................................................... 222
select data .......................................................... 221
select embedded .................................................. 223
switch ............................................................... 223
Chart area ............................................................ 226
Chart layout
change ........................................................... 370
Chart object
delete .............................................................. 227
move ............................................................... 227
resize .............................................................. 227
Chart sheet ........................................................... 220
delete .............................................................. 223
select .............................................................. 223
Chart toolbar
use ................................................................. 226
Chart type
change ...................................................... 223, 435
Chart Wizard .......................................................... 223
Charts .................................................................. 220
Check grammar ................................................. 16, 17
Check spelling ................................................... 16, 17
Excel ............................................................... 165
Click and Type ......................................................... 11
Clip art ......................................................... 110, 311
find on the Internet .............................................. 412
insert ............................................................... 325
Clipboard ....................................................... 50, 186
delete selections .................................................. 52
options .............................................................. 52
paste ................................................................ 51
Clipboard Task Pane ................................................ 51
paste a selection .................................................. 55
Collapse
outline .............................................................. 332
Collapse/expand ..................................................... 332
Color Fill
add .................................................................. 184
Color scheme .......................................................... 343
change ............................................................. 346
change color within .............................................. 346
Color to underlines
apply ................................................................. 71
Column .................................................................. 124
delete ......................................................... 190, 191
insert .......................................................... 190, 191
Column markers ...................................................... 124
Column width .......................................................... 130
change ............................................... 132, 169, 170
set .................................................................. 171
Columns ................................................................ 124
Columns or Rows
delete .............................................................. 191
hide ................................................................ 191
insert ............................................................... 191
unhide ............................................................. 191
Comma format .............................................. 181, 182
Comment ...................................................... 206, 207
create .............................................................. 207
Compatible file types ................................................ 59
Computer's clock ...................................................... 26

Condition .............................................................. 215
Content layout
work with .......................................................... 324
Contiguous ....................................................... 20, 178
Contiguous range ................................................... 178
Copy
slide ............................................................... 328
text ................................................................ 351
use ............................................................. 54, 55
Copy data ..................................................... 186, 187
Copy formula ......................................................... 188
Correct Grammar as You Type ............................. 15, 17
Correct Spelling as You Type .............................. 15, 17
COUNTIF
enter ............................................................... 217
COUNTIF() ............................................................ 217
Create bulleted list ................................................... 78
Create numbered list ................................................. 79
Currency format ............................................. 181, 183
Custom animation .................................................... 394
Custom show ......................................................... 406
Custom slide show
set up .............................................................. 407
Cut ............................................................... 50, 190
in Excel ..................................................... 190, 191
text ................................................................ 351
use .................................................................. 50
Cut and paste .......................................................... 51

**D**

Data
edit while typing ................................................. 159
format .............................................................. 181
select adjacent ................................................... 223
select non-adjacent ............................................. 223
Data label ............................................................. 373
Data series ............................................................ 220
chart ............................................................... 221
Datasheet .............................................................. 373
close ............................................................... 376
view ................................................................ 376
Date
enter in PowerPoint ............................................. 356
insert on slide .................................................... 355
Date and Time feature ............................................... 27
Date formats .......................................................... 168
Decimal places
increase/decrease ............................................... 184
Default .......................................................... 3, 154
Default width
cell ................................................................. 157
Delete
Excel ............................................................... 156
Delivery address ..................................................... 36
Design template ...................................................... 311
change in PowerPoint ................................... 320, 321
use in PowerPoint .............................................. 314
Destination ............................................................ 336
Destination file ...................................................... 337
Direct formatting
reapply ....................................................... 88, 89
Divider ................................................................. 124
Dock floating toolbar ............................................... 360
Document
attach to e-mail message ...................................... 100

close in Word ..................................................6, 7
create new ...................................................10
move insertion point.........................................11
open as read-only........................................59, 61
open from Windows ..........................................59
open from Windows Explorer.................................61
open recently saved........................................47
preview ...................................................11, 65
save new in Word ..........................................6, 7
send as e-mail .........................................100, 101
Document Properties ..........................................58, 59
use ........................................................61
Document Recovery ..............................................158
Document window ..................................................5
Drag-and-drop ....................................................50
in Excel ................................................191, 192
use ................................................51, 54, 55
Duplicate ........................................................328
slide .....................................................328

**E**

Effect details
set ........................................................396
Elements ..........................................................3
E-mail ............................................................99
receive in Outlook Express .............................101, 102
send from Word ........................................100, 101
E-mail address ....................................................99
Embed .......................................................324, 380
Embedded chart ..................................................220
End of cell markers ..............................................125
End of row markers...............................................125
Envelope
print........................................................39
Error
correcting ................................................6, 7
Excel
exit...................................................153, 154, 160
start...................................................150, 153
Excel menu .......................................................151
Excel window ....................................................150
Expand
outline ....................................................332
Expand/collapse .................................................332
Export............................................................336

**F**

Favorites Folder..........................................106, 107
Field ...........................................................140
File
basic search .............................................60
open in Excel .............................................162
File extension ...................................................58
File formats ....................................................336
File icon .........................................................58
File type ........................................................58
Files
search from open dialog box .............................62
Fill ............................................................183
Fill effect ......................................................110
Fill handle .....................................................186
Floating toolbar
dock .......................................................361
Flush...........................................................20
Font ..............................................31, 36, 181, 182

change .....................................................183
sans serif ...................................................37
script.......................................................37
select ..................................................37, 38
serif .......................................................37
Font color ........................................................71
Font effects ......................................................70
Font size..................................................181, 182
change .....................................................37
select ......................................................38
Font style .......................................................36
Footer .......................................233, 235, 354
insert on slide .............................................355
text, enter .................................................357
view in PowerPoint ........................................356
Format .......................................................181, 343
of numbers .................................................141
Format a business letter .........................................26
Format a one-page report ........................................93
Format Painter .........................................71, 349, 350
Formatting .......................................................88
check .......................................................89
check as you type..........................................89
clear ...................................................89, 90
copy.......................................................71
Formatting toolbar .................................................5
customize view ............................................154
Formula ......................................................140, 173
edit ........................................................203
enter .......................................................174
use in Excel ...............................................173
Formula bar .............................................150, 151
use ........................................................203
view .......................................................154
Formula palette
use ........................................................203
Full block ........................................................26
Function ......................................140, 200, 215
arguments .................................................200
enter in formula ...........................................203
name ......................................................200
nesting....................................................200
use .......................................................200
Function name ...................................................200

**G**

Graphic objects ........................................110, 362
Graphics lines .................................................110
Gridlines .................................................124, 125
show/hide ..................................................376
Group ...........................................................360
Group objects.........................................362, 363
Group sheets...................................................195
Grouping .......................................................194
Guide
create ....................................................363
delete .....................................................363
Gutter ...........................................................93

**H**

Handout Master..................................................401
Handout Master slide
edit .......................................................403
Handouts........................................................401
create ...............................................401, 403

Hard copy ..................................................................... 10
Hide slide ................................................................... 392
Highlight ..................................................................... 20
Highlight color
    change ..................................................................... 71
Highlight formatting ................................................... 70
Highlight text ........................................................... 71
Highlighted ............................................................... 21
Horizontal alignment ............................. 10, 20, 22
htm ........................................................................ 110
HTML (Hypertext Markup Language) ......... 100, 110, 311, 408
HTML document
    open ...................................................... 111, 112
Hyperlink ................................................................. 115
    change a destination ............................. 117
    create ................................................................. 115
    insert to a different document ................ 116
    insert to a Web page ............................... 116
    insert to an E-Mail address ..................... 117
    insert within a document ........................ 116
    remove ................................................................. 117
    select ................................................................... 117
    set Word to follow on click ..................... 117
    use ...................................................................... 107
Hyperlink destination ............................................. 115
Hyperlink source .................................................... 115
Hyperlinks or links ................................................. 105
Hypertext ................................................................ 115

**I**

IF Function ............................................................. 215
    nested .................................................................. 216
Imaging company .................................................. 412
Import ..................................................................... 336
Incremental series ................................................. 172
Indent text ....................................................... 83, 84
Indents .................................................................... 83
Insert data between cells ...................................... 192
Insert mode ..................................................... 46, 47
Insert symbols ....................................................... 75
Insert text ............................................................... 47
Insertion point .................................................. 5, 10
    movement ............................................................. 12
Internet .................................................. 99, 100, 105
    features in Word ............................... 106, 107
Internet basics ....................................................... 105
Internet service provider (ISP) .............................. 105
Intranet ................................................................... 99

**J**

Justified .................................................................. 345

**K**

Keywords ................................................................ 58
Kiosk ...................................................................... 389

**L**

Label ...................................................................... 156
    create ................................................................... 39
    enter ..................................................................... 157
    run ........................................................................ 170
Label prefix ............................................................ 167
Landscape orientation ..................................... 93, 94
Layer objects ......................................................... 362
Layout

change in PowerPoint ........................................... 320
Leading .................................................................... 82
Legend .......................................................... 221, 376
Letter
    delivery address .................................................. 38
    format ................................................................... 26
    full-block .............................................................. 26
    letterhead ............................................................. 36
    modified-block ...................................................... 26
    return address ...................................................... 36
    salutation ............................................................. 26
Letterhead ............................................................... 36
Line spacing ............................................................ 82
Line style ................................................................. 140
Line weight .................................................... 140, 141
Link ......................................................................... 336
    defined .................................................................. 380
    Excel worksheet to PowerPoint presentation .............. 337
Links ....................................................................... 106

**M**

Mail service provider ............................................. 99
Margins ................................................................... 93
Master slide
    Handout ................................................................ 401
    Notes ................................................................... 401
Mathematical operators ......................................... 173
Meeting feedback ................................................... 402
Meeting Minder ...................................................... 402
    create action items in ............................. 403
Menu bar ................................................................... 4
Menus
    shortcut ................................................................ 313
Merge and center entry .......................................... 170
Merge cells ............................................................. 135
Message window ..................................................... 99
Mode buttons ............................................................ 5
Modem .................................................................... 105
Modified block ......................................................... 26
Mouse selection shortcuts ...................................... 23
Move
    in Excel ................................................................ 190
    text ........................................................................ 50
Movie
    add to presentation .............................................. 399
Music
    add to presentation .............................................. 484

**N**

Name box ............................................................... 210
Named range .......................................................... 210
    insert ..................................................................... 212
    select cells ........................................................... 212
    set print area ........................................................ 212
Narration ................................................................. 406
Natural language formula ....................................... 206
    create ................................................................... 207
Nest ........................................................................ 200
Nesting .................................................................... 215
Noncontiguous ............................................... 20, 178
Noncontiguous blocks .............................................. 23
Noncontiguous range ............................................. 178
Nonprinting character ....................................... 3, 10
    show/hide .............................................................. 12
Normal view

in PowerPoint.................................................319
Notes .............................................................401
    export to Word ........................................381
    read/enter after presentation.....................403
    take during Slide Show ............................403
Notes Master ...............................................401
Notes Master slide
    edit.......................................................403
Notes Pages
    create..........................................401, 403
    print......................................................403
Number format.............................................181
Numbered lists................................................78
Numeric label................................................167
Numeric label
    enter.....................................................169
Numeric values.............................................167

### O

Object ...................................................226, 324
    animate.................................................393
    defined..................................................380
    embed....................................................324
    insert from file.........................................337
    insert into placeholder..............................325
    insert using no placeholder.........................325
Objects
    draw.....................................................363
    graphic, draw .........................................362
    group....................................................363
    group/ungroup........................................362
    layer.....................................................362
Offline ............................................................99
Online .............................................................99
Online meeting
    start......................................................413
Open a document not recently saved .........47, 48
Open a recently saved document ....................48
Options
    set for style and consistency......................391
Order of mathematical operations....................173
Organization chart .........................................369
    create....................................................370
    edit.......................................................370
    insert.....................................................369
Outline ..........................................................332
    export PowerPoint to Word........................381
    export to Word .......................................337
    import from Word ....................................337
    import/export..........................................336
    print......................................................333
Outline pane
    in PowerPoint..................................319, 332
Outline toolbar
    display ..................................................333
Outline view ..................................................332
    display titles ..........................................333
    move text ..............................................333
    select slides ...........................................333
Outlining toolbar............................................333
Outlook ....................................................99, 100
    disconnect .............................................102
Outlook Express ........................................99, 100
    disconnect .............................................102
    receive e-mail .........................................101

Overhead
    export to ...............................................413
Overhead transparencies
    export to ...............................................412
Overtype mode........................................46, 48

### P

Pack and Go .................................401, 402, 403
Page Setup
    in PowerPoint ........................................321
Paragraph
    move ...............................................51, 52
Paragraph mark ................................................3
Paragraph spacing .................................82, 349
    increase/decrease............................349, 351
Paste.............................................................190
    in Excel..................................190, 191, 192
    text.......................................................351
    use ...........................................50, 54, 55
Paste data .....................................................187
Paste formatting options
    select................................................88, 90
Paste function
    use ......................................................203
Pattern..........................................................181
Pen color, change...........................................399
Percent style .................................................183
Percentage
    format ..................................................182
Percentage format..........................................181
Personal business letter ...................................36
Pick From List ........................................163, 164
Placeholder ...................................................311
    copy......................................................351
    copy/move.............................................350
    delete ............................................350, 351
    insert object into .....................................325
    insert object not using .............................325
    move .....................................................351
    size................................................350, 351
    use in PowerPoint ............................313, 315
Placeholder border .........................................349
Places bar .......................................................46
Plot...............................................................220
Plot area .......................................................226
Portrait orientation ....................................93, 94
PowerPoint
    about ....................................................311
    exit.......................................................315
    export slides and notes to Word ................380
    screen ..................................................312
    start ..............................................312, 315
PowerPoint screen .........................................313
PowerPoint text
    export to Word .......................................381
Preprinted letterhead.......................................36
Presentation ..................................................311
    add slide to ...........................................314
    blank....................................................312
    close.....................................................315
    open existing ..................................318, 321
    open new...............................................315
    preview as Web page...............................410
    print ..............................................319, 321
    publish..................................................408

read/enter notes after .................................................... 403
save ............................................................... 314, 315
save as Web page ...................................... 314, 315, 410
save as Web site .............................................. 408
set up and run ...................................... 406, 407
show .................................................... 389, 403
unpack ............................................................ 403
Presentation
make more efficient for Web ................................ 409
Presentation conferencing ...................................... 413
Preset animation ................................................ 393
Preview
a closed document ........................................... 64
document .......................................................... 65
Print .......................................................... 11, 12
document without opening .................................... 65
multiple files ................................................... 65
named range ................................................... 212
presentation .......................................... 319, 321
worksheet .................................................. 187, 188
Print options, list of
PowerPoint ...................................................... 320
Print Preview ......................................... 11, 12, 186, 187
worksheet ...................................................... 188
Proofreaders' marks ............................................... 46
Properties dialog box
display automatically ......................................... 61
Publish .......................................................... 408

**R**

Range ............................................................ 178
enter ............................................................ 179
enter using Collapse button ................................ 179
name ............................................................ 211
naming .......................................................... 211
Range name .................................................... 210
Read-only ......................................................... 58
open document as ........................................ 59, 61
Real time ........................................................ 412
Redo ........................................................ 3, 7, 156
Excel ...................................................... 157, 159
use ............................................................... 6
Relative cell reference ............................................ 186
Repeat ............................................................ 7
Replace Selected Text .................................... 21, 23
Return address ................................................... 36
Return address labels ........................................... 39
Right-clicks
use in PowerPoint ............................................ 315
Rotate text ...................................................... 137
Word table ...................................................... 136
Row ............................................................ 124
delete ................................................... 190, 191
insert .................................................... 190, 191
Row height ...................................................... 130
change ........................................................ 132
Ruler
show/hide ........................................................ 7

**S**

Salutation ........................................................ 26
Sans serif ........................................................ 36
Save ............................................................ 12
document .......................................................... 11
Save a compatible file ............................................ 61

Save As ........................................................... 48
Save Files
Excel ........................................................... 160
ScreenTip .......................................................... 5
Script ............................................................ 36
Scroll .................................................... 150, 153
in PowerPoint ......................................... 319, 321
Scroll bars ......................................................... 5
Section ...................................................... 21, 93
Select ............................................................ 20
text ............................................................ 21
using keyboard ................................................ 23
using mouse ................................................... 23
Select grammar style ............................................. 17
Select range of cells
using keyboard ................................................ 179
using mouse ................................................... 179
Selection
cancel ......................................................... 23
Selection bar .................................................... 20
Series ............................................................ 167
create .................................................. 168, 170
Series labels .................................................... 221
Serif ............................................................ 36
Set line spacing ................................................. 84
Set margins ...................................................... 93
Set margins in any view ......................................... 94
Set margins in Print Layout view ................................ 94
Set page orientation ............................................. 94
Set paragraph spacing ........................................... 84
Shading .................................................. 140, 141
cell ............................................................ 141
Shareware ....................................................... 105
Sheet
select .......................................................... 195
Sheet tabs ....................................................... 150
Sheets
copy ........................................................... 196
delete .......................................................... 195
format .......................................................... 195
group .......................................................... 195
insert .......................................................... 195
move ........................................................... 196
rename ......................................................... 195
select all ....................................................... 195
select consecutive ........................................... 195
ungroup ........................................................ 195
Shortcut menus .................................................. 313
Show
setup options .................................................. 406
Show Presentation .............................................. 403
Show/Hide ....................................................... 10
Shrink to Fit ................................................ 32, 33
Sizing handles .................................................. 349
Slide
advance ........................................................ 390
background, change ........................................... 345
color scheme, change ........................................ 344
copy ..................................................... 328, 329
delete ................................................... 328, 329
duplicate ................................................ 328, 329
embed in Word document ..................................... 380
export to Word ................................................ 381
hide ........................................................... 392
layout, change ............................................... 320
move .................................................... 328, 329

move from slide to ................................................ 319
new, insert .......................................................... 315
paste .................................................................. 329
transistion, remove ............................................. 392
view in black and white ...................................... 321
Slide
embed in Word .................................................. 381
Slide layout .............................................................. 311
apply .................................................................. 312
change ............................................................... 321
Slide master ............................................................ 354
use ..................................................................... 354
view .................................................................... 356
Slide Master view .................................................... 355
Slide Number
enter ................................................................... 356
Slide numbers
insert .................................................................. 355
Slide pane
in PowerPoint .................................................... 319
Slide Show
custom ............................................................... 406
custom, set up ................................................... 407
pause and resume ..................................... 398, 399
start .................................................................... 391
take notes during ............................................... 403
Slide Show view
in PowerPoint .................................................... 319
Slide Sorter view ............................................. 328, 329
change to ........................................................... 329
in PowerPoint .................................................... 319
Slide views ............................................................... 321
Slides
check for style and consistency ......................... 389
hide .................................................................... 391
Smart tags ................................................................. 15
Sort ....................................................... 77, 78, 141
Sort a list ................................................................... 79
Sound
add ..................................................................... 390
add to presentation ........................................... 399
Sound clip ................................................................ 389
Source ............................................................ 255, 336
Source file ................................................................ 337
Spell check
in PowerPoint .................................................... 319
manually ............................................................. 321
Spell checking .......................................................... 318
Spelling checker ............................................... 162, 164
Split cells ................................................................. 135
Spreadsheet ............................................................. 140
Standard column width ............................................ 167
Standard toolbar ................................................. 4, 318
customize view ................................................... 154
Status bar ................................................................... 5
view .................................................................... 154
Style ......................................................................... 87
apply a ................................................................. 89
create ................................................................... 89
edit ................................................................. 88, 89
Style sheet ................................................................. 87
Styles ........................................................................ 87
SUMIF() .................................................................. 216
Summary information
add in PowerPoint .............................................. 315
Summary Slide ......................................................... 333

insert .................................................................. 333
Symbol ...................................................................... 74
Synonyms .................................................................. 15

## T

Tab ........................................................................... 31
set ................................................................. 31, 32
within table cell ................................................. 132
Tab color ................................................................. 196
Tab scrolling buttons .............................................. 150
Table ............................................................... 124, 373
align on page .............................................. 131, 132
calculate ............................................................ 140
change column width ......................................... 377
change row height .............................................. 377
change structure ......................................... 125, 126
columns .............................................................. 124
create in PowerPoint .......................................... 375
create ......................................................... 124, 126
draw ........................................................... 135, 137
enter data ................................................... 125, 126
erase borders ..................................................... 137
format text .......................................................... 126
format ......................................................... 125, 376
insert .................................................................. 376
move and resize ................................................. 136
move .................................................................. 137
resize .................................................................. 137
rows ................................................................... 124
select text ................................................... 125, 126
Tables and Borders toolbar ..................................... 135
display ................................................................ 137
Template .......................................................... 156, 366
add custom to AutoContent Wizard ..................... 367
apply custom ............................................... 366, 367
create custom ..................................................... 367
customize ........................................................... 366
Excel ................................................................. 157
save .................................................................... 366
use in PowerPoint .............................................. 315
Text
align ........................................................... 343, 346
animate ............................................................... 393
change appearance ...................................... 343, 346
copy .................................................................. 349
cut/copy and paste ............................................. 351
drag-and-drop ..................................................... 350
insert .................................................................... 48
move .......................................................... 50, 51, 349
select ......................................................... 343, 346
Text box
insert .......................................................... 325, 356
Text color
add .................................................................... 184
Text effects .............................................................. 70
Text format
copy ........................................................... 349, 350
Theme .................................................................... 110
apply .................................................................. 112
Web page ........................................................... 111
Thesaurus ................................................................. 15
Tick marks .............................................................. 226
Time
enter in PowerPoint ............................................ 356
insert .................................................................... 28

Timing
  add ...................................................................391
  check ................................................................392
Title
  Web page ........................................................ 111
Title bar ...................................................................4
Title master ...........................................................354
Toggle ....................................................................20
Toolbar
  add increase/decrease buttons ..........................351
  show/hide .............................................................6
  view ..................................................................154
Transitions ............................................................389
  add .............................................................389, 391
Transparencies .......................................................412
  export to ............................................................412
Typeover Mode .......................................................159

**U**

Underlines ...............................................................37
  apply ..................................................................39
Undo ..........................................................3, 7, 156, 325
  Excel ..........................................................156, 159
  use .......................................................................6
Ungroup objects .....................................................362
Uniform Resource Locator (URL) .............................105
Unpack presentation ...............................................403
Uppercase mode ................................................27, 28
URL
  go to in Word ......................................................107
Use symbols .............................................................74
Use Thesaurus ..........................................................18

**V**

Value .....................................................................167
  enter ..................................................................169
Value axis
  format ........................................................227, 229
Values ....................................................................167
Vertical alignment ..............................................20, 22
View ...........................................................................3
  change in Word ......................................................7
  full screen .....................................................32, 33
  in PowerPoint .....................................................318
  slide ..................................................................318
View buttons ..............................................................5
View menu ..............................................................152

**W**

Web
  search ...............................................................107
Web browser ..........................................................105
Web bullets ............................................................110
Web Layout view ..................................................... 111
  use ....................................................................112
Web page .......................................................105, 408
  background .......................................................... 111
  create a new blank page ......................................112
  publish ...............................................................410
  save a document as .............................................112

save locally ...........................................................106
save presentation as .........................315, 315, 410
set a Web page title ...............................................112
theme .................................................................. 111
title ..................................................................... 111
Web Page Preview ..................................................111
  use ....................................................................112
Web Page view .......................................................410
Web server .............................................................110
Web site ........................................................105, 408
Web site
  save presentation as ...........................................408
Web toolbar
  display ...............................................................107
Whiteboard ....................................................412, 413
Word
  exit .......................................................................7
  start ..................................................................3, 6
Word window .............................................................4
  change ..................................................................5
Word wrap ...........................................................3, 5
WordArt .................................................................324
  insert .................................................................325
Workbook ..............................................................150
  arrange several ...................................................163
  change ...............................................................164
  close ..........................................................159, 160
  create from template ...........................................157
  open ..................................................................164
  open blank ...................................................156, 159
  recover ...............................................................160
  save ..........................................................158, 159
Workbook sheets ....................................................194
Workbooks
  arrange ..............................................................164
Worksheet ..............................................................150
  crop ...................................................................337
  explore ........................................................150, 152
  insert new ...........................................................337
  link to PowerPoint presentation .............................337
  move ..................................................................337
  print ...................................................................187
  Print Preview .......................................................188
  save ...................................................................337
Worksheets
  change between worksheets ..................................152
World Wide Web ......................................................105
Wrap text
  around Word table ...............................................137

**X**

X-axis ....................................................................220

**Y**

Y-axis ....................................................................220

**Z**

Zoom percentage
  set .....................................................................154
  set using Zoom button .........................................154